BACK HOME

By the same author

Tarantino: Inside Story

Jeff Dawson

BACK HOME

England and the 1970 World Cup

ORION

First published in Great Britain in 2001 by Orion
An imprint of Orion Books Ltd
Orion House, 5 Upper St Martin's Lane, London WC2H 9EA

A CIP catalogue record for this book is available
from the British Library

ISBN 0 575 07158 3

Typeset in Great Britain by
Selwood Systems, Midsomer Norton
Printed and bound by
Butler & Tanner Ltd, Frome and London

Bliss was it in that dawn to be alive,
but to be young was very heaven!

WILLIAM WORDSWORTH

Contents

Acknowledgements

Of course, this book would not have been possible without the help of some good folks who gamely cast their minds back across the mists of time to recall the sights, sounds and smells of the World Cup, Mexico, 1970.

First and foremost, I must extend an enormous thank you to the members of that illustrious England party for their generous indulgence of me and their fond reminiscences – Alan Ball, Jack Charlton, Allan Clarke, Terry Cooper, Emlyn Hughes, Norman Hunter, Brian Labone, David Sadler, Alex Stepney, Peter Thompson and Dr Neil Phillips, the England team physician, whose ear was Sir Alf's throughout. Gentlemen, you are heroes all. It was a pleasure.

Enormous gratitude must be extended, too, to the brandishers of lip-mic and battered Remington, whose combat experience of three decades ago is still recalled vividly (even though there's been another World Cup in Mexico since) – Barry Davies, Hugh Johns (thanks, Joan, for a lovely cottage pie), Ken Jones, David Lacey and Jeff Powell. Cheers, chaps, for some real gems.

I am also indebted to everyone else who helped steer me in the right direction along this fascinating journey – David Barber at the Football Association, Joan Byrne at Liverpool FC, Peter Lockwood at Leeds United FC, Mark Rowan at Everton FC, the Manchester United Legends office, Fiona Williams at BBC Sport. Plus, the superb resources and helpful staff of the BFI National Film and Television Archive, the British Library, the National Sound Archive and, notably, the Newspaper Library branch of the British Library, an absolutely vital national institution. I'm much obliged, too, to Philip Parr for diligently sub-editing the manuscript.

Finally, especially, and extremely loudly, boundless thanks to the two splendid souls without whom this project would never have been realised – editor Ian Preece, a true gent of the highest order, who's nurtured this baby right from the off, and Kate Hordern, my wonderful, wonderful agent. To be believed in is a warm and tingly thing.

To everyone. I owe you all. BIG TIME . . .

Preface

I was only young when England won the World Cup. And, much as I'd like to think I was part of the collective experience – dancing a Nobby Stiles-ish jig as Big Geoff belted in his third; swinging my way across the Beatles-soaked, Mini-driving sixties in a Paisley-clad celebratory frenzy – the reality is I have no recollection of the game whatsoever.

It was just recently I learned the awful truth. Far from sharing in the country's greatest post-war moment, I had been removed ignominiously to the back garden early in the second half for 'incessant talking' – fit enough punishment for a boy of three.

And yet I *feel* like I remember the match – every move, every kick – the glories spoon-fed over the coming years, sealing that notion of English footballing supremacy and general British invincibility that we, the so-called Airfix generation, carried with us through our junior years.

England – Champions of the World. *Fact.*

By my reckoning, you'd have to be well into your forties now to have any substantial recall of the events of that July afternoon, which means that, for most of the population, the 'Boys of '66' are but legend, their exploits burnished by the golden glow of hindsight, which tends to obscure the truth that, at the time, England were quite unfancied to win the tournament at all.

Indeed, critics and Scotsmen will oft point out that, but for some gerrymandering of the draw and benevolent officiating (what price now a Zapruder-style film of Hurst's controversial goal?), they mightn't have anyway.

Though boo-sucks to all that.

If there is one complaint, it's that this unique and fleeting achievement in our sporting history has become the ball and chain shackled to the leg of our collective consciousness ever since. Had England never won, at least that victory wouldn't loom so large.

Better – had England bagged *other* trophies, it might ease the weight of the '66 crown that bears so heavily.

Such was nearly the case.

Sport historians will gleefully tell you that, had the Football Association bothered to enter an international team for the first three World Cup tournaments in the 1930s, it might have been a different story. Though that is mere conjecture. What is more reasonable supposition is that with a superior pool of players at his disposal than in 1966, and with everything going for them, Sir Alf Ramsey's England squad should have triumphed in Mexico in 1970.

They didn't, of course, Alf's lads crashing out to the Germans in exceptional circumstances – due in no small part, as everyone knows, to the last-minute strickening of England's and the world's number-one goalkeeper.

'I still think to this day if Banksie had played we'd have won,' says Jack Charlton, who watched that game as a reserve. 'I still think to this day if *I'd* have played we'd have won.'

But what a terrible moment it was.

For those youths reared on that misplaced notion of English supremacy, the scars have remained. Do not underestimate the psychological legacy of defeat. The Battle of León is the Airfix child's Dunkirk.

No, for a whole chunk of thirtysomething society – too young to appreciate 1966 but dosed-up on all the triumphalism – it is *that* World Cup which holds a special place in our affections – the crackly commentary of David Coleman and the fuzzy, solarised images, broadcast for the first time in colour (not that many people had it), only going to cloak events in a surreal, mythic glow. Pelé and Bobby Moore hugging in the centre circle; Banks's save; altitude; heat; a mass of sideburns and wristbands; the Esso coin collection.

And yet, perhaps due to England's failure – like some errant cousin that the family has excommunicated – the Mexico World Cup has, in this country, been consigned to a far-flung corner of the archival field – few books or videos available, the occasional clip of those quarter-final goals replayed, seemingly, only when it's time to lose to the Germans again.

'All I ever see now is Müller scoring that goal,' Brian Labone tells me. 'I wish I'd been on royalties. Twenty pounds a go, I'd have been a millionaire by now.'

Strange really, for Mexico 1970 remains arguably the most important World Cup of all. It gave us the greatest team of all time (Brazil); the best-ever player (Pelé); three of the most dramatic international encounters imaginable (England v. Brazil, England v. West Germany and the West Germany v. Italy semi-final).

It was, too, the only occasion England have entered such a tournament as World Champions with the general public fully justified in believing that they could succeed again.

Somewhat perversely, it might be said that two of England's most sublime World Cup performances of all time, against Brazil and West Germany, came in games in which they actually lost – the heat, altitude and humidity reducing England to playing a type of slow possession football more in keeping with the global game than they have ever achieved since. (Or perhaps this says more about our inordinate capacity to assume the role of the heroic loser.)

Mexico 1970 was the first 'modern' World Cup, shaping everything about international football as we know it today. Aside from the practicalities of the game (the introduction of substitutes, the first use of yellow and red cards), it marked a TV revolution. A year after satellite technology has brought the world together to watch the moon landing, such modern marvels were employed to forge a global village for the world's biggest sporting event, making the goings-on at the Guadalajara Hilton as nonchalantly familiar as those at the Crossroads Motel.

On the home front, it was media heaven – blanket coverage, for one, and the first real 'tabloid' tournament, the country whipped into a patriotic fervour such that, come the arrest of Bobby Moore, in the infamous Bogotá bracelet affair, it seemed only right and proper that John Bull would mete out vengeance on Johnny Foreign-Trouser. (And not eat his stinking muck, either. With the 1970 World Cup deemed the footballing equivalent of the package Torremolinos jaunt, the FA decided they should take all their own food with them to Mexico – as well as the team bus.)

Fish fingers aside, it was certainly the last romantic World Cup – the ending of an era of free-flowing football before it became submerged by tactical negativity; when the great players were chainsmoking matadors rather than sinewy robots; when extra-time meant socks round ankles and soldiering on through agonising pangs of cramp. Certainly, too, an enlightened time for the roving sports reporters who travelled with the squads as members of their parties and could wander in and out of camps and speak to players at will.

'I remember going to Puebla to this little two-star hotel in the high street and being able to walk in and go and chat to the Israelis,' says the *Guardian*'s David Lacey, rather poignantly, given what was to follow.

Two years later, the Munich Olympic massacre changed everything. The staging of international sporting tournaments was now an entirely different proposition – security became tight, 'Access All Areas' was duly denied, sportsmen were no longer 'us' but 'them', and football, anyway, was about to enter a new dark, cynical age.

Alas, by the time of the 1974 World Cup, things had changed for England – 'Clown' Tomaszewski and Poland had seen that Ramsey's team no longer had a seat at the top table; Alan Ball had started wearing white boots.

Sadly, too, the same Brazilians who won so exuberantly in 1970 had turned into spiteful Afro-ed assassins, hacking their way to an ignominious exit. And, in tune with club football around the world, the concerns of commercialism started to dictate the international game.

It seems symbolic that, soon after Brazil won the 1970 tournament, keeping the Jules Rimet Trophy outright, this totem of football's golden age should have been stolen and lost for ever.

There are still some wondering how the hell it wasn't England who were bringing the cup home again. With this whole competition seemingly set up for an England–Brazil final, the cataclysmic showdown between Europe and Latin America, somehow it went awry, England's demise at the hands of the West Germans flummoxing players even now.

'I still can't believe it to this day. I've never been so in control in an England side in all my life,' laments Alan Ball. 'To think we were ever going to get beaten is a bizarre thought.'

('I still blame Terry Cooper,' quips Jack Charlton, at least able to extract some humour out of the situation.)

But England's demise, too, coincided with the end of an era at home. If the swinging sixties marked the last hurrah of Britain's post-war jubilation, and the World Cup its sporting highlight, then it was fitting that the loss of the trophy four years later should be synchronised with the slide into a new age – Conservatism, industrial decline, a fall in hem-lines, hooliganism and Enoch Powell's attempted race war. Even the Beatles' split in the run-up to the tournament seemed entirely in keeping.

Britain, too, was facing stark questions about its own role – integration into Europe? What to do about Northern Ireland? *Plus ça change*. And, with the nation riddled with strikes and rising inflation, there was the sense that Old Girl Britannia, having gorged herself on success over the previous decade, was now developing an excessive amount of cellulite.

It was twelve years before England would play in a World Cup again – an entire childhood – by which time the 'Boys of '70' were but memory, too, England having moved into a new phase of bubble perms, Admiral shirts, and shorts so tight it still leaves Kevin Keegan with an expression of permanent anguish.

Not that the Mexico World Cup was *quite* as innocent as we might think, for though on the field it amounted to the last great football carnival, behind the scenes affairs could not have been in sharper contrast. Cloaked in the murkier aspects of Latin American politics – war, espionage, blackmail, kidnapping, corruption, the machinations of military regimes, rumoured CIA involvement, an alleged poisoning, even voodoo – Graham Greene or Ian Fleming could not have scripted Mexico 1970 better, exemplified for England by that whole Bobby Moore business, the full details of which have only just come to light with the release of the files from the Public Records Office.

Moore, of course, is no longer with us, passing away, sadly, well before his time, as did another unsung hero of that Mexican June, Keith Newton; Sir Alf Ramsey and trainer Harold Shepherdson, old soldiers both, simply fading away in the ensuing years.

For Ramsey, the 1970 World Cup marked the beginning of the end, and it is touching to hear old pros still talk of the man with such great affection. With no time for the press, no time for the authorities, Alf was a players' man through and through. If the loss of England's crown were not bad enough for those who went to Mexico, it is the subsequent treatment of their boss that still rankles most.

'If Alf Ramsey had been born in another country, after being sacked by the FA, I wonder if he'd have been lost to the great game we all love, for the rest of his life, which he was really,' mourns Allan Clarke. 'I hope we've learned lessons from that.'

The answer to which, sadly, is probably not. But we can always live in hope.

In 1970 the air was full of it. This, then, is the story of what happened . . .

Introduction

A Rumble in the Jungle

Summer 1969

No one's sure who started the damn thing, each side laying blame squarely at the foot of the other. Though whether the territorial integrity of Honduras has been brutally violated by El Salvador (as Honduras protests) or such action is a pre-emptive strike to ward off an imminent Honduran invasion (as El Salvador claims), the result is still the same.

On 14 July, at sundown, eight P-51 Mustangs of the Salvadorean Air Force – the *entire* Salvadorean Air Force – groan across the Honduran sky and release their bombs. Creaking relics of World War Two – fighter planes at that, with minimal payload – the damage inflicted is more symbolic than material. But, having barnstormed Toncontin Airport in the Honduran capital Tegucigalpa, the mission is enough to satisfy El Salvador's military dictatorship, which makes a grand song and dance about smiting the eye of its neighbour...

Until dawn that is, when eight Honduran Corsairs of similar vintage – the *entire* Honduran Air Force – are dispatched to repay the courtesy.

Faring marginally better, the ageing rust-buckets – US cast-offs all – set fire to a fuel depot at Acajutla, creating just enough smoke to remind the locals of the perils of tweaking the mighty Honduran tail. And, moreover, spelling out the diplomatic state that now exists between the two countries: war.

It does not take long, however, for Ruritanian farce to turn to international tragedy. With El Salvador's four-tug-boat navy being of little use – its shores lying on the Pacific, Honduras's on the Caribbean – the Salvadorean Army launches a land offensive, thrusting a motorised division forty miles into Honduran territory.

1

Running into stiff resistance at Nacaome, seventy-five miles from Tegucigalpa, vehicles get bogged down in the rainy season mud, fuel and ammunition soon run out, and, with all planes now grounded due to a lack of spare parts, the fighting becomes rather more primitive. Soon both sides abandon professional pretence altogether to become nations at arms, and thousands of rural peasants without guns, uniforms or boots are duly press-ganged into service, unleashed into the swamps and forests to machete each other with glee.

With a common ethnicity and language and the fact that the border has never been clearly defined, execution of military strategy is somewhat haphazard. But with carnage extending now along the full length of the 860-mile frontier, and refugees pouring into adjacent Guatemala, the Organisation of American States (OAS), the international mutual security organisation, becomes concerned.

As the conflict escalates, power is cut, phone lines go dead, El Salvador and Honduras are severed from the outside world. And with each side proclaiming 'great patriotic victory' and 'heroic resistance', the American continent is given its biggest headache since the Cuban Missile Crisis . . .

When Maurício Rodríguez belted in the winner for El Salvador in a World Cup qualifying match, vanquishing Honduras 3–2, he probably did not imagine his actions would prompt such an outbreak of hostilities. But then national sport, and especially football, has long been a tool of the military dictatorships which run virtually every country in Latin America – the tin-pot regimes appreciating the worth of harnessing national sporting prowess in order to foster patriotism or divert from domestic turmoil.

The Mexican authorities certainly know the value of it. Two days before the Mexico City Olympics, President Gustavo Díaz Ordaz, behind the smokescreen of the Games, and hardly pursuing the Olympian ideal, sanctioned the shooting and bayoneting to death of 250 protesting students in one of the capital's plazas. The staging of the World Cup in 1970 will prove very useful, too, in the run-up to the shrewdly timed national elections.

In Brazil, President General Emilio Garrastazu Médici has hitched his star securely to the football wagon, meddling in team affairs, placing the 1970 World Cup squad under his generals, in the realisation that, just as the World Cup victories of 1958 and 1962 brought a great surge of patriotism, failure, as happened in 1966, can plunge the country into despair. Indeed, it is said that the CIA, in order to prevent destabilisation of South America's largest state, will go to any lengths – *any* lengths – to ensure that Brazil's footballers emerge victorious.

In Uruguay, where President Jorge Pacheco Areco has put the country under emergency rule, a strong Uruguayan performance in the 1970 World Cup will be a very welcome relief. And in Argentina, riddled with strikes and discontent, President General Ongania – without this time the crutch of sporting achievement, given the national football team's miserable, faltering qualifying campaign – knows his days are numbered.

Poor old Argentina still believes it should be hosting this, the ninth World Cup, the awarding of the tournament, during the 1964 Olympics in Tokyo, coming after a controversial and narrow vote, racking FIFA with internal wrangling and the type of unseemly bidding wars that will characterise all sports politics henceforth – underlining once and for all what a valuable political prize the hosting of such a major event can be...

In the context of the political tension that existed between El Salvador and Honduras, it was only a matter of time before the football match became the Football War.

In truth, conflict had been simmering for ages. El Salvador, with a population of three million, is the smallest and most densely populated country in Latin America. Honduras, with a third fewer people but five times the land mass, has long been the destination for thousands of Salvadorean peasants crossing the vague border in search of spare soil – the 'fourteen families', the coffee barons who own most of El Salvador's land and call the shots for the military government of President Colonel Fidel Sánchez Hernández, tacitly encouraging the exodus.

When Honduras, the region's poorest state, began a policy of land reform, then, trouble was inevitable. Conveniently avoiding the tracts owned by the large American fruit corporations that control the economy of this genuine banana republic, the military-backed regime of President Oswaldo López Arellano began going for the softer touch, dispossessing the 300,000 illegal Salvadorean settlers, blaming these interlopers for all the country's ills.

The Salvadorean government, aside from having its nationals bad-mouthed, did not appreciate the flood of returnees, either, many now with inflamed leftist sympathies. An ambitious charge of 'genocide' was duly levelled against Honduras. And from that there was no turning back.

It was against this backdrop that the countries confronted one another on the football pitch, each side contesting for leadership of Qualification Group Thirteen – the CONCACAF (Confederation of North, Central American and Caribbean Association Football) region – the top team assured of a place in next year's World Cup Finals. Mexico usually won the group easily but, as hosts of the 1970 tournament, and therefore qualifying automatically, a rare opportunity had arisen for another nation – El Salvador, Honduras, the USA or Haiti – to shine upon the global stage.

On 8 June 1969, before a crowd resembling something only slightly removed from a lynch mob, the El Salvador team contested the play-off opener in Tegucigalpa, losing, perhaps wisely, 1–0. Intimidated, sleep-deprived, spat at and beaten up on the way back to the airport, they escaped to El Salvador to be greeted as heroes.

With its citizens whipped into a patriotic fervour, it seemed only probable that for the return leg in the capital San Salvador, the hosts would supply an even ruder welcome. And thus, on 15 June, defeated 3–0 (probably the safest result under the circumstances), the Honduran players were duly whisked back to the border in an armoured car while the home fans went to work on the travelling support, killing two and setting fire to 200 cars bearing Honduran number plates. In Honduras, a further 1,500 Salvadorean settlers were chased out. And, on 26 June, diplomatic relations were broken off, the frontier closed.

Not that the soccer contest was over. With aggregate score not applying, a third, deciding game was required, staged at a heavily policed ground in neutral Mexico City. And, in the wake of El Salvador's ultimate triumph, a series of border incidents followed that pushed the countries towards the inevitable – El Salvador's land incursion conducted, officially, to protect its brethren from Honduran persecution...

*

4

And so now, in Washington, at a hastily convened meeting of the OAS, diplomats do their best to contain the dispute and prevent the conflict spreading to surrounding countries – all of which have fractious military regimes and, under the guise of exterminating revolutionaries and Castro-ites, are all itching for a pop at a neighbour.

Representatives from El Salvador and Honduras are dragged by the ear before the OAS to explain their actions. And, on 18 July at 10 p.m., a temporary ceasefire is obtained while a seven-man team, led by Dr Guillermo Sevilla-Sacasa, the ambassador from Nicaragua, shuttles back and forth between the combatants' capitals on a series of fifty-minute flights.

The United States, meanwhile, somewhat embarrassed that it had armed both sides to the teeth, and with President Nixon's military brass preoccupied with the small matter of Vietnam (not to mention the American public currently enthralled by the twin fascinations of the Apollo XI moonshot and Ted Kennedy's exploits at Chappaquiddick), is happy to let the natives patch things up. After all, an ongoing mission by Nixon's special envoy Nelson Rockefeller to build diplomatic bridges down south is proving to be a disaster – rebuffed by Chile and Peru, protested in Venezuela, forced to cut short his trip to Bolivia, Rockefeller-owned stores firebombed in Buenos Aires.

Deadlines for an El Salvador withdrawal come and go, angry ambassadors thump tables, and President Colonel Sánchez Hernández, having visited the front line and realised that he's never been more popular back home, reveals his grand design of pushing right through to the Caribbean, making mighty El Salvador mistress of two oceans.

Enough is enough. With the Pope expressing concern, the UN getting agitated, and El Salvador showing no signs of withdrawal, at midnight, 29 July, OAS Secretary-General Galo Plaza drives to the Salvadorean embassy in Washington and bangs heads together.

A diplomatic solution is reached. With Honduras's wrist duly slapped for mistreatment of its Salvadorean immigrants, El Salvador, in return, will be allowed to save face. To a roomful of cheering diplomats, the Salvadorean Foreign Minister, Dr José Guerrero, reads a terse statement citing not *withdrawal* of his army, but 'troop redeployment' to back behind the border. And so, on 30

July, two weeks after it kicks off, the Football War comes to an end.

The fighting has lasted four days, killed 3,000 people (80 per cent of them Honduran) and caused $50 million worth of damage. In a year's time a demilitarised zone extending 1.8 miles each side of the border will be established to ward off threat of repetition.

Not that the El Salvador football team are yet through to the World Cup proper. Forced into a final play-off series against Haiti (who beat the USA), they lose 3–0 at home, gain a 2–1 reverse away in Port-au-Prince, and prevail 3–2 in the decider in the safe remove of Kingston, Jamaica...

Someone somewhere should have given the English Football Association a few words of warning about the passions football can arouse in these parts. A thousand miles north, after a goalless draw against Mexico in the Azteca Stadium, on their 1969 World Cup warm-up tour, a grumpy little Englishman in a light blue tracksuit is doing his best to prompt a diplomatic incident of his own.

At an ad hoc press conference outside the dressing rooms, Sir Alf Ramsey, England team manager and the man in question, declines to thank his hosts for their hospitality and instead runs through a litany of complaints to a stunned Mexican press: there was a band playing outside the hotel till 5 a.m.; the motorcycle escort to the stadium never showed up; the players were booed during the pitch inspection. 'I would have thought the Mexico public would have been delighted to welcome England,' he growls.

Three days later, after an FA XI have trounced a Mexico XI 4–0 in Guadalajara, he gives short shrift to local pressmen who, as is the custom, had wanted access to the dressing room, in particular to photograph a presentation being made to the England team by the state governor.

With the officials and the journalists harried out by an angry Ramsey, it is left to one Mexican paper to express its displeasure in print, harking back to Ramsey's previous encounter with men of that continent in the spiteful World Cup quarter-final of 1966. 'What can you expect,' it asks, 'from one who referred to the Argentinians as animals?'

El Salvador's qualification for next year's finals means no United States, the great 'Yankee imperialists'. Though there will be other

Anglos to take their place – England. A gringo is still a gringo. And Sir Alf has already fired an inadvertent salvo.

Whoever said sport and politics are separate entities had better think again. The 1970 World Cup looks set to be extremely eventful indeed.

It takes El Salvador twelve games and a war to secure a place in the World Cup Finals for the first time in its turbulent history. The team will finish bottom of its group in Mexico and come home after the first round without scoring a goal . . .

Chapter 1

Splendid Isolation

Thursday, 8 January 1970

Two unassuming, crusty Englishmen in crumpled suits board a morning commercial flight from London Heathrow and jet off to Caracas, Venezuela. Travelling business class, and clutching a small hard-shell case that never leaves either's hand, they arrive at their destination in the early afternoon, local time, and shuffle rather uneasily in the sticky heat of the transfer lounge before connecting with an onward flight to Mexico City.

The trip to Caracas, as it turns out, is a purely diversionary manoeuvre, a safer bet than flying from London to Mexico direct. The security of their cargo, it seems, is of paramount importance. An £83 insurance policy, putting its actual value at £9,000, three times its intrinsic worth, does not reveal the true extent of its importance, however. The fact is that the item they are transporting would be a priceless asset to any person, state or organisation – legitimate or otherwise – that came into its possession.

That night, on arrival at Mexico City airport, the two men are whisked off the plane by plain-clothes policemen and fast-tracked through Customs and Immigration. Then, with 200 undercover law officers lurking thereabouts – not one of them ever more than a few feet away and ready to spring into action, putting life on the line if need be – the two men clamber into a bullet-proof limo. Driven at break-neck speed through the city's streets, escorted by an armoured car and a dozen motorcycle outriders, they arrive at the Banco de Comercio, where the case is taken to the strongest bank vault and locked behind a ten-ton steel door under twenty-four-hour armed guard.

Mindful that its previous guardians once lost it, the Mexican security adviser assures the Englishmen that, from hereon in, until

21 June, the scheduled day of the next transfer, only a replica of the object in the case will ever be used in public. The tired men nod, one of them expresses profound sorrow about the handover but hopes that in five months he will be back to redeem the goods. And with that, Dr Andrew Stephen and Denis Follows, chairman and secretary of the Football Association, retire to their hotel – the Jules Rimet Trophy, the World Cup, having been conveyed safely to its new custodians . . .

The idea of England failing to retain their world crown does not bear thinking about, of course. And, ever since Kenneth Wolstenholme proudly burbled his bit about some people being on the pitch, the words 'World Champions' have, in footballing terms, been attached as a prefix to 'England'. Indeed, though less than four years since that epochal triumph, it seems incredible now that there was ever a time when England weren't.

The exploits of that glorious afternoon have long been burnished into legend: Hurst's disputed second, the Russian linesman, Nobby's toothless jig, Moore wiping his muddied hands on the Royal Box velvet. And when even little old ladies who, before 30 July 1966, could not tell the difference between Ray and Harold Wilson can now reel you off those eleven names – Banks, Cohen, Wilson, Stiles, Charlton, Moore, Ball, Hunt, Charlton, Hurst, Peters – argue the merits of the 4–3–3 system; know that 'wingless wonder' is not some strain of Emu, you know that the effect has been profound.

Wilson, Harold, certainly thinks so. He has made great political capital out of the victory, milking his part in England's triumph (or at least his presence at it) for all its worth – if only because it gives him something with which to break the ice with foreign dignitaries. Anything that makes the nation happy and diverts from all those nasty strikes which are currently plaguing the country will surely stand him in good stead if, as the pundits predict, he goes for an election in May or June.

And, if Britain is still in the late throes of sixties swing, the evident feelgood factor is due in no small part to the feat of the men who gave the nation its finest footballing hour – proud pictures of the heroic team, beaming in their famous red shirts, adorning every pub, greasy spoon, launderette and classroom from Cornwall to

Cumberland. As ubiquitous as the portrait of Her Maj – trainer Harold Shepherdson to the left, Sir Alf to the right, Bobby Moore, the talismanic white knight at the centre, cradling the overpolished Jules Rimet and its spanning angel, like a proud, scrubbed schoolboy.

No one now remembers the other poor blighters, the squad members, even the ones who played – Ian Callaghan, Terry Paine, John Connelly – though the obligatory bit of sympathy is still reserved for poor old Jimmy Greaves – Greavesie – the world-class finisher who would have walked into any other international side and who had his 'life's greatest moment' snatched away.

Never mind the fact now that England were never expected to win it in the first place, reckoned to be a quarter-final shot at best. England are World Champions, and we're all rather happy with it, thank you very much – far too content to have to compete for it all over again.

Back home, football is certainly reaping the benefits of that World Cup win. Attendances have boomed in the ensuing years, there is more money in the game than ever, the likes of George Best – 'El Beatle' – with his colourful extra-curricular activities, are elevating the profile of footballer to that of pop star. Not entirely unconnected with that, women have started going to matches, too.

Though football is still only on the eve of that shift into 1970s flamboyant hedonism. By and large, footballers, and we're talking of a Football League where older players started their careers before the abolition of the maximum wage, and dutifully did their National Service en route, still exude a sort of collar-and-tie, Brylcreem decency. Not quite the ride-on-the-bus-with-the-fans cliché of yore, but certainly a sport where the players are still 'us', the Saturday afternoon on the terrace is a safe and sacred ritual, only with those pitchbound idols now, thanks to the glories of television, all household names.

Managers are still largely martinet Scotsmen (Bill Shankly, Matt Busby, Tommy Docherty), or avuncular trilbied Englishmen (Don Revie, Joe Mercer, Bertie Mee). The disciplined players are still their 'boys'. Though, tearing a strip off Bestie, a new breed of flair player has emerged to give the old guard the willies – Peter Osgood and Alan Hudson at Chelsea, Rodney Marsh at Queens Park Rangers, Tony Currie at Sheffield United (there's even a flash coach in Manchester City's Malcolm Allison). Too cocky and 'Continental' by half, they say. Objects of mistrust. Lacking the perceived Anglo-Saxon virtues of hard graft and discipline, the very kind epitomised by the England 1966 side (no room for mercurials like Greaves) and which has provided the model for all club sides to emulate.

Whether it makes for beautiful football is another matter entirely, but it certainly does the trick. In the 1969–70 season alone, Leeds, Manchester City and Arsenal are odds-on to sweep the European, European Cup Winners' and Fairs Cups. It is entirely accurate to say that at this very moment in time, English football, both at international and club level, is at the very height of its power.

Most of the men responsible for the boom are still around. Given that four years is a long time in football, though, it is perhaps surprising that most of the boys of '66 are still in the reckoning for the 1970 England squad, for which a preliminary twenty-eight names must be finalised by 15 April. Only George Cohen (retired), Ray Wilson, whose career has entered its twilight at Fourth Division Oldham, and Roger Hunt, who left Liverpool for Second Division Bolton, are no longer in the frame.

Hunt, 'Sir Roger' to his teammates, has been typically gallant. Mindful of Sir Alf Ramsey's loyalty to his old boys, but knowing that the future of England's strike force rests with younger legs, he has asked Ramsey not to consider him for Mexico. Greaves, now thirty, back in the England fold in 1966–67, had apparently done likewise, though in less intentional terms. He will not join an England party unless he is definitely going be playing. Ramsey, who would never cut such a deal and considers squad selection an honour in itself, has declined to get back to him on that.

Of the eleven men who took on West Germany that fabled afternoon, the spine of the team is still there. Bobby Moore, though enjoying indifferent form with West Ham, has been imperious on the international stage, a better defender now than ever. Geoff Hurst, 1966's surprise hero, has smoothed off the rough edges and become a sophisticated leader of the line. Banks, too, though stuck with another middling side, Stoke City, can still raise his gloves as the best keeper in the world. And little Alan Ball, who has moved from Blackpool to Everton, no longer a mere wide scurrier, is enjoying life in the engine room of club and country, on course for a Championship medal – 'playing some of the best football of my life,' he says.

Others are fading. Jack Charlton, still the rugged rock of all-conquering Leeds, but pushing thirty-five, has found his England centre-half shirt taken by the powerful Everton captain Brian Labone. And Nobby Stiles, who has suffered badly with injury, has lost his snappy defensive-midfield slot to the equally combative Alan Mullery of Spurs.

Some regulars, however, are patently off the boil. Bobby Charlton, the hub around which Alf built his World Cup winners, has, since skippering Manchester United to the European Cup in 1968, been brushed by the sense of impending decline that has enveloped Old Trafford in the post-Matt Busby era, his England place taken on occasion by the Manchester City workhorse Colin Bell.

And Martin Peters, who – but for a few seconds of injury-time – might have gone down in the history books as the scorer of the winning goal that Wembley afternoon, is suffering a patch of such poor form that he has asked his West Ham manager, Ron Greenwood, for a transfer to kickstart his career, granted for the close season.

Not that Peters doesn't know a thing or two. Just as he is used to ghosting in on the blind side of a defence, so he does the same with the press. On Monday, 16 March, the twenty-six-year-old becomes Britain's record transfer in a secret £200,000 swap deal taking him to Tottenham Hotspur and the disaffected Jimmy Greaves – an old mate from their days in Essex schools football – in the other direction. Officially, the move will give Peters a maximum of seven games at Spurs before the season's end, a risky move if he is hoping to book his Mexico ticket. Peters, however, practically knows that he'll be going anyway, as Alf's recently gone on TV and proclaimed him 'ten years ahead of his time'. Peters knows Alf, and Alf is not one who willingly eats his words. And just to prove a point, Peters scores on his debut against Coventry.

(Greaves, deemed 'finished' on ITV's *On the Ball* that same Saturday lunchtime – and by Bill Nicholson at that, the manager who just let him go – has a bone to pick, too. The striker scores nonchalantly on his West Ham debut, casually chewing gum on his way back to the centre circle, with a smirk that suggests he can do this sort of thing with his eyes shut.)

Other replacements for the '66 retirees have figured enough to be considered regulars. In place of Hunt has arrived the barrel-chested Manchester City forward Francis Lee, mischievous with the ball, a powerful shot on him, and not without a trick up his sleeve when the ref's back is turned. In defence Keith Newton and Tommy Wright of Everton, the Leeds pairing of Paul Reaney and Terry Cooper, and the young Liverpool dynamo Emlyn Hughes – 'Crazy Horse' – have all had a crack at full back. Norman Hunter, the bone-crunching defender of Leeds – a '66 squad member – has had the odd outing in Bobby Moore's shirt. Though, up front, only Jeff Astle, the big West Brom target man, has been given any real opportunity instead of, or alongside, Hurst.

Other deputies have had less chance. In goal, Chelsea's Peter Bonetti (also in the '66 squad) and Manchester United's Alex Stepney, despite distinguished club careers, have had little occasion to guest for the injury-free Banks...

In football terms England are still ranked number one, and their record as an international team in the games since '66 bears this out. Since winning the World Cup, they have played thirty-four matches and lost only four, which takes some doing. Though their grip on the game is perhaps less assured than they would wish. Success has come with the luxury that it has been seven years now since they last had to play a competitive qualifier against foreign opposition (entering automatically the World Cups of 1966 and 1970, and with the Home Internationals substituting as the group stage for the European Nations Cup). Indeed, a recent announcement that, for the 1972 European Nations Cup, England will have to scrap it out with the great unwashed of Greece, Switzerland and Malta is deemed to be well below England's lofty station.

Their status as World Cup winners, though, has certainly made England marked men, with even the most insignificant of friendly matches turned into ones as cut-throat as cup ties – every opposition desperate to put one over on them – a case proved by the Auld Enemy, Scotland, who caused red faces at Wembley in 1967 by becoming the first team to beat the new champions. Scotland, being Scotland, applied boxing logic. Having contended for the title successfully, it declared, Scotland was therefore the new Master of the Universe. Though England were having none of that.

Drawing the return in Glasgow saw them, not their northern neighbours, through to the final stages of the 1968 European Nations Cup (though a semi-final defeat against Yugoslavia – who lost in turn to Italy – has shown that staying on top is a tough proposition). As per historical convention, Britannia may rule the waves, but is no longer mistress of Europe, where, with the rise of new powers, storm clouds seem to be brewing.

England's relationship with world football, though, has never been a particularly comfortable one. Until 1966, and for all the bragging about bestowing on the world the beautiful game, England was a relatively new actor upon the global stage, a World Cup participant of a mere sixteen years, preferring instead the favoured state of splendid isolation.

The very first international match may have taken place between England and Scotland way back in 1872, but England's priorities within the international game, certainly for the first fifty years, had been confined largely to the Home International series – deemed a more challenging alternative to racking up a cricket score against Continental opposition.

When FIFA (Fédération Internationale des Football Associations) was formed in Paris in 1904, the British nations predictably remained sceptical: damn foreigners meddling. Though the English FA, with a rush of liberalism to the head (having just decreed, domestically, that players' shorts need no longer cover the knees), relented and soon joined for fear that laws might be made without the creator's consent.

The Great War interrupted proceedings, with the British nations still refusing to play former adversaries or neutrals in peacetime. And when, in 1928, a row over expenses for Olympic footballers blew up, the English, Scottish, Welsh and Northern Irish FAs withdrew from FIFA altogether. Though the British Associations allowed FIFA representation on *their* own committees to at least keep them in touch with the outside world (or more likely vice versa).

Wooing continued, such that in 1938, on the FA's seventy-fifth anniversary, FIFA sent a Rest of Europe team to Wembley for England to beat 3–0. But the upshot was that, excluded from FIFA, no British side was eligible for the first three World Cups – 1930, 1934 and 1938. England fans will often add – quite disingenuously –

that had they been able to send a team to each of those tournaments, they might, by World War Two, have already had a hat-trick of World Cup triumphs to crow about, especially given that the winners were invariably invited to Wembley for a chastening wallop.

Though it is a fanciful notion. In 1946 the spirit of rapprochement prompted the Home associations to join FIFA once and for all (and a united British team thumped a Rest of Europe side 6–1 at Hampden Park in front of 135,000). But England soon found herself in for a rude awakening. Having already begun to lose abroad in the inter-war period – to Spain, Hungary, France, Czechoslovakia, Austria, Switzerland, Yugoslavia and Italy – then sliding, eventually, to the famous Wembley defeat by Puskas' Mighty Magyars in 1953, England's hopes of waltzing into its first World Cup and claiming what was rightfully hers turned out to be a delusion of grandeur.

For the World Cup of 1950 in Brazil, England were given safe passage, FIFA having generously decreed that the Home International series would double as a qualifying group, the top two teams granted entry (the Scottish FA, rather parsimoniously, declaring they would only travel if champions and breathing a sigh of relief at finishing runners-up). But oh, how the world had passed England by. The long shorts, heavy ankle boots and button-up shirts of the England team were out of place in the Tropics, with the modern athletic gear and nimble gymnastics of the South Americans. Burdened by a panel of selectors who changed the team without rhyme or reason from game to game, not even a party containing Stanley Matthews, Tom Finney and Billy Wright could prevent what remains England's greatest humiliation: crashing out 1–0 to the amateurs of the USA in Belo Horizonte, the cold bucket of water on England's international ardour.

To one of England's defenders, a stocky full-back named Alf Ramsey, the South American debacle scarred deep, and England's forlorn return heralded what has forever been perceived since as the Latin hoodoo – the notion that little dark men, with their fancy tricks and spitting and foul play and gamesmanship, would always be the nemesis to the gentlemen of Albion. Thus followed defeat by Uruguay in the 1954 finals and a number of hidings by the new darlings of world football, Brazil. It was Brazil that knocked

England out of the World Cup, when the competition returned to that continent, in Chile in 1962 – a tournament at which Sheffield Wednesday's Peter Swan nearly died of dysentery. And lurking behind it all was the feeling that English, even European, football was locked in some cataclysmic struggle with Latin America.

The 1962 World Cup, most notable for the 'Battle of Santiago' between Chile and Italy, one of the most violent internationals ever played, told everyone in English circles all that needed saying about the volatile Latin temperament (the Italians, Latin themselves, included various ex-patriate South Americans in their line-up). More recently, World Cup Championship games between Celtic and Racing Club, and Manchester United and Estudiantes had been marred by mass brawls. And then, of course, there was the experience of 1966, the expulsion of two Uruguayans in their quarter-final against West Germany, eclipsed, rather more famously, by the antics of the Argentinians at Wembley, Ramsey running on to the pitch to stop his players swapping shirts, then lambasting the opponents as 'animals' while – unbeknown to the press at the time – the accused duly lived up to their billing, venting their spleens, quite literally, against the England dressing-room door.

And so now, for the forthcoming tournament of June 1970, England can justifiably take the moral high ground. For the first time officially, rather than fancifully, England can go into battle as a world power, the defending champions . . .

Except to those in Latin America. There, with that 'animal' remark ringing in their ears, the 1966 triumph has never really been regarded as bona fide. European refereeing practices – over-tolerant of the physical – had put paid to Brazil's assault; it was fussy and vindictive officiating, they claim, that did for Uruguay and Argentina.

Plus, wasn't there the question of home advantage? That last-minute switch of England's semi-final back to Wembley from Goodison? And, of course, that disputed Hurst goal? It was a conspiracy, no less, something sure to be prolonged under FIFA and the stewardship of Sir Stanley Rous – the 'English King' . . .

For England, the awarding of the World Cup to Mexico has raised obstacles way beyond the field of play. It would be tough enough defending any trophy away from home. With the World Cup only ever having been won once by a team outside its own continent (Brazil in Sweden, 1958), the odds would already appear to be stacked against England mounting a successful defence.

Promising the biggest and best football extravaganza the world has ever seen, it is likely that Mexico – backed by American money and infrastructure – will live up to its word (the 1968 Mexico Olympics were a success, and the Azteca, its football stadium, is light years ahead of any sporting arena in Europe), though the alien conditions that most teams will have to play in may prove to be Mexico's Achilles heel as a venue.

This summer, each of the thirty-two games, at the designated five venues – Mexico City, Guadalajara, Puebla, Toluca and León – can expect to kick-off in temperatures between 90 and 100 degrees Fahrenheit. With a seven-hour time difference and the demands of European TV audiences dictating that games either kick-off at 4 p.m. or, for the key Sunday clashes, noon, it is going to be an almighty strain on those countries unaccustomed to such a climate. Given, too, that these venues are all situated on the central Mexican plateau between 5,000 and 9,000 feet in altitude, the rarefied air will, in addition, place an incredible demand on hearts and lungs.

England, as holders, will play their games in the country's second-biggest stadium in Mexico's second city, Guadalajara (the Azteca, of course, providing the 'home' for the Mexican team). What they don't know yet is the identity of the opposition they will meet there.

The furtive mission of the FA to Mexico has been for a reason. On the afternoon of Saturday, 10 January, at Mexico City's Hotel Maria Isabel, and presided over by Rous, a thousand people, including sixteen dignitaries and a contingent of around 250 press men, gather for the World Cup draw. Stephen and Follows, also present, are discreetly assured that the Jules Rimet Trophy on display is a fake. And, as befits the new global televisual age, the events over the coming half an hour will be broadcast live by satellite around the world – quite timely for those back home for whom the proceedings fit neatly into that night's special edition of *Match of the Day.*

Not that people are getting too worked up about the outcome. 'The Draw. It's just a formality,' proclaims the morning's *Daily*

Express. They are not wrong. Though FIFA never *officially* seed the entrants, in reality they do (after the draw they will even admit as much). Though it only requires logic to work out how it's all going to pan out.

There will be sixteen nations competing, four groups of four teams, the winners and runners-up of each group going straight into an eight-team knock-out. Groups One and Two will constitute the top half of the draw, Groups Three and Four the bottom. Mexico, as hosts, will head Group One in the top half, which means that, due to the quaint notion that hosts and holders should meet in the final, England will be in the bottom half, Group Three. With West Germany already hinted to head Group Four, based at León, it's a toss-up between Russia and Brazil to head Group Two – most likely Brazil, playing in fixtures spread between two small stadiums in Toluca and Puebla.

Or so it would seem. FIFA, however, has other obligations. The three South American countries – Brazil, Uruguay and Peru – must be kept apart and are unlikely to feature in Mexico's group. Arabic Morocco and Jewish Israel must be separated lest Morocco toe the Arab party line and pull out. And these two, plus El Salvador, must be split up anyway to balance out the weaklings. It is also known that FIFA would prefer to separate Western Europe from the Eastern Bloc, meaning Belgium, Italy, England and West Germany are unlikely to be pooled together; the same going for Russia, Czechoslovakia, Romania and Bulgaria. And in the certain event that not all these criteria will be fulfilled, inoffensive Sweden will be used as the 'wild card' when shuffling things around.

To many observers and journalists there are mutterings. However much FIFA witters on about this being the world's supreme soccer tournament, it, in no way, contains the best sixteen teams in the world. Indeed, the continental tournaments, the European Nations Cup and the South American Championships, seem far more meritocratic by comparison, genuinely representing the best teams of those regions. In this draw Europe, the cradle of the game, will get only half of the sixteen places (England are already there as hosts). South America, for all its rich World Cup history, will have only three. While FIFA's evangelical mission to spread the game to Africa, Asia and Oceania has rewarded three amateur sides that have come through flimsy qualifying groups and who are not in the same league as several European teams – Spain, Hungary, Scotland, Poland, Austria, Portugal, Yugoslavia and the emerging Dutch – who came within spitting distance of the Mexico plane.

A twenty-four-team tournament, it is argued, would allow the best of both worlds, and Rous, mindful of the criticism, has suggested that for the next World Cup, in Munich 1974, there may well be restructuring. But until then El Salvador, Morocco and Israel (who won their Asian group when '66 darlings North Korea refused to play them) proudly take their places among the world's sixteen most powerful footballing nations.

Morocco owe their presence to a good deal of fortune. Though coming through a tough eleven-team African group, their play-off against Tunisia was won on a coin toss. With Tunisia having correctly guessed the initial flip, it took some bright spark in the Moroccan camp with a book of FIFA regulations to realise that the referee, by making the toss in the tunnel and not in his dressing room, had violated the international code. Amid heated Tunisian protest, he was forced to spin again. Tails it was. Morocco went through.

As in 1966, England are the UK's sole representative, a Scotland side imploding against West Germany, while Wales and Northern Ireland never stood much of a chance – the former given a stiff what-for by both Italy and East Germany, the latter placed unfortunately in a group with the USSR. George Best – Pelé's favourite player – will be denied his one chance to appear on the world stage.

In South America, with Brazil, for the first time since 1958, having to go through the indignity of qualifying, the competition has provided genuine shock. Argentina, failing to acclimatise for a vital away match in the Andes of Bolivia, and resorting to such thuggery that President General Ongania himself warned them about their conduct, are out. The Peruvians under the managership of former Brazilian World Cup winner Didi, and topping their three-team group, have qualified instead, playing some spectacular football. And so, as expected, have Brazil, scoring hatfuls of goals, looking strong as the tournament favourites.

Despite the prior second-guessing, there is a dramatic inevitability as Monica Maria Cañedo, ten-year-old daughter of the president of the Mexican Football Association, draws the name of England's first group member out of the hat – Brazil. And while other nations sweat that they are not pulled out to appear in the same group, the realisation of the awesome task ahead for England begins to dawn. They will have to scrap like hell if they want to hang on to that trophy.

It will be Czechoslovakia and Romania who will make up Group Three's other two teams, not makeweights either one. The World Cup has got its Group of Death – every one should have one.

The tournament will commence with the opening ceremony at the Azteca on Sunday, 31 May, and conclude in the same stadium on 21 June, exactly three weeks later. In Group One, in Mexico City, the host nation will face the USSR, Belgium and El Salvador. In Group Two, at Puebla/Toluca, Italy will do combat with Uruguay, Sweden and Israel. In Group Four, at León, West Germany will take on Peru, Bulgaria and Morocco. And in Group Three, in Guadalajara, England will play Romania, Czechoslovakia and, according to the game schedule, Brazil, on Sunday, 7 June, at high and roasting noon.

Statisticians are duly summoned. Since May 1963 England have only won one out of seven games against the teams in their group (beating Czechoslovakia 4–2 at Bratislava): they drew 0–0 with the Czechs at Wembley; drew 0–0 with Romania in Bucharest in November 1968, and 1–1 at Wembley the following January. And while they drew 1–1 with Brazil at Wembley in May 1963, they were whipped 5–1 in Rio the following summer, and only last year lost there again (2–1).

But for all the divided opinion – 'I'm backing England to win again,' says Alan Barham of the *Guardian*; 'A South American team will probably win and my bet is Brazil,' claims Don Revie – and for all Denis Follows's diplomatic pronouncement about it being a 'group fit for champions', and how you've got to beat the best if you're going to win the trophy, England know they're going to have their work cut out.

It's only the group stages, but still. If 1966 had been characterised by Ramsey's perceived arrogant assertion that England *would* win the World Cup, there is none of that now.

'I have always thought it will be hard to win the World Cup in Mexico, but it will be harder still to get the trophy away from us,' he says.

He'll have to ask the staff at the Banco de Comercio about that . . .

Chapter 2

Dead Man's Shoes

Season 1969–70

Everybody's got a story about Sir Alf. George Cohen still chuckles about the time, during the last World Cup, when Ramsey took his squad to the set of the new James Bond film at Pinewood, introducing his players to the actor 'Seen' Connery.

Then there's that post-'66 banquet when Sir Alf, enjoying a rare drink and struggling to prevent his Essex accent from protruding through the elocuted veneer, supposedly declared to a waiter, in his poshest voice, 'I don't want no fuckin' peas.'

Allan Clarke, the young Leeds goal machine, will tell you about Alf's legendary ineptitude with humour and how, on his first England flight, chatting to Bobby Moore and Alan Ball, Alf approached him from the back of the cabin.

'Enjoying yourself, Allan?' said Alf.

'Aye, smashing,' replied Clarke.

'Well you're not here to enjoy yourself, you're here to work,' Ramsey snapped, the intended quip – an art he's never quite mastered – leaving three grown men to quake in their boots.

Peter Thompson of Liverpool does a good impression of the boss. Big Jack Charlton can dine out on an evening of Alf anecdotes. Though all of them, every England player, will walk through fire for the grumpy little bloke.

When Alf trudges through a players' lounge at 10 p.m., looks at his watch and declares, 'Time for bed,' you will not see twenty-two young men move faster. When Alf decides that the lads must be up at 6.30 a.m. for a cross-country run, you'll not hear a single peep.

'Very strict, a disciplinarian,' says Emlyn Hughes. 'But every one of the players has the utmost respect for Alf.'

In an interview on BBC radio, Big Jack tells David Coleman

what it's like to be on the wrong end of one of Ramsey's legendary icy stares. 'Every England player fears him in a very funny sort of way,' he confesses. 'I know I'm frightened of him a little bit.'

Inspirational, too, though, surely, fumbles Coleman. And what about respect?

'Frightening might be the better word,' echoes brother Bobby, sharing the Q&A. 'He frightens you. Call it respect if you want.'

Poor old Ramsey. He's a man out of his time. Fêted, knighted, but he's still the same old Alf – he of the short temper; the mistrust of foreigners; suspicious of the media; and the elocution lessons, legacy of the days of self-betterment, which have flattened his Essex accent but left a trail of clipped participles a-hangin'.

The boys of '66 were fashioned somewhat in his own image. Still mindful of their ps and qs, still in short back and sides while the rest were letting it all hang down – one reason he never saw eye to eye with a Bobby Dazzler like Greaves.

Now in 1970, though the sideburns have grown and the hair is brushed forward (except in the case of Bobby Charlton), his clothes-conscious players squeezing into tight slacks and turtle necks, they are not that different in core value from the squad of yore. Financially they are still only on the eve of realising their earnings potential. But there are yet no agents, no business managers, no distractions – Ramsey's footballers are just content to make a living at the game. Though they have each been given an honour beyond price: playing for England.

No, you'll not get an England player to say anything against Alf, even the ones he's discarded. Alf's been there and done it just like them; 100 per cent a players' man; doesn't give a damn about the critics, the FA and certainly the press. As a siege mentality has built around his squads over the years, it has only fostered bonding; Ramsey, with a unique gift of being authoritative yet able to be one of the players when needed, joining in practice games at every opportunity.

'I went to Mexico for him as much I did for anyone else,' Norman Hunter will say later, not one known to get overly sentimental. 'You'll never hear one of the players have a bad word about him.'

'By the far the best manager I've ever had,' adds Clarke, and so says everyone else.

Though for all Alf's conservative approach – commutes every

day to London from Ipswich, a non-smoker, has a rare glass of sherry, dotes on his Dachshund – the man is a contradiction. For at heart Alf is a moderniser, having dragged the England national set-up kicking and screaming into the modern age.

When he declared, before the '66 tournament, that England would win the World Cup, and said it so emphatically – and contrary to popular judgement – he was merely stating what he believed.

Still only fifty – though some records put him at forty-eight, having fudged his papers in the army – Ramsey's grounding is strictly old school, his formative days spent before the almighty conflagration that cleaved the century in two. It was the war, rather serendipitously, that brought Ramsey into professional football, allowing him to guest for Southampton as an amateur while commanding an anti-aircraft battery in Hampshire with the Duke of Cornwall's Light Infantry. And his late blooming, as Spurs and England right back – and the reason he knocked those years off – was borne by one whose gifts came from hard work and the coaching manual rather than any God-given talent.

His subsequent managerial exploits are now legend. In 1955, his playing days over, he took over as manager of lowly Ipswich Town, struggling in the Third Division South. And, with scant resources and a motley crew of old pros, fashioned a side whose meteoric rise through the divisions culminated with the 1961–62 League Championship. That same year, when Walter Winterbottom quit the England managership and none of the favoured successors would touch the assignment with a barge-pole, the FA came calling. Ipswich, as a thank you, gave Ramsey their blessing. Though, a loyal old sort, he refused to take the job full time till he'd finished the season at Portman Road. In October 1962 Ramsey became England caretaker. In May 1963 he was England manager...

On one condition: the Selection Committee, which until then had chosen the team, presenting it as a fait accompli to the man nominally in charge, was to be scrapped. Alf would only do the job if he was in sole control – the seniors, the under-23s, the youth team, the lot. Rather desperate, the FA agreed, though the suits, now with nothing to do, rather embarrassed when he went and won the World Cup, and since then rather jealous of his knighthood, have spent the rest of Ramsey's reign conspiring to get rid of him.

It's been a long haul. Early games were lost, old stars like Johnny Haynes were discarded. And, by December 1965, Ramsey climaxed the first segment of his stewardship with a 2–0 away win over Spain, unleashing a positional tactic known as 4–3–3, the blueprint established for future glories.

Plus, Alf's a great motivator: doesn't rant, doesn't rave, just has a canny knack for quietly instilling players with an unshakeable confidence. It's done with great conviction. Not only did Ramsey play in that infamous game in Belo Horizonte (indeed, he was to blame for the American goal), but Alf's final act, during his thirty-second cap, was to score a late penalty in that Wembley defeat by Hungary. Party to the two greatest humiliations in English football, he's had a point to prove ever since. And now, with great satisfaction, he's rammed it right down their throats.

Not that it's been made easy for him. Whereas in 1966 the Football Association bent over backwards to ensure Alf's wishes were accommodated in the build-up to the finals – it was, after all, their party and they wanted to be seen to be throwing a good one – in the years since, the crusty old duffers have shown him no favours.

In a rare moment of generosity, the League and FA have conspired to help on one score. The 1969–70 League season will finish three weeks early, allowing England to depart for Mexico on 4 May, a month before their first game. But just that one thing, that's it. Len Shipman, Football League president and chairman of the FA International Committee, has openly declared that the League will no longer be helping the national team.

In the *News of the World*, Alan Hardaker, secretary of the Football League, a body that has benefited enormously from the 1966 triumph, spells out the party line: 'World Cups, European Cups, we can live without them. I get annoyed by people talking about nothing but the World Cup. What possible difference can it make to our football?' he asks.

That huge rise in football match attendances, perhaps?

'It was the weather which made the difference,' says Hardaker. 'Good weather always does.'

And so, in the 1969–70 season, the one which will culminate in the defence of their crown, and before the season's-end Home

Internationals, England have played just four internationals – Belgium, Portugal and Holland twice.

At a time when the machine should be being fine-tuned, club concerns, once again, have overridden those of country, with the paradox that the more successful the top clubs – like Leeds, involved in three competitions – are, the less their players are made available for international selection.

So few games has hardly left room for experimentation, hence Ramsey's reliance – not necessarily out of choice – on the old guard. Coupled with Alf's determination that England, champions or not, but especially since they are, should not lose games to *anyone*, even in friendlies, England, with its steady regulars, has adopted a posture of being hard to beat. There is a downside to this. For all its success, the England team has begun to bore the pants off everyone. And, with the odd exception – beating Scotland 4–1 last May, a successful 1969 Latin American tour – their unbeatable keeper, impervious defence and sturdy, workmanlike midfield are not matched by imagination in the last third of the pitch. England, the critics charge, do not *play* like champions.

In January 1970, after a dull 0–0 draw with Holland, the Wembley crowd boo England off the park, perhaps understandably, though the lust for glory has got out of check. The previous March, after trouncing France 5–0, an unusually rabid audience at the national stadium demanded double figures and derided Ramsey for not recalling Jimmy Greaves, who would have helped them to a more 'respectable' scoreline.

'You boobed, Sir Alf – England need that Osgood flair,' blasts George Best in the *News of the World* in February, echoing a clarion call for the mercurial Chelsea forward, rather than leaving him in the under-23s where he has twinkled yet again. 'Goal grabbing Astle flying high for Mexico,' adds the *Sun* after the Throstles forward dominates the air in a Football League versus Scottish League representative fixture.

Still, if Alf's good at anything it's his meticulous preparation. As far as he's concerned, the press can bitch all they like. His job is to go to Mexico and win, not put on a pantomime in north London. And winning in Mexico, in intense heat, thin air and against opposition who play the game in a completely different manner, will require a very particular type of football . . .

Altitude can do strange things to a footballer. It'll make him horribly short of breath, for one. At 5,212 feet, around a mile high, the pitch at the Jalisco Stadium, Guadalajara – even though the lowest of the five World Cup stadiums – is still above the critical mark at which physical capability begins to diminish. At such an elevation, the oxygen content of air is 20 per cent less than it is at sea level. Go straight out to play there without sufficient acclimatisation and it can be extremely taxing. While the body goes through its usual exertions, lungs strain vainly to provide adequate recovery, causing the heart to go into overdrive, pumping depleted blood round an exhausted body as breath is sucked in frantically to top up the oxygen content. Stagnant, polluted air makes the job even more difficult; 100-degree heat makes it downright dangerous.

During matches in Mexico, players can be expected to lose eight to ten pounds in sweat per game. A body secreting fluid causes the blood to become more viscous. Thicker blood makes the heart pump even harder than it is already. Throw in the idiotic decision that world-class sportsmen should compete at noon – when even the locals won't venture out – or that fair Northern European skin is vulnerable in a thinned atmosphere which does little to filter the sun's rays, and you are asking for trouble.

Alf knows all this because he's been doing his homework. Two years ago, with the FA's grudging permission, Ramsey went to the Mexico Olympics (the FA wouldn't countenance the England team doctor's attendance alongside Alf's, which had been lobbied for, preferring to send one of the blazers to do the G and T circuit). There the athletics yielded some strange results. In the field events, the throwing and jumping, records were shattered left, right and centre as the thin air reduced resistance and aided aerodynamics – Bob Beaman's famous long jump record being way in excess of any previous achievement. The same conditions were favourable to the sprinters, too, who found minimal air resistance conducive to speed and anaerobic performance – that which requires minimal breathing during the event – unaffected by lack of oxygen. But the middle- and long-distance runners – the *aerobic* athletes, the endurance performers – that was a different story. While avoiding serious harm (and thanks to officials on hand with oxygen at every turn), they found themselves suffering – the marathon being the slowest recorded in modern times.

However, importantly, the Olympic football tournament passed off without serious medical incident. Indeed, though the final in the Azteca was marred by four sendings-off, it was two European teams, Bulgaria and Hungary, which contested it.

The professional opinion was that, in order to perform at optimum level in Mexico 1970, it would take at least three weeks to acclimatise fully and allow the blood to produce the extra red-blood cells necessary for comfortable athletic performance; not to mention a week to get over the jet lag fully. It was on this basis that the League season would be truncated.

Not relying solely on textbook analysis, or his personal observations, Ramsey had decided to test the conditions for himself. Last year, on a twelve-day end-of-season tour, he took an England party to Mexico, Brazil and Uruguay for three full internationals and one 'B' fixture under battle conditions.

Aside from the PR gaffes in Mexico, it had presented all the predictable physical difficulties. None the less, it was a valuable exercise. Arriving exhausted after a long League season and without time to acclimatise, on 31 May England drew 0–0 with Mexico in the Azteca, the stadium they hoped to be visiting again in the final stages the following summer. A good result under the circumstances.

On the eve of the game, however, Gordon Banks had received news that his father had died and was released to head for home on the first available plane. Gordon West of Everton, the established number-two keeper, had taken his place. West then got injured himself, and followed Banks home a few days later; he had not enjoyed the tour and subsequently told Ramsey he would not be available for selection for the World Cup. With no cover, and Bonetti and Stepney unavailable, an SOS was put out to nineteen-year-old Peter Shilton of Leicester, who was on an under-23 tour of Europe, and he arrived hot foot, still clutching his dirty kit.

On 3 June in Guadalajara, in the not-yet-completed stadium where England would be playing in 1970, a 'B' team, an FA XI, as it was called, with Shilton between the sticks and the likes of budding squad players Allan Clarke and Colin Harvey in the line-up, played a Mexico XI and won 4–0. Though it was treated as a minor frill to the proceedings, the match was significant in that for the first time ever England tried tactical substitutions, Ramsey getting Peters and Ball to run themselves ragged in the first half with the idea that they would be withdrawn for fresher legs at half-time. There were no subs in 1966, one had been permitted in international football since 1968, but now football was to become a thirteen-man game.

Plans went awry when Alan Mullery was sent off, and the problems of the conditions were already becoming apparent. Poor old Bobby Charlton, with his futile, wispy comb-over, said he wished he could have played in a hat.

And the players found that in the thin air the ball did some strange things. It could be struck for miles, seemingly at constant velocity, so a good deal of restraint was required by those fresh off the mud of the Football League and used to wellying sodden leather casers. Plus, it could be made to swerve violently, completely flummoxing goalkeepers, whose reading of angles and trajectories would have to be totally rethought under such circumstances.

England, it seemed, would have to play an alien game – slow, with passing accurately to feet – to avoid teammates having to expend energy retrieving stray balls.

'In these conditions passes must be measured to the last refined inch,' Ramsey announced afterwards. 'In that way the playing life of colleagues could be prolonged for another ten years.'

On 7 June it was all taken manfully in their stride as England unravelled Uruguay 2–1 in the Centenario Stadium, Montevideo, site of the original World Cup, with goals by Hurst and Lee and with Banks having returned. No mean result. Uruguay will be serious contenders in Mexico. It also gave England an unbeaten run going back two years. The watching João Saldanha, manager of Brazil, was mightily impressed, proclaiming the '69 England side better than that of '66.

While it didn't get the attention it deserved back home, news dominated by the forthcoming Investiture of the Prince of Wales in Caernarfon, Ramsey was rather more glad that he could continue his work away from prying eyes.

On Thursday 12th, England played Brazil in the Maracanã. Fortunately, England had learned a few things from their previous trip in 1964. Then, told to go out on the pitch for the scheduled kick-off, they had had to wait half an hour for the Brazilian team, who, without letting England know, and in a cruel piece of gamesmanship, had put back the start time. This time Alf would have none of it. When he got a knock on the dressing-room door, he marched down the tunnel to check that Brazil were out there first. They were. And before a 150,000 crowd, England gave their hosts one hell of a game, taking the lead through Colin Bell, then flagging to a 2–1 defeat and a late winner by Jairzinho (while 'the bongo drums beat a wild tireless rhythm,' according to Geoffrey Green of *The Times*).

England had covered 20,000 miles and played four games in twelve days. And, just to illustrate the physical strain involved, Bobby Moore, while walking back down the tunnel, puked down Martin Peters's back.

It was England's only defeat that season and the World Cup holders were showing World Championship pedigree. As if to crown it all, in the Queen's Birthday Honours List, Bobby Charlton and trainer Harold Shepherdson got an OBE and an MBE.

England, though, with an air of foreboding, had not done themselves any favours with the locals. In an incident seemingly blown out of all proportion, the players were accused of boorish behaviour by the Uruguayan FA. Their crime, it turns out, had been a refusal to indulge the hospitality in Montevideo, at a 'do' laid on in their honour, by eating the local speciality black pudding.

'We went to a barbecue,' remembers Brian Labone. 'The Uruguayans, God bless them, they eat everything. There were yards of intestines, which we wouldn't touch. And that was put down as, "Oh they insult the hosts." There was a real campaign against us.'

And later, at Rio airport, when generously supplied with a drinks cart after their plane was delayed and Jeff Astle began serenading fellow travellers, Ramsey knew he would have another factor to cope with on a long trip away: boredom . . .

The trip, though, had clarified an issue in Ramsey's mind: the players who, injury permitting, would constitute his first XI this summer, as well as the identity of most of the reserves. Having sampled the conditions, knowing the draw, he now understood exactly the type of players needed to combat Brazil, Czechoslovakia, Romania and whoever else would cross England's path.

The way circumstances have had it, he's been able to blood a few players in the games this season, though with no time for great experimentation. And, with the deadline for registering his squad with FIFA set for 15 April, it is inevitable that some who will go to Mexico will be uncapped at full international level, especially in the forward department, a possible problem should anything – God forbid – happen to Hurst.

A cap for Nottingham Forest wide player Ian Storey-Moore in the home game against the Dutch (supplying crosses for Leeds's Mick Jones) suggests Alf hasn't written off the possibility of including a winger or two in his party as strategic options. The presence of Peter Thompson, 'the Maestro', the somewhat erratic, but always entertaining Liverpool dribbler, who got a game in Holland, and has come back into the fold, adds weight to the theory.

The question of wingers has enveloped all criticism of the England team ever since Ramsey took over. By eschewing them for his 1966 triumph, Alf has never endeared himself to the romantics – the Matthews-ites – whose pleasure in the game is to see a juggling flank player tying a full back in knots (no matter his contribution to overall team play) and who bemoan a team fashioned purely on industry.

But, to the chagrin of the critics, England keep on winning without wide players. The following month, on 25 February a wingless England go to a muddy national stadium in Brussels and notch up an impressive 3–1 win over World Cup finalists Belgium, who themselves have come through a tough qualifying group, knocking out Yugoslavia and Spain. Ball gets two, Hurst the other, and, most significantly, there is finally room for a darling of the press. Peter Osgood, having a cracking season both at club and under-23 level, banging in thirty-one goals for Chelsea, at last gets his chance as England turn in their most impressive performance since last summer. Though Alf has oft eyed Osgood with suspicion – a lippy medallion man, not known for his graft when not in possession – there is little doubt that Ossie must have booked his ticket.

Damn right he has. On 25 March, earlier than required, when the FA releases the names of the twenty-eight players who will constitute Ramsey's preliminary squad – to be whittled down to the official twenty-two for the FIFA deadline on 25 May – there Osgood is.

'Twenty-eight men to beat the world,' proclaims the *Sun*, which is quite possibly true, though their subtitle says most of all about the names that Ramsey has chosen: 'Nobby's call up is top of the shocks.'

Nobby Stiles: a player more unlike Osgood you could not find. Uncultured, a scurrier, a destroyer; the talismanic tiger who leaves his teeth and specs in the dressing room; the devout Catholic who crosses himself before taking the field then commits devilish acts on the shins of the opposition. Nobby hasn't played for England for over a year. In fact, with a knee operation keeping him out, he hasn't played for Manchester United for much of the season either – though he did return to the United side to give a thumping performance in their FA Cup semi-final defeat by Leeds.

'Stiles is a good player, a very good player,' says Alf. 'He is certainly good for England, he is certainly good for the party and he has been chosen because of that.'

There has never been any doubt in Alf's mind. Stiles is a Ramsey player through and through, fits the pattern perfectly, does exactly what you tell him. And though Mullery – surprisingly a year older than Stiles (the latter having looked like an old man since he was twelve) – is the surer starter, Stiles is a lucky charm.

'Nobby had had a pretty bad time since '66, an unlucky time with injuries,' says David Sadler, his club and international team-mate. 'But he was a bit of a lucky mascot for Alf. Alf just liked him along, as much to do with what he gave to the squad.'

And so there they are, the twenty-eight who will go to Mexico, eight of whom played in the '66 final, six of whom will, at one point, receive that dreaded 'quiet word' which will signal an early departure, as the final twenty-two are named in the week before the tournament.

Goalkeepers: no surprises with Banks, Chelsea star Peter Bonetti and Alex Stepney, a European Cup winner with Manchester United, who was capped against Sweden in 1968, and young Shilton.

Centre backs: pretty much as expected with Moore, Labone, Jack Charlton and Hunter. Although the inclusion of the versatile Manchester United player David Sadler defies predictions.

Full backs: Newton, Wright, Reaney, Cooper and Hughes (with both Hughes and Hunter doubling as defensive midfielders).

Midfield: with the exception of Stiles, nothing untoward – Ball, Charlton, Bell, Stiles, Mullery, Peters.

Only with the forwards, predictably, is there perhaps the biggest gamble. Aside from the expected Hurst, Lee, Astle and latecomer Osgood, there are three uncapped players in the ranks – Clarke, Brian Kidd of Manchester United and the Burnley wide player Ralph Coates. And there are smiles all round. The Maestro's made it. The popular Thompson, one of those in the original '66 party given the tap on the shoulder when pruning down to twenty-two on that occasion, gets a second, welcome, chance at participating in a World Cup.

A lot can happen in two months and, in case of injury, Ramsey also names twelve reserves, making forty in his total pool. There is a practical reason here. With the players requiring inoculations and medical certificates, Ramsey must be able to call on replacements who can fly at a moment's notice – and so Mike Bailey (Wolves), Colin Harvey and Joe Royle (both Everton), John Hollins and Alan Hudson (both Chelsea), Mick Jones (Leeds), Roy McFarland (Derby), Bob McNab and Peter Simpson (both Arsenal), Alan Oakes and Mike Summerbee (both Manchester City), and keeper Jim Montgomery (Sunderland) are jabbed for typhoid just in case.

'I believe it is a stronger party than the one that won the World Cup in 1966,' declares Alf. But he would say that, wouldn't he?

Inevitably the critics can't resist a pop, bemoaning certain exclusions. Tommy Smith of Liverpool has his champions, as do the Forest pair Ian Storey-Moore and Henry Newton. And there is one absence which causes unanimous surprise – the omission of Paul Madeley from even the forty. The others of Leeds's 'Magnificent Seven' have made it into the pool – Big Jack, Clarke, Hunter, Cooper, Reaney, Jones. The ones in the twenty-eight now constitute a 'Famous Five'. Madeley, 'the most versatile footballer in Britain', according to Tom Finney, an elegant defender and utility player who's played in every position at Elland Road, including goalkeeper, and was considered to have been a good bet on account of his adaptability, is out in the cold. He says he's not disappointed, blames it on a 'stinker' he had when Alf came to watch him recently, but you know deep down inside he must be hurting.

And for the twelve on stand-by, 'the men who lurk in the shadows', as the *Sun* puts it, there is an eerie feeling. Though they'd never wish ill on a fellow professional, sickness and injury will become of morbid interest over the coming weeks.

Back at the League, it's business as usual. Everton storm to the title on 1 April with a club record of 63 points. They are followed in order by Leeds, Derby and Chelsea – Derby on the verge of a fine and European ban for 'administration deficiencies'. Muscling behind them come unfashionable Coventry, who clinch a Fairs Cup place by winning at Wolves, making their own unique contribution to English football in the process. On the way back from the game, 300 Coventry 'skinheads' (as the euphemism for troublemakers goes) riot on a football special train, leading to sixty arrests – a strange turn of events that has got sociologists scratching their heads as to the business of why on earth violence should be linked to football.

At the bottom, Southampton and Crystal Palace scrape vital points to avoid relegation, sending Sunderland and Sheffield Wednesday down into Division Two, to be replaced by Huddersfield and Blackpool, with Huddersfield manager Ian Greaves getting a congratulatory telegram from none other than Terriers fan the PM. Way down in the basement, Bradford Park Avenue finish bottom of Division Four. Failing to get re-elected on 30 May, they will be replaced in the Football League by Cambridge United.

Manchester City look good to beat Schalke '04 in the Cup Winners' Cup semi-final. Arsenal have got Ajax in the same stage of the Fairs Cup, and Chelsea have rented a medical 'wonder machine' from America to get whiz-kid Alan Hudson over his leg injury for the FA Cup Final against Leeds, the Yorkshire side seeing captain Billy Bremner voted Footballer of the Year by the football writers at the Café Royal, London.

It was perhaps inevitable, though, that it should be a Leeds player who would also come a cropper.

There is something up with Leeds. Jack Charlton thinks so. They're a superstitious lot – always come out of the tunnel in the same order, stick with colours or numbers that did them prior favours. Sometimes, on the way to an away game, they'll drive miles out of the way so that they can go to a 'lucky café' that earned them good fortune on a previous visit. This season, though, Jack'll tell you, Leeds are jinxed. League Champions in 1969, they'd looked a good bet all season until spring when Everton started to leave them trailing. And now, with the season pulled forward, it has caused inevitable fixture congestion.

In the knock-outs, Leeds are going strong. They have come

through a bruising FA Cup campaign to meet on-song Chelsea in an early Cup Final on 11 April. They are into the semi-finals of their first European Cup, drawing Celtic. But it is taking its toll. Indeed, as the season builds to a crescendo, they are even scheduled to play some League matches on consecutive days. On sodden, heavy pitches, it is tough going. But because Leeds are a robust outfit it has accentuated the problem – players left limping into line-ups when ordinarily they would not have been available for selection. As the *Observer*'s Hugh McIlvanney puts it, if Billy Bremner were a boxer, he would be deemed unfit to fight.

It's showing, too, in Leeds's play. In the first leg of their European Cup semi-final at home they concede a goal in the first minute and the 1–0 scoreline duly remains, of delicious joy to the Scots, who seem to have a point to prove on the eve of England's great adventure. Leeds are in danger of ending the season with just the FA Cup.

There is another problem: tired players get injured – mental fatigue and weary limbs making a player a split-second slow when it comes to riding a tackle, throwing himself into a challenge, putting his head in where feet or elbows are flying.

Something is bound to go horribly wrong. And on Friday, 3 April, the *Daily Mail* devotes half of its front page to a picture of a young woman clinging on to a couple of little kids – a 'World Cup wife'. 'He'll fight back,' says Mrs Sandra Reaney, at her Gosforth home.

The nature of the injury is irrelevant, as is the opposition. All that matters is that it has happened. Reaney, Leeds's twenty-five-year-old right back, breaks his leg in a League match at West Ham, stretchered off unconscious by the St John's Ambulance people, his legs strapped together, before anguished teammates. No FA Cup Final, no European Cup run-in, and, above all, certainly no Mexico.

Reaney's misfortune, though, will bring a sick case of good news to one other. Though it remains unannounced, it is a near certainty that, being the only full back among the twelve reserves, one who played in Guadalajara last summer, and was perhaps unlucky not to have made the twenty-two in the first place, Bob McNab will now get his crack.

'I'm still hoping against hope that I will get a chance to go,' he had told the *Daily Mirror*, somewhat presciently, the previous week. 'Yet for that to happen some poor so-and-so will have to suffer a bad injury. I wouldn't wish that on anyone. It is a horrible thing to even think about, like waiting for a dead man's shoes.'

Strangely, the call never comes. On Tuesday, 7 April, strolling off the Leeds United training ground, Paul Madeley is informed by a *Daily Mail* reporter with good intelligence that it is he who will drafted into the twenty-eight in his stricken clubmate's stead. Madeley is a little suspicious. Surely wires have been crossed? It must be that McNab is in the full squad and he has been elevated to the reserve. After all, he wasn't even in the original forty. But soon it's there in black and white.

McNab says he's gutted – he has, after all, been effectively dropped twice – but swallows hard, expresses optimism for the future, time is on his side. And though Alf doesn't bother himself with explanations, the guessing is that as it is a right back who is now required (McNab is essentially a left back), it was a necessary step. Either that or Alf made a mistake first time round.

It is suddenly rendered moot. The very next day, Madeley comes back with the rather surprising news that, after talking it over with his wife, he doesn't want to go to Mexico after all – he was told originally he wasn't going, has booked a holiday in Cornwall, they have a baby due and he has family business concerns to take care of. After a long, hard season, he won't be mentally right.

Laymen cry treason ('I was too tired for Mexico my son,' mocks the *News of the World*, envisaging a haggard older Madeley explaining the grim truth to his disowning offspring). Some professionals lend support: 'Paul's an individual who's very strong minded,' says teammate Terry Cooper. 'He thought that was right for him and his family. There's no point in going if you're not mentally right.' Brian Labone even reveals that he passed up a spot in the 1966 squad after being called upon in similar circumstances: 'I wasn't in the original thirty, so in the meantime I'd arranged to get married,' he says. 'I'd had a long and exhausting season, Everton had won the Cup, England had no chance of winning the World Cup. I know it sounds a bit lacking in ambition, but that's the way I read the situation at the time.'

But in the middle of it all stands a happy player. For Bob McNab it is third time lucky. Less than twenty-four hours after being given the heave-ho, he takes a call during training at Highbury. He's in.

Barring disaster, England's squad is settled . . .

Chapter 3

The Celts

Outside the FA headquarters at Lancaster Gate, off Hyde Park, a middle-aged man named Sid Brown poses for a few photographers. A bus driver by trade, Sid is not used to all the attention, but makes a good show of it anyway. After polishing up the back of his luxury air-conditioned coach, making a big deal for the snappers over buffing up the Union Jack and 'Willie for Mexico' logo on the rear (the World Cup Willie lion wearing a sombrero), he climbs aboard and turns her over.

Sid drives down the block, hangs a right on to Bayswater Road, and the legend 'England Team – World Cup Mexico' disappears from view. Soon he'll be on the A30, heading down to Southampton. Tomorrow, Sid and his bus will be on a cargo ship setting sail across the Atlantic.

For reasons known only to themselves, the Football Association, grossly underestimating the state of civilisation in Mexico, has decided that England should take their own team coach with them all the way to the World Cup Finals – 'with tea, coffee and iced drinks available as they play cards or listen to the built-in hi-fi system'. Perhaps it's just superstition. Sid, after all, was the England driver during the 1966 finals. And now he's grabbed his own little slice of football history again by being the first member of the England party to head off for the 1970 World Cup, ready and waiting to pick up the lads when they arrive at Mexico City airport.

The Mexicans, when they find out, are not going to be very happy...

Being on the ocean wave, Sid'll have to catch the FA Cup Final on the World Service, but then you don't get to drive the World

37

Champions every day. In 1970 the Cup Final is still, by far and away, the biggest event in the domestic sporting calendar; arguably, to the man in the street, a more important trophy than the League Championship. It is an annual ritual that will see just about half the population sit down in their living rooms at 3 p.m. on the given Saturday to share the same experience, not to mention partake of the sacred custom of all flushing their toilets and boiling kettles at half-time, putting enormous strain on the nation's utilities.

Certainly, it's always a memorable match. With League games restricted to TV highlights packages on *Match of the Day*, *The Big Match* or its regional ITV counterparts, for many people – ones who don't go to games – it's their annual, only, chance to see a club match in its entirety.

With BBC and ITV trying to outdo each other with coverage, the Cup Final is fast becoming an all-day extravaganza. The build-up starts at mid-morning, the pre-match hours padded out with all sorts of novelties – breakfast with the teams, vox-popping Northern fans on the train south, quiz games, 'Abide with Me' – right through to the sweaty post-match interviews and a sing-song in the bath.

Hopefully, this year, the chat will be more cordial than it was last. After unseemly scrapping by TV reporters in 1969, in which punches flew, the event organisers have told the broadcasters to cool it when it comes to vying for post-match interrogations. When players come off the pitch, it's enough that they have pints of milk thrust into muddied hands by the Milk Marketing Board (an early piece of product placement).

This hasn't stopped BBC and ITV doing a bit of pre-World Cup muscle flexing, but now, when the players march back up the tunnel, they've been told to take turns with the questions, an arrangement that will carry on into Mexico. The Beeb, rather non-plussed by its upstart commercial rival, is having to lump it – although it has scooped the opposition by getting a live link-up to Paul Reaney's bedside.

Still, surely if there's one thing that'll make the Cup Final a spectacle, it's that beautiful bowling-green pitch.

Unfortunately not. Wembley, to put no fine a point on it, is a disgrace. The weather hasn't helped – snow before the League Cup Final necessitated straw to be put down – but the stadium authorities are the biggest culprits: in a moment of madness they agreed to stage the Horse of the Year Show on the hallowed turf. The pitch will be relaid at a cost of £20,000 during the summer, but now, churned up and cratered under several tons of sand, it looks like the last days at El Alamein.

It's a curious weekend. Aside from providing what will be the climax to the football season, things are happening in the wider world that, in their own way, make it a cultural watershed. On Friday, 10 April, at the offices of Apple Records in Savile Row, a statement is released by Paul McCartney citing his termination of musical and business interests with John Lennon, George Harrison and Ringo Starr. 'I'm fed up with the whole business,' he says. He doesn't do it directly, but with McCartney employing the politician's euphemism of choosing to spend more time with his family, it's now official – The Beatles are no more. It's been on the cards for a while, ever since Lennon started going off the rails, causing further controversy not two weeks ago by stating that while the erstwhile cheeky mop tops were getting their MBEs, the lads smoked pot at the Palace.

Against this backdrop no one notices what's going in America People are now so blasé about lunar missions that on the evening of Saturday 11th, Cup Final night, more people watch Yvonne Ormes, a twenty-one-year-old model from Nantwich, Cheshire, crowned Miss England than see the live blast-off of the latest lunar mission – Apollo 13.

We are becoming accustomed to the new technological era. Men walk on the moon and we can see it in our living rooms; Technology Minister Anthony Wedgwood Benn takes a trip in the new marvel Concorde; a 'test-tube baby' is announced as a very real possibility; and the *Observer* fantasises about a time when each house is equipped with a computer terminal where you can log into a central bureau for 'houses for sale, holiday tours, theatre programmes and prices'; on BBC1, a new series called *Star Trek* taps into the obsession with futurism; and, next month, the whole world will be able to sit at home and tune in to football matches beamed live from Mexico.

And so the Cup Final build-up continues – with Hudson definitely out, will Ron Harris and Eddie McCreadie still be fit for Chelsea? Will Leeds shake off what happened to Reaney? Every newspaper, even the posh ones, is chock-a-block with Cup Final pull-outs, special editions and all the attendant bumf. Chelsea, we know, will be going for their traditional dollop of lucky rice pudding, their pre-match meal, at a Gloucester Road hotel; it's the earliest Cup Final since 1897; if Leeds win, Don Revie will be the eighth manager to play in and manage cup-winning teams; 150,000 souvenir programmes, printed in advance, still list Reaney as the Leeds number 2.

In fact, the Cup Final is so huge that it even has a curtain-raiser, a game played the night before – this year a third-place play-off between losing semi-finalists Manchester United and Watford at Arsenal's ground. With Mexico approaching, it is very keenly contested, Brian Kidd scoring twice as United win 2–0 on a waterlogged Highbury surface. Arsenal have already announced they'll soon be at the cutting edge of seventies stadium technology by introducing a system of undersoil heating.

After all the hype, the Leeds–Chelsea clash lives up to its billing: a classic encounter that ends in a 2–2 draw after extra-time. The Ford Motor Company has recently offered a £100,000 incentive for clubs to clean up their disciplinary records. But if they thought they would have any influence here, or that some players would be inhibited with Mexico on their minds, they are wrong. It is a bruising encounter. Great for entertainment, but perhaps not for Alf Ramsey, who must be wincing as some of the tackles fly in. Mercifully for Ramsey, all the England players on show come through unscathed. The chief plaudits go to Leeds's Scottish winger Eddie Gray, who runs rings round Chelsea right back David Webb, but they all, Madeley included, do well, with Jack Charlton and Mick Jones on the scoresheet for Leeds and Osgood excelling for Chelsea.

Though there is now another problem. On top of an already overloaded season, and for the first time since 1912, the Cup Final will require a replay. The schedulers had never quite budgeted for this. And with Wembley a mess, Leeds otherwise occupied in Europe midweek and the stadium needed for the England–Northern Ireland Home International the Wednesday after, the rematch is shifted to Old Trafford, where Leeds and Chelsea will renew hostilities on 29 April.

Because of their exertions, the Leeds and Chelsea players are thus excused from the first Home International against Wales at Cardiff on Saturday 18th. For a moment it also looks like Ramsey might lose Bobby Charlton. Walking round the Wembley track with his hands in his pockets before taking his seat for the Cup Final, Charlton trips over and splits his lip. But Bobby's OK. With a black eye and a bruised face – and despite the suggestion by some tabloids that he's now out for Mexico – he assures there's no way he's going to miss anything. Stepney, McNab and Coates are called into a reduced party of sixteen.

Amid all this, and somewhat forgotten in the Madeley Affair and McNab's promotion, a vacancy still exists on the twelve-man reserve list in Ramsey's forty. Sheffield Wednesday full back Wilf Smith is recruited to fill the slot.

There is now a new fear. What if the Cup Final replay is also drawn? What if Leeds get to the European Cup Final? How the hell are they going to fit all these games in? The FA asks Coventry if Highfield Road can be used for a second replay, if needed. But if Leeds go all the way in Europe, they won't be free till the week beginning 13 May, a full nine days after England are scheduled to fly out to Mexico. A contingency plan is made to share the FA Cup for the first time in its history.

Such matters suddenly seem insignificant. On Tuesday 14th there comes breaking news that the Apollo 13 mission, which slipped away almost unnoticed, has run into trouble. A technical malfunction has left the astronauts in peril 257,000 miles from the earth, with rumours of an onboard explosion on the moonship *Odyssey*. The oxygen supply is dwindling, as is water. There is a very real possibility that astronauts Lovell, Haise and Swiggert won't make it back. Millions around the world who didn't give a damn are suddenly fascinated. For seventy-two hours the world is encouraged to pray.

It seems to do the trick – that and some ingenious NASA technical improvisation, which gets the spacecraft through what the *Sun* calls 'the greatest cliffhanger the world has ever known'. On Thursday 16th at 7 p.m. BST (followed by *Steptoe and Son* at 7.25 p.m.) and watched by a record British audience of 42 million, the astronauts splash down. Seven hundred million people see it worldwide, sitting through an agonising seventeen minutes as radio contact is lost during re-entry. The Age of Aquarius is over, but the global village has begun.

Football, of course, carries on. And it seems somehow fated that in the biggest game of their season Leeds crash out of the European Cup, losing 2–1 away to Celtic, 3–1 on aggregate. A staggering 135,000 fill Hampden Park to watch the match, and celebrate as Celtic book a place against Feyenoord in Milan's San Siro Stadium on 6 May. Manager Jock Stein will have to call on all his powers of motivation. To the Scots, the real final has already been won.

Elsewhere it's good news for the English. Manchester City beat Schalke 5–1 (5–2 on aggregate) and go through to the Cup Winners' Cup Final; Arsenal lose away to Ajax 1–0, but win 3–1 on aggregate to meet Anderlecht in the Fairs Cup Final.

Ramsey, despite the raft of absentees, can still call on the old guard as he names his team on Friday to trot out at Ninian Park: Banks, Wright, Hughes, Mullery, Labone, Moore, Lee, Ball, Bobby Charlton, Hurst, Peters. With the possible exception of the full backs, this is pretty much looking like his first-choice team: six players from the '66 final and 330 caps between the team. Emlyn Hughes, at left back, is the only novice, with three caps. As Dave Bowen, the Welsh manager, puts it, England at this rate could pick four teams to win the World Cup.

But this football is decidedly unglobal, thoroughly British. Though an official international, squelching around in the Cardiff mud seems light years away from the lush turf and baking heat of Guadalajara. Ramsey knows that he should perhaps experiment – blood the likes of Kidd or Coates – but such games are too important: England need to leave for foreign shores with their tails up. His players may be knackered, carrying injuries, and will have to steel themselves for the kicking and *schadenfreude* of the Scots, but if they can get on the plane with the Home International Championship, or at least finish it by turning over Scotland at Hampden, then this will be a great fillip. Alf will then have a whole month to gel the squad together. To achieve this, he has arranged two warm-up matches and second XI games in Colombia and Ecuador. He can give the youngsters a whirl then . . .

On Saturday, 18 April, England are in Cardiff for what is the beginning of a long journey, one full of hope and expectation. Beneath tight Ninian Park, with its steep terraces and sloping corrugated roofs, its quaint hand-painted advertising daubed on top of them, the team limber up in the dressing room. Games in the Home Championship never feel like proper internationals. They are like domestic games, played in British grounds, with British crowds and clubmates eager to put one over on each other.

More importantly, it is always a quintessentially British game – hard, physical, no quarter in the tackle, balls skimming across the mud, or rolling to a halt in heavily sanded goalmouths. No chance for fancy on-the-floor footwork – especially at Ninian Park, where the only grass, in the conventional sense, lies out on the wings and the corners. The keys to games like this are hard running, tight marking and brisk thumped balls through the midfield, or out to the flanks where a winger or galloping full back can belt the ball over for Hurst to nod down.

Wales are not ranked as an international team. They were cannon fodder in their World Cup qualifiers. Their club sides – Cardiff, Swansea, Wrexham and Newport County, all struggling against the popularity of the handling game – are strictly old-fashioned, lower-tier sides. And Bowen, in contrast to the riches of Ramsey, can raise only fourteen players for the match, some of them, like Swansea goalie Tony Millington, straight from the Third Division.

(In the Republic of Ireland it is even worse. Searching for players for two games versus West Germany and Poland, they've had to drag up a Warwick University student, a Dublin-born amateur with Skelmersdale named Steve Heighway, who's had this mighty honour thrust on him right in the middle of his Economics finals.)

The form book, though, counts for nothing. Wales will always raise their game where England are concerned, and the packed Ninian Park faithful, crammed in under great clouds of Benson and Hedges and Players No. 6, give lusty voice, drowning out the crackly Tannoy which is playing a selection of pre-Beatles pop.

At 2.50 p.m. the teams appear in the tunnel and emerge in two columns, the studs rapping hard on the concrete before they march out on to the mud. Arriving simultaneously will discourage the barrage of boos against England, though, to be fair, the crowds at the Welsh grounds are respectfully partisan, schooled in the sporting code of rugby crowds, by far the most courteous of England's three Celtic opponents.

Out they stride, Moore at the head of the English, Terry Hennessey (of Derby) the Welsh. Wales are in an all-red strip; England in their traditional colours, white long-sleeved shirt with its round collar and cuffs (exactly the same as '66), navy-blue shorts, white socks, on the left breast the famous three lions, on the back a big bold number in red; Gordon Banks in international yellow.

The teams line up for the national anthems, though first there is a presentation to Bobby Charlton. He's getting used to this, though it's becoming awfully like reading his own obituary. It's been that way ever since he nudged nearer his hundredth cap. This one is number ninety-nine. Fingers crossed, Northern Ireland on Wednesday will be the century. If all goes according to plan, and Alf doesn't drop him, he should get his 105th in the game against Brazil, which will put him equal to Billy Wright's record as England's most capped player. Not that Wales are going to go all soft on him.

The teams split up, run to their respective ends, hoof a few orange balls back and forth while the ref gives a few short, sharp blasts and Moore and Hennessey shake hands in the centre circle and conduct the coin toss and ceremonials.

It's only been a short hop over this morning. England stayed overnight in Bristol where they had a light training session yesterday afternoon in front of some local schoolkids who packed in eagerly behind Banksie's goal during shooting practice. Now, though, the hard work begins. And boy, is it hard. Wales are no mugs, a team that, on its day, can play well beyond its means. Smaller international teams like this play best when they stick to a plan. And, from the off, it's quite apparent what that plan is. Pulling eight or nine players back into the defensive third of the field and leaving only Dick Krzywicki up on the halfway line, they play effectively like an away side, soaking up pressure, waiting to hit England on the break. And they're not shy about it either. At Wembley last year they were 1–0 up, employing this method, until England managed to reverse it 2–1. Such a method relies on English fallibility, though on the sticky Ninian Park pitch, with a swirling wind, it only takes a defender to misplace a pass or mess up a tackle and a nippy attacker can dart in and zip past a defence that has pushed square up to the halfway line. Not that England haven't encountered this sort of tactic before. At Wembley it is commonplace. There, back home, the large pitch gives England ample space for people to attack down the flanks and get round the back. At Cardiff, turning a defence will take some doing, especially, as

England's critics keep pointing out, without wingers.

England do not rise to the challenge. It may be a question of avoiding injury for three more games – the players perhaps with an image of Reaney in the backs of their minds – but it's a poor game. England's attack looks blunted, and as for the centre of defence, Moore does not have one of his better games. Labone, the stopper, is used as a stepladder all afternoon by Southampton centre forward Ron Davies, he of the uncanny ability to hang in the air. Five minutes before half-time, Krzywicki – a Wrexham native of Polish parentage – runs on to an Alan Durban through ball and scores without a challenge.

On it goes. Peters is quiet, seemingly out of sorts, Alan Mullery has his work cut out. And with Hennessey holding the centre of midfield, and both Davies and Krzwywicki making Banks thankful that he'd got in that practice yesterday, Wales look set for their first victory over England in fifteen years.

Then, twenty minutes from time, just when it looks as though Wales might have nicked it, Charlton, who'd been anonymous, finds Ball, who hits it to Lee on the left of the Welsh penalty area. With a little shimmy and a couple of strides, and before any red-shirted defender has figured out what's happening, Lee belts it hard and it flies into the top corner. Though he doesn't disappear under a pile of celebrating bodies, the eagerness and glee with which his teammates slap him on the back suggests almighty relief. If there's one thing England know how to do, it's kill off a game. And so they do, playing it out for a 1–1 draw. The headline in the *Observer* the next day sums up popular consensus – 'WELSH BRUISE ENGLISH PRIDE.'

Alf Ramsey's concern for the game against Northern Ireland is that, with Labone's shin pummelled against Wales, he hasn't got a fit centre half to play alongside Bobby Moore. With Jack Charlton and Norman Hunter unavailable, heads are scratched during training at Hendon FC's ground as to how to contain lanky Derek Dougan, who might do to England what Ron Davies did last Saturday.

Ramsey is left with Keith Newton, Emlyn Hughes, Alan Mullery and Nobby Stiles who could play in the middle. He resists the temptation to call up Derby's young centre half Roy McFarland from the reserves and figures that he'll get by with what he's got.

This, after all, is a dress rehearsal. But just when it seems he'll switch the tall Newton to the centre and have someone else fill in at right back, he has a change of heart: Moore will wear the number 5 shirt, in the 'stopper' role, and his usual position, which involves sitting just behind, mopping up like a sweeper (though no one would dare use such a dirty foreign word), will go to Nobby Stiles.

And this time, at wide open, if sandy, Wembley, and with a partisan crowd behind them, Ramsey feels confident enough to give Kidd and Coates their debuts. Though the evening most definitely belongs to another. Ramsey is not generally given to sentiment, but tonight Bobby Charlton will be captain on his hundredth international. With Wembley a 100,000 sell-out, too, this is it – the last home game, the final send-off. The next time England step out here they will either have retained their world title or – God forbid – passed it up in the heat of Mexico.

There is a genuine well of affection for Charlton. Even the *Guardian*, not huge on sports coverage, devotes a leader article to the great man, under the header 'BOBBY CHARLTON – SPORTSMAN'. Charlton, a survivor of the Munich tragedy, has won everything in the game – three FA Youth Cups as a teenager, then the FA Cup, three League titles, the European Cup and World Cup. He's been Footballer of the Year and European Footballer of the Year. He's scored a record number of England goals. Now he has one hundred England caps. According to old teammates, Charlton's only ever lost his temper once – when up against Scotland defender Jimmy Scoular. When young Bobby started throwing punches, Scoular put his hand on the top of Charlton's head, keeping him at arm's length and laughing while Bobby kept on swinging. Since then, nothing. The perfect gentleman.

Charlton leads out a team that reads Banks, Newton, Hughes, Mullery, Moore, Stiles, Coates, Kidd, himself, Hurst and Peters. Northern Ireland (or rather just Ireland, as they are officially titled, the Irish Football Association technically representing the whole island) are no shrinking violets, with some useful club players, like goalie Pat Jennings, the aforementioned Dougan and without question one of the greatest players in the world, Georgie Best.

Best, though, is using up his favours fast. Having been sent off against Scotland, an aftershave lotion manufacturer, which pays him £12,500 each year to appear in its commercials, tells him, quite literally, 'to keep his nose clean'. It is estimated that Best's wages are now a staggering £30,000 a year, but there still seems something self-destructive about him.

For England it is a fond farewell. Charlton leads the team out to a hero's welcome, is given an almighty cheer whenever he touches the ball, instigates two of England's goals (scored by Peters and Hurst) and caps the night with one of his own in a 3–1 win. Best, predictably, is booed, but scores an excellent individual goal of his own to garnish the proceedings.

But this is still a scuffling England – no Ball, no Lee, a patched-up, uncomfortable defence. Coates, though, looks good scurrying up and down the left, but the truth is that Jennings, the big keeper with the oversize hands, is barely troubled for large patches.

And yet further problems. Manchester City boss Joe Mercer has asked Alf to withdraw Lee and Bell from the Scotland game because of the Cup Winners' Cup Final. There is nothing Ramsey can do; Uncle Joe has always been one of the most helpful club managers. That same night Arsenal lose 3–1 at Anderlecht in the first leg of the Fairs Cup, but Ray Kennedy scores the vital away goal in the eighty-fourth minute . . .

Sport is not all cause for celebration. Though Charlton is given generous column inches in the national press, the front pages are dominated by the question of the impending and highly controversial cricket tour by an all-white South African team. The 'Stop The '70 Tour' movement, led by twenty-year-old Peter Hain, is gathering steam – the beginnings of what will become an international anti-apartheid campaign – and looks set to disrupt the Tests with a series of protests. Black and Asian Commonwealth cricketers playing county cricket are being asked to boycott representative games against the visitors. The issue is the hottest political item of the day, Labour wanting the tour called off, the Tories, led by Shadow Home Secretary Quinton Hogg, giving it vocal support.

There is tension elsewhere. For the second time in a year there is a very real threat that all national newspapers might be halted, the spill-over from an industrial dispute by printing staff at the *Daily Mirror*. Vic Feather, leader of the TUC, is brought in for eleventh-hour conciliation and averts a walk-out. Fleet Street, though, remains on the brink of an all-out stoppage. Over 10 million copies of the *Daily* and *Sunday Mirror* have failed to reach readers in recent weeks and industrial action threatens to engulf the whole newspaper industry as a two-week deadline to resolve a pay dispute is laid down to management by union, the NGA. Bad news for politicians, who are about to embark on a general election. Even worse for football fans.

England and Scotland get down to the serious business of contesting British supremacy. It might prove a fanciful notion. Wales, on Wednesday, drew 0–0 at Hampden, and though only 30,000 turned up in the rain to see it, the Welsh look set for their first Home International title for thirty years.

Scotland will be back to full strength to play England, with the return of their Celtic players, who have declined the option of resting. 'Playing against England is a different matter. Every Scotsman wants to win this match,' says manager Bobby Brown.

England count their own wounded. Labone passes a fitness test and will play. The only other switches might be tactical, Ramsey stepping down Coates and Kidd for some seasoned pros in a game he doesn't want to lose under any circumstances.

'Alf, God bless him, was a real Englishman. I'm not saying he didn't like foreigners, but . . .' says Labone. 'That's what he used to say, "I don't mind the Irish, I don't mind the Welsh, but I hate the effin' Scots." '

The bulldog spirit suggests Stiles might get a second crack. Alf loves Nobby and confirms he'll be in midfield. There will, though, be no Bobby Charlton. During a morning training session at Kilmarnock's ground, in a loosening-up game of tag, he collides with Geoff Hurst and breaks a small bone in his hand. It's nothing serious – he is getting accident prone in his old age. The injury will delay his 101st cap. Nevertheless, another (this time ferociously whistled) presentation takes place.

England line up with Banks, Newton, Hughes, Stiles, Labone, Moore, Thompson, Ball, Astle, Hurst and Peters. Tricky Jimmy Johnstone troubles Newton and Hughes, switching between the flanks; Willie Carr, another flame-haired dynamo, gets the better of Ball; Bobby Moore can't cope with a rampaging Colin Stein; and Labone looks shaky. Peters is anonymous and, interestingly, the only flashes England show are when the defence plays the ball up to Peter Thompson, who runs at people, causing problems. Though Ramsey brings on Mullery for him and shuts up shop, playing for the draw.

The crowd do not like what they see, especially in the twentieth minute when, under the nose of German referee Gerhard Schuleberg, Labone, skinned by Stein, scoops him into the air in the area but no penalty is given. Later in the game, the decisions equal out as Hurst has a perfectly good headed goal ruled offside.

The game conforms to full-blooded type, but produces the first goalless draw between the sides since their initial encounter ninety-eight years ago. In a baying cauldron, 137,000 strong, much as Leeds had experienced ten days ago, England are fairly roasted by the crowd, who are left to believe that the World Champions are nowhere near as good as Scotland and certainly not worthy of bringing home the World Cup again. In three games Scotland's defence has conceded no goals.

At the end even Ramsey admits England were lucky, which means he must be *really* angry. With Wales beating Northern Ireland 1–0, the Home Internationals end in a three-way tie.

Graciously, from the Scottish camp, Bobby Brown and captain John Greig say that England are better than West Germany, and the Irish and the Welsh add their praises, too.

England should take heart. In São Paulo, World Cup favourites Brazil are held to a draw by travel-weary Bulgaria and the 150,000 crowd boo them off, Pelé having missed two penalties . . .

And so the domestic season winds to its close. There are odd diversions: Tony Curtis, on his way to London to film the TV series *The Persuaders*, gets pinched for possession of cannabis at Heathrow and fined £50 at Uxbridge Magistrates' Court. In Massachusetts, the judge accuses Senator Edward Kennedy of lying in the investigation into the death of Mary Jo Kopechne at Chappaquiddick Island. Kennedy's late brother John F. is back in the news as former President Lyndon Johnson goes on TV to dispute the Warren Commission's finding that the Kennedy assassination was the work of a lone gunman.

Then, in Europe, Arsenal and Manchester City do what Leeds failed to do, albeit in lesser competitions. On Tuesday 28th, Highbury is tense as Arsenal try to claw back the two-goal lead held by

Anderlecht and set out to stifle super striker Jan Mulder and a team containing several Belgian internationals. The away goal from the first leg proves vital and Arsenal come through 3–0 with goals by Kelly, Radford and Sammels – 4–3 on aggregate. It is Arsenal's first major trophy since they won the League title in 1953.

The following night, Wednesday 29th, Manchester City beat Polish team Gornik 2–1 in the rain-soaked Prater Stadium in Vienna, their third major prize in twelve months, Lee scoring twice (one penalty) and Young getting the other as the Poles are torn apart. Unfortunately, no one back home sees it. The FA and Football League committees refuse permission to broadcast it because it clashes with the FA Cup Final replay (shown on both the BBC and ITV). It is the first time a British side contesting a major trophy has not been seen live in modern times.

But what a replay it is. Still without Hudson, Chelsea do their homework to rectify the tactical errors of the Wembley game. Right back Webb, run ragged by Gray in the first game, is switched with centre back Ron Harris. 'Chopper' has a simple solution to the problem: at the first opportunity he fouls Gray so brutally that the Leeds winger is left as a limping shadow of his former self. No one complains; it's all part of the game. And to cap it all, the Chelsea winner in a 2–1 victory – in which Osgood is the star – is scored by Webb, his header going beyond the reach of David Harvey, Sprake's replacement in the Leeds goal. Though again there are some injury scares for Ramsey: Peter Bonetti gets floored, Jack Charlton struggles through.

Poor old Leeds, after a season of seventy-two games, they have lost the lot, and a miserable Don Revie cancels the civic reception at the town hall (as also happens to the one in Glasgow as Celtic are turned over 2–1 by Feyenoord in the San Siro). To add insult to injury, Leeds are fined £5,000 for fielding weakened teams at the end of the season. Can you blame them? Their Easter week schedule had them playing Southampton on Saturday, Derby on Monday, Celtic on Wednesday, West Ham on Thursday.

So in Europe there is no Triple Crown, but the dominance of English teams gives every encouragement that the national side has got what it takes. For the Leeds players, going to Mexico will be almost like a holiday...

Chapter 4

Hi-ho, Hi-ho

Monday, 4 May 1970
At 1 p.m. at a sunny Heathrow Airport, the England party prepare to board a BOAC Boeing 707 – flight number 675 – for the fourteen-hour, ten-minute flight to Mexico City, a full twenty-nine days before their opening encounter with Romania. They will enjoy a period of togetherness unprecedented in English international preparation. Not all the teams competing are so fortunate. England, the first overseas team to arrive, will touch down two weeks ahead of group rivals Czechoslovakia.

With twenty-eight energetic young men now deprived of access to wives and girlfriends, not to mention drink, Ramsey will have his work cut out to halt the onset of boredom. The physical conditioning and training work will fill large parts of each day, though Alf has also arranged an itinerary that will keep the players busy as the tournament looms. While their official World Cup base will be in Guadalajara, Mexico's second city, 300 miles north-west of the capital, the World Cup odyssey will commence in Mexico City itself, where England will be based for two weeks before flying down to South America for final warm-up games against Colombia and Ecuador on the eve of the tournament proper.

There, the venues at Bogotá (Colombia) and Quito (Ecuador) have been selected for good reason. Aside from tropical conditions and Latin opposition, the games will be played at altitude far in excess of that to be found even at the grounds in Mexico. Bogotá is at 8,500 feet, Quito, up in the Andes, at 9,500. Survive there, on the roof of the world, and descending to the 5,000-odd feet of Guadalajara will seem a breeze – the same logic applied by distance runners who stay at altitude till the last minute, then come downhill to compete.

In the departure lounge the spirit is almost carnival like, the players buoyed by that going-on-holiday feeling and all sporting their brand-new official England suits, the FA crest upon the blazer pocket. This being the age of sartorial concern, with men turned into primping peacocks, the players have been given a choice between white shirt and black tie or pale blue turtle neck sweater. Topped off with light blue cotton trilbies, which are to become a permanent feature throughout the trip, and with many of the players having already decided to don their Ray-Bans, the squad looks like sub-Bond agents on a mission to Havana.

Typically, given the FA's grip on modernity, they are wearing clothes that would have been more in vogue in the World Cup of 1962. Though the collar-and-tie ethic still runs deep in English football. No leisure wear or casual dress here, even for a long-haul flight. National duty requires best bib and tucker. And anyway, the players are just glad that the big day has arrived. For Jack Charlton and Peter Bonetti, who've been carrying knocks since the Cup Final replay, there's an almost palpable sense of relief that they've got their boarding cards in their hands.

Before they embark, while the porters load up the luggage and a pile of black England hold-alls sits on the tarmac, the waiting press are treated to a few final words. The mood is upbeat. Bobby Moore toes the company line:

'Without doubt the four years extra that most of us have had together has made us into a better side,' he says, trotting out how we've got the best league in the world, how Pelé's going to be the man to watch, and how one must never underestimate the Romanians. (The last part is a thoughtful addition, for Romanian captain Lucescu has just been saying some very nice things about England, telling everyone how he thinks they'll win it.)

It is Ramsey, though, whose words carry most weight: 'We'll be a hard team to beat,' he declares, as the flashbulbs pop. 'It will take a great team to beat us. If we are not successful, the responsibility is mine ... This is not sales talk. It is something I genuinely believe.'

With the flight half an hour late, now scheduled to leave at 2 p.m., the players sit around and do what players do: take the mickey out of each other; in the case of the Charlton brothers, smoke like chimneys; mostly they play cards. Over the coming month, the

England squad will play more hands of brag than in the entire history of gaming.

The airport workers though, are less blasé about England's impending adventure. In the spring sunshine, hundreds of ground staff surround the plane and cheer the players up the steps when boarding is finally announced.

Not all the squad is present. Francis Lee has just been given special dispensation to join the party later, staying behind because his wife has had to go into hospital for a minor operation. He said he'd fly if necessary, but needed to look after the kids. The FA kindly consented and so Lee will hook up with the party at the end of the week. In the meantime he'll be training alone at Maine Road, the rest of the Manchester City players having gone on tour to Australia.

With England, as ever, come the gentlemen of the press. The papers make much about sending their boys overseas, treating them like war correspondents about to dive into foreign foxholes, and, in a manner of speaking, the sportswriters of the day *are* going to be sending back missives from the trenches. In the last days of an open, unrestricted era, the scribes – Ken Jones of the *Daily Mirror*, Desmond Hackett of the *Daily Express*, Brian James of the *Daily Mail*, Peter Batt of the *Sun*, the *Observer*'s Hugh McIlvanney, Geoffrey Green from *The Times* – are accustomed to travelling with the team as almost part of the party, right there in the front line, mingling with the players, getting access later journalists would kill for.

Despite the pack of hacks, the England departure does not achieve the headlines it would have done normally. Once again, America has stolen the thunder. Over the weekend, President Nixon has ordered the invasion and bombing of Cambodia, expanding the Vietnam War into a new theatre. Despite his proclamation that it is merely a brief incursion to sniff out the Vietcong who'd been operating beyond American reach, the move provokes outrage. In London, thousands of angry marchers rally in Grosvenor Square, outside the US embassy. In the USA there are mass protests on university campuses across the country. On Monday 4th, at Kent State University in Illinois, national guardsmen open fire on demonstrators and kill four students. America is stunned. The issue is sent spinning off on a whole new tangent.

Civil unrest seems rife across the Western world. In Northern Ireland, a civil rights movement has begun to highlight the lot of Ulster Catholics and, with sectarianism at its ugliest, what seemed the odd flashpoint last year is now descending into a fully fledged summer of rioting as Protestants and Catholics beat seven bells out of each other.

On the mainland, the flames of discontent are being fanned. The question of race is now firmly on the agenda. The Tory Monday Club calls for repatriation of coloured immigrants on a massive scale. And Enoch Powell begins a series of provocative speeches, in strongly immigrant areas, in the West Midlands and London, advocating that black citizens should be given £30,000 to go back to their place of birth (quips TV personality Kenny Lynch, 'It'd come in very handy in Camden Town').

And what with the hoo-ha over the South African cricket tour continuing, a number of African and Asian Commonwealth countries are threatening to boycott the Commonwealth Games in Edinburgh this September if the cricket goes ahead.

Jack Charlton's concerns are rather more basic – he bemoans the fact that while he's away he won't be able to get a decent cuppa. The *Sun* sympathises and advises the boys to take their own teapots and brewing gear with them, 'due to the fact that these foreigners have their own peculiar customs ... like coffee'.

On arriving at Mexico City airport, immigration officials have trouble believing that Nobby Stiles, with his thick specs and false teeth, is a genuine member of the England football squad.

Actually, the Mexicans love Nobby, 'Terrible Stiles' as they call him. Here he ranks alongside Moore and Bobby Charlton in popularity. It's just that he doesn't look the same without that gummy grin, haring down on a nervous centre forward. But, with the matter soon cleared up, Stiles and co. emerge into the arrivals area before a cheering crowd of locals, to be picked up by Sid Brown and driven to the Parc des Princes Hotel, a chalet-style establishment near the capital's Reforma district. The World Cup adventure has begun.

There, before being medicined with sleeping tablets, they are divvied up into twos and threes for room-sharing. Traditionally paired off according to their clubs, Ramsey has always done it according to personality type – the quiet ones, like Bobby Charlton and Keith Newton; Londoners Martin Peters and Peter Bonetti; cocky Merseyside clubites Emlyn Hughes and Tommy Wright; cool wind-up merchants Bobby Moore and Peter Thompson; the bubbly ones, Nobby and Ballie, up to their usual mischief.

'Alf was always good like that,' says Alex Stepney. 'He'd mix it up, which was always good for team spirit and getting to know players.'

Though, according to the great package tour cliché, when they emerge the next morning and blink into the bright Mexican sunlight, all is not quite as expected. Not only, in the finest tradition, is there extensive building work going on, to a constant backdrop of drills and hammers, but England find themselves sharing the place with the Mexican squad. *Their* training facility, a space-age centre next to the Azteca Stadium, has not yet been completed, and so they've been billeted at the Parc des Princes since the beginning of March, with no evidence to suggest they are in any rush to be moving out.

Ramsey, to put it mildly, is not best pleased, as it destroys all his plans for seclusion and privacy. And, to make matters worse, he is informed that, in a couple of days, the Italian team will be coming to share the hotel, too.

There is nothing England can do. And so they go about their business, which essentially entails taking it easy for the first few days, getting used to the heat, which is not as bad as everybody expected at present, peaking around the high eighties in midafternoon.

On Wednesday 6th, after a rest day, the squad goes up to the national park at La Marquesas – at 12,000 feet, twice the altitude of Guadalajara – where the Olympic marathon runners trained, and have a light-hearted game of cricket. In the evening the players sit in the hotel TV lounge and watch a training match between Brazil and a Guadalajara XI.

On Thursday, in the morning, they are taken to a rodeo by people from the British embassy. And, in the afternoon, at the Reforma Club, a country club run by wealthy British ex-pats, where they'll do their training, they have a game of golf – the non-players asked to caddy or score.

The team-building activities continue – more cricket, darts, dominoes, cribbage, all sorts of equipment having been shipped out with them – with a daily routine of loosening-up exercises.

On Friday, England have their first official practice session, largely for the benefit of photographers, which involves Banks and Peters running around with Nobby Stiles on a stretcher, pretending to be flaked out, and David Sadler and Jack Charlton adjudicating a light practice match, giving marks to players – Big Jack being ruthlessly tough on his kid brother, Sadler having fun winding up Alan Ball, not the most difficult of tasks. The day is rounded out when Francis Lee arrives, clutching his England hold-all, his wife Jean now safely back at home. Straight off the plane, Lee joins right in and charges around, thumping in a few goals, bagging a quick fifty at cricket and beating everyone at darts. The other players exchange knowing glances. The problem of altitude is not immediately apparent. It takes a few hours to catch up with you. Soon, Lee is so exhausted he's nearly out on his feet. And the day ends with England taking a trip to the Azteca to see the full Mexican side play a friendly against visiting German club side Borussia Dortmund.

Though England would be unlikely to play Mexico in the tournament, and even then not until the semi-finals, some satisfaction is to be had as Mexico, against an unacclimatised, jet-lagged Dortmund, shorn of its German internationals, can only scrape an undeserving 1–0 win.

England do manage one serious, behind-closed-doors work-out, but the frivolities resume on Saturday as they indulge their hosts at the Reforma Club with a knock-about game of football, then play a match against the gentlemen of the press, the tormenting of whom is of particular amusement to the players . . .

The leisurely introduction to Mexico is all part of a calculated plan. Until recent times, the England football team never much bothered with medical detail. Indeed, until Ramsey brought Dr Alan Bass into the fold when he took over the national managership, England had never travelled with a doctor at all, culminating in the near-disastrous situation in Chile, 1962, with Peter Swan. Until then, the men in suits had deemed a doctor superfluous to requirements (and, one assumes, depriving them of an extra spot at cocktails). Ramsey, by bringing in Bass, had gradually exposed the England set-up to the notion of sports medicine, moving it beyond the stage where the trainer and his magic sponge were the panacea to all known ills.

Taking over from Bass in 1968 came the genial Dr Neil Phillips. He'd fallen into sports medicine surreptitiously when, as a GP in the North-east, he happened to be on hand to treat West Ham's John Byrne ahead of an under-23 international at nearby Middlesbrough FC. A football fan, as well as a capable amateur cricketer, Phillips subsequently became the club doctor at Ayresome Park and eventually a director. He was soon recommended to the England fold by ex-England boss Walter Winterbottom and Boro associate Harold Shepherdson. And, since his elevation – a Welshman at that – had assumed a unique role within the England set-up, a permanently tracksuited member of the bench, becoming part of Ramsey's inner sanctum.

It brought criticism from some, like Brian Clough, who questioned what a doctor was doing taking part in training sessions, becoming second only to Shepherdson as Ramsey's confidant, though Phillips was merely carrying out Alf's instructions 'to be a friend to the players and just one of the squad,' he says. 'I never missed a team talk, I never missed whatever they were doing – going to the pictures, playing in the five-a-sides.'

Indeed, he had duties way beyond the medical. In the England camp, an extra and steady pair of hands was much appreciated. As Phillips soon found out, everything on an international trip – from booking hotel rooms, flights, transport, arranging meals, entertainment, training facilities, down to sorting the kit – was left to just three men: Ramsey, Shepherdson and himself (four, when for big championships, like this, trainer Les Cocker was drafted in from Leeds).

Unfortunately, even with Phillips's efforts, England, medically speaking, were on borrowed time. Though they had known since 1964 that the 1970 World Cup would be in Mexico, and that since winning it in '66 they would definitely be going, by 1968 there had still been nothing done by way of preparation for the rigours of heat and altitude.

On appointment, Phillips sprang into action. In two years, squeezing his missions into half-days and weekends and unpaid for his pains, he devoted every moment of spare time to researching the physiological problems that Mexico would bring. He drew together a think-tank of top football-friendly physicians to act as consultants (including Dr Roger Bannister) – orthopaedic surgeons, haematologists, a dentist and others – travelled to foreign medical sports organisations, and compiled dossiers. His first trip, to the Sports Medicine Institute in Bucharest, a state-of-the-art unit (the communist countries placing great value on national sporting prowess), told him what he already knew – that England was woefully deficient in such resources.

'I remember coming back to the hotel to Alf and saying, "How the hell do you expect me to provide you with similar medical cover? I'm a GP in Redcar. I'm only part time with the England set-up,"' says Phillips. 'I always remember Alf saying, "I don't care how you do it, but make sure ours is better than the Romanians'."'

Between heat and altitude, heat was perhaps the easier issue to combat. Much scientific information existed in military circles about desert warfare and heat-survival methods. Phillips also had well-versed colleagues to contact in Addis Ababa. On a practical level, the biggest problem with playing football in the Mexican heat would be salt loss. Traditionally this had been rectified with salt tablets, though swallowing such things before sporting activity had always been tricky: they were huge; too much salt in one dose makes you sick; and all the salt is released in one hit, not beneficial for sustained performance over two hours.

In conjunction with Hugh de Wardener, professor at the renal unit at Charing Cross Hospital, and one of Phillips's team, a novel idea was hit upon which they took to the UK branch of the pharmaceutical company Ciba-Geigy to manufacture. This was an innovation known as 'slow sodium' – a smaller tablet, structured like a honeycomb, with individual salt cells, each cell covered with a soluble membrane of varying thickness, which would thus release pockets of salt into the body at steady intervals. Taken with the pre-match meal, three hours before kick-off, by the time the tablet kicked in, it would provide an internal sodium drip over two and a half hours of activity. Already tested at League level during the 1969–70 season, the advent of slow sodium had already done much to alleviate cramp in the late stages of games.

Altitude, however, was more of an unknown quantity. Given that the highest League ground in the UK is West Bromwich Albion's Hawthorns, at 550 feet, it was never something that had cropped up in the domestic game. And even internationally it was a real concern for top-class sides only when playing in Mexico or the Andean countries. So there was little information available.

Much material was gained – some of it by calling in favours, the rest by subterfuge. A major breakthrough was made when journalist Peter Lorenzo managed to get hold of a copy of a detailed Argentinian study compiled (then ignored) for Argentina's World Cup qualifier at La Paz, Bolivia. Then came the pièce de résistance. The Dutch Olympic Committee had been known for a long time to have produced a groundbreaking report compiled to prepare athletes for the '68 Olympics. It was now in possession of the Dutch FA, who were holding it for the World Cup. Phillips had become friendly with the relevant medical big-wigs in Amsterdam and, when Holland failed to qualify (and for fear that it might slip into German hands), they kindly passed it on to him.

'I remember rushing back to the hotel with this book in my hand because it was the thing I'd been looking for for ages,' he says. 'Everything I wanted to know was in this book.'

Blood profiles had to be compiled on all the players, weights taken, tests run, jabs administered. In advance of approaching the squad, Phillips used a number of the sportswriters who accompanied England as guinea pigs in his research. There was clearly much work to be done. When Phillips took over the position of team doctor, not one England player had ever had a blood test in the line of national duty.

For the preparatory time in Mexico, a programme was devised so that, as pulse rate and body temperature gradually declined over days, with acclimatisation to altitude, this decrease was matched by an increase in the body's production of sweat to combat heat. The two lines on the graph were set to cross at the crucial point before England's first fixture against Colombia on 20 May.

'We were as well prepared as any European side could be – other than having lived there all our lives,' deadpans Brian Labone.

With England players set to lose between eight and ten pounds of sweat per game – up to six pints – and still plenty more besides during training, fluid replenishment was a crucial issue. This led to another problem – Mexican water was not the most reliably hygienic. Indeed, Phillips had already been warned by the British vice-consul in Guadalajara, also a doctor, about the particular conditions there.

'He said, "We've got a big problem. We can't separate the water from the sewage,"' says Phillips. 'He said, "Don't let them have any frozen ice in their drinks because they'll be consuming raw sewage."'

England's arrival in Mexico was thus accompanied by 15,000 bottles of Malvern water.

Former Leeds player Freddie Goodwin, now on the verge of becoming Birmingham City manager, had informed Phillips of something else that might help. While playing in Florida at the end of his career, Goodwin had been turned on to the wonders of a glucose and saline drink which had been pioneered by the US Army and was now commercially available as Gatorade. Unfortunately, England cannot bring in sufficient quantities of Gatorade from the States because they have no import licence. Instead they sneak it in in crystal form. And so, on every morning of the Mexican sojourn, Phillips will get up well before breakfast to make up thirty litres of the stuff in his hotel room, mixing it in buckets with the Malvern water, pouring it into twenty Thermos flasks and packing them in ice (not for consumption) in his bathtub, ready for that day's action.

Ramsey takes some of the health precautions a little too seriously. Obsessed with the sun, he rigorously keeps his players out of it when not training, and also out of the pool – not easily done when the Italians and Mexicans are enjoying the facilities. After several days of sitting in the shade, watching the Italians strutting round the pool, or swanning about in their sharp shirts and tailored slacks, it gets too much. Fed up with sitting pallid in the shade in their standard-issue light blue tracksuits ('boiler suits', as they call them) – all way too tight and making them look like members of a chain gang – the players have a diplomatic word with Ramsey.

'We talked Alf into letting us have a bit of sun,' says Jack Charlton. 'We were all down by the pool. He blew a whistle and we all lay down. Then ten minutes later he blew a whistle and we all turned over. After about another ten minutes he blew again and we could all go in the pool. But we couldn't swim in the pool, we had to play around.'

The spectacle is of much amusement to onlookers, though Ramsey had made his point.

'You're not there to sunbathe,' says Allan Clarke. 'You're there to do a job of work for your country.'

It does not stop one of the lads from having a bit of fun, though. Each night a note is slipped under Ramsey's hotel door from a player, signing himself anonymously as 'The Thumb', detailing secret stashes of Ambre Solaire, illegal sunbathing activity and girls being sneaked back to rooms.

'It wasn't me. I'm sure Alf *thought* it was me,' says Big Jack. 'Alf was going berserk. If he found out who this guy was who was writing these letters, there was going to be real trouble. I never found out who it was.'

It will not take long, though, for the Mexicans to take umbrage with the eccentric goings-on in the England camp. And this concerns the matter of food. The eagerness of companies to be seen supplying England had resulted in a deal being struck with frozen-food people Findus. 'Shows you how amateurish we were in those days,' says Phillips. 'She wouldn't like me to say it – but my wife worked out with Findus what we needed for thirty people for six weeks in Mexico and Findus shipped it all out there. The sad thing was, when it arrived in Mexico, the Customs and Excise people wouldn't let it into the country because they were certain that Great Britain was a foot and mouth country.'

The Mexican authorities decree that all dairy products must be destroyed there and then at the quayside. The beef products must go, as must eighty pounds of English butter.

'I had to go down and certify that it had all been burned,' says Phillips.

With the steaks and burgers now gone, England's finest sportsmen are left to subsist on fish fingers and ready-meals for the duration of the trip.

'Other countries did it but they didn't make a fuss about it,' says Ken Jones. 'The companies that were providing England with the facilities created the publicity out of it.'

'England didn't do themselves any favours at all,' says Hugh Johns, the ITV World Cup commentator. 'That was very, very silly. It was "the nig-nogs the other side of the Channel," "don't drink the water," typical Anglo Saxon nonsense and, of course, the natives didn't like it and I don't blame 'em.'

But still the lads seem in good spirits – and start getting quite cocky. Though they are supposed to be concentrating on the opener against Romania before they turn a thought to Brazil, everyone knows the showdown with the men from Rio is going to be the pick of the first-round games.

Last year, on tour, though Brazil won, some of the players remarked that Pelé was a bit 'flash' – could do all the little tricks, but didn't really contribute much to the overall game. Having seen Brazil on TV winning only 3–0 against a weak Guadalajara XI – a team nicknamed the Striped Goats – some England players are prompted to suggest that a pub team could have done better. Of course, this is all just shadow boxing. Brazil know exactly what they're doing.

What the England camp cannot fail to have noticed is the rapturous welcome reserved for the Brazilians by the local fans. Indeed, Brazil have already done the missionary work. They go straight to Guadalajara on arrival, rather than spend any time in the capital. Before the game they throw bunches of flowers into the crowd. Then, the whole team does a lap of the pitch with an oversized Mexican flag. In the daytime Brazilians have been ingratiating themselves, giving interviews proclaiming the wonderful hospitality of the locals and the beauty of the Guadalajaran women. Brazilian banners have gone up proclaiming the longstanding (if spurious) friendship between the two nations. Hats and T-shirts are given away by Brazil showing the two national flags intertwined.

For Brazil, England's Findus faux pas could not come at a more opportune moment. The story of the English and their burned offerings soon becomes widely known. Throw in the bus and the English are branded as 'rude' and 'arrogant'. What's more, it turns out that the food shipment even contained imported fruit, something not exactly in short supply in these parts. In one Mexican newspaper, a headline proclaims, 'IF YOU ARE GOING TO THROW FRUIT AT THE ENGLAND TEAM, REMEMBER TO WASH IT FIRST.'

Ramsey, not quite fully aware of the implications, makes encouraging noises about Guadalajara – a little hollow given that England have chosen not to go there till the last minute – saying how they 'will appreciate every cheer' and hope that the locals will respect their privacy and show some self-restraint once the team checks in at the Guadalajara Hilton, right in the centre of town. Just short of drawing them a map, it is an open invitation to disruption.

Brazil are certainly not all show. Their programme has been carefully calculated. Having completed their missionary work, they are then whisked away to their Guanajuato training camp, sixty miles east of Guadalajara, where they are locked away under armed guard while they get down to the serious business of training. They are way more secretive than England in this respect. Though with the presence of the military in the security set-up, this is not surprising. The fate of the Brazilian government rests on the success of the football team and there must be no distractions. A firm hand is needed to ensure stability. Brazilians are no strangers to coups. Indeed, the military have just inflicted one on the team's managership.

Only weeks before the tournament, the all-conquering manager João Saldanha has had his services forcibly withdrawn.

To the military regime of General Emilio Garrastazu Médici, Saldanha had always been a bit of a thorn in the side – a free-thinking left-winger, an economist with a degree from Prague University, a former war correspondent who still had a bullet lodged in his shoulder – a bit of a folk hero, second only to Pelé.

Saldanha was a man of huge personality. Though he had played and coached in his earlier days, he got his first managerial job – at Botafogo – when, in a later phase as a sports journalist, he criticised the team so often that he was asked simply to put up or shut up. He had done so well that he was eventually elevated to national manager, appointed in 1968 to clear the hangover that still existed from the 1966 World Cup, replacing previous manager Vicente 'El Gordo' (The Fat) Feola. He had an immediate impact, with Brazil scoring twenty-three goals for and two against as they stormed through the six games of the World Cup qualifiers.

Saldanha had never been shy of courting controversy. In 1967, when his Botafogo side won the Rio state championship, he accused opposition keeper Manga, of Bangu, of taking a bribe. When Manga confronted him he pulled out a pistol and fired off two shots. More recently, as national boss, when Flamengo's manager Yastrich called him a coward, Saldanha headed straight for the Flamengo hotel and, once more, whipped out his piece. Challenging journalists to punch-ups, too, was a regular occurrence. ('He did have a slight screw loose but he was a fascinating character,' says the BBC's Barry Davies, who encountered Saldanha later in Mexico City.)

None of this was as shocking as his next move. As Brazil entered the final stage of its run-up to the World Cup, Saldanha had announced he would be dropping Pelé from his starting line-up. Although possibly a piece of kidology designed to reinvigorate a flagging player, it was deemed publicly to be more a sign of Saldanha's deepening mental torpor.

None of the above curried favour with Médici, especially since the general himself was trying to preserve his position, caught between feuding military factions and needing some happy symbol of national unity to cling to. The situation was complicated by the fact that he was also a keen football fan and had already started sticking his oar into soccer affairs. A Flamengo supporter, Médici still went to games, standing on the terraces of the Maracanã. He loved the club so much that he personally arranged the transfer from Atletico Mineiro of his favourite striker, Dario. As the World Cup came around, he was in the process of trying to land Paulo Cézar from Botafogo.

When Médici invited the national team to the Presidential Palace in Brasilia and Saldanha refused because it would interfere with his training schedule, the president was left fuming. More so when Saldanha, although forced to include darling Dario in his squad, refused to play him.

Saldanha was on borrowed time. A warm-up game in Porto Alegre was the last straw. Losing 2–1 at home to Old Enemy Argentina, the excuse presented itself. And, on 15 March, Saldanha was removed from his post for reasons of 'emotional instability'. He left a morning training session for a meeting with the Brazilian FA (the CBD), told his squad he might not be back, and, true to his prediction, didn't return. The bemused players were informed some time later that he had been removed.

Saldanha's job has passed to thirty-nine-year-old Mário Zagalo, a former player and World Cup winner himself in 1958 and 1962, though only third choice for the job. But there is a problem. Zagalo and Pelé, former teammates, do not like each other. What's more, to several players, there is something foreboding about the manner of Zagalo's arrival. 'The Ant', as Zagalo, a former midfielder, is known, seems to owe his successes to the misfortunes of others. His place in each of those World Cup teams was due to timely injuries to other players (Pepe, then Germano). Now he has gained the managership through highly dubious circumstances. To the superstitious players, third time is most definitely not lucky.

Ironically, Zagalo was a former protégé of Saldanha's at Botafogo, and now he has had to lock himself away with Saldanha's players to try to mould them into a cohesive unit.

Médici also still has a role to play. He has installed retired army captain Claudio Coutinho, a physical training expert, to oversee the camp, along with help from other brass, like Admiral Jeronimo Batsos. 'One thing people tend to overlook about that Brazilian team,' says Ken Jones, 'is that it was very much government controlled. Even the freer spirits like Pelé had to conform. They were under very tight control, which doesn't seem to marry with their flair in the field.' To get their physical preparation right – nothing short of a Brazilian victory being acceptable – the team has even been to Houston to work with NASA on the conditioning of heart and lungs. It's tough on a team laden with heavy smokers. Gérson, it is said, is such an addict that a reserve with a lit fag is always waiting for him when he comes down the tunnel at half-time.

Nevertheless, Brazil seem to be overcoming their difficulties and step up a gear. At the weekend they beat the far more proficient club side León 5–2, Pelé scoring twice.

As Brazil ride out their problems, other camps are troubled. Just arrived in Mexico City, the Uruguayans are coming off the back of a strike over expenses payments for games outside Uruguay which resulted in the cancelling of some of their warm-up games. A similar problem has afflicted tiny El Salvador due to their FA's alleged reneging on an agreement over remuneration.

England also have some niggles of their own. While the games against the Reforma Club and the press prove a laugh, beating them 9–3 and 6–0 in two short matches, toying around at quarter pace and teasing Ramsey, who has filled in for a missing man on the Reforma side, the day's training has not been without casualties. Stiles has to have a hand X-rayed after getting in the way of a point-blank shot from Hurst, though it turns out to be OK. Then Les Cocker injures his back while unloading the team kit and is confined to bed for the day. If anything is to be gained from the Stiles injury, it's the realisation of just how hard the ball can be hit in this atmosphere.

Venturing out for the first time, the England party soon gets an idea of the reception that will lie in store for them when the tournament begins. On Wednesday 13th they hold a public practice at the 103,000-capacity Olympic Stadium. Thinking that it will be an exercise in greeting the natives, they are astonished to step out on to the pitch to the boos and jeers of the two thousand locals who hurl bottle-tops at them and chant for Brazil. Afterwards Ramsey stomps off, uttering only a terse, 'I do not speak to the press until Thursday.'

Despite the assertion from Peter Batt of the *Sun* that 'the early taunts of the local sleekheads were silenced by goals', the general feeling is that it was all rather lacklustre, perhaps deliberately so.

The teams are split, as at all practice games, into 'Whites' versus 'Reds', on this occasion deliberately mixed up between first and second teams. There are more injury scares – Lee and Bonetti clash, Wright limps off, Stiles struggles, gasping for breath near the end, Sadler gets blisters and hobbles away without boots, Jack Charlton and Kidd are hurt in tackles, Moore, for the Reds, is replaced in the second half by Hunter to avoid aggravating a muscle strain.

The weather – drab, cool, with occasional rain – does not simulate battle conditions. But the players give it a good go. The Whites win 4–0 (Hurst with two, Bobby Charlton and Clarke), with Charlton strolling around like he owns the place. It is an interesting experience for him. He played in this very stadium in 1959 as a twenty-one-year-old England man of one year's standing. Coates, not unlike Charlton at a distance, with his prematurely balding thatch, looks equally sharp. The Burnley man is the only player who gets any extended attention from Ramsey, receiving a long pre-match talk in the centre circle. His position in the squad is looking increasingly secure.

On Thursday, after their exertions, the players have a 'fun' day with a mini-Olympics – sprinting, jumping, bench hurdles, javelin-throwing, shot-putting, throwing the cricket ball – to which the press are cordially invited. Bobby Charlton proves best at the fifty-yard dash, and this from a thirty-a-day smoker. Alan Ball is the tops at pull-ups, done on a goal stanchion, though Colin Bell, 'Nijinsky' (named after the racehorse, not the ballet dancer), famed for his stamina, wins just about everything else – seven golds in all.

The afternoon's frivolity seems at odds with the security cordon placed around the pitch at the Reforma Club and the twenty-four-hour watch now being mounted by the security men of the Mexican government. This is a new turn of events, and though the lads joke about it, when Ramsey gathers them to explain, they find him deadly serious. A statement from the British embassy has warned them all to take care. The German ambassador has just been killed in Guatemala, an Israeli official has been murdered in Paraguay. Now there are threats of kidnapping and terrorist activity in Mexico. 'You are all valuable property,' Alf tells them. 'Go out in groups and lock your doors at night.'

Training continues through the weekend under the same guarded circumstances, but Ramsey remains pensive. On Sunday 17th, after training, he gives a press conference by the pitchside sitting in a deckchair. Although he does his modest best to exude an air of calm he knows that the hard work is about to begin. According to all the charts, graphs, weigh-ins and blood tests, the England players are now fully acclimatised and ready for action. Tomorrow, Monday 18th, they'll be leaving the hotel at 5 a.m. to catch the 7.20 a.m., five-hour flight to Bogotá, Colombia. Hopefully it will not be goodbye for good to Mexico City. Depending on the draw, they could return here to play at the Azteca if they reach the last four. They will certainly be back if they make the final.

They've got every chance, they reckon. The lads are in fine fettle. A unit now. Making jokes, even at Alf's expense. As they enter the dining hall and Ramsey asks them in his most headmasterly fashion whether they've washed their hands, Moore quips, to raucous merriment, 'Why? Haven't they any knives and forks?'

Back home life goes on. Frank Sinatra plays the Royal Festival Hall at £300 a ticket; Christy Brown's book *Down all the Days* comes out, having taken him fifteen years to type with just his big toe; Mike Winters (of he and Bernie) is nicked for speeding in his Aston Martin in Buckinghamshire, and now his brother will have to drive twenty-seven miles out of his way each night to pick him up for gigs; fears grow that barmaids – bless their pretty little heads – won't be able to add up come Decimalisation Day next 15 February; *M*A*S*H* wins the Best Film award at Cannes; and residents of Riston Close, West London, formerly known as Rillington Place, do double takes as film actor Richard Attenborough appears in their street dressed as serial killer John Reginald Christie.

And the big news: after taking time out to sing 'Cockles and Mussels' with Violet Carson (*Coronation Street*'s Ena Sharples) on a TV awards show, Harold Wilson, on Monday 18th, decides to go to the people. He announces 18 June – Waterloo Day – as the date of the general election, Parliament to be dissolved on 29 May. As the vote looms, a Scottish Tory Party conference gets into gear by advocating the hanging and birching of criminals and 'using them as target markers' on rifle ranges.

To herald the start of a gender-bending decade, in Buckley, North Wales, six-year-old Michael McGrath joins the Brownies. And, with every tabloid obsessing over the bottom-pinching epidemic which is sweeping the nation, with managers, civil servants, even vicars arrested daily, the latest culprit, in Iver, Buckinghamshire, turns out to be none other than the ghost of an eighteenth-century stable boy – 'It borrows my wife's jewellery, too, and leaves it in a different room a few days later,' says the haunted home-owner.

Elsewhere people are spending their hard-earned on the by-products of a very big event indeed. Whereas 1966 had seen souvenir manufacturers go into a patriotic huddle and knock out merchandise in an unaggressive, or certainly uncoordinated fashion, much as they would for a royal jubilee, or like a hawker trading his knick-knacks outside the Tower of London, the 1970 World Cup has seen commercialism reach an unprecedented level. Just about every newspaper issues a souvenir poster or wallchart. The *Daily Mail*'s costs 1s from newsagents and can be completed by attaching stickers of the players obtained by sending off a series of cut-out coupons; with the *Express* you can write off for a 22" × 16" colour poster, sending a bunch of coupons and a 6s postal order. The Co-op produces a transfer book; the Official World Cup programme goes on sale at local newsagents for 6s; *Football Monthly* (June issue, 3s 'Out Now') gives away a free 'at your fingertips, unique dial-a-match spinner', with all the kick-off times and TV schedules; an official World Cup England table lamp costs 30s; and drinks suppliers have a field day urging their customers not to run out of Double Diamond and Blue Nun (for the wives) over the coming month. The biggest hit of all the promotional gimmicks is the coin collection by Esso, 'the action station', comprising '30 gleaming silvery coins, each bearing the sculptured head of one of England's greatest soccer stars ... each coin has a milled edge and is minted in exactly the same way as a coin of the realm'. They're free with every gallon of four star, and for 2*s* 6*d* you can buy the splendid mounting board to put them all on. Most souvenir manufacturers have had to take a guess on which players will make the final squad. But the announcement of the official twenty-eight has left Esso particularly blue, with Sadler, Stiles, Kidd and Coates failing to make their own cut, preferring instead Madeley, Storey-Moore, Henry Newton and reserves Jones, Oakes and Simpson. They also promote Bobby Moore from an OBE to a CBE, but no one seems to mind.

The cartoonists have fun with this sudden spate of merchandising. One in the *Daily Express* portrays a Mexican in a sombrero (what else?), outside a ground with boxes of toilet rolls, being pored over by quizzical natives. 'For the crazy British,' it says. 'They take them like so and throw them all over the pitch – don't ask-a-me why.'

And there is a new customer – 'the bird fan', as the tabloids call her. A London company called Marida capitalises by knocking out a series of floppy, Australian-style bush hats (5*s* each), with Esso coins dangling off the brim ('not too tall to block the view of patrons behind'). On 30 May the 'bird fans' get a team of their own as players' wives Tina Moore, Judy Hurst, Kathy Peters and Frances Bonetti fly out from Stansted to Mexico, Mrs Moore ('Bobby's shapely wife Tina', according to the *Daily Express*) having spent the past month posing in the papers in a series of fashionable summer accoutrements.

The presence of this foursome in Guadalajara will be a source of great consternation to Ramsey, who does not appreciate distractions from the business of football. Ramsey is not, however, in a position to object. On 19 April, while waving off the *Daily Mirror* World Cup motor rally, the question of a fee for such a task left hanging, he simply requests that the organisers foot the bill for his own wife, Vicky, to be flown out for the tournament.

The rally turns out to be an epic event worthy of a book in its own right, the biggest such race ever staged. Full of colourful characters, a bizarre array of vehicles and constant incident, it sees 96 cars and their 240 drivers embark on a 16,244-mile race across 25 countries from London to Mexico City via Central Europe,

Lisbon, Rio de Janeiro and a long haul over the Andes, all the way up to Central America.

Twenty-five thousand turn up at Wembley see the cars set off, sent on their way by Ramsey with an oversized Union Jack. Both he and Moore give an affectionate thumbs-up to a certain driver by the name of Jimmy Greaves, who, with Tony Fall, is co-driving a Ford Escort. The Escort cars will feature prominently.

The gallery of entrants is like something out of *Wacky Races*: serious drivers like Paddy Hopkirk and Roger Clark; Australian driver 'Gelignite' Jack Murray, a demolition expert, whose speciality is lobbing lit sticks of dynamite out of the window to amuse the crowd; a collection of chinless cavalry officers led by Prince Michael of Kent; some keen women competitors ('bird drivers'); and a group of mysterious Russians who motor along in five Moskovich saloons. Greaves is a bit of a star. Greeted by football fans even in the remotest places, he will eventually finish sixth when the cars limp home. The race ends with a final push into Mexico City on Wednesday, 27 May with the first prize of $10,000 going to 'Flying Finn' Hannu Mikkola and Swedish co-driver Gunnar Palm in their Escort, which had led through the latter stages of the rally.

England's footballers are certainly not badly paid, but naturally they have been eyeing all the commercial activity surrounding the World Cup – people cashing in on their success. In 1966 the players had netted a paltry £1,000 each for winning the World Cup. Stressing, naturally, that they were not in it for the money and would have played for free, the bone of contention seemed not the appearance money but a lack of a stake in all the commercial spin-offs. 'Even though the '66 side had won, they didn't make any money out of it,' says Emlyn Hughes. 'You look at what that side did. Bobby Moore's the only England player ever to pick up a World Cup and he didn't make two shillings out of doing it. That was the way it was.'

This time the players organise themselves. They employ, collectively, the services of the agent Ken Stanley – a former table-tennis international who looks after George Best – deciding to pool all their earnings and share them evenly between the squad members and the two trainers (Ramsey keeps managerially aloof). They extend it to thirty-one by retaining Paul Reaney after his injury. Rather than pursuing sponsorship deals, the England party has instead struck up arrangements whereby certain products – the aforementioned Findus, Ford, Esso, BOAC – can sport the prestigious lion rosette logo and the legend 'Chosen by England' (netting each player an estimated £5,000).

For some sponsors it's a case of wishful thinking – the Linguaphone Company, last winter, supplied language-lab equipment so that the boys could all become proficient in Spanish. Findus is a bit more practical, though their full-page newspaper ads say more about prevailing attitudes than the product. Under a picture of quizzical Bobby Charlton and Norman Hunter, with an anxious Ramsey in between, Findus proudly ask the question, in massive type: 'What happens if foreign food gives our boys bellyache?' ('Don't worry it's no risk a team manager will take in a foreign country,' they assure us.)

During a squad get-together at the Hendon Hall Hotel, in March, the England party are approached by a songwriter/producer called Bill Martin who, with partner Phil Coulter, had scored hits with 'Puppet on a String' and 'Congratulations'. Martin, a Scotsman, but a former professional footballer who'd played in South Africa, is a big hit with the players. He manages to entice them into a one-day recording session at London's Pye Studios to sing, as a chorus, a number of pub standards and assures them that, if they get it down on vinyl, it will sell a lot more copies than they think.

Ramsey encourages the project as a diversion, and the lads get into it. For the album, playfully titled *The World Beaters Sing the World Beaters*, Martin and Coulter throw in a composition of their own, a catchy rabble-rouser called 'Back Home', the lyrics of which affectionately suggest that whatever the boys achieve in Mexico they'll be doing it for the fans in England.

Released as a single on 18 April 1970 (Pye 7N 17920), the record spends sixteen weeks in the charts. Within two it has climbed to number three; the following week it dislodges Norman Greenbaum's 'Spirit in the Sky' from the coveted number-one spot, staying there for three weeks (and reappearing in the chart in August before the start of the new season). The football record is born. The squad, dressed in their dinner suits, makes three appearances on *Top of the Pops*, one of which involves the London-based players – Bonetti, Osgood, Hurst, Moore and Mullery – surrounded by fans, co-presenting some of the acts with Jimmy

Savile, even joining in the freestyle dancing as the end credits roll.

The *Observer* mourns such tackiness, suggesting that only George Best has got what it takes to pull off this sort of thing. 'Here Jimmy Savile brought on the unlikely short-haired blazered figures,' it says, 'got them to announce the numbers and then spent most of the time suggesting that while the hairy freaks were belting out the music, the dollies were queuing up to be serviced by the *real* men.'

'Back Home' enters football legend. The fans love it, the England lads love it. Usually led by Jeff Astle, it is sung on the coach to every game . . .

And so to Colombia. The evening before flying, a jewellery salesman is invited to the team hotel to show the players some of his wares, sold at cost price, so that the dealer can then claim to have been yet another England team supplier. 'About six limousines pulled up. Out got a little guy, about five foot, with shades on,' says Peter Thompson. 'He had bags of watches, diamonds, emeralds, everything.' They are asked to select items that will be reserved and paid for on their return. Some of the players buy, some don't, and they gradually drift out to sit by the pool. A short while later, Ramsey comes out. There's been a problem, he explains. An Omega watch has gone missing, and the little man in the shades is going bananas, accusing one of the players of stealing it.

The squad, led by Geoff Hurst, baulks at Ramsey's suggestion that they have a whip round to cover it, even if it's only to keep it out of the papers. They are innocent, Hurst says. There were staff wandering in and out all the time and God knows what's been happening inside since they've all been sitting out here.

'So Alf said – and he was smashing – said, "Fine, I understand that. I'll pay for it myself," ' Thompson explains. 'It was quite expensive. So we had another meeting and all chipped in. That never got in the press. It would have been a terrible start.'

It is an ominous portent of what is to follow . . .

Chapter 5

Bogotá

Monday, 18 May 1970

As England fly to Colombia, the final round of warm-up games for other participants gets under way. After the Dortmund debacle it does not bode well for the Mexican team. Playing against a decidedly casual Dundee United, in town as part of the pre-World Cup jamboree – as jet-lagged and unacclimatised as the Germans – Mexico can only scrape home 2–0. The Tangerines even enjoy the luxury of missing a penalty.

Duly enthused, Dundee United offer to play England for a box of cigars a man, but Alf politely declines, stating his preference for serious international fixtures rather than this type of friendly. Plus, there is no room in the finely tuned England schedule – certainly not for a bunch of Scotsmen who, with all the best intentions, might get carried away in the tackle. England, unlike many national sides, have traditionally avoided playing club opposition. Colombia and Ecuador may not feature highly in the FIFA rankings, but international football is a different kettle of fish. These games will be the *real* test of England's potential.

Across the world the summer touring season is well under way. Manchester United beat Celtic 2–0 in an exhibition game in Toronto and Spurs lose 1–0 to Malta. More strangely, it's Rhodesia 3, Kilmarnock 4 (in Bulawayo) and, in Colombo, Ceylon 1, Southampton 2. In Mexico itself, El Salvador, newly arrived and filled with the thrill of the big event, surprisingly thrash Mexican club side Liverpool 11–1 – of concern, again, to the Mexican national side, who will be playing El Salvador in Group One.

None of this matters to England. They now have the serious business of two tough international games to contend with, another hectic timetable, more time-zone changes. They will play Colombia on Wednesday night and Ecuador on Sunday lunchtime. This is no mere short hop: despite apparent proximity when viewed from Europe, it is about a twenty-hour round trip. While the players are physically prepared and the mood is upbeat, the atmosphere in the party is a little more tense than usual. In just a few days, depending on what happens in South America, six players will be jettisoned from the squad. For the fringe members – and they know who they are – these will be the games of their lives, they *have* to be. The last chance for them to impress.

It does not help relieve pressure that on the way the plane is diverted via Panama for an unscheduled thirty-minute stop because a damaged aircraft is blocking the runway at Bogotá. The players are allowed to leave the plane briefly to walk around, but they just want to get down to Colombia and put this show on the road.

When England finally arrive at Bogotá airport, it is not quite what they expect. 'It looked like you were at the end of the world,' says Brian Labone. 'There was a dead horse, bloated up. Looked like it had been there for months.'

There they run into the Soviet national squad headed in the opposite direction. A few quizzical nods and pleasantries are exchanged. The USSR are on their way back from their own secret trip to Ecuador, where, it turns out, they were just held to a goalless draw by Ecuadorian club champions Liga Deportiva Universitaria, in Quito, having had defender Dzodzuashvili sent off by a local ref (for kicking an opponent in the head).

This is of interest, for Liga will be involved in the proceedings against England. So that all twenty-eight players in the party can get a run-out, Ramsey has arranged for two supporting fixtures to be played as double-headers with the full internationals. In Bogotá the England Bs (the FA XI) will play Colombia's reserve team. In Quito England's second string will face the same Liga side that just drew with the Russians. Sadly, for six players, battling against Liga will just mean going through the motions. That morning, before the lunchtime game, Ramsey will announce his twenty-two, to be communicated to FIFA to accord with Monday's deadline.

Ramsey is not looking forward to this. He has often said that, given the need to include three goalkeepers, a better squad count would be twenty-three, so that every outfield position could be duplicated. But it would still not spare him the difficult task ahead. Discharging the same unpleasant duty in 1966, on the training ground at Lilleshall, cutting the squad on that occasion down from twenty-seven, he still ranks as 'one of my worst moments in seven years as England manager'. For the players axed it was also one of the lowest points of their football careers.

Two of those poor unfortunates that solemn day are here again now – Keith Newton and Peter Thompson. It says much for them that they stuck at it and clawed their way back into the England fold. Indeed, Newton – then at Blackburn, now at Championship-winning Everton – is a regular starter. But both know what an awful business it is receiving such unwelcome news. In England four years ago they could slink off home and lick their wounds. Coming all this way, training so hard, only to be given a sudden ticket out of here will amplify the sense of rejection for the unlucky souls not nominated. But they understand one thing, as do all the players. Alf is in this tournament to win it, nothing less, and he will choose his men accordingly, with no room for sentiment.

When England eventually get to the opulent Tequendama Hotel in downtown Bogotá at around 6 p.m., they find a good-luck telegram waiting for them from former England international Neil Franklin.

Now forty-six and running a pub in Lancashire, Franklin's name is notoriously synonymous with Colombia. The once-time Stoke and England centre half had, on the eve of the 1950 World Cup, at a point where he was a regular international and teammate of Ramsey, shocked football by turning his back on the English game. Covertly, he had disappeared off to Colombia and signed for club side Santa Fe in a new rebel league that was throwing crazy money at foreign mercenaries. The vision of El Dorado had failed to materialise and, with Colombia then outside the jurisdiction of FIFA, coupled with the manner of his sudden departure, Franklin faced a lengthy ban by the Football League on his return to England. His career eventually petered out at Hull City.

Franklin wishes England all the best and assures them that, having played his first game in Bogotá after only five days, the 1970 squad will not have any problem with altitude, even though, at 8,500 feet, it is 3,300 above Guadalajara.

The gesture is appreciated, though the name of Franklin still sits rather uneasily, a hint at the murky nature of the way things are done in Bogotá – 'a sombre city of criminals and cripples', as Brian Glanville of the *Sunday Times* so unflatteringly puts it. Even the nature of the full international that England are playing here has been shrouded in rather unseemly haggling, with Colombia getting the game on the cheap – for a low-rent £5,000 fee. None of the players has ever been to Colombia before. It is a step into the unknown, and the sense of estrangement is reinforced when they are greeted at the hotel by an employee of the British embassy who gives them the run-down of all the dos and don'ts in the city – detailing the problems with kidnappers, pick-pockets, rip-off merchants, and, as with Mexico, the prudence of not venturing out alone.

As the mass check-in begins and rooms are assigned, players mill about, gradually wandering off upstairs when their number is called. Some agree to come straight back down for a bite to eat, others sit on the foyer couches starting up fresh rounds of brag, the rest wander along to browse the row of smart boutiques. The hotel is definitely of the luxury variety. In Latin America, where extravagant wealth sits cheek by jowl with obscene poverty, such places seem like little oases of splendour, vastly at odds with the acres of slums that were passed on the way in from the airport.

Aside from a burgeoning cocaine trade, Colombia's official wealth comes from its emeralds, and the gift shops at the Tequendama are stuffed full of rock-encrusted finery. Some players look for presents for wives or girlfriends from the cheaper end of the scale. Others stare in amazement at the ostentatious, and often quite tasteless, jewelled trinkets. Bobby Charlton and Bobby Moore pop into the Fuego Verde (Green Fire), a small jeweller's shop about twelve feet square. Charlton is looking for a gift for his wife, Norma. They nod hello to the young shop assistant, a pretty, tall woman in a skirt-suit, and a chic short hairdo, and peruse the wares, displayed on chunks of coral, all locked away under the thick glass of the counter and in a case on the wall. Others wander in and out. Peter Thompson is there briefly before returning to reception to check on some mail and tells Moore and Charlton he'll be right back. Then enters Dr Phillips.

As the two Bobbies saunter back out to the lobby and look in on the latest card school, however, there is a sudden commotion.

'Next minute there's alarm bells going off and this and that and everyone's looking around thinking there's a burglary,' says Emlyn Hughes. And, true enough, the assistant from the Fuego Verde runs out rather agitated, insisting that an item of jewellery has just been removed from her store. What's more, she knows who took it.

'We came out of the shop and the three of us sat on the settee and this girl came out then and accused Bobby of *stealing*, to his *face*,' says Phillips. 'He denied it and said that it was a load of nonsense. And I always remember, I said, "You two stay here. I'm going to find Alf."'

The tourist police and hotel manager are suddenly on the scene. There is confusion. In a mix of Spanish and English, the shop assistant repeats her accusation. Something is missing. Moore and Charlton are responsible.

'Our Kid and Bobby Moore were the two people that were pointed out as having been in the shop,' remembers Jack Charlton, one of the card demons. "The woman walked up and said, "*Him* and *him*." They didn't even know what she was talking about . . . just sitting in the foyer. They hadn't been to the rooms anyway, so they said, "Well, *search* us," you know. And they [the hotel authorities] went, "No, no, no."'

With Ramsey arriving, there is a bit of a kerfuffle. Moore and Charlton are left utterly bemused. They are led off for a while to be questioned, as a matter of protocol. Moore happily makes an official statement, but the pair return with apologies proffered to them for the inconvenience. Whatever the specific accusation is, and despite the protestations of the shop assistant, the matter has been swiftly resolved . . .

Colombia – in spite of its political problems – is football mad. Because of the turmoil in the wake of a recent presidential election, the country has been placed under emergency rule and an 11 p.m. curfew has been imposed. Given that the Colombia–England international is not scheduled to kick off till 9.15 p.m. – after the B international – many citizens will be risking breaking it, and serious trouble, to see England in action, knowing they must disperse in double time at the final whistle.

On Tuesday 19th the team trains at a military school near the stadium. As they do so, word circulates among the press as to the events of yesterday and that bizarre incident outside the Fuego Verde shop.

No one really knows the full details – with the exception of one photographer, none of the journalists was immediately on hand and the players have remained deliberately tight-lipped – but certainly nothing has happened in the hours since to suggest that there is any problem or that any of the players looks concerned. All thoughts turn to the likely composition of the teams that Ramsey will field the next night at Bogotá's El Campino Stadium.

From the games over recent months and the set-up now in training, it seems that Ramsey knows his first team. In which case it is the game preceding it which is of greater interest, certainly to the press anyway. Here, the players will be doing their darnedest to catch Ramsey's eye.

The B team lines up as follows: Bonetti, Wright, McNab, Stiles, Jack Charlton, Hunter, Kidd, Bell, Osgood, Clarke, Hughes. The guessing game is confused by the fact that the same set of outfield subs – Sadler, Coates, Astle and Thompson – will sit through both games. With Shilton as Banks's reserve and Stepney due to sub for Bonetti in the Bs, logic says that, with only three keepers needed, it's Stepney who won't make the cut. The four subs, though, would appear to be holding the revolver of World Cup Russian roulette. Add Stepney and that's still only five on the critical list. One of the starting players in the B game is probably going to get a tap on the shoulder, too. As wide players, at least one of Coates and Thompson will stay. Thompson was the best player against the Scots, but Coates, in training, has looked the perfect Ramsey soldier, a team man, a hard-working wide midfielder rather than a flash dribbler. Would Alf have messed McNab around like he has, then brought him all this way just to drop him again? Probably not. So maybe Kidd, whose better days will surely come with Munich in '74, is for the chop?

The nerves are getting to everyone. Even Ramsey flaps when, in the dressing room, he loses his wedding ring, before finding it later in a kit bag.

The hosts are generous: before the game, Cesar Lopez Fretes, the Colombian team boss, an imported Paraguayan, reaffirms his belief that England are going all the way in Mexico. And just for good measure the Colombians have, quite accidentally, even laid on a suitably muddy pitch, churned up by recent heavy rain, with cool weather redolent of an English spring.

So to the football. And, in the first game the FA XI put on a good display, not yielding an inch as they win 1–0 against the Colombian Bs and showing what strength in depth the full squad now has. A fired-up Astle, desperate not to be given an early ticket home, comes on in the second half and drives home the winner. And elsewhere the team plays enthusiastically and competitively, the bit between their teeth. McNab looks assured at left back. Bell, who surely knows he's Bobby Charlton's understudy, runs around like a man possessed, making tackles, stroking the ball about, manning the ramparts. Hughes, pushed forward on the left of midfield, rather than full back, is unfussy and extremely efficient. Allan Clarke, cool and clinical up front, just as he has been throughout the monumental Leeds season, looks a class act. Each of these players leaves the field feeling quietly confident. This is the best send-off they could have asked for.

And then, fifteen minutes later, comes the first team – lean and sinewy after their training, gleaming like white knights in their new-style tropical kit. The strip England sport is of interest: while running around and cutting deals on medicines and frozen foods, Dr Phillips has also enlisted the help of Umbro, the England kit manufacturers. In 1970 sports clothing is not yet a heavily marketed business. Though the trademark Umbro diamond appears discreetly on tracksuits – and boots, more often than not, bear the three stripes of Adidas – the notion of vaunting a designer logo is considered somewhat vulgar. Labels stay firmly on the inside. Indeed, commercialism was partly responsible for England's first ever defeat against West Germany, in Hannover 1968. There, due to cash incentives, the England team took the field in brand-new, unbroken Adidas boots (and left it a blistered mess). Phillips enlisted Umbro to come up with an entirely new England uniform, but without concerns for fashion or marketability. It was designed for one thing only – keeping the players cool. Previous experience had shown that, with great sweat loss, the traditional cotton jerseys, which soaked up the moisture, were left slapping on the backs of players, up to eight pounds heavier than at kick-off. Not particularly helpful given all the other physical difficulties. And so out have gone the heavy cotton shirts of yore, and in has come a lightweight, shortsleeve shirt, made of aertex material, like a finely meshed version of a string vest. Shorts, too – white, rather than dark blue – have aertex vents down the sides, and the players are all equipped with white towelling wristbands. Due to the heat absorption of dark colours, England's famous 1966 red has been abandoned as the team second strip for an outfit of all pale blue.

At the start of the main feature there is yet another presentation to Bobby Charlton. If this is the pattern for the World Cup then he will be needing an extra suitcase for the voyage home. This time it is made by former Yugoslav international Dragoslav Sekularec, who poses for a photograph with the man of the hour. Now thirty-two and playing for Santa Fe, Sekularec was the forward who scored in a 5–0 thrashing of England in Belgrade back in 1958, just as Charlton was coming into the team.

Then the white knights go about their business with clinical efficiency. No sooner have the anthems, handshakes and formalities been dispensed with than they set about slicing up their opponents with the ruthlessness of a lab technician dissecting a pegged-out rat. Their 4–0 win is 'the most impressive victory since they took the World Cup in '66', according to the *Daily Express*'s Desmond Hackett. Roll on Guadalajara, 'where they will begin what I am more than ever convinced will be another World Cup'.

Impressively, a player who had been lacking in form suddenly comes good: Martin Peters asserts himself well and plays some intelligent balls down the left, bursting well into the box. What's more, he scores two, both headers. There's something about Ramsey in this regard – bringing out the best in people, confounding the critics, just when you need it most.

The others do as expected. Hurst throws his muscular physique about in the Colombian defence. Charlton, though misplacing a few balls early on, altitude messing up the accuracy, utterly dominates the midfield once he finds his range, banging in a goal from a lazy right-foot drive. Mullery scampers tirelessly. Ball, who nuts one in himself, looks eager. Moore is imperious. And both Cooper and Newton scurry up and down the flanks. Banks, confused a couple of times by the movement of the ball, makes three fine saves towards the end.

However, the victory is not as easy as it appears. 'I remember playing that first game at altitude and it was like we couldn't run,'

Winston the bulldog, the England team mascot, flew with the squad to Mexico, but was eventually banned from the Jalisco Stadium pitch prior to England's opening game. Captured here in happier times, January 1970

A bespectacled Nobby Stiles and the rest of the squad board the coach for the airport, 4 May 1970 (both Hulton Getty)

Above left: 'English King' Sir Stanley Rous (centre) and the VIPs at the opening ceremony in the Azteca Stadium, 31 May 1970 (Hulton Getty). *Above right:* England's first game, against Romania in the Jalisco Stadium, Guadalajara (UPI). *Below:* The tournament curtain-raiser, Mexico v the USSR: 'a classic stalemate opener' (*Mirror* Syndication)

Above and below: Martin Peters, Geoff Hurst (the goalscorer), Bobby Charlton and Alan Ball help England grind out a 1–0 win against Romania (both *Mirror Syndication*)

Above: 'Pelé's cunning accomplice' Tostão – the 'Little Coin' – takes charge in Brazil's 4–1 thrashing of Czechoslovakia (*Mirror* Syndication). *Right top:* To the anger of the crowd, masters of negativity Italy and Uruguay play out a mutually beneficial 0–0 draw in Group Two. *Right bottom:* Franz Beckenbauer, 'The Kaiser', directs operations in the 3–1 victory over Peru (both *Mirror* Syndication)

View from the touchline:
Dr Phillips and Sir Alf Ramsey
witness the epic encounter: "A
veritable masterclass in football."
(Empics)

But it's Jairzhino's goal that separates the
two sides. The Brazil forward leads the
celebration behind the England bench
(Sporting Pictures)

England and Brazil
line up for the
Guadalajara
showdown game,
7 June 1970
(Popperfoto)

Below: Francis Lee
and Bobby Charlton
are tireless in the
1–0 defeat (*Mirror*
Syndication)

Félix comes off worst in a 50/50 challenge with Lee. Brazilian vengeance is swift.
(*Mirror* Syndication)

says Terry Cooper. 'And we thought, If it's like this in Mexico, we've got no chance.'

Encouragingly, Brazil only achieved half this margin when they played in a qualifier recently. And after the match, Fretes is quick to point it out. 'I have seen Brazil, West Germany and Russia but England impressed me as a wonderful and powerful football machine,' he says at the quick post-match press conference before everyone darts off to avoid a police clubbing. 'I am impressed by their cohesion. I am not surprised by their acclimatisation because they have trained for this. They have always been a wonderfully physical side but this team is more mature than the team of 1966. The big difference between England and Brazil is England's ceaseless challenge for the ball and the terrific power they impose on the opposition.'

And Ramsey, though he would never betray it, is surely feeling smug. 'I am very pleased,' he says, matter of factly. 'The players started out of touch because many had not played in a match for several weeks. No players complained about the altitude. And they felt much better than after the practice matches in Mexico.'

Back home, while the nation sizzles in a heatwave, hoping it will carry over into the coming Whitsun Bank Holiday weekend, England are, in an oft-repeated phrase, 'on top of the world'.

On Thursday 21st, on *Sportsnight* with David Coleman, sunburned Englishmen can tune in to see the highlights. Ecuador is next.

Rather excited about the coming business in Mexico, there is little thought given to cricket – certainly not in the playing sense. Politically, however, the question of the South African tour is now resolved. With the South Africans due to fly in on 1 June for their opening game five days later, the matter reaches crisis point and the government finally exerts pressure. On 22 May the Springbok tour is officially cancelled and the Test and County Cricket Board rushes to organise a substitute England versus the Rest of the World series.

Ramsey has his own problems with the clash between sport and politics. His main truck with the authorities over the last few days has been with news coming out of Ecuador about the forthcoming game.

Football in Ecuador is not all sweetness and light. The last national team manager, Gomez Nogueira, was recently sacked after declaring his players were more interested in marijuana and women than playing football. The Saturday before England flew down from Mexico, Ramsey had been informed of a fresh squabble within Ecuadorian footballing circles concerning the venue for the England match. This was due to a dispute between the two top national clubs, one in Quito, the capital, the other in Guayaquil, the second city – the latter having suddenly lodged an appeal against Quito's choice as the venue to stage the game.

Because Russia played in Quito last Sunday, the authorities in Guayaquil claim that it is their turn to host the next international. All well and good, but Guayaquil, the country's principal port, is, naturally, at sea level. For England, playing there would not only defeat the exercise of coming to Ecuador, but would undo, possibly harmfully, the painstaking altitude work they have been undertaking.

Acknowledging this as England's purpose in visiting – as well as for the honour of playing Ecuador, of course – it had seemed that Guayaquil would concede to Quito on this occasion, but, in protest, not release any of their players (of which there were several) to the national team. Perversely, this would mean that the Liga side, scheduled to play the FA XI, might prove tougher opponents than the weakened full international Ecuador team facing England A. Requesting that the Ecuadorians switch their teams would be an insult.

However, just as it looks like the long haul down to Ecuador might have been a worthless exercise, Guayaquil complies. Interestingly, the notion of Ecuadorian players going back and forth from sea level to altitude is not an issue.

On Saturday morning, as the team trains at a Quito sports club, the clock is ticking for six players, but the handful of newspapermen watching the session are being nagged by something else: it's that Bogotá business again. Normally, this would not worry anybody. Aside from the fact that the matter was quashed, there is no way anyone would believe for one second that Bobby Moore would be involved in anything like that – let alone Moore *and* Bobby Charlton. Short of anything sinister, it was just some kind of over-zealous security procedure. Things like this happen in tin-pot countries. Any old ruse to extort a bit of cash out of the gringos.

However, the England travel arrangements, as they stand, involve the team flying back through Bogotá, where they will be stopping over for a few hours before making their connecting flight back to Mexico. What's more, it is learned that Ramsey has arranged for the squad to revisit the very same hotel, where they can relax for the daytime layover. A couple of the pressmen raise the issue with Ramsey – a case of erring on the side of caution, not going back into the lions' den.

'I remember saying, "Alf, why are we going back through Bogotá?"' says Ken Jones. 'And he said, "It's because it's the only way we can get back." I said, "When you think about all that bloody nonsense last week, couldn't you have found an alternative route?"'

Ramsey's wrong: it isn't too late to change the plan. It is revealed that England can still fly back directly to Mexico City if they wish, or certainly connect via Panama rather than the Colombian capital. Ramsey, Shepherdson and Phillips huddle together at various points during the morning session. 'Both Alf and Bobby Moore were of the view that we haven't done anything wrong, so we're going back,' says Phillips. Ramsey repeats his line on the matter – neither England nor Moore has anything to hide, the police had tossed out the accusation and the matter is closed. What's more, England had stayed on in the same hotel for three nights without any bother. Why start behaving like a bunch of fugitives?

The writers are presented with a conundrum. As journalists they are professionally bound to report news. Really they should have mentioned the jewellery-shop incident in their stories when it first occurred. But was it genuine news or just a ridiculous bit of farce? By writing about it, they will be elevating an unsubstantiated non-story – an old story now, at that – into an issue. Being close to the England party, they know that, given the growing antipathy towards England in Mexico, something like this will upset a build-up that is going exceptionally well. The hacks are so close now that they have lost all objectivity. They agree not to mention it. Indeed, in questioning Moore on the eve of the Ecuador game, none of them brings it up at all.

Ramsey, though no lover of the press, privately appreciates their restraint. He is then asked, by Frank McGhee of the *Sunday Mirror*, for a small favour. Ramsey had not planned to reveal his final twenty-two till Sunday morning, shortly before the Ecuador game.

With the whole country back home hanging on news of the unfortunate six players who will be dropped, and given the time difference, the details will not make the UK national newspapers till Monday – looking rather old into the bargain, especially as it will already have been scrutinised on radio and TV. (The press are already having a bit of trouble with time zones. They can wire over, or phone in stories by early afternoon for publication the next day, but any story that requires analysis or quotes or happens later in the day is generally thirty-six hours old by the time it hits the streets in Britain.) How about this? What if Ramsey revealed the twenty-two names to the travelling press in the strictest confidence on Saturday? That way they could meet their deadlines for the Sunday editions. Given the isolation of the England camp, especially in a place like Quito, Ramsey could still tell his players as planned and they'd be none the wiser. The sportswriters give their word that they will keep the information strictly to themselves and ensure their editors in London treat it with all due discretion, embargoing the news until the last possible moment.

Remarkably, and uncharacteristically, Ramsey agrees. On Saturday afternoon, after training, he takes the little band of reporters into a meeting room at the Intercontinental Hotel, where they are all staying, and, with grim seriousness, imparts the classified information. 'It was a difficult job. It had to be a difficult job,' he says with great solemnity, giving them the obligatory quote. 'For those who have been left out, being with us has been an invaluable experience. In any case they may be in a position no different from some who are already in the twenty-two.'

The press reiterate that this news will be treated as a matter of national importance before retiring to their rooms to try to beat the clock.

Whether his mind was preoccupied with the match, or perhaps with Bogotá, for Ramsey it is a grievous error. At breakfast on Sunday, David Sadler, beside himself with anger, storms into the hotel canteen and demands an audience with Ramsey. No one ever speaks to Alf like this. Ever. But Alf complies. In the corridor, Ramsey is backed up against the wall while Sadler, an articulate, thoughtful man, not normally given to ranting and raving, lets him have what for. Confirming Ramsey's worst fears, Sadler has already found out the horrible truth. He informs Ramsey that his wife had telephoned him late last night. She had been called at their Manchester home by a London journalist, seeking a reaction to the fact that her husband had just been axed from the squad. ('David said, "You're in, I'm not," ' remembers Alex Stepney of that trip downstairs to breakfast. I said, "How did you know that?" He said, "Bloody hell, Christine phoned me." ')

'She said she knew how disappointed I would be that I hadn't made the final twenty-two,' states Sadler. 'She didn't know that I didn't know ... So she was pretty upset. *I* was pretty upset. I got pretty angry about it and set off to front up Alf with it. My wife was crying on the phone and I found out that I'd been left out of the final twenty-two. So I flew at Alf a bit.'

Indeed, from what Sadler has discovered, and from the frantic calling that was going on back home late last night, reporters have been out in force, crawling all over the place to track down wives, girlfriends, family members of the unlucky six, all fishing for disrespectful quotes about the England boss. No matter how discreet the travelling sportswriters may have been, they have been undone by their news desks. For Ramsey, the fact that his players were still contactable by phone, even in Ecuador, had been foolishly overlooked.

Sadler admits he had half been expecting it – was really only there as cover for the three regular centre backs of Moore, Jack Charlton and Labone, and, though disappointed, had steeled himself for the worst. But he tells Alf that is not the point. After a whole season of promise, three weeks out here working his socks off and blind loyalty to England, he would have expected to have been treated with greater respect than this – and told directly. Ramsey is sheepish, cannot look Sadler in the eye. Sadler, he says, is perfectly entitled to his anger. For the first and only time in his managerial career, Ramsey apologises to a player.

'Alf calmed me down, then we went off, which is what we should have done in the first place. I'd gone off in front of some of the other players, which was wrong,' says Sadler. 'He took me to one side, explained the situation and really that's it. That's the end of it. He apologised. I understood.'

Ramsey walks back into a hushed room. His hand forced, he calls away five other players – Peter Thompson, Peter Shilton, Brian Kidd, Ralph Coates and, for all the highs and lows over the last few weeks, Bob McNab. They have served England well, he tells them, and thanks them for all their hard work, but their services are no longer required.

Some of the players have more reason to be disappointed than others. Shilton and Kidd, who did not play that well in Bogotá, are young and know that they have great international futures ahead of them, especially as an inevitable 'clearing out' phase will take place after this World Cup. Coates and McNab, though, have not put a foot wrong. Ramsey tries softening the blow by saying that even within the twenty-two, only maybe fifteen can expect to play; the rest are effectively there as insurance.

'But you know the way the team's forming itself,' says Brian Labone. 'I know there are a couple of peripheral positions. There may have been one or two were shocked, but I'm sure the majority of them are realistic enough to know that if they haven't played in this game or that what the squad is going to be.'

Inevitably, the news falls hardest on Peter Thompson ('POOR THOMPSON THROWN OUT AGAIN,' screams the *People*). To have this happen to him on the eve of *two* World Cups is cruel indeed, though demonstrates Ramsey's ruthlessness when it comes to such decisions.

'Well, '66 for me was the biggest disappointment of my career, because Alf said to me, "You're in the twenty-eight. I think you'll be in the twenty-two." I was training really hard and I was one of the six and I was really upset,' says Thompson. 'But '70 for me wasn't that big a disappointment. I just felt that he wouldn't play me. When he told me, I was really upset for about ten minutes.'

At twenty-six, it is unlikely he'll be in the frame for 1974. He admits that his Liverpool manager, Bill Shankly, had long been telling him to prepare for such news. 'I played against Scotland and Shankly said to me, "You're not going to Mexico. If he pulls you off and you're the best forward . . ." But I said, "No, I want to go." '

'This decision is hard for everybody,' says Ramsey at a press conference later. 'Obviously it is unfortunate that a thing like this should happen twice to Peter Thompson. But the fact that I had to drop him for the World Cup in England did not make it any harder this time. There could not be any sentiment involved. I was not looking to the past but to the future.'

The task was made difficult for him, he says, given that all the players came through the training with no adverse effects, which might have done for a couple of the older players. The bottled oxygen and resuscitation equipment they brought with them on the trip have been completely surplus to requirements (except to revive a member of the press during that Reforma Club kickabout!). So it is purely a strategic decision. And, in the axing of Coates and Thompson he has decided to go without wingers. Some critics bemoan the preference for industry over art, argue that if George Best were English, Ramsey wouldn't select him either. It is undeniable, however, that the quick passers are obviously better suited to Ramsey's game plan in these conditions than those who can dribble the ball. The flank running and crossing now rests squarely on the shoulders of the full backs.

It is a sad day for everyone. A spirit of camaraderie has built up and now some of their comrades have fallen. The ones who have made the cut and are bursting with joy inside – Emlyn Hughes, Jeff Astle, Peter Osgood, Allan Clarke – do their best to put a diplomatic lid on it.

The jilted six are given the option of staying on with the party or flying home. Ramsey tells them they are welcome to remain for the duration of the tournament. They will train as part of the squad and play in the practice games, their worth no less than any of the twenty-two. Indeed, their presence will be valued. However, if leaving is the preferred option, tickets for their departure have already been arranged. Whatever their decision, Ramsey informs them, it will not prejudice his opinion of them one way or the other.

The players confer, go off, think about it, make those calls back home. McNab just wants to get the hell out of there, he's been up and down like a bloody yo-yo. The youngsters, Kidd, Coates and Shilton, though with the most to gain from staying, feel that their long-faced presence will only be a distraction to the others. Sadler and Thompson, perhaps the two with the biggest justifications to leave, decide to remain. Though their pride is wounded the England cause is greater. Their participation in training can still be of use. Plus, it's not every day you get an all-expenses-paid trip to watch a World Cup.

'Bill Shankly rang me in Mexico and said, "I want you home *now*," ' says Thompson. 'I said, "No, I've done three weeks in South

America. I'm staying at the Hilton. Might as well watch it." '

'He said, "Come home now. He's embarrassed me, Nessie" – that's his wife, I don't think Nessie was embarrassed – "the people of Liverpool, Liverpool Football Club." I said, "No, I'm not coming home." '

It means there will be no celebration of Brian Kidd's birthday. A quiet sort, who went to the same Manchester Catholic school as Nobby Stiles – St Patrick's – Kidd's twenty-first falls on 29 May. The players had been given special dispensation for a drink that night. Kidd was used to having birthdays on tour and, most famously, had celebrated his nineteenth with a goal for Manchester United in the European Cup Final. It also means that Peter Shilton and Bob McNab will have to wait to resolve the contractual disputes that they are currently involved in with their clubs; Shilton, in particular, is unhappy about spending another season in Division Two with Leicester. Their managers Frank O'Farrell and Bertie Mee will be in Mexico for the tournament, flying out on a 'managers' special'. It had been hoped that they could settle the matters out here.

Amid all the furore there is still the business of the two matches against Ecuador. Despite all that has happened, Thompson will start on the left wing for the B team, while the four other outfielders of the six remain subs in both, and Shilton is Bonetti's understudy for the second team. More significantly, the squad numbers are distributed, which gives the biggest clue of all to the team which will take the field for the opening game against Romania: 1 Banks, 2 Newton, 3 Cooper, 4 Mullery, 5 Labone, 6 Moore, 7 Lee, 8 Ball, 9 Bobby Charlton, 10 Hurst, 11 Peters. FIFA, knowing how superstitious some players are, give consent for the number 13 jersey to be omitted if so desired, going up to 23 instead, though Alex Stepney takes it anyway. The rest are made up as follows: 12 Bonetti, 14 Wright, 15 Hughes, 16 Stiles, 17 Jack Charlton, 18 Hunter, 19 Bell, 20 Osgood, 21 Clarke, 22 Astle.

The games in Ecuador go as expected. In a rickety stadium set against spectacular snow-capped mountains – incongruously for a nation whose very name denotes its situation on the Equator – the two England teams do their business. The B team, perhaps through sheer exuberance at squad selection, wallop Liga – the team which Russia couldn't beat – 4–1. The game is not pretty. On a well-worn pitch and with a threadbare ball, Jeff Astle, by far and away the biggest player in the Ecuadorian box, and, as it turns out, the most lethal, scores a hat-trick, plus two more disallowed headed goals. The fourth goal sees Hughes get his name on the scoresheet, hitting a post initially and then diverting Astle's thunderous follow-up past goalkeeper Montoya. Astle seems already to have proven his worth.

The 30,000 crowd, swelling to 36,000 for the main game, largely barefoot, some walking for miles to get here, or riding on donkeys and mangy horses, reserve their biggest roar for the main attraction. At the beginning there is the inevitable fuss over Bobby Charlton. Next, the anthems, with a tone-deaf military band doing their best to approximate 'God Save the Queen'.

Then, 9,500 feet up in the Andes, England set about their business. It is efficient more than exciting, but the sense of purpose is shown when England takes the lead. Moore finds Mullery, who sends Newton running down the right. While the defence rush to smother Hurst, Lee pokes another misshapen ball past keeper Mejia. Ecuador, to their credit, fight back. Ball has a mishap in defence, trying to find Newton but gifting Penaherrera to race through to a one-on-one against Banks. While Ramsey glowers, Banks rushes out to block.

In the second half, already out of the squad, Kidd comes on for Bobby Charlton and, with eight minutes to go, dives in to head home – 2–0. The crowd, who were gingerly booing England at the start, politely clap them off. The manager, Ernesto Guerra, utters the same smitten valentines as his Colombian counterpart . . .

Back home the sizzling bank holiday weekend has precipitated the traditional rush to the seaside, filling newspapers with pictures of 'bathing belles' at Brighton, Southend and Great Yarmouth, wearing Kiss Me Quick hats, slurping 99s, or splashing merrily in polluted surf.

The seaside proves less favourable to Conservative leader Edward Heath, who sails his yacht *Morning Cloud* on to a sandbank at Ramsgate and eventually has to be rowed ashore. And, of course, the bank holiday weekend witnesses another great British tradition: the punch-up – though not this time mods and rockers but, in keeping with new sinister new political forces at work, skinheads and Asians. They take to the streets of Wolverhampton, hotbed of Powellism, whom Heath still refuses to disown. The police, meanwhile, are playing with their new toys: a pioneering piece of technology, a radar box the size of a stand-up piano, is 'hidden' along various traffic trouble spots. The speed trap, or 'tender trap' as the wags in blue dub it.

Elsewhere, John Alderton and Pauline Collins get married, hot new musical act the England Football Squad are knocked off the top spot by Christie's 'Yellow River', while, in the album chart, the honour goes to the Beatles, with the soundtrack to their post-humous and lukewarmly reviewed film documentary *Let It Be*. Though, according with their split, none of the band turns up to the premiere of the movie in Leicester Square. Another British film – Ken Loach's *Kes*, complete with PE master Brian Glover as an aspiring Bobby Charlton – is getting raves for its previews.

In the *Daily Mail* the regular cartoon, Jon's Sporting Types, shows six glum footballers, suitcases in hand, facing Alf Ramsey. 'Oh thanks, Sir Alf,' reads the caption. 'Now we can vote in the election.'

In the wider world, Russian dissident writer Andrei Amalric is arrested after predicting that the Soviet Union will disintegrate by 1984. In Germany, not far from where the Nazis threw in the towel in 1945, an international gunnery exercise is taking place – 'BRITISH ARMY WIN NEW TANK BATTLE AGAINST PANZERS,' screams the *Daily Mirror*.

Though such news will soon pale into insignificance. While the back pages vaunt their votive praise of the England footballers, the new conquistadors, vanquishers of a tropical paradise, the breaking news columns on the front pages and stop-press boxes in the wee small hours of Tuesday 26th contain alarming news: 'BOBBY MOORE COURT SHOCK,' as the *Daily Express* puts it. '2 a.m. – soccer star accused...'

Chapter 6

'A Team of Drunks and Thieves'

Monday, 25 May 1970

For the England party there had been nothing out of the ordinary about this day – another victory under their belts, further travelling, more games of brag. Flying into Bogotá, they had been taken to the Tequendama Hotel as planned. To kill the four and a half hours' waiting time, a couple of diversions had been organised. Some of the press boys – for reasons known only to themselves, perhaps in an act of self-penance over the miserable business of the squad leak – had arranged their own tourist jaunt to some local salt mines.

The alternative time-killer, cards permitting, as Nobby Stiles points out to the reporters, while sitting there having his shoes cleaned, is to stay in the hotel, where there has been laid on a screening of a film *Shenandoah*, a five-year-old American Civil War drama starring James Stewart. Duty bound to stick together, the press, to their later chagrin, will be absent from the hotel over the next couple of hours.

Ramsey is fond of Westerns (though this isn't strictly one). Not perhaps the most dynamic choice of viewing for his players, but with a weary day's travelling to contend with, most of them watch it anyway. And it is here, while waiting in the darkened room, with all attention turned to the screen, that two plain-clothes detectives enter, discreetly tap Bobby Moore on the shoulder and ask him to accompany them outside. There they formally charge him with the theft of an emerald bracelet from the Fuego Verde the previous Monday. When the film is over, amid the throng, no one particularly notices Moore's absence, especially as he is often called away to give an interview or perform some honorary function on behalf of the team – his lot as captain.

When the squad boards the coach for the airport, Martin Peters is asked to carry Moore's hand luggage. He has a funny feeling about things, but assumes, as do the other players, that Moore, along with Ramsey and some of the other FA officials, also absent, will be along soon.

Ramsey arrives in time for the plane, the team board and they are soon headed skyward. It is only then, in the air, that the players are told the news by a grim-faced Ramsey – 'The captain's been left behind.' He has been arrested on a charge of theft and detained according to procedure. Denis Follows and Dr Andrew Stephen have remained behind with him.

The players are speechless. Apart from the ridiculous accusation, their friend, skipper and star player has been marooned under God knows what conditions in an alien and hostile land. Dr Phillips walks down the aisle to the front of the plane, where some of the sportswriters are sitting, and imparts the same information. They, too, are shocked, kicking themselves that they hadn't pursued a more insistent line about flying by a direct route. But they are furious for another reason: they are 30,000 feet above the world's hottest news story, jetting away from it at 500 m.p.h. Why on earth couldn't they have been tipped-off before take-off? At least then some of them could have stayed behind. They have become used to doing reporting tasks in rotation and pooling the information. They could easily have handled it. Indeed, it might even have been to Moore's advantage to have a friendly conduit of information on the scene.

For Ramsey, the press are no longer a consideration. They've already burned their bridges. He doesn't give a damn. And the respective newspaper editors, when they find out that the travelling press knew about this whole business and had been sitting on it for the past week, will be exchanging rather harsh words with their charges. 'There was only about six of us knew about it,' says Ken Jones of the *Daily Mirror.* 'Afterwards we were criticised for not doing the story – but there was no bloody story to do.'

The news desks back home go into a flap, dealing with the scant information available. On arrival in Mexico, some of the travelling press pack are called by their editors to turn right around and get back down to Colombia, renting cars if need be – as if it were just a short hop rather than a journey of over 2,000 miles – the problem of coverage being solved in some instances by diverting journalists who had been reporting the World Cup rally.

But until then, there is general confusion, often based on the erroneous assumption that the alleged theft and Moore's arrest happened at the same time and not days apart. On BBC radio, sports reporter Bryon Butler gives as much information as anyone knows at this moment. 'What happened was the players, together with officials and some journalists, had gone to this little shop in the Hotel Tequendama,' he explains. 'And after they'd left the shop, the complaint was made. The people in the shop claim to have a witness. He's a man in his twenties. He claims he was on the other side of the glass partition and saw everything that happened and, in fact, he also claims that Bobby Charlton, of all people, shielded Bobby Moore while he put the bracelet into an inside pocket.'

There are conflicting details about the value of the item. Initially it is said to be an eighteen-carat gold bracelet worth about £600. It quickly becomes one studded with emeralds and diamonds and now worth £5,000. No one knows whether Moore ever even handled the thing.

'I have been in touch with the party. I've spoken to an official and some of the players and the word "fix" is one they're using quite frequently,' says Butler. 'The official was confused and said that he was very disappointed; that everything had been going so swimmingly. But he knows for certain that Bobby did nothing wrong. This was his opinion. But that some mud was bound to stick. He felt it was a simple case of someone trying to make some easy money.'

By Tuesday afternoon, the whole of the English nation downs tools to await word of their captain. The situation is stated in dramatic terms; as the London *Evening News* puts it: 'BOBBY MOORE HELD AS THIEF.' And, by the next day, when the papers can devote their full editions to it, a nation's anger becomes vented at the shop assistant who accused Moore in the first place. Suddenly, Miss Clara Padilla, twenty-one, is a household name. 'This is the girl', snarls the *Daily Mirror* contemptuously, 'who has accused him [Moore] of stealing a bracelet.'

Padilla has been quite forthcoming about events, explaining how Moore pocketed the offending item – now confirmed as an eighteen-carat gold bracelet with twelve diamonds and twelve emeralds embedded in it, worth £600. 'It all happened very quickly,' she tells a crowd of reporters in competent, accented English. 'Bobby Moore and two of his teammates came to the counter and started talking to me. Then I saw Mr Moore open a glass case, take out the bracelet and put it in his pocket.'

Duly charged, Moore, meanwhile, had been taken to a waiting car, then questioned at the Bogotá police headquarters. At first it is hinted that he will be released within the hour and taken to the airport to connect with his party and their 4 p.m. flight. That deadline comes and goes. Alarmingly, and with no idea what is going on, Moore finds himself being led to a cell. To his relief, just as he is about to be incarcerated, it is explained that a legal compromise has been reached. He will be placed under house arrest at the suburban residence of Mr Alfonso Senior, director of the Colombian Football Federation and president of club side Millonarios, who has put his home at Moore's disposal.

In the interim, Dr Andrew Stephen and Denis Follows rope in the brand-new British ambassador of three days' standing, Tom Rogers. He assures Moore that they will do everything in their power to clear up this mess. A lawyer, Vincente Laverde Aponte, is found to represent Moore, and, at the embassy, First Secretary Keith Morris has talks with the acting Colombian Foreign Secretary. It had been Morris's fortunate intervention, apparently, that facilitated the discreet apprehending of Moore at the hotel rather than under a more formal – and public – scenario at Bogotá airport.

It turns out, too, that the alleged accomplice, Bobby Charlton, though uncharged, volunteered to remain in Bogotá with Moore. Ramsey told Charlton that absolutely no way was he going to risk losing him as well, especially as he is a nervous type, less equipped mentally for such an experience. 'They could have chosen Bobby Charlton, and if they'd done so, that would have finished Bobby,' says Ken Jones.

'Our Kid breathed a sigh of relief when he sat on the plane and it took off,' adds Jack Charlton. 'He was worried to death that him and Bob were going to be kept back.'

It was more a case, as Alex Stepney puts it, of 'getting us out of the bloody place'.

Peter Thompson, who had also been in the shop, offered himself up, too. Anything to help. 'I went to Alf Ramsey and I said, "I'm the third man," ' says Thompson. 'And actually, footballers are stupid. I then looked in my pockets [and thought], If someone's stuffed something in my pocket...' But Ramsey, sensing the set-up, and with all due respect to Thompson, tells him that they're not after him. 'They had Bobby Moore, captain of the World Champions. Bobby Charlton, one of the most famous players in the world. I was a nonentity,' says Thompson. 'He said, "They're not interested in you, Peter."'

England are fortunate in that, at the moment of the alleged theft, Dr Phillips – a medical man, trained to make copious notes ('We were always told to write down things of importance as a record') – is on the scene. His first instinct at the time of the initial incident, after running to fetch Ramsey, had been to write his observations down in detail. Stirring the increasing murk surrounding this allegation, Phillips's testimony is never requested.

Fortunately, Moore has officialdom on his side. Though the allegation is taken very seriously, and the twenty-nine-year-old skipper vigorously protests his innocence – 'I know nothing about the theft. I have never seen the bracelet' is his terse response – he is brought before a judge, Justice Pedro Dorado. Dorado confesses he does not like football, in fact knows nothing of Moore and his reputation. There is no agenda here. He will be judging the case purely on its legal merits.

On Tuesday Moore arrives at Dorado's office and undergoes a four-hour interrogation. The judge is not sufficiently impressed by the conflicting information laid before him by the prosecution and would like to see the scene of the crime for himself.

Moore, as cool as he ever is on the pitch, gives a few words to the press via Senior: 'My only wish right now is to leave ... I am absolutely innocent,' he reiterates. 'I really don't know why I was involved in this matter ... Just as much as my team colleagues believe in me, I do believe this issue will not affect them whatsoever.'

The next day the judge, Moore, Padilla, their attorneys and a surrounding swarm of 300 people, including, police, photographers and rubberneckers, descend on the Tequendama Hotel. Moore arrives two hours late after his guards refuse to release him before getting the order from the chief of police personally.

After swearing an oath, Moore and Padilla go through a ninety-minute reconstruction of the alleged incident in the small room with its cream, gold and red decor.

Padilla, quite the fashion bombshell in her light brown bob, subtle make-up, beige suit and purple scarf, and now the centre of attention, simpers before her audience and tells a BBC TV reporter, 'I love football very much. I have never seen England play, but I imagine they play very beautiful. I am depress [sic] and I can assure you that I feel very sorry for Bobby Moore. But it's not my fault. I'm sorry.'

So why have the Colombian police suddenly decided to press charges when they had originally dismissed the allegation as bogus? As had been correctly reported by the BBC, the case had been reopened by the emergence of a key witness, an antiques dealer named Alvaro Suarez, a twenty-seven-year-old twitchy man in a grey suit. Due to his testimony, a warrant had been issued for Moore's arrest on return.

Moore, still in a pale blue buttoned shirt and his England blazer slung over his shoulder, looks on. He must be taking some satisfaction – the case rapidly appears to be full of holes, and he's casually playing it all like the world's best centre back against a talentless forward line.

From swearing on the Bible that she saw Moore put the bracelet in his pocket, Padilla, chainsmoking, now confesses she didn't actually see him take the bracelet from the wall-mounted cabinet because it was obscured by his 'wide shoulders'. She only saw Moore put *something* in his pocket and deduced it was the bracelet on Suarez's say-so.

It is Suarez who claims he had actually seen the crime take place, walking past the shop window at the point of theft. And though Suarez says yes, he registered everything, and reported it at once to the police, he then admits it took several hours for him to get round to doing so (and he may not have done so at all, for the policeman he claims to have spoken to denies all knowledge of such a conversation). And besides, why did it take four days to dig up this witness, one who was never mentioned when the initial charges were being levelled?

Suarez, too, asserting himself as a completely impartial witness, turns out to be an associate of the shop's owner, Danilo Rojas, having sold antiques to him in the past.

Rojas, aged twenty-eight, who is demanding £6,000 in 'moral and material compensation' for the bracelet – which has still not been found – starts to distance himself from the accusations and refers back to a conversation he had with Suarez on Friday 22nd. 'Suarez said, "Did he give you the bracelet back?" explains Rojas. 'I said, "My God, why didn't you mention this earlier if you knew something about the case?"'

With supreme irony, it is hinted by some that Rojas wanted to extort money so that he could take his friends to Mexico to see the World Cup.

Moore casually tackles his opponents. Padilla claims she saw Moore put something in his left jacket pocket; the England captain promptly dons his blazer: there is no left pocket.

As Moore is driven away to the house in the suburbs, and Padilla is led away in tears, cries of 'Viva Bobby' ring out.

Though the case is not open and shut. Judge Dorado informs Moore that it will take up to five days to clear this stage of the charge, and even then he might not be released right away. He must remain in the custody of Alfonso Senior until such time.

His words are a coded reference to what has suddenly become a horrible possibility. While nobody remains in any doubt about Moore's innocence, there is a very real chance that he might not be released in time for the opening game of the World Cup. Worse still, he might miss the tournament altogether . . .

On the plane back from Bogotá, Ramsey is in a black mood – so angry and upset over the arrest of Moore that he does not speak. 'Alf sat there impassively,' says Ken Jones. 'He never moved. There wasn't one flicker in his face.'

Matters are not helped by the fact that, running into a violent electrical storm, the plane is forced to land in Panama once again. Allowed to disembark, the players stand around in the airport concourse area, while the press race off to seek phone lines to London. Ramsey just paces around in a big circle – round and round, round and round – like a man possessed. 'He never stopped. Couldn't stop him,' says Jones. 'Just kept walking.'

Jeff Astle, meanwhile, a nervous flyer, deeply troubled by the violent lurching and dropping of the plane – not to mention the heavy condensation in the cabin air which he takes for smoke –

finds himself a calming drink. Back on board, with the usually watchful eyes of the England managership distracted, he has another – quite a few in fact – though the players will close ranks, insisting that it is travel sickness medication which has made him all woozy.

Fortunately for Astle, Ramsey has bigger things on his mind. When the plane touches down in Mexico City, with Mexican press all over the arrivals lounge, Astle is helped off the plane, plonked in a chair, and Nobby Stiles does his best to smarten a slumbering Big Jeff up. Mirror lensman Monty Fresco throws a photographer's cape over Astle's head to keep his identity secret and the players shield him from the cameras.

'The lads mucked in, got both sides of him [Astle] and sort of walked him to the coach,' says Stepney. Though it is to little avail. 'By now the shit's hit the fan and there are people waiting everywhere – reporters, photographers,' says Ken Jones. 'And Astle is legless. Alf just doesn't know where he is.'

The Mexicans have already got their story. As the sports daily *Esto* puts it the next morning, in a huge headline, with an accompanying picture of a lolling Astle: 'ENGLAND – A TEAM OF DRUNKS AND THIEVES'. The squad, it claims, had been drinking 'with the spirit of pirates'.

Back home in the Midlands, Mrs Lorraine Astle, 'a non-drinker', admits that husband Jeff 'has a pint or two' after a game but is not one for over-indulgence. And, with superbly undiplomatic timing, a Midlands brewery announces the same day that it has sent twelve dozen cans of beer to the West Brom man – a further six dozen cans will follow. It was shipped after Astle mentioned in a postcard to his local in Stourport that he misses his favourite tipple. The landlord told the brewery, and they stress the delivery is unsolicited.

'It was a personal gift,' says an official.

The next day at the England hotel, some British reporters sit around talking to Astle and others. Says the *Guardian*'s David Lacey, 'The conversation stopped abruptly when Alf came out of one of the little bungalows around the pool with a copy of *Esto* saying, "Jeffrey, could we have a word?"'

Back in London, on arrival at Heathrow, Ralph Coates and Brian Kidd explain their shock to Stuart Hall on BBC radio and give voice to what is now being taken as part of a huge Latin American conspiracy campaign against England. 'I think it's just to disrupt the party,' says Coates. 'It's diabolical the things they've accused us of. You can't find the words to describe what's going on ... They're a bit frightened of England really. We must be favourites to win the cup and they're doing everything they can to stop us from retaining it.'

They might be being a little harsh on England's hosts, though, when it comes to events in Bogotá. Indeed, the serious Mexican press stand firmly behind Moore. As British embassy spokesman Eric Vines, the man acting as middleman between the Mexican press and Ramsey, explains to the *Daily Mail*: 'The embassy has been flooded with calls from Mexicans wishing to declare their belief that Moore is innocent. But it is the newspapers that have changed the most. The affair has completely drowned most of the continuous criticism we had been getting. In a political sense this incident in Colombia has been a good thing for England. To understand the political implications, you have to understand the Mexican character and particularly their insistence that they are not *South* Americans. This whole incident gives them the chance to declare that such things could only happen in less civilised parts of this continent.'

And another weighty advocate steps in. João Saldanha – who has made his way to Mexico, despite being kicked off a scheduled flight by the Brazilian military (for fear that he'd hijack the plane) and come by a circuitous route, with a visa on the verge of expiry. In his daily column in *Esto*, he talks of Colombian 'shopping habits' and of the hassle that Brazilian players have had there in the past. In that very same hotel two years ago, it seems, Pelé's team Santos was subject to similar allegations, as, elsewhere in Bogotá, was the club side Portuguesa. And once, when his own Botafogo team had come under similar suspicion in Colombia, Saldanha had locked all the players in a room until the jewellery was found elsewhere, stashed away in a janitor's closet. All had been done with the intent of a quick cash pay-off to avoid a scandal. Other celebrities had become similarly unwitting victims. Moore, Saldanha says, is an excellent fellow. 'This is slander, it is against nature. It is against football. Bobby Moore is an honourable man.'

'All these stories quickly started circulating about it happening to other people prior to that, which just seemed to add up,' says

David Sadler. 'It just seemed designed to upset the morale in the camp, but it just binds you even tighter together. If they thought they were going to upset Bobby, he would have been upset at the [original] allegations. He was far too strong an individual to let anything like that weaken him.'

'They could have picked any one of fifteen,' says Terry Cooper. 'But we were very annoyed, I can tell you that, because the last bloke that would have done that was him.'

The England party have clearly had enough of it all. Having transferred to their new digs at the Guadalajara Hilton, they go to ground, leaving David Coleman and others to do TV stand-ups outside the hotel, reiterating what is patently fact – that none of the England party, players or officials, will say a word on the matter till their skipper is returned to them.

With no news forthcoming on Moore, things get surreal and comic.

'It didn't affect us at all. We treated it as a joke,' says Jack Charlton.

'We knew there was no way they could make it stick,' says Alan Ball.

Kenny Lynch, just arrived in Guadalajara, manages to get a phone call through to Moore, pretending he is the player's brother (Moore telling him he'll get ten years if they ever get a look at the comic). And Lynch and humorist Clement Freud pay a visit to the England team, with Freud's monotone monologues having the players in stitches. And so it goes. In Guadalajara, a chum of Moore's phones the England camp asking for an insurance quote for some jewellery, and Moore's roommate Peter Thompson is inundated with calls from the captain's celebrity pals, including none other than Sean Connery. 'He thought I was Bobby Moore's butler,' says Thompson. 'I swore at him and said, "Excuse me, who did *you* play for?" ' News comes in, too, that Bruce Forsyth has incorporated some Bobby Moore gags into his act at the Talk of the Town. And when Moore's wife Tina arrives in Guadalajara, she even brings her husband an ID bracelet as a novelty.

'It was an absolute joke, a complete set-up job,' says Allan Clarke. 'We just thought it was one big laugh. We felt sorry for Bobby, obviously, but we just laughed it off.'

The lads, though thinking of Moore constantly, get on with things.

Training continues at the team's new facilities at the Atlas Club and they get up to their usual japes. Mullery and Stepney, out walking one day, get stopped by a man with a gun and ordered to get in his car (it turns out he's a secret policeman under instruction to bring them back to the hotel); Jeff Astle keeps the squad amused with his impressions of Football League managers; some players are invited to have tea at the home of a kindly old British couple, the players scoffing all the cake that had been laid out the moment their hosts' backs are turned. And, at a local dance, a few of the England footballers have a 'dogfight' – drawing lots for ugly dance partners...

For Moore, training continues, too.

'I spoke to him on the phone a few times at Alfonso Senior's house,' says Jeff Powell of the *Daily Mail*, later Moore's official biographer. 'He would say, "I'm just going out running." The guards were sleeping on their chairs by the door and he went out running through the park and signing autographs for the kids – bizarre, really.'

It seems, fortunately, that everything is coming to a satisfactory conclusion. On the morning of Thursday 28th, after kicking a ball about for forty-five minutes on the grounds of the Millonarios club with his two guards, Moore is summoned for another meeting with Judge Dorado. It lasts just ten minutes. Moore is told that, due to insufficient evidence to bring a prosecution, he is essentially freed from the charge of theft.

The release is conditional, however. Dorado has thirty days to submit his report to another judge and it is this second arbitrator who will then decide whether to quash the case officially, a process of deliberation without a fixed time limit. In other words, Moore can still be recalled to court if need be. It is therefore necessary that Moore report to the Colombian consul while out of the country.

Technically it is not over, but to all intents and purposes what remains is mere red tape. Moore's ordeal is at an end.

'I am happy to have been set free and that the accusations made against me turned out to be groundless,' says Moore in a prepared statement. 'If necessary I will cooperate with the Colombian authorities and do all I can, just as promised ... Now all I want to do is forget the incident and return to my work as a football player and help England to retain the World Cup. I am grateful to the Colombians for the many expressions of sympathy and support which I have received from them in the last few days.'

The news is relayed by an official to a rather relieved fifty-year-old Englishman in Guadalajara. 'This is the first official news I have had,' comes Ramsey's official response. 'If what I have heard is true, I am very happy. I shall smile even more when Bobby is here.'

Still in the same clothes he has worn for the last four days, Bobby Moore is, within hours, on a plane bound for Mexico City, upgraded to first class and finding himself in the company of Omar Sivori, an Argentinian ex-international.

'I must insist this is the first time I've enjoyed flying,' he tells the BBC reporter on the plane, with a smirk, 'and I'm delighted to be heading back to Mexico to meet up with the rest of the lads.'

At Mexico City airport it is chaos as Moore is led off the plane by David Coleman and Peter Lorenzo. 'The place was mobbed by journalists and photographers. And all the barriers at customs and immigration were down and everyone charged through – this great heaving mass,' says the *Guardian*'s David Lacey. 'Mooro was the calmest man in the place.'

That night the England captain stays at the residence of Eric Vines. The next day, Friday 29th, he will take the first flight on the short hop to Guadalajara. In Mexico City he gets a surprise visitor. Jimmy Greaves, in town having finished the rally, evades the security cordon and simply strolls in through the back door of Vines's house. The two old mates share a quiet and extremely welcome drink.

In Guadalajara all other news is irrelevant. Les Cocker's revelation that Nobby Stiles is carrying a shin injury barely raises an eyebrow. England's belated PR drive of presenting a set of shirts to boys' team Estrellitas, ten-year-old kids from the poorest part of town, champions of the local junior league, hardly gets a mention.

Bobby Moore arrives triumphantly in Guadalajara on a small business plane. Though the whole squad had wanted to turn out to welcome him, only Shepherdson accompanies Ramsey. There is confusion as Alf's car is sent to the wrong runway, but he gets there in the nick of time to meet Moore. Ramsey is not normally given to displays of emotion. Indeed, although Moore is his lieutenant, their relationship has, in the past, been less harmonious than suggested. None the less, Ramsey scampers across and, with the nearest thing you'll ever get to a hug from the man, clasps Moore's hand, thumps him on the back and asks, 'How are you my old son?', telling him it's the most wonderful sight since he saw Moore lift the World Cup. Shepherdson quietly puts his arm around the captain's shoulders and, with a lump in his throat, adds to the sentiment. Alf has never been so bubbly, like an excited puppy. 'I feel ten years younger just putting my arms around this lad,' he tells everyone. 'No, not ten; make it fifty years younger.'

Alf, Shep and Moore get in the car and speed off to the Hilton. When they get there, all twenty-three players are lined up either side of the entrance, like a guard of honour, to clap their captain home. Then Moore disappears under a weight of hugs and backslaps.

For the benefit of the world's media, a press conference has been arranged at the hotel. The unflappable Moore simply has a few words, apologising for 'looking like a tramp', and expressing profound regret for missing the last few days' training. 'Once I had got over the shock of what had happened to me I decided I was not going to let this thing get me down,' he says. 'As the days went on it was not so much the psychological strain as the boredom.

'Until you are on your own in a strange land, even though people are being really kind, you do miss having the lads around. I have no anger about what has happened. I suppose the people had to do their job and that is that. As far as I am concerned, it is all behind me. All I want to do is get on with the job of keeping the World Cup.'

'They picked on the wrong bloke,' says Norman Hunter. 'He could take it all in his stride. He was used to being an England captain. He'd been in the England team since he was twenty, so they definitely picked on the wrong fella there.'

But there is also an icy tone to Moore now to suggest there is no doubt that, when it comes down to football, England can go all the way. 'Bobby was unbelievable. He was so cold,' says Ken Jones. 'I remember saying to Brian James [of the *Daily Mail*], "Christ, I wouldn't want to play against *him*." '

Ramsey ends the press conference by throwing down the gauntlet: 'I insisted in 1966 England would win the World Cup. Without wishing to appear too repetitive, I say in 1970 England will win the

World Cup. This squad contains all the qualities to do it again. Their enthusiasm, confidence, skills and, above all, their peak physical fitness command the respect of the rest of the world'...

What really happened in Bogotá will never fully be known. Certainly no one, players, public or otherwise, ever suspected for one minute that Moore would do anything as daft as steal a bracelet. 'Bobby Moore needed it like a hole in the head,' says Brian Labone. The widely held notion that the whole thing was a frame-up for the purposes of extortion was given great credence later when the Colombian police published possible evidence of an extortion plot, with Padilla even fleeing to the USA under harassment over the issue. The Fuego Verde shop closed soon after.

'It was a set-up,' says Peter Thompson. 'A complete sham,' says Emlyn Hughes. 'A lot of baloney,' says Labone. 'Anyone who's ever met that wonderful guy would know that it's a ludicrous suggestion,' says Alan Ball.

The case, however, did not go away. On 27 October 1970 the Colombian authorities moved to reopen it on the basis that there was a genuine theft from the store and that, while Moore and Charlton were not necessarily responsible for it, there was an unidentified England player still required for questioning, one for whom, it was suggested, Moore and Charlton might have possibly been forced to cover. A letter was sent to the British government by Colombian Ambassador Camilo de Brigara, who moved to get Moore and Charlton to appear at Bow Street Magistrates' Court on 17 December. There, they were to swear a statement to this end – though when the two England players repeated their line that there was no theft and that they knew of no other player involved, the case came to nought, and was dropped officially in November 1972. Moore, however, did not receive Colombian legal notification of such until December 1975 (even then it was not worded to Moore's satisfaction).

The Colombians, though, had been put under great pressure to release Moore, with Colombian President Carlos Lleras personally involved, and British Foreign Secretary Michael Stewart rushing out of a NATO council meeting in Rome to deal with proceedings. Certainly Moore's house arrest, rather than his going to jail, was a result of strings being pulled in the highest places, sanctioned by the Colombian Ministry of Foreign Affairs.

As the hours wore on, Harold Wilson himself had stepped in. On 26 May he cabled FA President Lord Harewood, already in Mexico, and assured him that everything was being done to secure Moore's release. He even asked British diplomats in Colombia if he should contact the Colombian President directly to raise the question of the 'administrative deficiency' that was delaying the release of Moore. (Privately Ramsey was panicking, too. Allegedly, plans were drawn up to play Norman Hunter in Moore's position, with the captaincy passing to Alan Mullery.)

Grim statements about the consequences for Colombia followed ('We ensured that the magistrate concerned was privately made aware of the awkward implications of the case for Colombia,' Michael Stewart communicated secretly), as well as news of death threats to the Colombian ambassador in London. It was all taken on board. Commissioned by President Lleras, two senior politicians were dispatched to have words with Judge Dorado and see what could be done to make this embarrassing affair go away. The first, a lawyer, tried the tactful route, but when Dorado refused to divert from the due process of law, he was paid a night visit at home by General Leyva, the heavy-duty head of the secret service, the DAS (who had questioned Moore and Charlton at the time of the original incident). Leyva informed Dorado it would be 'highly counter-productive' to pursue the matter. Dorado, who had been in no rush to dismiss the case, suddenly had a change of heart and released Moore at the first available opportunity. On the player's swift exit, he even told Moore that he wished that the player would 'score many goals'.

One source, who today deals with England Old Boys in a commercial capacity, confirms that there is private speculation among some of the 1970 players that the whole incident may have been the result of a misfired prank by a younger player, with the unfortunate Moore, as skipper, singled out and reluctantly taking the rap.

'You've got a group of twenty-odd young men, some younger than others,' says David Sadler. 'Some that would lark around, others that just quietly went about their business.'

'Footballers do stupid things,' counters Peter Thompson, 'but I don't think that happened.'

In Jeff Powell's biography of Moore, however, the player suggested, cryptically, that this may well have been the case: 'He was the victim of a frame-up and he carried it off with such dignity,' says Powell, 'but I think there is no question that one of the young lads on the squad was messing around and causing the problems.'

No one will ever know. Moore, who died tragically young in 1993, took the secret to his grave . . .

Chapter 7

Azteca

At 5.30 p.m. BST, on BBC1, the words 'World Cup Grandstand' flash up on the screen. Following the style set down for all official tie-ins with the tournament, they are written in a new triple-stroke, rounded sans-serif typeface – not dissimilar (and perhaps not uncoincidentally) to the graphics of sportswear manufacturers Adidas. It is followed by the official Mexico theme music, a sort of jolly, Tijuana brass theme with a chorus of referees' whistles worked into it, composed by Joan Shakespeare and Derek Warne. The programme credits roll over split-screen footage of the 1966 final. It's been a long wait, the Bogotá ordeal has put a painful drag on proceedings, but finally we're here: the opening ceremony and then, when it's done, and with merciful relief, the first match – Group One, Mexico versus the USSR.

Cut to the satellite broadcast and the legend 'David Coleman, direct from the Aztec Stadium.' And there, suddenly, from the other side of the world, is Coleman standing in an open-neck shirt, mic in hand, on the greenest baize of grass you will ever see. 'Welcome to a Mexico morning in the Aztec Stadium,' says the Beeb's favourite sports broadcaster, his instantly recognisable tones coming echoey, distorted, crackly – as if he's speaking to you over a cheap Tannoy system from the bottom of the garden. The visual and aural assault only go to reinforce one thing: that he's talking to you from a long, long way away, beamed right into your living room via a satellite orbiting the earth. An unbelievable technical feat.

The camera pulls back and pans up. The picture, always a little fuzzy, blurs even more when the camera sweeps, but Coleman is put in context of his surroundings. There, towering, shimmering in the heat haze, is the huge concrete bowl of the Azteca, packed to the rafters, a blaze of colour – flags, banners, brightly coloured clothing and banana-leaf hats. And, ringing the stadium about a third of the way up, a continuous flash of advertising – Esso, Cinzano, Martini, Philips, Corona, Hoechst – as if you were trackside at a Grand Prix. Some First Division grounds in England still refuse to carry perimeter advertising, our football seemingly designed for performance before a drab, grey, overcoated backdrop. This is glorious Technicolor.

At pitch level, in a frieze around the playing area, are the flags of each of the sixteen competing nations, with a single word next to each – 'welcome', 'wilkommen', 'bienvenidos' 'bemvindos', 'benvenuti', etc. And the crowd: not the roar or chanting of home, nor the tooting klaxons of the Continent – instead a constant din, a buzz almost, insect-like, as if the stadium were being plagued by locusts.

'The sun bright, the day still, the temperature already in the high seventies,' enthuses Coleman, 'and a scene that really is quite remarkable with this huge arena filling for the start of the 1970 World Cup which gets under way in just about half an hour.'

And thus, on BBC1, roll clips of all the finals to date – from the grainy, jerky sepia of Uruguay in 1930, playing at double quick time, through to that day at Wembley three years and ten months ago only yesterday.

Back in London, Frank Bough takes over, explains how the early tournaments, without England, were 'hardly representative'; how, although the South Americans dominated, never forget that the 'idea came from Europe'; why Pelé will really have to shine if he expects to take over from Puskas as the greatest player of all time; how, among the favourites, one must never write off the Germans – what with their 1954 final comeback, and, of course, that scare they gave our boys last time. Yes, say it loud and savour it once again – England are the World Champions.

But what about that stadium? The Aztec, or Stadio Azteca, to give it its correct title – a 105,779-capacity all-seated arena. Unrestricted views – no pillars, no posts. Light years beyond anything on offer in the Football League. Streets ahead of creaking old Wembley, built before the World Cup was even a twinkle in Jules Rimet's eye, thrown up in a cod Imperial–Raj style for the 1923 FA Cup Final – not by any means intended as a permanent facility, and now surviving largely on the strength of its dog racing and the occasional speedway event.

Completed four years ago to the day, just before Mexico's players set off to London for the '66 tournament, the Azteca cost £7 million to build. Its roof is 125 yards high. Its pitch is 7,349 feet above sea level. It has in-built TV studios, acres of parking space, and circling the structure above the first tier of seating are 900 luxury private apartments. Literally – like hotel suites, each built into the stadium, comprised of a flat, with a kitchen, shower, TV and balcony on to which twelve people can step out and watch the game. An 'executive box', as some commentators are referring to it, the kind of thing, culturally speaking, that will never be accepted in England. What's more, you can drive your car round the peripheral road, up a ramp, and park the damn thing right outside your apartment door. The suites are not cheap. Bought largely by companies to facilitate corporate entertainment, each box has been purchased on a ninety-nine-year lease – the means by which Emilio Azcárraga, the Mexican TV magnate, owner of America FC, and chief inspiration behind the Azteca, has been able to raise the stadium capital.

The World Cup is big business. Ten million pounds in income will be obtained from tickets (with a £400,000 bonus as the Mexican government grants tax exemption on sales). But that's OK, £5.5 million will pour into the Mexican economy from an estimated 26,500 visitors (6,500 from Britain). Proceeds from the Juanito emblem (the Mexican World Cup Willie – a fat kid in a sombrero) will gain £1 million. Press and media fees will net the authorities another £2 million.

Of course, it is offset by the £25 million cost of broadcasting the television pictures – a massive logistical operation, the responsibility of Telesistema, Azcarraga's company – but the sale of these pictures will make Mexico '70 a very profitable exercise indeed (and Azcárraga even richer than he is already, which is extremely).

Of all the tickets for the tournament, only 30,000 are available to foreigners. England have put in the biggest request – 16,000 for Guadalajara. Fans will be pleased to know that the ticket prices are the lowest in the whole history of the World Cup: at the Azteca it's 5 pesos (3s 4d) for the cheap seats; 1,000 pesos (£33) for a package of ten games in the front row, including the final.

Mexico is taking the ticketing very seriously. This very morning a special squad of undercover agents arrested twelve touts in a dawn raid. Tickets for the opening game were going for up to £200; even the cheapest on the black market costs £10. The scalpers have been thrown in jail for the duration of the tournament.

Back on the pitch, Coleman has been joined by two others. He introduces Joe Mercer, sporting a trilby, and Don Revie, who looks a different man out of his sheepskin coat. 'There isn't a footballer in the world worth his salt who wouldn't give his eye teeth to be playing here,' gushes genial Joe, giving the impression he might have brought his boots along just in case. Revie is impressed too: it's a great stadium; a *fantastic* stadium; better than Wembley; England should have one just like it. 'And I'll be very proud on the twenty-first [the date of the final] when England walk out on this turf.'

'They're a football-loving nation,' adds Uncle Joe, filled with a Woodstock-esque feeling of togetherness. 'And they play football. Wherever we go, we see kids play. Couldn't play it anywhere else.'

And with that Coleman and co. retreat to their seats in the gods.

Opening ceremonies to sporting events are strange affairs. They are traditionally half-baked pageants, usually featuring lots of kids, doves and balloons (but no jelly), and with great overtures made about peace and friendship. No one likes them. In a World Cup all anyone wants to do – fans, broadcasters and, especially, players – is to get on with the damn game.

For politicians and dignitaries, however, it is another matter. This is their moment, and, like tin-pot Caesars, they're going to milk the pomp and circumstance for all they're worth.

At 11.30 a.m., in accordance with an instruction over the PA system, the official 105,779 present (though in fact more like 115,000) start waving the red, white and green squares of paper that have been planted on their seats to welcome President Ordaz – he of the student massacre.

And with that, from an underground tunnel, but not quite in the spirit of peace, a military band – men from the Mexican Naval Infantry – start filing out, their braided tunics and stove-pipe hats adorned with quivering plumes.

'Rather like the Royal Marines,' says Coleman, without unintended disrespect, for within thirty seconds – and accentuated by their white gloves and spats – the soldiers are horribly out of step, out of synch, bumping into each other, treading on each other's heels, the trombone players ramming their slides into the necks of the grunts in front.

A section of the sailors carry the flags of 119 FIFA nations which didn't qualify ('Football's own United Nations,' burbles Coleman). At the back flaps a forlorn Saltire.

Back in the BBC studio, to fill in for a bit of signal lapse, Bough introduces some goals from '66. Spectacular, but hardly relevant – Bobby Charlton's screamer versus Mexico, a powerful Beckenbauer shot against Switzerland. Behind Bough, under a big stencilled football, is a grid for all the World Cup groups, left tantalisingly blank. On two rows of desks below it, as if they were competitors on *University Challenge*, sit the studio guests: Noel Cantwell, manager of Coventry; Ian St John of Liverpool; Ray Wilson, hero of '66, now sporting an ill-advised mullet haircut; Johnny Haynes, Fulham veteran and former England captain whose barnet, unlike Wilson's, has remained exactly the same as when they played for England together at the end of the fifties – a heavily greased DA, like he's an extra from *The Wild One*. Then come former Arsenal and Wales player Wally Barnes, now a BBC commentator; another Arsenal boy, their current keeper Bob Wilson, who seems shrewdly intent on forging a media career for himself when his number's up; and Jim Finney, a referee from 1966, who had been hotly tipped to be part of '70, too. Each, Bough explains, has written down his predictions on a piece of paper of the two teams who will make it to the final, then the winner itself – nothing more than a million punters have been doing over the Double Diamond for the past few weeks.

Barnes reckons Brazil and Russia, with Russia to win; St John thinks Brazil, too, but after a final with Italy ('Tremendous talent, the Italians,' Bough agrees, 'bit short on character'); Haynes fancies Brazil but, perhaps stuck in his earlier England days, still sees Uruguay as a world power, giving Brazil a trouncing; so too does Cantwell, who envisages them doing over a super-fit Russia ('They've been up the mountains'); while Finney and Wilsons Bob and Ray all go for an England–Brazil showdown, but only Bob Wilson fancies England.

Suddenly, another guest pipes up. Sitting at the front, slightly apart, he has remained aloof, not mucking in with the others, his voice whiny and patronising. 'I don't like this type of thing, Frank, because, out of the sixteen sides, I know very little about over half of them,' he moans. When pushed, he says England will win, but can't see any other team getting to the final than 'dark horses' Romania. Watching somewhere in a dressing room at a small-town Hippodrome, Mike Yarwood has struck upon a new impression. The age of Brian Clough has dawned ...

Television is where the greatest changes will be in the 1970 World Cup. The '66 final was watched by 450 million people; 600 million people witnessed last year's moon landing. Even more will tune in to Mexico 1970. And while in Britain only a million homes have colour sets, this will be the first football tournament broadcast in living colour, pictures beamed live by satellite right into the nation's sitting rooms.

For the first time in a major sporting event, television is going to be in the driving seat of proceedings. Whereas coverage of the 1966 World Cup had been sterling, it still conformed to the idea of reverential and unobtrusive reporting of an event in progress, a bit like a royal wedding. Now the TV companies are dictating the tournament, gearing the event around their needs. Given that the bulk of the commercial power lies in Europe and its huge audiences, match schedules have been arranged purely to coincide with prime-time European viewing hours.

As already mentioned, this is not without severe consequences for the nature of the tournament. Britain currently operates an experimental British Standard Time (introduced in 1968, to be abandoned in 1971) – essentially British Summer Time retained throughout the whole year (causing public safety hazards in the winter months as children are dispatched to school, still in the dark, clad in fluorescent arm bands and sashes). London is seven hours ahead of Mexico City. Thus, to accommodate the UK and the rest of Europe – while still conforming to some sense of normality in Mexico and Latin America – weekday games will kick off at 4 p.m. local time. Worse – the planners of the weekend schedules have decreed that the showpiece Sunday games will all be broadcast at 7 p.m. BST – noon in Mexico. With no night games at all, the players will be doing battle in the heat of the day.

Given the size of the ratings at stake, in the control rooms of the

BBC and ITV the battle has been hotting up. The BBC has been piling on the frivolities in an attempt to hook viewers in from the start. Immediately prior to the opening ceremony there is a special pre-recorded *Question of Sport* with David Vine featuring Moore, Hurst and Mullery (the London boys again) versus Johnny Haynes, Tom Finney and Stan Mortensen. In the countdown to the big kick-off, the Beeb has been replaying England's games from 1966 on a nightly basis in a series entitled *England, Champions of the World* – culminating on the eve of the tournament with a rerun of you know what (unless you prefer Peter Wyngarde in *Dept S* on the other side).

For some time, the rival TV networks have been trying to outdo each other in a series of grand pronouncements. On 25 March the BBC had declared it would provide a staggering seventy hours of soccer coverage during the finals. ITV hit back that they alone would broadcast England versus Brazil live (this operation costing over £250,000). ITV director of sport John McMillan added that ITV had also captured England–Czechoslovakia, as well as a scoop, the third–fourth-place play-off. Plus an ambitious plan to do their own breakfast show. Sixty hours in total.

The breakfast show is ultimately dropped, leaving the BBC with the daytime hours to themselves. *Good Morning Mexico*, going out daily at 8 a.m., presented by Frank Bough, will replay one hour's worth of highlights from the night before. It will be complemented by ninety minutes of further replays in a lunchtime edition of *World Cup Grandstand* with David Vine. In the early evening *World Cup Grandstand* will continue with an update of news from the England camp and a preview of the night's games, fronted live from Mexico by David Coleman. Plus, of course, it will resume for the games themselves, from 10 p.m. till 3 a.m., introduced by Bough again. Eight and a half hours a day. In actual fact, nearly *80* hours in total.

ITV will go head to head in the early evening slot and with its own live games package from 10 p.m. under the banner *World Cup '70*, anchored by Brian Moore. All a great boon to the TV rental people (very few people own sets) – DER offering a 'World Cup colour bonanza' on its new 24-inch models.

With presentation on ITV, it's straightforward: Hugh Johns commentating on all the big games, Gerald Sinstadt for the secondaries and a lot of stuff on the ground. Conversely, within the

BBC there is a bit of a power struggle going on, a rivalry between its two leading microphone men – the established Kenneth Wolstenholme, hero of '66, and rising star David Coleman, who is equally adept as front man, interviewer and commentator. BBC politics decree that Coleman will get the opening ceremony and England games, Wolstenholme the final. This means, essentially, that between the showpiece games which bookend the tournament, Coleman will work out of Guadalajara, Wolstenholme will do the León games, Alan Weeks (and a newcomer called Idwall Robling, who won his slot in a BBC commentating competition) will cover Mexico City, and young Barry Davies will work from Puebla/Toluca. Coleman, who got rather carried away when David Hemery won the gold at the 1968 Olympics, has been accused of being too patriotic in some quarters. But no one in the general public sees this as anything other than an admirable quality.

The BBC produces a special edition of the *Radio Times* crammed full of every conceivable detail about the World Cup, full of illustrations of dirty Latin foul play and containing a colour pull-out profile of the whole squad, featuring such descriptive gems as 'Alan Ball: "Carrot hair"'. Of greater importance is its very solemn pledge to the British public about the comprehensive coverage, between TV and radio, of every single kick in Mexico. Soccer for breakfast, soccer for lunch, soccer at night.

Somewhere amid all this there's a general election about to happen. Robin Day, *Election Panorama* and all the party political broadcasts barely get a look-in...

Back at the Azteca, the commentary positions are not great. Most of the broadcasters have to crane forward to see over the wall in front of them. Also, the seats in the Azteca are not seats as such, but long concrete benches. Small boys in Scout uniforms dart around selling cushions, an absolute necessity, especially with a buttock-numbing opening ceremony to sit through (useful, too, if your team is losing – Mexicans love to hurl them on to the pitch).

'I called this little lad over, extended to him a fistful of notes and sent him off to get about a dozen of these cushions,' explains Hugh Johns. Said kid is never seen again. 'When it was over, Coleman and Wolstenholme came over and said, "Thanks, Hugh, that was absolutely brilliant." This little boy had got all the cushions. He knew it was for English television people, but he couldn't remember which ones, so he took them all to the bloody BBC. We were sitting on bloody concrete. I could have killed him.'

On the pitch below, the ceremony is shaping up. As has been the custom with all the World Cups, it has commenced with teams of schoolboys marching, dressed in the colours of each country – here, as at Wembley four years ago, parading behind a flag and, mounted on a pole, the name of each team. Each is greeted with a cheer as they file across the turf to take up their carefully rehearsed positions opposite the presidential box.

Though unlike Wembley, where polite clapping was the order of the day, in Mexico it is a popularity contest. West Germany comes first – no real reaction either way – but favouritism is soon revealed. Czechoslovakia, invaded two years ago, gets a sympathetic hurrah. The Russians, their conquerors and Mexico's opponents today, get a muted boo. Then, as more teams enter, more cheers. Until midway, that is, when the England boys appear. As the Union Jack precedes a group of kids all in white, a bloodcurdling din of booing and catcalls reverberates around the stadium. Cans of Coke are hurled towards the pitch, the drink fizzing out like spinning liquid Catherine wheels. In the upper tiers, youths set fire to newspapers, waving them like torches before flinging them out to float down, falling on to anyone below. Despite the sympathy towards Bobby Moore – and there is even one little blond boy included to represent him, a Mexican national whose parents come from Weybridge – the degree of hostility to England is now apparent, catching the Israelis by surprise who follow England out and wonder what the hell it is they've done this time.

The Union Jack, as any Briton knows, is officially the flag of the United Kingdom rather than England. Though in 1970, as in 1966, before the resurrection of St George's cross, the Union flag has featured in all official FA publicity. Incorrect as it may be to wave it – being a composite representation including the crosses of St Andrew and St Patrick – to fans and officials alike, the Union Jack and England are synonymous. Whatever the Scots may think, these boys are representing Britain, and the flag, symbolically, seems all about inclusion.

The booing doesn't last long: Brazil get a massive cheer; for the final team, Mexico, the roof comes off.

In the commentary position there is trouble already. While Coleman reminds us that the Jules Rimet Trophy is twelve inches high, nine pounds of solid gold, was worth £400 in 1930, that Rimet kept it under his bed in Paris during the war, that a million bums will sit in the Azteca throughout the tournament, that 3,000 Brazilian fans are already in Guadalajara, that the England team is watching all this up there in a special BBC studio, there are, so far, no team sheets and no team news.

It turns out that the Russians have staged a protest. They don't want their players to go out, as is planned, and stand in the fierce sun for half an hour while the big-wigs deliver the opening speeches. The crowd grows impatient. Where are the teams? Coleman mutters something about the Russians not being too generous with the 'hand of friendship'. But then, before you know it, and to thunderous applause, something's happening down in the subterranean tunnel. Three black specs emerge, coming up the ramp – referee Kurt Tschenscher from West Germany and linesmen Keith Dunstan of Bermuda and Jack Taylor from Wolverhampton. And behind them, two columns, green and red, the Mexican and Russian teams, march (or, in the case of the Russians, trudge) across the pitch in front of a podium, all ceremonially red with gold braid ropes, that's been wheeled on to the turf below the VIP area. Mexico are in green shirts, white shorts, green socks, each trimmed with the red, white and green of the Mexican flag, colours that are being waved frantically all round the stadium. Russia are in traditional red, white, red, their shirts looking distinctly old-fashioned with a big flapping 1950s-style collar, that familiar CCCP flashed across each player's chest.

While the camera closes in on the officials, back in London, and largely because referee Jim Finney is in the BBC studio, this cues an obligatory talk about the officiating and how it might be a problem in this tournament, that this opening encounter's a test case.

'I don't wish to appear rude, but a foul is a foul in anyone's language,' interrupts Brian Clough, indicating that players will accept a referee's decisions if consistent. 'Jim's looking for an expense account,' he adds, exacting glowers from the brooding Finney.

Bough tap dances, talks about the tactical use of subs; a clip of

Pat Jennings getting beaten in Moscow; a clip of a 1969 game in Mexico, a 1–1 draw in which Italy equalise with a long-range, bending shot and then cushions rain down on the pitch. Clough will only agree on one thing. That now, with the big kick-off imminent, and the lads watching in Guadalajara, England will be 'on their toes ... ready to go'.

On the pitch, the Mexicans look edgy, the Russians unfamiliar. With no team sheet, the commentary area is full of frantic broadcasters fumbling through notes, making panicked gestures to assistants and runners, while they themselves try to project a semblance of calm and authority to the folks back home.

With no news, they can buck it with the Mexicans – their captain Peña, number 3, at their head; the colourful goalkeeper, Ignacio Calderón – 'Nacho' to his fans – a sometime film star and cult hero in Mexico. As for the Soviets ... the captain? Yes, that's Shesternev, all right. But the rest? Word comes up from the dressing room. True to their objection, the Russians have sent out their reserves. Indeed, one of them might not even be that. Forty-ish and sporting a beer gut and quasi-breasts, it would be fair to say that he hasn't stepped on a football pitch in anger for quite some years – possibly one of the Russian backroom staff.

It seems to take for ever, but down the walkway come President Ordaz, a sprightly, Asian-looking man with glasses, Stanley Rous, the president of FIFA and, lastly, Guillermo Cañedo, president of the Mexican FA and chief organiser of the 1970 tournament.

Cañedo gets a warm reception, his words reverberating round the several hundred speakers of the PA system. He extends a 'cordial welcome', hopes for brotherhood and sportsmanship between all nations and creeds – 'We are sure the ninth World Cup will be an exhibition of gentlemanly behaviour.'

Then comes Rous – the 'English King'. He gets whistled. A round, portly old duffer of seventy-five years, with white hair, moustache and a pair of tortoiseshell specs, he takes it all in his stride. This erstwhile head of the FA and former referee has heard far worse.

'My lords, ladies and gentlemen,' he begins, as if addressing a Round Table supper. He talks of 'television', a word that seems to sit awkwardly on his lips, and 'association football', then invites the opening of the ninth 'Jules Rimet Cup'. 'All is ready for a memorable feast of top-level football.'

Rous gets off lightly compared with Ordaz. At the end of his presidency he was hoping for a bigger valediction than this. To yet further whistles, he declares the 1970 World Cup open.

Huge bunches of colourful balloons, threaded together like DNA strands, rise slowly in the still air. A peashooter bugler blows a Vulgarian fanfare. The military band plays the anthems. The Mexicans, with hands across hearts, sing theirs with gusto. It takes a while for the ovation to subside. Then comes the Soviet one, a great socialist dirge. With cries of '*bastardo*' and '*puta*' (whore), the Mexican crowd does its best to drown it out.

As the teams go off, Coleman waffles something about El Salvador, and Don Revie chips in with his new hobby horse: 'The Football Association must think about building a stadium of this type in our country.'

When the personnel and detritus have been expunged from the playing surface, the Mexico and USSR teams – the real ones in the case of the latter – emerge again. Aside from avoiding an 80-degree frying, for the Russians, sending out the reserves was a useful exercise. The Mexicans are familiar with the playing surface at the Azteca – indeed, they have defied FIFA's ruling that the surface should not be used for a month before by playing friendlies on it in recent weeks, citing England's advantageous use of Wembley last time. But for the Russians, Shesternev and the reserves have confirmed what was already suspected: that the grass is too long, ankle deep in places. Long studs have duly been screwed in and the players prepare for exertions on a turf that would sap energy at sea level.

As the teams line up for kick-off, the locust buzz of the Azteca has reached a level of intensity that would do for lesser mortals. The Soviets have never been very popular, but this almost physical wall of noise will be hard to batter down.

Mexico need all the help they can get. Aside from their poor showing in the warm-up games, it's now become even worse. On Wednesday, 27 May at the height of the Bobby Moore scandal, their star player, twenty-two-year-old midfielder Alberto Onofre, broke his leg in two places during a collision at a lunchtime training session. He will be hospitalised for four months. It's a national tragedy, especially as, given the passing of the date for squad nomination, the Mexican party is now short of a player . . .

Or not. Despite the fact that Mexico had already angered FIFA over the pitch business, team manager Raul Cárdenas has thrown himself upon its mercy. The president of the Mexican Selection Committee once again spits out the word 'England', now almost a euphemism for favours done on behalf of a host, even if not remotely relevant in this case. FIFA does not wish to upset Mexico: it's their party and they can cry if they want to. A new revised squad deadline is set for 3 p.m. the next day and in comes Marcos Rivas.

With or without Onofre, the Mexican pedigree is poor. The crowd may act like a twelfth man, but in the business of the World Cup, and despite home advantage, they are still outsiders. Last year, with no qualification tournament to occupy them, Mexico came on tour to Europe and won only one of seven games (against feeble Norway), even losing 2–1 to Luxembourg. Though they could produce the odd surprise: in 1968 they beat Brazil home and away with a 2–1 score in each case – the win in Rio their greatest ever footballing achievement. Then, in October, at the Olympics, playing all their group matches at the Azteca, Mexico did enough to convince the public that they might do OK in 1970.

But, though admittedly they have won only one of the 17 World Cup Finals games they have ever played in, they have appeared in the finals of six tournaments, a record bettered only by Brazil. In fact Mexico played in the first ever World Cup Finals match, against France in Uruguay in 1930.

And they mean serious business. The European tour cost manager Ignacio Trelles his job. His successor, Raul Cárdenas, coach of champions Cruz Azul, is no pussycat. Two of his 1966 players – Ernesto Cisneros and Gabriel Nuñez – who could have expected to feature in 1970, were suspended after breaking a team curfew in Acapulco. Plus, crucially, time has been on their side. Since August 1969, under Cardenas, the team has been meeting twice a week. Since 12 January, and despite the incompletion of their training facility, they have been together as a squad. And while they have used thirty-eight players in the training games, with no clear first team to emerge, Cardenas has drilled them into an organised 4–3–3, with the best players all from his own club: Mário Pérez in defence, Javier Fragoso in attack and captain Gustavo Peña, who played at Wembley as a nineteen-year-old in 1961 when Mexico lost to England 8–0. Their stars are Enrique Borja, of America FC, a nippy centre forward who debuted in the '66 World Cup and scored Mexico's only goal, and goalie Calderón. Quite a character, a snazzy dresser with long dark sideburns, Nacho's known largely for his off-field antics. He didn't play for much of 1969 as he was on a one-man wage strike against his club, Guadalajara. Athletic and unnecessarily spectacular, he can, almost inevitably, also be a colossal liability.

The Soviet Union, on the other hand, is a powerhouse in world football. Given the size of their population (at 234 million, the biggest by far in the tournament, three times that of Brazil, its nearest rival) they have a big pool to choose from. Though their famous club sides – Moscow Dynamo in particular – are not as dominant as they should be.

None the less, they have qualified for all three World Cups they have entered – not arriving on the scene till 1958 – won the Olympic title in 1956 and the first European Nations Cup in 1960 (though there was no England or West Germany that year). In 1966 they were World Cup semi-finalists.

With most of their old stalwarts – Yashin, Voronin, Chislenko (though the great Yashin, most famous goalie in the world pre-Banks, is still in the squad) – now past it, their manager Gavril Katschalin, recently reinstated, has rebuilt the side, focusing on youth, but constructing it round his trusty twenty-nine-year-old centre half and captain, Shesternev of CSKA Moscow.

Youth has not bred excitement, but, in keeping with the Russian stereotype, a dour workmanlike side – one with a very bad disciplinary record at that. The Russian domestic season has been plagued with a sending-off crisis unprecedented in the major leagues. Still, there are some great players – Anatoly Bishovets of Dynamo Kiev, the deep-lying centre forward; midfielder Vladimir Muntian, his club teammate and Soviet Footballer of the Year; their 1966 success Murtaz Khurtsilava of Dynamo Tbilisi, now one of the best defenders in Europe and who plays stopper while his skipper sweeps in a defensive system based on the Italian model. Plus they're certainly prepared. They've spent the last 200 days on tour together or training. All for the glory of the motherland.

Unfortunately, the Soviet state machinery has also extended its arm into the team camp. The squad is staying at a bland, austere, carpetless Soviet-style hotel. Locked away, the players have been denied access to the decadent culture of the West (right next door to the USA, the great Satan itself) to such an extent that they are driven to training in a bus with darkened windows so they can't even see it. Some players, speaking to local schoolboys, have their actions deeply frowned upon lest they get a capitalistic brain-washing. England may be the ones in the boiler suits, but the Russians are the team of convicts...

At a little before noon on Sunday, 31 May Mexico – the world – comes to a standstill. Around the Azteca and throughout the capital, traffic will be in total gridlock for the next two hours while everyone stops what they're doing, right there and then, and makes for the nearest TV.

The Russians are lucky. As they line up opposite the hosts, the lip of the stadium roof has kept back the sun, sparing them the worst of the blaze until the second half, though the mercury's rising fast. And, with a short, shrill blast on Herr Tschenscher's whistle, the 1970 World Cup kicks off. Number 11 Asatiani rolls the ball to 16, Bishovets, who plays it back to the playmaker Serebrianikov. And, after a few interchanges, Serebrianikov blasts the ball into the face of Tschenscher, whose whistle is unceremoniously disgorged on to the lush turf.

Opening games in tournaments are never exciting affairs. There is too much at stake. Too much tension for sides to run any risks. On a competition of this scale, with the whole world watching, such caution is magnified. Wanting to settle down, the Russians play it straight and sensible, directing operations through Shes-ternev, the sweeper who wears number 9, patrolling behind the defence.

With only a minute or so gone, something very weird happens. Evriuzhikhin runs down the left, bangs in a long, looping centre, the sideburned Calderón, in an all-white Vegas-Elvis combination, flaps, and Russian forward Nodia, charging in like the clappers, going by instinct to where the ball will arrive, misses it, only for it to make harmless contact with his knee. The effects of the notorious thin air are suddenly apparent.

Unfortunately it is about the only issue of excitement in the first half. Whenever a Mexican gets the ball and looks like pushing forward, the locust buzz intensifies, but invariably subsides as the players square it off, stroking the ball across the lines rather than taking a defender on and risking losing possession. It is all posture and no potency. Until midway through when the atmosphere again comes into play. The Mexican number 10, López, sneaks in behind Logofet, and picks up a low diagonal cross from the right by number 18, Velarde. The normally assured Shesternev doesn't read the high ball, but López, free and unmarked, pings his close-range header straight into the arms of goalie Kavazashvili (wearing, unusually, number 2). Then, Pérez runs down the left and lobs one over for Fragoso, who misses it with his head altogether.

Undoubtedly swayed by the partisan crowd, and with their tails now up, the ref starts letting Mexican infractions go, getting over-fussy with the team in red. Kavazashvili is penalised, rather ridiculously, for holding on to the ball too long. A bit of penalty-box bagatelle follows the Mexican free kick, which ricochets off the wall.

Then a moment of history. Lovchev leaps innocently over a prone Valdivia. The Mexican number 19 makes the most of it and rolls around as though he's being disembowelled in the Inquisition. Bishovets and Lovchev are summoned over and – like an infantryman proffering a picture of his sweetheart before going over the top – referee Tschenscher removes a lemon-hued oblong from his breast pocket and palms it under their noses. Only one of the pair, it turns out, Lovchev, is the object of this curious exercise, though even he is not really sure. But he has already gone down in history – the first ever player to be the recipient of the new-fangled caution known as the yellow card.

For Mexico 1970 refereeing has been revolutionised. A bone of contention in international football, England has long been contemptuous of 'Latin' gamesmanship, play-acting and a standard of officiating that seems to punish what is perceived as good honest physical play, the very foundation of the English game. England, it is figured, play hard but fair. When the Latins do it, in the Americas, or closer to home in Spain and Italy, it's a case of hard but dirty.

'They've never been particularly sporting, these duskies.' So writes Mr H. E. Lowe of Chessington, in a letter to the *Daily Mirror*, complaining how once, in 1926, when his ship pulled in at Tampico and the sailors hoofed a football on the dock, they were chased around by an opponent brandishing a sword.

Any doubts about the gulf in standards have been brought into focus by the Anglo-Italian Cup, a new club competition that has been lost somewhat in the build-up to the World Cup. In this tournament, some middling English teams (Swindon, Sheffield Wednesday, West Bromwich Albion, Wolves, Middlesbrough, Sunderland), and some average Italian ones (Juventus, Napoli, Lanerossi Vicenza, Fiorentina, Roma, Lazio) had been chosen to extend the hand of friendship in a brotherly end-of-season football fiesta, opening games played in England, the returns in Italy.

It had been an unmitigated disaster, culminating in savage violence. A match in Vicenza between Lanerossi and WBA led to a riot, and was abandoned by English ref Kevin Howley after seventy-five minutes; a game between Wolves and Lazio in Rome's Olympic Stadium turned into a shambles after the Lazio goalie clobbered Bernie Lutton and got sent off; the final between Napoli and Swindon was abandoned by the Austrian ref eleven minutes from time when the players were stoned from the terraces and a pitch invasion met with police and tear gas. Swindon, 3–0 up, were awarded the game.

The question of refereeing has prompted fierce debate. Before England's opener against Romania, Jimmy Hill on ITV speculates about where it's all going. He shows a clip of Bobby Moore cleanly tackling a Belgian forward, but penalised when the player falls over Moore's trailing leg; a clip of a ref being pushed by the French after giving a penalty to Sweden; lots of South Americans barging keepers Lofthouse-style. Why, only last week, our very own Jack Charlton was being punished against Ecuador, tackling through a screen and winning the ball. 'This', declares Hill, 'is the prospect that will confront European teams in the next week.'

It has not been helped by a press campaign predicting (and hoping for) disaster, especially when Jim Finney (who sent off the two Uruguayans in the '66 quarter-finals and regarded as one of England's top refs) doesn't make the final FIFA list.

Mexico, it is feared, could not organise the proverbial drink-up in a brewery. Look at the 1968 Olympic Final between Hungary and Bulgaria. Referee Diego de Leo, an Italian-born Mexican (what else!), became the centre of attention in one of the most bizarre of major finals. At 2–1 to Bulgaria, he sent off one Bulgarian and then two more, then a Hungarian. At ten players to eight, Hungary won

4–2, though the game was jeered and whistled and suffered the inevitable barrage of cushions.

Worse, by a process of logical deduction, the *Daily Mirror* has worked out that England may get this clown, the 'four-off ref', in one of their group games (close – he gets Czechoslovakia–Romania instead).

Fanning the flames, the *Sun* has brought to the fray the 1954 World Cup ref Arthur Ellis (last seen overseeing Rhyl and Llandudno in the new TV series *It's a Knockout*), who bemoans the dubious Latin standards and how the referees have been chosen politically, to fulfil quotas from the African and Asian federations, rather than going for simply the best thirty officials in the world (including absentees Finney and highly rated Leicestershire ref Gordon Hill). 'Not so long ago an official of FIFA told me he didn't think they'd be able to find six Mexican refs capable of doing the job,' says Ellis.

The Latin Americans reply in kind that with the mistreatment of Brazil, Uruguay and Argentina in 1966, there will be an English-led conspiracy against them – especially with King Rous at FIFA's head and the Referees' Committee run by its deputy chairman, Ken Aston, the quivering English gent from the no man's land of the Battle of Santiago.

But in truth the ultimate confrontation over refereeing comes not with England versus the rest but Europe against Latin America. In particular, in Northern European countries the tackle from behind is part and parcel of the game, while in Latin America it is a strict no-no. There is nothing in the rule book to say that a tackling player mustn't approach from the rear but, in spirit, the South Americans are correct – any attempt to remove the ball from behind will result in playing through the man. When done quickly, it all appears simultaneous, ball and man removed in one, though the reality is that the physical contact comes first. The South American disdain for physical play can be taken too far. Perfectly legal shoulder barges and inevitable aerial collisions are oft treated with Academy Award displays of injury. But as the tackle from behind is part and parcel of the game in Europe, so gamesmanship is in Latin America.

Somehow, and in the interests of the World Cup, all this has had to be ironed out. Fortunately, Stanley Rous is a former ref himself.

It was he who devised the system of the referee patrolling the pitch diagonally, from one corner to the other, while the linesmen each work a coordinated beat on opposite sides of the pitch, from goal line to centre circle, each responsible for one half of the field of play. Rous has laid down the law in no uncertain terms, branding 'unfit and morally cowardly' referees who are swayed by the crowd or, the most heinous crime of all, rely on their linesmen to make difficult decisions for them.

On 25 May, a full week before the tournament began, Ken Aston got the disparate bunch together (including a ref each from El Salvador, Morocco and the USA, a fifty-year-old Egyptian and two British officials, England's Jack Taylor and Scotland's Bob Davidson) and put them through their paces. The main object was to ensure uniformity in decision-making, players at least respecting consistency of decision if not the decisions themselves – any confusions arising on the field of play over discipline (given the variety of languages to contend with) to be dealt with clearly by the new system of cards: yellow for a caution, red for a dismissal. True, they haven't yet figured out matters of subsequent suspension – that seemingly being determined by the Referees' Committee on the hoof. But now there will be no repeat of 1966-style scenes of referees being mobbed.

The refs, in effect, have become the seventeenth team of the tournament, shut away in their own Mexico City training camp, divided into four linguistic groups – English, French, German and Spanish – and thrashing out ideas till consensus is reached, this group of schoolteachers, company directors and bank managers also undertaking the business of getting fit. Such preparation is unprecedented in World Cup terms where the norm has been a one-hour pep talk beforehand on the eve of the competition.

Having decided what is legal and what is not, Aston has compiled a film of sixty challenges and incidents which he takes to each training camp and forces each team to watch.

For their opener against Romania, it is known England will be getting English-speaking referee Vital Loraux of Belgium ('Monsieur can catch England swearing,' warns the *Daily Mail*), with Abraham Klein of Israel for the Brazil clash. England duly devote time in training to the question of tackling, perfecting the art of not sliding in willy-nilly. 'Basically, against these teams, jockeying them was the great thing,' says Brian Labone. 'Alf said don't be throwing yourself in and giving away free kicks. You had to adjust and use your brains a bit. But certainly against Brazil you didn't get much of a chance!'

The choice of Tschenscher, a West German, for the opener is to ensure rigidity and set the pattern for the rest of the World Cup. Over-fussy maybe, but it does the trick. Though there will naturally be refereeing controversies, not a single player will be dismissed in the whole tournament.

Back at the Azteca at half-time, Mexico and the USSR retire goalless. In the second half, Bishovets has a chance fall to him from a Muntian cross but can only head it wide. Tschenscher now takes centre stage. The number 11, Asatiani, is booked for standing before an opponent. The Russians are not happy. What the hell is all this about? Then, as the game wears on, predictably the Russians run out of steam. Puzach comes on for the tiring Serebrianikov to shore up the midfield. The number 19, Nodia, a forward, also booked, staggers around quite exhausted and is replaced by Khmelnitski. Let no one be in doubt, this is now a thirteen-man game.

Later Shesternev, too, is given the yellow-card treatment. When they pick the game up again, Guzman fires on goal but his shot is saved. Two Mexicans are booked – Vantolra and Peña.

And there it ends, 0–0, a classic stalemate opener – a heroic achievement for Mexico, none the less, whose reaction would lead you to believe they'd just won the final. Satisfactory for the USSR, too. A point next against Belgium, without such a hostile crowd, and only little El Salvador stand between them and the quarter-finals.

In England, the papers focus on the reffing: 'If this one match was an example of their government then I fear for England,' says the *Daily Mirror*. 'Asatiani, Lovchev and Logofet were booked for incidents which in England would not have inspired more than a passing glance of condemnation from the ref.'

There is the fact, too, that, as the same paper puts it, 'England get the bird!' There is nevertheless an overwhelming sense of relief, what with the torments of the past week, that the competition is finally under way, and 25 million Britons tune in for the most watched 0–0 draw of all time. The country is going into overdrive. One London dealer is doing a roaring trade in a line of new Japanese mini-TVs at £80 each. 'They're ideal for late night viewing,' he says. 'A chap can put them on the bedside table, plug in the earpiece and let the wife sleep while he watches.' In Harlow, Essex, newsagent Bernard Walker is laying on a free knock-up service to get house-holders to work on time during the three-week competition, employing his paper boys to add an extra duty to their rounds. And power stations make contingency plans to cope with the surge in demand. Last night an extra 700,000 kilowatts was allocated to meet a sudden rush. It was all needed. Within minutes of the game ending, millions of viewers got up from their sets and switched on stoves, kettles and percolators.

They are not the only ones for whom the World Cup has meant extra business. The Ministry of Posts and Telecommunications reveals that it has dispatched a fleet of twenty detector vans to track down the million viewers who are watching without a TV licence, patrolling the streets until 3 a.m. – game time – to recoup the dodged £6 million a year in revenue. It's a bit unfair on the 13 per cent of the country that still can't get BBC2 – East Sussex, Wales and parts of the North. Though in the North-west they're mighty thankful for the Beeb right now. For the last five days, viewers in the Granada region, seven million of them, have had ITV blacked out altogether due to an industrial dispute (300 technicians demanding a 12 per cent wage increase), and keeping Granada-produced programmes like *Coronation Street* off screens nationally. Yet another one for Vic Feather to sort out.

He'll have his work cut out. The GPO is taking measures to stop a series of lightning strikes by telephonists – under normal circumstances not good for the government, but nobody seems to be noticing that the general election scrap is now under way. There are only eighteen days to go between now and polling day – that's an awful lot of World Cup games. In the *Daily Mail* the Trog cartoon sums it up perfectly – Wilson and Heath as boxers, slugging it out in the ring with the whole crowd turned away to watch football on a TV in the corner of the room. A *Sunday Times* poll puts the Tories ahead by 2 per cent, the first time they've led for ages. It's not been a good week for Harold. Voted Pipe Smoker of the Year in that heady annus of 1966, he gets short shrift from a British Rail conductor on a London to Cardiff express for lighting up under a red no-smoking triangle . . .

Chapter 8

The Italians

Monday, 1 June 1970

No one should ever write off the Italians. The *Daily Express* certainly doesn't think so. It's programmed every conceivable bit of information into a huge computer – form, history, player strength, everything – and come to a conclusion: Italy will win the World Cup. But it hedges its bet: computers will not decide this tournament, and with their histrionic, self-destructive temperament, who knows what those crazy Eyeties will do? At 6–1 in the official betting, they still come in third behind England (3–1) and Brazil (7–2) – the World and European Champions, the best team in South America.

The old criticism about the Italians not having the stomach for the fight is misplaced and harsh. Rather the Italians have developed a complex. In 1966, in England, when they had every chance of winning the tournament, and perhaps on paper should have done, they were sent packing by rank outsiders North Korea. Forget England and the USA in 1950, this was, and still is, the greatest humiliation in modern international football. England, in Belo Horizonte, could at least protest that they dominated the game and lost to a freak goal. Italy, however, had no such excuse for their 1–0 defeat. They were utterly outplayed. Outclassed.

And when they flew home to Genoa airport, a welcoming party was organised to pelt them with rotten fruit . . . unwashed . . . and with considerable velocity. An Italian's pride and joy is his clothes. This was punishment indeed.

Since 1966, the Italians have lost only once in twenty internationals (beaten by Bulgaria in the European Nations Cup, the tournament they eventually won). And they beat Mexico over here last year in preparation. What's more, Italy have got some blinding players. Their domestic league, though the English won't like it being said, is probably the best in the world. Cautious, but astutely tactical, their top club sides and national team are built on the destructive system of 'catenaccio' – the blanket, sweepered defence – all offence lying with the speed and thrust of counter-attacks. Not pretty but effective.

The Welsh certainly think so: they found the Azzurri way too much to cope with in the qualifiers. The people on the telly agree, with Jimmy Hill taking us again and again through the three goals Luigi Riva put past Gary Sprake at home, highlighting his great control, acceleration and 'nice pair of shoulders'. Riva is the golden boy of Italian football – an orphan of Cagliari whose hometown football club, Italian champions for the first time, will do anything to keep him. Rumour is they put 6d on the rates to help afford his staggering £40,000 a year wages. In only fifteen starts for his country, the big, muscular twenty-five-year-old, a late bloomer as far as strikers go, has scored seventeen goals, blasting them in with his left-foot cannon. You think Martin Peters cost a lot of money? Cagliari just turned down a bid of £900,000.

Still, the Italians always were a bit flash when it came to getting their man. Pietro Anastasi, at Juventus, cost a diabolical 666 million lire (£400,000). Though Anastasi isn't even in Mexico: on 18 May the twenty-one-year-old striker pulls out of the squad, in need of a cartilage operation and is replaced by the diminutive Boninsegna. Not that it'll worry them unduly. Under manager Ferruccio Valcareggi, who took over from Edmondo Fabbri after the fiasco of 1966, Italy have been forged into a formidable unit.

Valcareggi is a chainsmoker, and no wonder: the Italians expect success, the pressure on them enormous, but even this hasn't stopped Valcareggi proclaiming that 'it should not be beyond us to reach the semi-finals'. He has every reason to justify such an assertion for, besides Riva, his side is bristling with talent. The giant Giacinto Facchetti, his captain, a quality left-sided defender with forty-five caps, has rarely put a foot wrong for his club, Inter Milan, or country. Nor has Burgnich, his defensive Inter Milan partner. Sandro Mazzola, another Inter player, is a quick, scheming, moustachioed midfielder – another one of those players who seems thoroughly modern, can defend, can attack, with twenty goals in his thirty-six internationals.

Far and away their most influential creator is the enigmatic Gianni Rivera of rivals AC Milan, European Footballer of the Year, holder of League, European Cup and European Cup Winners' Cup medals. And something of a former child prodigy, having made his League debut at sixteen.

Then there's their World Cup pedigree – twice World Cup winners and current European Nations Champions. But it could be suggested they're not great travellers: the 1934 World Cup and the 1968 European crown were both won on home soil; the 1938 World Cup – secured under the patronage of Mussolini – required a short trip next door to France. Dump the Italians in a hostile environment, the theory goes – like breezy Ayresome Park, where the Italians endured their darkest hour – and they haven't got the right stuff. Not because of the conditions but because, simply, an Italian squad thrown together for any length of time will soon be beset by infighting.

And, you know what? It already is. Valcareggi has always had a problem motivating players used to big win bonuses, though that is not the main gripe. What's up is this – that with too much talent, an embarrassment of riches, and especially an overload in the forward half of the team, the manager has been left to fit too many square pegs into too few round holes. Only one thing is certain: with Riva currently on fire, attacking tactics will all be geared round him – the ball played fast and direct. And, for all his talents, the slight Rivera, an artist, is too flamboyant and flash for such economy. Mazzola, older and less gifted technically, is certainly less fussy, and while he had been out of favour for some time (both he and Rivera played in the North Korean humiliation), when Mazzola appeared in the 1968 European Nations Cup Final, standing in for the absent Rivera, it all worked a treat. And though they have tried all permutations since, Valcareggi has come to the conclusion that Rivera and Riva just won't mesh. Like Ramsey facing the terrible question of dropping Jimmy Greaves, Valcareggi has had to make a tough decision.

'Valcareggi seemed to have some suspicions of him,' says the BBC's Barry Davies, detailed to cover the Italian camp. 'One of those players who would disappear in a match then suddenly produce the pass which decided the match.'

Of course, it's a thirteen-man game these days, but for an Italian star, notoriously fragile of ego, a place on the bench is like an insult to his mother. On 26 May when Rivera finds out from a journalist of all people that he will not be figuring in the starting line-up for the opening game against Sweden, still a full week away, he blows his top and publicly condemns Valcareggi and Walter Mandelli, the head of the Federal Technical Centre. The officials tell Rivera that unless he apologises he will be sent home. A stand-off ensues, eventually mediated by some high-ups from the Italian FA and Nereo Rocco, Rivera's manager at Milan.

'If they want to toss me out, they should have the guts to stand up and say so,' says Rivera, a veteran of both '62 and '66.

The officials agree. In future, word will come directly to him rather than via the press – though it may still come all the same. Valcareggi has now had his hand freed. He can do as he wishes ..

Puebla, its citizens reckon, has the prettiest stadium. The Cuauhtemoc arena, a clean, concrete, modernist construction, is certainly not unpleasant. With its Aztec ruins near by, a mosaic frontice and lines of flags ringing the concourse, it certainly projects a provincial splendour. Its 30,000 capacity is not in the same league as the Azteca or Guadalajara's Jalisco Stadium, but, built only a couple of years ago and spankingly modern, it is infinitely better than the Bombonera Stadium at neighbouring Toluca, which, with its slanting corrugated-iron roof, square wooden goalposts, breezeblock walls, barbed wire and rivers of urine, has a distinctly lower-division feel. Take away the mountains, the sun and the sizzle of tamales and you could be at, well, Ninian Park.

Toluca and Puebla will share Group Two of the World Cup. At 7,052 feet, Puebla is a little lower than Mexico City. At 8,744, Toluca is the highest of all the grounds. Though that is not really the problem. With Puebla less than a hundred miles from Mexico City, and Toluca not fifty, the media folks, administrators and even a fair portion of the fans can all bus in and out of the capital. The World Cup, it seems, is happening elsewhere.

'I don't think I ever felt, doing the group matches in Puebla and Toluca, that I was at the heartbeat of the World Cup,' says Barry Davies, for whom the Italy–Uruguay game will be his first ever live match commentary. 'It was clear by going back into Mexico City that I was, and it was also clear from what we were able to see from our own coverage that things were happening in Guadalajara and León.'

Even the Italians are based in the capital, still at the Parc des Princes, trudging out only for the pre-game training sessions and the matches themselves. The other three teams felt it their duty at least to stay locally – Uruguay in Puebla, Sweden in Toluca and Israel in both, decamping from their first Toluca hotel because of noise, the second because of theft and ending up in another one in Puebla where they all get ill. No, with Mexico City currently in the throes of post-0–0 euphoria, Puebla/Toluca just does not feel like the World Cup.

The commentators do their best to suggest a bit of atmosphere, but the truth is, this is the bum assignment. Apart from the venues, the teams are bad enough. Italy – cautious; Uruguay – dull; Israel – no-hopers; Sweden – boring.

'It doesn't matter how good you are when you do the commentary,' explains Davies. 'You're dependent on what sort of match you've got.'

Sweden have got the best chance, still slim, of taking one of the top two slots from Italy or Uruguay – but it's just a green light for those two old warriors to shut up shop, not lose, and nick the odd goal – recipe for an even more unattractive stalemate than is anticipated.

Still, there's always Israel, a new state of only twenty-two years' standing. Like a Southern League team that's crawled its way into the third round of the FA Cup and drawn a First Division giant, the amateurs of Israel – tradesmen, salesmen, students, a PT instructor – might just grab a few headlines.

Italy are probably glad for Israel's appearance. It was North Korea's withdrawal from the Asian qualifiers on political grounds that allowed Israel to advance through Group Fifteen, a far-flung qualifier including Australia, New Zealand, South Korea, Japan and that well-known Asian country Rhodesia. They are the first members of the Asian section ever to qualify for the finals. Israel harbour no illusions about their prospects. Before their opener with mighty Uruguay, the *Jerusalem Post* carries the self-deprecating headline, 'LET US HOPE THAT THE WORST TEAM WINS'. But it is a case of nothing ventured, nothing gained. And maybe, just maybe, their £80-a-month part-timers can pull off a shock.

There is no professional football in Israel, but the team has been training hard at the hi-tech Wingate Sports Centre in Tel Aviv.

Their fortunes as a national side are somewhat mixed. Winners of the Asian Cup in '66, '67 and '68, many of their players featured in the 1968 Olympic team that lost a quarter-final on a coin toss to Bulgaria. Recently they have been training at altitude in Ethiopia and, in their last full international before leaving for Mexico, beat their hosts 5–1. Such pluses are strongly countered by defeat against the Romanian B team, Holland and, just recently, club side Borussia Mönchengladbach (losing 6–0). A 4–4 draw with a New York representative team on their way here makes them definitely a minnow.

They've really only got one star player in Mordecai Spiegler, their main forward, a Russian-born pools agent who, next year, will be playing professionally for Nantes (though West Ham, too, have declared an interest). For the last two days, Spiegler's been in bed with a stomach bug, but for tonight's game with Uruguay the doctors have restored him with injections.

OK, there is Giora Spiegel, his midfield partner, a university student studying accountancy; and David Primo, who played in the USA with the Baltimore Bays. But their busiest player is likely to be Yitschak Vissoker. A bus driver by day, he doubles as their goalie.

Keeping it all together is their coach, the German-born Emanuel Shefer. The players don't like his hard, disciplinarian regime. There have been internal rumblings about drilling into them what Shefer calls the 'German method'. Quite what he means is not exactly clear, for Shefer is a survivor of a Nazi concentration camp. 'I have been to hell and back,' he says. 'It has taught me that all is never lost in this world.'

It is highly unlikely that Israel will dent Uruguay, which, though a small country, is a giant of global soccer. The original winners in 1930, their greatest moment was when they repeated the feat twenty years later, devastating hosts Brazil right there in the Maracanā.

Twenty years on and history is due for repetition, they claim. Like Italy, should they win this time, they will keep the Jules Rimet Trophy outright. In 1966 they went out in the quarter-finals, prematurely amid player dissent, and their relations have never been particularly harmonious internally, either. All their players come from rival Montevideo clubs Peñarol and Nacional. Both are very powerful within the Uruguayan Football Association and forever disrupt the planning of the national team. They have been especially uncooperative with releasing players for the build-ups to international tournaments, which, as for most South American countries, fall in the middle of the domestic season.

Manager Juan Hohberg, an Argentinian by birth who has lived in Uruguay for years and played for them in the 1954 World Cup, has already got his work cut out: players Julio Castillo and Dagoberto Fontes have been fined for fighting during a training session.

Still, they've definitely got the talent: Nacional's Luis Cubilla, an ageless winger, once of Barcelona and their main source of goals; captain Pedro Virgilio Rocha, Peñarol's elegant link man; clubmate Roberto Matosas, their solid left back in a ruthless defence. And their goalie, of Polish extraction, Ladislao Mazurkiewicz of Peñarol, is, some critics argue, equal to Banks as world number one. Like Italy, Uruguay are famous for their defence – dull, stifling, dense, but even more brutal.

Confounding poor Israel's hopes, Uruguay push forward in Group Two's opening clash and win 2–0. Whenever Israel get the ball, the Uruguayans scuttle back and assume their defensive positions, like basketball players massing round the zone. After twenty-two minutes a cross from Mújica comes over and the resultant header by Maneiro gives the 1970 World Cup its first goal; Mújica adds a second in the second half. The game is not without severe misfortune: it is barely ten minutes old when, reaching for a high ball, Rocha comes down hard and rips a groin muscle. Uruguay have lost their most influential playmaker and captain, his tournament over before it's hardly begun. The 22,000 have seen incident, even some goals, but it is not beautiful.

It seems only appropriate that such a dull group should contain Sweden, the poor Scandinavians neither wholly good nor wholly bad, their presence in the World Cup largely anonymous – make-weights in a group already decided. Getting a team together is still not easy for Sweden, their mercenary players cast across Europe. Orvar Bergmark the 'selection/coach' has some good players in Ove Kindvall of Feyenoord, the striker who plagued Celtic in the European Cup Final and scored nearly all of their goals in qualifying. Part-timer Leif Eriksson of Orebro, their midfield artist, is a lawyer, who consistently declines offers from professional clubs.

With Italy's tough reputation going before them, Sweden try to match them physically, making a busy afternoon's work for ref Jack Taylor. Olsson and Axelsson try to shut Riva down and little Bo Larsson darts about in midfield, though Italy always look comfortable. In the end Italy win: a fluky Domenghini shot is dived over Sprake-like by goalie Hellström. With the onfield battle and the thin air, both teams are dead at the close.

To the satisfaction of many an Italian official, Valcareggi only uses one sub, Rosato, leaving Rivera to stew on the bench.

Perhaps the only thing to be said for both games is that after the nervous refereeing at the Azteca, here two British refs (Bob Davidson takes the Puebla game) do their best to keep their cards in their pockets, Davidson even waving up Uruguayan forward Losada who got too theatrical on the deck.

But by the end everyone's forgotten it all. And, after the conclusion of the opening salvo in Group Two, everyone piles back to Mexico City, where the real action is . . .

It is a world away from Bodmin, at the disused Methodist church which Paul Madeley and his brother are converting into a DIY wallpaper, paint and accessory centre. 'The paint seller who snubbed Ramsey', as the *News of the World* has it, the paper having followed the Leeds player to Cornwall where he spends his evenings at Cobbler's Cottage, Little Helston, and the daytimes working on the store.

'But it wasn't just because I was tired after a hard season that I didn't want to go to Mexico,' Madeley tells them. 'That's a misunderstanding. Some people would have me drawing my old-age pension. If I had been in the original forty Alf had picked, I'd have been raring to go, but I was the forty-first choice for England and, by that time, I had already arranged my holidays with my wife.'

He was hurt, he says, when not picked originally – never got any explanation, and didn't see the logic when he leap-frogged over Bob McNab, who got sent home anyway, vindicating his feeling that he'd never have got a game. His 'charming brunette wife' Ann, who works behind the till, sadly says that people think it's her influence, but it's not at all: the decision was all Paul's.

Meanwhile, his clubmate, the hospitalised Paul Reaney, makes a vow: 'I'll be back with a vengeance', he says, 'for Munich '74.'

Elsewhere, life chugs on. Dana, the eighteen-year-old Londonderry singer of the hit 'All Kinds of Everything', sacks her manager of two years only a week after he gives up his day job as a headmaster to do it full time; Benjamin Spock, the world's most famous paediatrician who has enraged the USA because of his anti-Vietnam War views, arrives in the UK; in a school in Penryn, Cornwall, kids are left distraught as the object of dissection in their biology exam turns out to be none other than Dylan, the school's pet rabbit.

In the Himalayas a British team conquers Annapurna One. The Reliant motor company launches a new car called the Bond Bug. Intended for seventeen- to twenty-five-year-olds, it is a bright orange doorless, climb-in three-wheeler that does 70 m.p.h., though experts say it is liable to turn over. In New York the Apollo 13 astronauts parade through a tickertape welcome down the 'canyon of heroes'. There's a new giant oil find in the North Sea only 200 miles from Aberdeen. The Met Office predicts a flaming June.

On TV, the World Cup dominates all, guillotining children's programmes like *Lost in Space* and *Junior Showtime* on ITV and, on the Beeb, *Shazzan*, *Hector's House* and *Abbott and Costello*. *Z Cars* and *Star Trek* ('The Trouble with Tribbles') provide the lead-ins to the first big games.

In football, Peter Shilton eventually agrees a four-year contract with Leicester. Out-of-favour Arsenal forward Bobby Gould joins Wolves. Crystal Palace look set to sign Chelsea's Bobby Tambling and Alan Birchenall for £140,000. And globetrotting Southampton draw 3–3 in the second of a four-game series with Japan at the National Stadium in Tokyo. Meanwhile, Boy of '66, John Connelly, is given a free transfer by Blackburn.

Symbolically, as every newspaper goes into a last-minute World Cup frenzy and proclamations of 'Good Luck England' and pictures of Union Jack-waving tots appear everywhere, the *Daily Express* patriotically recalculates its odds: it's official – England will meet Brazil in the final...

Chapter 9

Guadalajara

Tuesday, 2 June 1970
Gerald Sinstadt stands beside the pitch at the Brazilian training ground. As with every time Brazil appear on the telly, samba music plays. The players are ranged in rank and file and formed into a square, running up and down, turning rhythmically on instruction from a trainer, like a well drilled infantry unit. Sinstadt, in his appearance – open shirt, shades and sideburns – but mostly in his delivery, seems a little like Eric Idle from the new comedy troupe Monty Python's Flying Circus, which is becoming cult viewing over on BBC2.

'Well, here we are on another roasting afternoon at Guadalajara,' he informs the nation. 'Brazil are already halfway through their training session. After an impressive display of gymnastics and ball skills, they've gone on to give the goalkeepers Félix and Ado a workout in the aerial department, in which they could be weak when challenged by Geoff Hurst and Martin Peters.'

Balls are pumped over high, and the two goalies do their stuff. Though not for too long. And before Sinstadt can finish the observation that 'Some Brazilian critics say they haven't got a goalkeeper who can catch a ball ...' manager Mário Zagalo comes over and shuts the filming down. This information is classified.

When it comes to Brazil's strengths, however, it's a different ball game. Too much has been written or screened about their greatest ever player to make him much of a mystery. Today even the great Pelé is only doing light training. 'In boxing language,' says Sinstadt, 'he didn't want to leave his fight in the gymnasium.' However great he may be, there's a lot riding on Pelé this time. Twenty-nine now, he's already announced it's going to be his last World Cup, and that in three years' time he will retire altogether. He is still bitter about what happened to him in England in 1966, getting booted out of the tournament by Bulgaria, Hungary and Portugal. This, then, will be his fourth and final series. Despite his amazing career, since his remarkable turn as the seventeen-year-old boy wonder of the 1958 tournament (an impudent goal and one other in the final against Sweden) his World Cups have not been so happy. In 1962 he was injured and didn't make it to the final. Add in the England performances, where he limped out, and he has not completed a Brazilian World Cup campaign for twelve years.

Nevertheless, Pelé is a legend. 'The most complete footballer in the world,' according to Jimmy Hill. Earnt 150,000 a year. Together with Muhammad Ali, the most famous sportsman on the planet – both black men, a sign of changing times. As every smart-arse kid will tell you, Pelé's real name is Edson Arantes do Nascimento. His mother would have kept it that way too, beating her son for playing football, like a delinquent, in the streets of Três Corações, in the state of Minas Gerais, where he soon became known by his more famous moniker – a contraction of 'pelada', it is rumoured, the Portuguese word for 'kickabout'. (Pelé never cared much for his nickname.) Ma Nascimento, it seems, had been less impressed with the life of a footballer as evidenced by the heartbreak of husband Dondinho, a player who dreamed of the big time, only for it to be snatched away cruelly, invalided out of the game on his very debut for giants Atletico Mineiro. This didn't deter Dondinho's son. As the legend goes, young Pelé stole peanuts and sold them to buy a secret pair of football boots. He had an old ball, too, and would devote every waking hour to practice, initiating the pick-up games from which he derived his sobriquet. His talents did not go unnoticed. Like another boy genius who would later be doing amazing football tricks in the back alleys of Belfast, Pelé soon came under the watchful eye of a devoted scout – in this case, Waldemar de Brito, a veteran of the 1934 World Cup, and friend of Dondinho's, who implored that such gifts must not go to waste.

The family had, by this time, relocated to Bauru in São Paulo state and there young Pelé was duly fixed up with his local club, FC Bauru, staying there for four years till, aged sixteen, he was snapped up by rising club Santos – an outfit with big ambitions. Pelé advanced through the junior teams and soon, in his famous number 10 shirt, was banging in goals in the first XI against the top sides in the land. Within a year, he had won the first of what currently stands as eighty-seven caps. Within two, he had a World Cup winner's medal.

Pelé had always made plain the debt he owed to de Brito for showing faith in him so young. He has been incredibly loyal to Santos: though a good team, with which he has won six National Championships, he has resisted a king's ransom to take his gifts elsewhere – within Brazil, Europe, anywhere he damn well pleases.

Seven months ago, in November 1969, Pelé notched up another record, scoring his thousandth top-class goal versus Vasco da Gama, one of the teams that had been courting him. His record speaks for itself. In all his games he has averaged 0.939 goals per match; he has 93 hat-tricks to his name and has scored 4 goals or more 37 times.

But memories of 1966 still linger. While still a fixture in the national team – the dropping by Saldanha notwithstanding – only recently did he agree to play in Mexico. 'I cannot live for ever,' he pronounced. 'I need a good dream to chase it away.'

Privately, too, Pelé's business ventures – in transport, farming, the rubber industry – are leaking money.

This time, the on-field burden of responsibility will not lie squarely on Pelé's shoulders. He has a cunning accomplice – Tostão. The Brazilians love diminutives – every player's title whittled down to a mononym. Jair Ventura Filho becomes Jairzinho, 'little Jair'; Jonas Eduardo Américo is Edu; Gérson de Oliveira Nunes is just Gérson (or 'Papagaio', the Parrot). Eduardo de Gonçalves Andrade – small, frail, his looks deceptive as to his true worth – is the 'Little Coin', Tostão. 'The white Pelé,' as Sinstadt puts it. 'Though doubtless he would prefer it if Pelé were known as the black Tostão.'

The Cruzeiro forward has had a turbulent couple of years. A free-scoring foil to Pelé in the qualifiers, Tostão got ten of their twenty-three qualifying goals, romping home over Paraguay, Colombia and Venezuela. But, just as he was becoming a national hero in Brazil, in a club match against Corinthians in September 1969, he got hit in the eye with a ball which detached his retina. For a while it seemed that the injury might – at age twenty-three – have prematurely curtailed Tostão's career, and even cost him the sight in that eye. But Tostão, a man with a medical training (indeed, in only three years' time he will turn his back on football to become a doctor), consulted the top ophthalmic surgeon in the country, who then took him to Houston, USA, for make-or-break surgery. Dr Abdala Moura (a Cruzeiro fan), who performed the operation himself, reassured Tostão that everything would be fine. And though the Little Coin must go through a routine of eye-drop application before each game, has had to have certain medication specially certified to get round the doping rules, and the eye still bleeds occasionally, disturbing opponents more than it does Tostão, he is fit to play. But he mustn't head the ball. However, he and Pelé have got enough tricks to overcome any such deficiency. No longer the out-and-out centre forward he is for Cruzeiro, Tostão has dropped into a deeper role to service the Master – holding the ball and laying it off for Pelé and Jairzinho.

And while Houston has been good to Tostão, so it has been too for the other players. The squad have been together from 14 February, including six weeks at altitude with games in Ecuador and Colombia. The final stage, at Houston, has been for Dr Cooper of NASA to fine-tune them physiologically on a programme designed for astronauts, including a top-secret technique to avoid dehydration.

Even on a fundamental level, though, the Brazilian preparation has always been a bit different. Stories of famous foreign players visiting Rio and barely able to hold a candle to the urchins juggling oranges on Copacabana Beach are legend. Whereas in England the ball is a weapon, a hand-grenade, to be relinquished at the first opportunity, detonated at the right moment good and hard, in Brazil it is an object of beauty, to be stroked, caressed, fondled. As part of their training, the Brazilian players love to play volleyball, using head and feet instead of hands. After their training routine, they go about it gently at a net, respectfully knocking the ball back and forth, tenderly and barefoot with beautiful close control. Dark skinned, sinewy and strolling round in their little trunks, medallions a-flapping, they are football Lotharios – in stark contrast to the pasty English players, ruthlessly kept out of the sun.

In this World Cup Brazil have more stars than anyone. Son of Italian parents, Roberto Rivelino, with his playboy bandido moustache, has, according to the Brazilian coaching staff, 'a gun in his feet'; Jairzinho, the powerful black right winger from Botafogo, hot under his former club coach Zagalo, is assured of automatic selection; and then there is the great Gérson, the shuffling, balding orchestrator, deliverer of the pinpoint forty-yard pass. The defence, as everyone keeps pointing out, is mighty suspect – certainly in the goalkeeping department, with little Félix as eccentric as they come – but when you've got a great surging right back like the captain Carlos Alberto (Pelé's Santos clubmate) steaming down the wing, it can offset a few deficiencies. Brito, too, who's grown a professorial beard and says he won't shave it off until Brazil reach the final, can be a tough customer on his day.

Brazil have assessed their strengths and weaknesses and come to a conclusion: as Napoleon decreed, attack is the best form of defence; why worry about conceding two goals when you can always score three . . . ?

Back home, for the past six months, the great meeting between England and Brazil has been hotly anticipated. It is the set-up for what is tipped to be the final. If England and Brazil qualify from their group as everyone expects – nay, demands – they will go into different halves of the draw and won't renew acquaintance until the ultimate showdown.

Every interview with an England player in the interim has been about how best they will conduct the battle. All rave about Pelé, though Mullery, having snuffed him out in Rio last year, singles out Tostão as the danger man. But all enthuse reverently about the ball-playing skills of their rivals. If you think George Best is a bit fancy, well, let me tell you, there are a million Georgie Bests in Rio alone.

All are keen to point out that to regard England as a kick-and-rush outfit is a mistake. The muddy pitches of the Football League tend to diminish skill, but on his day, under good conditions, the English player can cut it with the best of them. And, adds Hurst, though defences at this level are inevitably tight, there's always the odd bounce or knockdown. It's the taking of them that counts.

But England, and especially Ramsey, know that at this point the clash of the titans, next Sunday, 7 June, is a long way off. There is the small matter of the Romanians to deal with first, and they are a team which must be treated with every respect.

At the end of a short training session in the Jalisco Stadium itself the day before their game, Ramsey sits the players down around him – some in red shirts, some in white, in keeping with a further mocked-up battle strategy. Alf goes through the plans one more time and reminds them of the quality of tomorrow's adversary. Aside from the three or four major powers in this tournament, just about every team is described as a 'dark horse'. In Romania's case it may be true: they are a mystery team on the world stage – this being their first appearance in the finals since France in 1938. Their coach, Angelo Nicolescu, a firm but fair disciplinarian, has earned growing respect. And, as Dr Phillips has already found out, their facilities and preparation are second to none. The players have long come to terms with altitude at their training camp in Poyana Brasov in the Carpathians and, previously, on two Latin American tours.

And they've got some star players, too. Nicolae Dobrin of Argesul Pitesti, a deep forward, is to Romanian soccer what Rivera is to Italian. With a similar temperament, too, it would seem. Dropped once for refusing to attend a team training camp, he is now back in favour. By the same token, twenty-two-year-old Florea Dumitrache is the Romanian Riva. In 1968 the Dynamo Bucharest goal machine was the Romanian Footballer of the Year. And then there is his clubmate, midfielder Radu Nunweiller, the 'General' – Nunweiller the Sixth, as he is known to the fans, one of seven brothers to play for the club. Past goalkeeping problems have been solved by Necula Raducanu. And there is a strong defence with Ludovic Satmareanu at overlapping right back. Midfielders Mircea Lucescu, the captain, and Dembrowski are not to be messed with.

Romania's form, however, is inconsistent. They were beaten by France, though drew twice with West Germany recently. Then they forced a draw in Peru with their typically tight, committed defence and possession game in midfield.

Alf points this out, though the players have been briefed on the dangermen before. All Ramsey really cares about is sticking to the simple plan, stripping the game down to its elements – simple passing to the man, running off the ball, giving the man on the ball options – and the importance of laying it out to the full backs to bang in the crosses. Tidy stuff.

He knows exactly what they're up against. Romania have recently held England to draws twice – a 0–0 in Bucharest in November 1968, and a 1–1 at Wembley in January 1969. There was only one previous fixture – England winning 2–0 in Bucharest before the war.

By and large, Lucescu and the Romanians have said some very positive things about England – that they are full of respect and will be very wary. For both teams, points on the board from the first game will be a massive psychological lift. Though they are not completely gushing. The odd sarcastic comment has come out about England wasting their time with the altitude training as they're never going to get as far as Mexico City. They are fine ones to talk. Despite all the hi-tech facilities back home and the arduous altitude programmes they have completed, the Romanians are being troubled by the climate: Dobrin, their 1967 Player of the Year, is out for the England game, having developed heatstroke. Because the game kicks off at 4 p.m., Nicolescu has withdrawn him and the Romanians are now training with shirts tied round their heads, like crash survivors in the desert. On Tuesday they will be smearing themselves in sun lotion. Lucescu has already lost ten pounds; he reckons any European team is only good for an hour.

And further trouble: giant goalie Raducanu has been disciplined after having thrown some officials in the hotel pool, fully clothed. Though that is not the formal explanation. Raducanu has been dropped because too many of his saves are thought to be extravagantly spectacular – 'for the benefit of the photographers and not the footballers,' says one Romanian official.

The weather will be a problem for England, too, but perhaps it won't be as bad as expected. Miguel Rodríguez, head of the Jalisco State Meteorological Department, assures the Europeans that the climate is so reliable in June that there will be six straight days of rain between now and the 15th, but only one day of over 0.24 inches before 5 June. Hopes are that it will fall on Tuesday to make the boys feel at home.

All that remains now is to name the teams. The Romanians have already submitted theirs: long-haired Dinu will anchor the defence as usual in a 4–4–2 formation; Lucescu and Dembrowski are in midfield; Tataru and Dumitrache will be up front, the latter having recovered from an ankle twisted in training. Ramsey, by contrast, has given away nothing. Though, given the adherence to the same eleven in the last few games, and the issue of the squad numbers, the opening line-up is unlikely to differ from that. On Saturday they play that way – 1–11 versus 12 and up – in a full-scale practice match at the Atlas Club. The B team wins 3–1 – running the As ragged in parts, with Osgood and Thompson combining well. Osgood gets two, Bell the other, and Ramsey is a little concerned. This first game, he knows, is the most important of the lot.

There is interest in who the subs will be, especially as two will likely play, certainly if Ramsey pursues last year's policy of running Ball and Peters into the ground. Bell and Stiles, it is reckoned, will be waiting to take over should either flag. Stiles might come in useful: it's just been revealed that the stadium authorities will not sanction the presence of Winston the bulldog, the official England mascot, on the playing surface. Of the remainder, Bonetti will be there automatically, so the other two spots are open to debate. Perhaps Osgood and Astle, if England go into the last quarter still without a goal. Alf keeps his cards tight to his chest – he'll announce his team, as ever, forty-five minutes before kick-off.

His main concern right now seems to be with the Jalisco Stadium pitch. It's not as good as last year, that's for sure. Importantly for a man for whom precision is everything, it's shorter, by about five yards, and lacking a few feet in width. You can still see the previous markings etched into the grass. When you've planned moves and strategies down to the nearest inch, such things are not welcome. An angry Alf tells the Mexican press so. 'There is a piece three yards square near the centre which has just been retouched,' he adds with a huff. 'I am extremely surprised.' There's the roof, too. An addition since their last visit, turning the 70,000-capacity ground into a vast bowl, like a three-quarter-scale version of the Azteca. At match time, the new roof casts a sharp shadow down the length of the pitch, bisecting it almost exactly into two. It will be tough on defenders and goalies who must keep switching their vision from blinding sun on one flank into gloomy shade. Problematic, too, for the TV cameramen who, as it will turn out in Guadalajara, will find parts of some games almost unfilmable, constantly losing the play while apertures are furiously adjusted . . .

But there's nothing England can do about that.

England finish off the 45 minute match with some shooting practice against the three goalies. No complaints there. Banks looks sensational . . .

*

Bobby Moore: 'The talismanic white knight – imperious on the international stage.' (Empics)

It's the real thing. Alf holds court
after training (Popperfoto)

Clodoaldo can't contain Bobby Charlton:
"El Calvo Divino." (Empics)

Below: Peter Osgood carves through Czechoslovakia (Sporting Pictures). England's 1–0
win sees them through to the quarter final and West Germany . . . where [*opposite above*]
Mullery opens the scoring but is then sidestepped by Beckenbauer [*opposite below*] to
concede "a soft, silly, stupid, goal." (both Empics)

Terry Cooper tries to muster strength for an extra 30 minutes against West Germany: 'I was out on my feet.' (*Mirror* Syndication)

Charlton, Ball and Labone contemplate the inevitable: 'A late German equaliser, 2–2, and extra time. Exactly the same as '66.' (*Mirror* Syndication)

Gerd Müller's volley ends it all (Sporting Pictures)

Moore in resignation: 'England, kings of world football, abdicate.' (Empics)

Chaos breaks out on the pitch as Bobby Charlton confronts the end of his England career (*Mirror* Syndication)

Carlos Alberto raises aloft the Jules Rimet trophy. Brazil's to keep for ever
(*Mirror* Syndication)

'Sheer spellbound admiration' for El Rey Pelé (Empics)

'The last great football carnival': Pelé and the 1970 Brazilians celebrate their appointment as the greatest team of all time (*Mirror* Syndication)

At 3.50 p.m. local time on Tuesday, 2 June, the England team files up the concrete steps from the underground tunnel and out into the bullring of the Jalisco Stadium. It is 88 degrees but overcast, taking the edge off the heat. As they witnessed yesterday, there is that damned shadow, but the question of light is not the first thing that hits the players. What does is the noise – a hellish siren wail of whistles and catcalls. England, it seems, are now officially anointed as the World Cup's villains. Throughout the presentation, anthems and everything else – whistles, whistles and more whistles. The England players, veterans of Liverpool, Manchester and London derbies, claim the day you let a crowd begin to bother you, you might as well pack it all in – nothing worse than Hampden last month where twice as many baying Scotsmen were after either Leeds's or England's blood. 'We were battle hardened, we were World Champions, and expected everything that went with being World Champions,' says Alan Ball. 'Every team would be up for trying to knock us off our perch.'

Then there is the smell. Not the great cloud of cigarette smoke, or pungent aroma of greasy pies, the stale wafts from a lunchtime session, nor the unmistakable smell of wet English mud, here it is tortillas and burritos, and tobacco of a different scent.

Despite their status as World Champions, the ground is not full. Of the 40,000 who are in, there is a 5,000-strong merry band of Union Jack-waving fans who are willing, if not always audible. The majority – Mexican and some Brazilian – will be honorary Romanians for the day.

'If you go away expecting to be hated, you're not going to be surprised,' says Brian Labone. 'We're not very popular, are we? It's lovely being the best and being hated.'

After a barely discernible 'God Save the Queen', lost in a racket of ululation, England run off to one end and what is already known is announced over the PA, each player getting a shrill wail from the crowd – 1, Banks; 2, Newton; 3, Cooper; 4, Mullery; 5, Labone; 6, Moore; 7, Lee; 8, Ball; 9, Charlton; 10, Hurst; 11, Peters – the long-suspected first XI.

And then come the five who have been chosen to sit on the bench: Bonetti, Wright, Hunter, Bell, Osgood. Not as predicted, but a sensible spread – keeper, obviously; full back; centre back; midfielder; forward. All bets covered if anyone flags, though more suggestive of caution than of a great tactical game plan.

Back home, a nation gathers round its tellies, perching anxiously on the edge of sofas. Though the England party are not immune to the tension either. On the way to the stadium, Alf has already had a row with some attendants as the coach was driven down the ramp into the underground parking bay. The players look similarly tense now: furrowed brows and flexed muscles; giving each other battlefield yells. And then, before you know it, England are in the 1970 World Cup.

In the opening minute there is a scare as Dumitrache goes clear of Labone, and Cooper allows a cross to drop to Dembrowski, who prods it wide with his knee. The Romanians, in their national colours – yellow shirts, blue shorts, red socks – send the crowd wild.

As predicted, there is no Dobrin, no Raducanu. But, as expected, the Romanians are a physical outfit. There is an inkling of it early on when Cooper charges down the left. As he is about to attack the Romanian number 2, Satmareanu, the number 15, Dumitru, thunders up from behind Cooper, launches himself, and hacks him down. The referee, the 'monsieur who can catch England swearing', is going to have his work cut out. He blows a shrill whistle but takes no further action. Instead he makes a downward pushing action with the palms of his hands, as if to say, 'Come on chaps, let's keep a lid on that sort of thing.' But the pattern is set, and, while his ability to discern English cursing is now being tested, the Romanians exchange knowing winks.

Moments later, when Alan Mullery runs through in the inside-right channel, facing up to a defender, here comes Dumitru again, purposefully lumbering over to take his legs away. Just for good measure, while Mullery lies face down, barely moving, not something he is given to doing when not seriously hurt, Dinu blasts the ball into the top of his head. The England supporters scream a chant of 'off, off, off' but again there is no card. Eventually Mullery gets up. He will later confess that he gave Dumitru a wallop when the ref's back was turned. He is not the only one. 'I can remember kicking the right winger because they were dishing it out,' says Terry Cooper. 'But you could get away with things then because there were probably only two television cameras. When I played you could usually get away with the first tackle. It's how you were brought up, and all footballers used to test the winger. If you whacked the winger and he didn't come back at you, you were in for an easy afternoon.'

Play goes back, forth, but mostly nowhere, the ball stroked slowly by both sides around the middle, the question of not losing overriding any reckless attempt at a win. And that crowd again, with its constant high-pitched buzz, gets higher or lower, louder or softer, according to the action rather than the punctuating chants of Kop or Kippax.

At half-time it's a cautious, nervous 0–0.

In the second half Dembrowski gets the ball in the same spot where Mullery was felled in the first. Peters shows the difference in approach. In complete contrast to Dumitru, he simply runs up, hustles, and whips his foot in to flick the ball cleanly away. Moore gathers, looks up in that characteristic alert, erect manner, and plays it to Ball in the centre circle. Ball holds, waiting for the team to move forward as a unit – a well-rehearsed drill – and the Romanians reply with their own obvious, though no less finessed, strategy, pulling ten men back behind the ball.

Ball processes the options, strokes it along the halfway line to his right to Mullery, who plays it up the right wing to Lee. With back to goal, Lee gathers it up, turns and then runs full pelt at the Romanian left back, number 4, Mocanu, who responds by bundling both man and ball into touch.

The Mexicans love every minute of it, and let England know it in no uncertain terms. It is the best England can do to keep their cool.

Seven minutes into the second half, Mocanu is at it again, felling Newton brutally on an overlap. Newton seems to be in trouble: he's down for a long time, wincing genuinely while Shepherdson and Phillips test the leg's mobility. Ramsey thinks about it, but it's no good pretending. He gets the nod. Newton's knee is buggered. A shame, for Newton had been playing well, but it's not worth the risk of him aggravating it. Alf signals to Wright. And once the necessary bureaucracy has been surmounted – players have to have a signed chit which must be handed in to the referee – Newton's Everton teammate takes over.

Romania get the odd break but seem to dither. The much vaunted Dumitrache dallies way too long in the England half.

Cooper scampers in, deflects the Romanian pass up to Charlton and the elegant number 9 brings it under control. A pattern is emerging here. There are no solo bursts without sufficient back-up. This is a team moving as one, players holding while others hit their marks. Charlton lays it off to Ball, who has to scurry to keep possession, though he swiftly finds Lee on the right, repeating his running charge. As he squares up to Mocanu again, Dumitru charges in to do his duty, running halfway across the pitch, flying horizontally with both sets of studs up. But Lee's wise to stuff like this – English League players aren't angels, either. He waits, feints, then dances over the challenge, does a jink inside and leaves a flat-footed Mocanu stranded as he pushes the ball forward and charges through on the edge of the area.

Though Mocanu has other ideas. He steadies himself, kicks Lee hard across the shins. Lee, rolled in a ball, clutching his wounds, tumbles across the turf. Mocanu stands there, the very picture of innocence, raising his arms in a 'search-me-if-I-know-what's-going-on' kind of fashion. But it is a horrendous foul – a good eight yards off the ball, deliberate, malicious, dangerous and, what's more, thwarting a clear goalscoring opportunity. The ref does not even speak a word of caution to the defender.

That's it. Alan Ball has had enough. In the sixty-ninth minute he gathers the ball up from Wright and gives the Romanians a dose of English medicine by lobbing the ball into the box – good old-fashioned route one. Lee attempts a half-hearted back-headed flick-on and fails, but it simply allows the ball to land at the feet of Hurst loitering on the corner of the six-yard box. Hurst nutmegs a static Satmareanu, swings and scuffs a left-foot shot across the goal-mouth. The keeper, Adamache, makes an athletic but ineffective feet-first lunge, and a perfectly stoppable ball bobbles under him into his left-hand corner.

The England supporters go wild. The players just look relieved. Back home, at precisely 12.24 a.m., 25 million people leap out of their armchairs. 'That is the goal they needed so much,' screams David Coleman. 'Nineteen minutes of the second half gone. Geoff Hurst, who got a hat-trick in the World Cup Final, England's last World Cup match.' Across the screen reads the simple evidence – 'Anotador [scorer]: 10 Hurst' – and that's all anyone needs to know.

Peters runs up, plants a palm either side of Hurst's face, and gives him a hug. Lee scurries over to join in the love-fest. A lone and brave England fan in the Mexican section waves a Union Jack with 'Leeds United' written across it. The Mexicans may be catcalling, but for England's barmy-army there'll be a hot time in the old town tonight.

And, fifteen minutes from the end, around the time that Osgood comes on for the battle-weary Lee, it even starts to rain for them.

There are other moments. Lee smacks a Cooper cross against the bar with goalkeeper Adamache nowhere. At the end, Hurst and Peters are still running strong. Cooper and Moore are solid, the captain seeming to have put the whole Bogotá thing well behind him. Wright and Osgood fit into the pattern with no difficulty to themselves or upset to the team rhythm. There is only one real scare. In the seventy-third minute, a shot from Dembrowski appears to be deflected and Banks can't hold it, but pushes it up on to the bar and safety. Banks looks altogether unfamiliar: forced to change his shirt at half-time by the ref because his traditional yellow clashed with that of the Romanians, he comes out with a short-sleeved red one, an outfield shirt from England's training kit.

It is definitely Hurst's day. He has become something of a national treasure since that golden afternoon in 1966. Go back only four years before that and there were questions asked as to whether this average half back – son of a Rochdale footballer but who grew up in Essex and had just made his cricket debut for the county – really had a future at West Ham, let alone England. It was the diligence of Hammers manager Ron Greenwood that transformed him into a robust centre forward, winner of FA Cup then Cup Winners' Cup medals. Seeing that his ability was being wasted in the wrong position, Hurst's transition, plus his strength and guile, had seen him become understudy to hero Jimmy Greaves in the national squad in 1966. A surprise inclusion in the quarter-final, the rest is history – though Greaves is now his clubmate, and the two are friends, running a clothing business together. Now, much more than in 1966, when he got by on raw talent, Hurst has become a true world-class player, a forward in the very modern sense – a holder of the ball, a layer-off of chances, not the battering-ram forward of old. In four years he, perhaps even more than Moore, has come to personify England's World Cup victory, and his talismanic effect rings still, picking up exactly where he left off in the previous episode.

At the final whistle Ramsey, uncharacteristically, skips across the pitch to congratulate the players. Not pretty, but effective.

'It was like every World Cup opening game,' says Ball. 'We went there as champions. We were a little bit cautious, but we knew we couldn't get beaten. It was a tough game but we did a professional job and got on with it.'

In the press room at the stadium soon afterwards, all is geared to getting Ramsey to say a few words to the folks back home. In two or three precious moments of satellite time, BBC and ITV must share the questions. It is not always an easy proposition, prompting Ramsey. 'Alf was not at all keen on press or television getting deeply involved,' says Hugh Johns. 'I was standing to attention when I spoke to Alf. He held you in such contempt. You had to stand there and say "Sir" to him.' Still, he gives it his best shot. England didn't seem completely to get to grips with the game, ventures Johns for ITV. Ramsey agrees. Why, they might even have lost an early goal due to 'a lapse in defence'. Other than that, though, he claims he is pleased, says there was a lot of tension, never seen that before in an England team. Says they took a long time to settle down, but once they did 'they became the force that we know they are'.

Coleman's turn. Alf must be pleased with this first win. 'It's important to win any match,' says Ramsey. And the next match 'will be the first match'.

Johns suggests that from where they were, some of the tackles looked 'vigorous'. Ramsey says yes, they were from where he was, too; that they had seven men in defence. He holds back with criticism and won't rethink his strategy for the Czech game: they, one assumes, will be employing the same sort of tactic.

Ramsey says it was tough – 90 degrees down there on the pitch and the humidity higher. They 'perspired quite a lot', did the lads, their 'shirts ringing wet'. But Peters took his goal well. Actually it was Hurst. 'I was so delighted,' says Ramsey, 'I didn't look at him.'

So delighted that he's even making jokes, saying the overlapping play for Cooper was easier than it was for Newton, because he got to play in the shade.

Still, there's no time for slackening off – there's still much work to be done, but he feels confident of beating both Brazil and Czechoslovakia, whom he'll be watching play each other here tomorrow...

Back at the Hilton later, Hugh Johns is joined by Bertie Mee and Ipswich manager Bobby Robson for a post-match discussion. Standing around talking off camera, they don't realise their mics are open. It can't have been 90 degrees, says Johns, but Bertie Mee thinks it was. No, says Robson, it was like an August opener back home. They get their cue and walk out from behind a bush towards the camera. Mee thinks it was 'a tremendous performance ... the boys did extremely well'. Robson is none too impressed with the physical approach of the 'Bulgarians'. Says it's a good job Nobby wasn't playing or he'd have been off. Johns, resplendent in cravat, asks for forecasts. Mee thinks two more points should do it, 'a lot of English blood and guts there'. Robson, though, has a point: all well and good at the back, but he can't see where the goals are going to come from. He'd like to see Charlton push up and have a few pot shots. Something. *Anything.*

Overall, everyone, really, is just relieved that England have got the points.

'Triumphant England ... They're on their way,' screams the *Sun.* 'Hurst's super goal beats the hate,' says the *Daily Mail.* All reserve some harsh words, of course, for the brutal play of the opposition. The Mexican press, predictably, thought England savage cheats, and the frail Romanians robbed of victory. Mocanu is not even mentioned. And if, as England say, Romania did at times play it a little rough, then England deserve everything they get for only being about playing with muscle in the first place. A cartoon in the *Daily Express* sums it up. It is a picture of a cartoon English gent with a Union Jack sitting amid a crowd of sombreroed Mexicans, who are all screaming with joy as a white-shirted player is hoofed into the air. 'Come in our sweep, señor,' says the bubble. 'The one who getta kicked highest into the air is the winner.'

Although the Mexicans do utter praise for Moore – 'The king of world football,' one daily puts it. 'He shone with gold. For a man who has been burdened with vile accusations and imprisoned, he commanded the game like an emperor.'

Mullery, despite getting chopped, is sanguine. He tells *The Times* that it was 'no worse than a hard game with, say, Liverpool, in the mud of White Hart Lane'. And, as a reward for their exertions, the England players are allowed a night off, can go anywhere they want, provided they observe the strict 11 p.m. curfew.

It is rigorously observed. Earlier in the trip, when given a similar isolated evening of leisure, some of the players had ignored such a deadline at their peril. 'We had to be back for twelve. I sat between Bobby Moore and Bobby Charlton. I thought, Well I'm safe with these two,' says Peter Thompson. 'Got to twelve o'clock. Got to one. Somebody said, "We'd better go," and they were, "Oh, we'll be all right for another half an hour." ' They had returned to the hotel to find Harold Shepherdson casually sitting on the landing jotting names and times in a notepad. 'Some were *really* late,' says Thompson. 'Alf was very quiet. We had a meeting the next day. He said, "I gave you permission to go out last night and have a drink. You've let me down. I said twelve o'clock. Next time I don't want anybody to come and say they're sorry, which I've had some players do today. All I'll do is say, 'Thanks for joining me in Mexico and there's your flight home.' " Nobody messed him about again.'

'Alf was a nice man,' says Brian Labone. 'But bloody hell, when he said "jump", you jumped.'

There are two absentees from the revelry: Keith Newton and Terry Cooper are whisked off to the local hospital for precautionary X-rays. No breaks, but it gives Ramsey pause for thought. Newton has a badly bruised knee (courtesy of Mocanu); Cooper has a damaged right foot which was danced upon by a Romanian (looking on the bright side, Cooper says at least it's not his left).

With their rare moment of freedom, some players pile on down to Willie's, the local mock-English pub, where Tommy Wright and Francis Lee explain to some of the press that the lads thought the hostile crowd was 'a bit of a laugh' – just away-ground stick. The others head to the bar on the twentieth floor of the Hilton where a number of England fans have congregated.

Among the new arrivals is a team, the Mount Street Football Club, a Sunday kickabout side comprising Alvaro, a restaurateur; Douglas Hayward, the Mayfair tailor who dresses Terence Stamp, Michael Caine and Bryan Forbes; actors David Hemmings, Tom Courtenay and Nicol Williamson; and friends. 'Spruced up and fitted out with new plimsolls', they have been running up and down

Hampstead Hill in training and are here on a promise by Bobby Moore that they'll get a kickabout with England's finest.

Here too, more famously, are Roger Hunt and Charlie Cooke, who were besieged at the airport by autograph hunters. Hunt is in Mexico as a courier for a travel company and will pen some articles for the Liverpool *Echo*. Scottish international Cooke even admits, through gritted teeth, that he will support England.

As the beers flow, Jeff Astle leads the players into some friendly banter and mickey-taking with some Stetsoned Texans who happen to be staying there . . .

Brazil, though, are less impressed with what they have seen. Not quite to the extent that the *Sun* claims, with its comment that 'Brazilian team manager Mário Zagalo has practically written off England's chances of even qualifying for the quarter-finals of the World Cup.' But the fact is that Zagalo has said now of England that he doesn't fear them as much as Czechoslovakia. Defender Brito enters the fray, too, talking about how the Czechs have a more impressive record than England over the past year. It's not a million miles away from what Ramsey was muttering before the Romania game – talking up the opposition; all eyes on that one first before the big showdown next Sunday.

In Guadalajara the Brazilian bandwagon is rolling with irresistible force. And the players, after their Guanajuato training camp ordeal, are now locked up under Coutinho's watchful eye at a suburban motel called the Suites de Caribe, under armed guard and ready to explode.

But the Czechs are no push-overs. They failed to qualify in '66 but have a good history in the tournament and are twice beaten finalists – in 1934 and 1962. It was Brazil who overcame them in the encounter eight years ago.

With the turmoil of the 1968 Prague spring, football has not exactly been a priority in Czechoslovakia, but for the people it has assumed a useful role – an outlet of patriotism. And the Czechs are fighters. In their qualifying group, after losing to Hungary in Budapest and being 3–1 down at home in the return, they seemed dead. But they salvaged a point with two late goals and finished level on points with the Magyars, winning a play-off 4–1 in Marseilles.

Most of the players are Slovak rather than Czech, more specifically from the club side Spartak Trnava. Manager Josef Marko comes from that team, too. Slovak clubs have done well in Europe, Slovan Bratislava even beating mighty Barcelona 3–2 in the 1969 Cup Winners' Cup Final.

Unlike other Eastern Bloc countries, where true amateur status is questionable, players often having spurious army roles, in Czechoslovakia the footballers are genuinely part time, a factor that only goes to enhance their club and national achievements. And under Marko they are a useful outfit, quite solid in defence and, with a 4–2–4 set-up, boasting some sharp forwards.

Their star player is Josef Adamec, another Trnava boy, and a veteran of 1962 (though he has only twenty-nine caps), who is an expert in that rare art of curling free kicks round walls. Lanky Ladislav Kuna, Czech Footballer of the Year in 1969, is their midfield distributor. Right back Karel Dobias, also of Trnava, is pretty useful, as is left back Vladimir Hagara, who line up in front of solid goalie Viktor. Andrej Kvasnak, who played in '62 (then a striker, now a midfielder), is one of the few full-time professionals, playing in Belgium. And then there is their new kid on the block – Petras – a nippy striker whom no one knows much about. All are organised by Alexander Horvath, of Slovan Bratislava, their centre back and captain . . .

Though Czechoslovakia have had a few problems. The first is that they didn't bother to come to Mexico until quite late. More recently, they have been training in a rough field and turned a few ankles. They've now moved to a new pitch near the local brewery. But after all that, Horvath and Adamec might not play . . .

On the afternoon of Wednesday, 3 June the England players go with Alf to the Jalisco Stadium to watch the game between Brazil and Czechoslovakia. Predictably the atmosphere is as if it were a Brazil home game. And for all the talk of sympathy for the Czechs, little seems to materialise. At the start of the game there is a bit of a mishap when a huge Brazilian balloon catches fire on the pitch and fries some of the doves that were going to be released, but the Mexicans are no great animal lovers and watch with an air of curiosity more than shock.

As the kick-off comes, the shrieks for Brazil intensify. It's those sublime ball skills, cunning artistry and flamboyance that everyone's come to see and it doesn't take long before the crowd witnesses such wonders. In the eleventh minute a nimble striker dances into the box, cheekily slots the ball under the goalkeeper and skips off to the left-hand corner flag where he drops to his knees in a praying position, crosses himself and exalts the heavens, while the whole team rushes in to pile on top of him.

The only thing that's off the script is that it is Petras, the Czech number 8, who is the executor. The Czechs are a goal up, and all the smug predictions about the slack Brazilian defence suddenly seem completely founded.

Order is soon restored. Twelve minutes later, ambling along in the Czech penalty arc, Pelé takes a half-hearted dive. Even the Czechs seem awed by his reputation. Though it is a dangerous free kick to give away, a couple of them check that the maestro's OK and help him to his feet, patting him on the head, almost as if it will win them credit from the crowd.

Pelé shapes to take, but storming in comes Rivelino and his left-foot gun. As Jairzinho ducks out of the wall, the ball flies like a bullet through the gap and nearly bursts the Czech net. 'Rivelino; oh what a goal,' rhapsodises Coleman. 'How did he find a way through?'

Brazil exert their dominance. Who cares about weak defence when you've got such an attack? And, then, something that shows this is no ordinary team at all. Pelé, inside his own half in the centre circle, and seeing the goalkeeper Viktor off his line, casually shoots. Not a wild skyward howitzer, but an aimed chip. *From inside his own half!* Amid audible gasps the ball flies a couple of feet wide.

In the second period, running into the box from the inside-right channel, Pelé takes the ball on his chest, allows it to drop, and casually thumps it past Viktor. 'Oh yes,' screams Coleman, like a just-released convict indulging in his first voluntary act of coitus. '*Pelé!*'

Ten minutes before the end, Ramsey ushers the England squad out of the ground to get the coach back and beat the traffic. Ramsey and Moore are not impressed by what they've seen. They've been allowed way too much space. The Brazilians won't get a kick if they play like that against England.

Who are they kidding?

Having already worked himself up into what will set the standard for his excited commentary for the rest of the tournament, Coleman only confirms what the world is witnessing: 'These Brazilians – brilliant in attack.'

Back home, the TV viewing public has suddenly been exposed to football the likes of which it has never before seen. Minutes from the end, against an admittedly flagging Czech team, Jairzinho lobs the goalkeeper, runs round him and fires into an empty net. Then, almost on the whistle, he scores again from a similar spot – beating three men before shooting home. Final score: 4–1.

A goal direct from a free kick? A player nearly scoring from the halfway line? Unheard of. And the sheer exuberance of the celebrations. Exotic coloured men in exotic coloured shirts turning the beautiful game into some riotous party. Whatever would the neighbours think...?

Chapter 10

Small Fry

The city of Lima, capital of Peru, is shaken by a violent earthquake. Those who have experience of these things – and Peru gets more than its fair share – reckon it is bad. The worst-hit area initially seems the city of Huarás, 180 miles to the north, though no one is absolutely sure. The first guess from the Associated Press agency is that there are some 200 dead in the capital. Radio Pan-America says 140 dead in Huarás, too. But with the shock measured at 7.75 on the Richter scale they are surely being extremely conservative.

Sure enough, word starts coming in of appalling devastation – there are estimates that 85 per cent of all houses have been destroyed in the Huarás region alone. The Peruvian Air Force reports whole communities have simply vanished after dams burst and rockslides eliminate flimsy adobe homes. At this rate, experts say, the death toll must be huge. They are right. The next day the Peruvian government puts the figure at more like 30,000. Foreign experts sombrely concur. The worst is confirmed when President General Juan Velasco Alvarado goes on national television and radio to announce it.

The epicentre is officially placed at 210 miles north-west of Lima, in the Pacific Ocean, off Chimbote. The details don't really matter: it is a disaster. A cloud of dust sits over the entire northern region at 18,000 feet, darkening the sky like the onset of the apocalypse. Aid and relief workers fly in from Chile and elsewhere.

Earthquake survival people will tell you that, unless you have a solid doorframe to stand under – which most Peruvians don't – the safest place to be during a major tremor is outside. Unfortunately the quake started at 3.24 p.m. local time. Just about the whole country was indoors listening to the radio for the opening

157

World Cup game. Cruelly, the whole nation had come to a stand-still. Peru's achievement in reaching the finals had been a cause for national celebration. With only a rich few having TVs, the country had become glued to its radio sets as the build-up to the tournament began.

Over coming days there are amazing tales of survival and heroism – the Peruvian Air Force find 2,500 survivors in the city of Yungay clinging to a mountainside cemetery after their whole town was demolished by a wall of ice water.

On Wednesday 3rd, Lima is rocked again by a huge aftershock and will continue to be so over coming days. It is a catastrophe of biblical proportions. With phone lines down or jammed both in and out of the country, the Peruvian footballers in Mexico are at their wits' end. Information from Peru is variable. There is no confirmed news of the fate of loved ones. The players do their best to find out, but the country is in chaos.

To a man they decide that, for all the World Cup's worth, this is no place to be when their kinfolk are in such peril. They ask to leave Mexico immediately. As news from the Peruvian camp itself becomes muddled and confused, one message does get through to the players: it is from President Alvarado. For the good of Peru, for the sake of national morale, the team must play on . . .

On 2 June, when the team takes the field against Bulgaria, the opener in Group Four, they have black ribbons pinned to their jerseys. Somehow, in Latin America, football and tragedy never seem far apart.

Understandably, the minds of the Peruvian players are not really on the game. They gift a goal to Bulgaria after twelve minutes and then another five minutes into the second half. The 18,000 in the León stadium are sympathetic to their plight. Even the Bulgarians look guilty about taking advantage of a clearly distracted foe. Then, suddenly, a strange calm seems to descend on the jittery Peruvians. Against all reasonable odds, they play twenty-two minutes of the most sublime football in the tournament, comparable even to the mighty Brazil.

A minute after the second Bulgarian goal, Alberto Gallardo thumps the ball home off the underside of the crossbar. On fifty-six minutes, a free kick is blasted in by the captain, Hector Chumpitaz.

Then, on seventy-three minutes, Teofilio Cubillas jinks his way through half the Bulgarian team to crash the ball home before disappearing under a pile of joyous Peruvian bodies: 3–2.

It is wonderful stuff and none other than Helmut Schoen, the watching West German manager, declares it to be the best international football he has seen since the Brazilians in 1958. Which is some compliment.

The Bulgarians – for whom Dermndjiev and Bonev had scored – can barely believe it. It will take a long time for Peru to recover from their tragedy but, for just a brief moment, the national spirit has been lifted.

Group Four is the most interesting one in the World Cup. Based 200 miles north of Mexico City in the provincial town of León, it has an air of self-containment about it. Out in the desert. Hot, but with a cooling breeze. Not the stifling airlessness of the big urban grounds or the mountain surrealism of Puebla/Toluca. But at 5,934 feet, it's marginally higher than Guadalajara, and the runners-up in England's group will have to come here to contest a quarter-final.

With a 30,000 capacity, the Guanajuato Stadium is moderately sized – one side stacked high with a teetering wall of executive suites and commentary positions, as if designed by some kid let loose with a pile of matchboxes. But there's a real World Cup atmosphere about León, and its Group Four teams are the most eclectic mix of the lot. In the true spirit of the tournament they couldn't be more diverse – Latin American Peru, communist Bulgaria, African Morocco and European giants West Germany.

Peru are perhaps the most intriguing team in the whole tournament. No one ever doubted these South Americans had talent, but under manager Didi, a Brazilian, and star forward of their 1958 and 1962 World Cup triumphs, they have welded the fancy stuff on to solid teamwork. Indeed, England played no small part in this transformation, Didi using the '66 winners as a shining example of what can be done by playing as a unit.

It has worked handsomely. Peru's place in the finals comes at the expense of mighty Argentina, whom they beat and drew with en route, heading a three-team group, consigning Argentina to bottom spot, below Bolivia. Before the tournament, Peru drew 0–0 with the USSR and could quite easily have won it, and have looked good in the friendlies they've played against club sides. What's more, the players have lived all their lives at altitude and wonder what all the fuss is about.

Hector Chumpitaz, the captain and centre half, plays as a free sweeper behind the defence and, as has been evidenced, can swerve a demon free kick; Hugo Sotil of Deportivo Municipal is the top scorer in the national side; his strike partner is Teofilio Cubillas; Alberto Gallardo of Sporting Cristal is a left winger who has played with both AC Milan and Cagliari. Then there is the twenty-two-year-old outside right. Jimmy Hill reckons Julio Baylon could be the star of the tournament, having amazing touch for such a big boy – 'the new Pelé'. A kiss of death indeed.

Fitting in with their mystique, Peru play in an outfit unlike any other in international football: an all-white strip with a red diagonal sash. Snazzy stuff.

The Bulgarians were never going to be pushovers, though, which makes the opening result all the more impressive for Peru. Bulgaria first qualified in 1962 but played no significant part then or in 1966. But they reached the Olympic Final in Mexico and drew 1–1 with England at Wembley in 1968. They have a solid base in that most of the players are drawn from a single club, CSKA Sofia, the army team which has won the championship ten times in the last fourteen years – all gratefully indulged by the Bulgarian government, which ensures no conflict between club and country.

Their manager is a veterinary surgeon, Dr Stefan Bozhkov, who won fifty-three national caps himself, although it is perhaps telling that their new star is their young goalkeeper Simeon Simeonov, who impressed Bobby Charlton when they came to London. But they have three great forwards: Dimiter Jakimov, with fifty-one caps; target man Georgi Asparoukhov, who's been chased by the big Spanish and Italian clubs; and especially a goal machine by the name of Peter Jekov, who scored thirty-six League goals last season – highest scorer in Europe no less.

Bozhkov seriously reckons that Bulgaria can reach the semi-finals and that once they have qualified from the group, anything can happen. It may be possible. After all, they made it to the World Cup out of a ten group ahead of Holland and Poland, and several players were in the Olympic team. They also held West Germany to a mere 1–0 in recent months and beat Peru 3–1 in Lima (losing a second game 5–3). Though there were other reverses. They drew 1–1 with Mexico and lost to them three days later 2–0. Interestingly, they also lost 3–0 to Morocco in a warm-up in December.

For the Moroccans, this is a major scalp. Unknowns, they are the first African team to make it this far since Egypt in 1934. Dab hands in the art of the coin toss (overcoming Tunisia), they nevertheless came through a tortuous qualifying group ahead of the emerging Nigerians. Good work for their manager, former Yugoslav international Blagoviev Vidinic. Last time they played West Germany, they lost 5–1 – but in a cup tournament, who knows, anything can happen. Kassou Allal, the goalkeeper, is probably the best player. Their one outfield star is captain Driss Bamous, of FAR Rabat, a midfielder who is being courted by a number of French clubs.

Confounding all expectations, 500–1 outsiders Morocco, for the first hour of their 1970 tournament, play like world beaters. For the last twenty-four minutes of that hour, it seems that all their wildest dreams have come true. For, in their first game, on 3 June, against the mighty Germans, before a paltry 8,000 crowd, they take the lead – Houmane Jarir seizing upon disorganisation in the German defence to tuck the ball home. Hottges heads it casually back across the box right to his feet, like the clumsiest of Sunday League players, and his error and Jarir's strike send the Moroccans into euphoria. Some players visibly weep with joy. And the Germans in the crowd, who'd been blowing plastic bugles, fall into stunned silence. Seeing little Morocco, skilfully and with great guile, toying with the mighty Teutons is great cause for alarm.

What can you say about the Germans except that they are the most consistently successful European side. They've qualified for every World Cup except the first one and the 1950 tournament (when they were banned for five years due to their misdemeanours of 1939–45). Winners in 1954, finalists in 1966, semi-finalists in 1934 and 1958, they have not lost a single qualifying match since they were let back into the fold after the war.

Of course, England beat them in the final four years ago, but Germany's overall World Cup record is superior. Plus, in 1968, in a friendly in Hannover, the last time the two teams met, they finally got their first win over England – quite astonishingly, England's first defeat on the mainland since 1963. England rather disingenuously dismissed the result as not being fair due to the fact that it came on the way to the 1968 European Nations Cup Finals in Italy and they had several key players rested. Plus, the only goal of the game, from a long-range Beckenbauer shot, took a bit of a jammy deflection off Labone.

Typically, the Germans are meticulous in their planning. Like many of the competing nations, last summer they came on tour to Mexico and got a 0–0 draw with the host nation, but unlike in England where the priorities of country over club were reversed after the amnesty of 1966, the Deutsche Fussball Bund has gone out of its way to ensure that the top players are always available for internationals, harmonising the whole set-up, getting the players together for regular training sessions even when they don't have a fixture. The only problem is with the availability of forward Helmut Haller and cultured right back Karl Heinz Schnellinger, who both play in Italy, but have not been absent from squad training as often as they might.

Their recent form is down to Helmut Schoen, who has provided continuity to the reign of Sepp Herberger, retiring as the national supremo in 1964. Herberger had been in charge of the national team that won the World Cup in 1954 and had been in the job for twenty-eight years, a world record. Schoen had been 'Uncle Sepp's' chief assistant for six years and was an automatic choice when the transition came. It wasn't a painless baptism, drawing with Cyprus in a World Cup qualifier (equalising in the ninety-second minute) and some erratic form over his first full season put his job in doubt. He has since steadied the ship and West Germany are back as a leading power. An ex-international himself, Schoen has vast experience as a tactician.

His team are no spring chickens, though. Like England, seven of the '66 finalists are still in the squad and all take the field against Morocco, but Haller injures his shoulder and seems doubtful for the rest of the tournament. Uwe Seeler, the captain, is thirty-four (playing in his fourth World Cup), as is Karl Heinz Schnellinger, but both are in good shape.

Tellingly, the Germans are the only senior team in the tournament not to be paid appearance money or win bonuses. They were consulted about it in '66 and voted it down unanimously. For them, the honour of playing for their country is enough. *Deutschland über Alles.*

Schulz can still sweep, film-star handsome Beckenbauer and the tireless powerhouse Wolfgang Overath run the midfield, little blond Berti Vogts is a solid left back. And, just to irk the English, their two star wingers, Reinhard Libuda and Johannes Lohr, are nicknamed 'Stan' and 'Tom', after Finney and Matthews. But, more than anything, they have found themselves just about the most effective marksman in the world. Number 13 may be unlucky for some but, for Gerd Müller, the stocky little forward from Bayern Munich, it has yielded nothing but goals. Müller is the German Jimmy Greaves – rarely breaks into a sweat, does little to help in team play, is a goal-hanger of the highest order. Twenty-four-years-old, he was considered a little too raw for the 1966 squad. But he's got 138 goals in five years in the Bundesliga, and a record 38 last season. In Germany they say there should be a law against him inside the penalty area. Müller also has a physique proportioned like that of a circus midget: tree-trunk thighs (he's called 'fatso' by his teammates), but, like the finest big-top tumbler, he can spring from a standing jump over men half as tall again to volley, head or gymnastically thump the ball home.

Not that the Germans don't have their fair share of problems too. With Seeler the perennial star of the team and long-term centre forward, roughly the equivalent of Bobby Charlton, whom he resembles physically to a degree, the arrival of Müller, quite a cocky little bugger, has led to an inevitable clash of personalities, if not roles.

At one point, neither player was speaking to the other. Schoen resolved the issue by making the pair share a room, leading to a complete transformation: they are now the best of buddies. And, more importantly, concerning the team, he has pulled Seeler back into a withdrawn Charlton-type role, which suits his slowing pace, while still allowing him to sneak in and score a fair amount of goals, adding to the inevitable hatful that the now unencumbered Müller racks up.

Despite the early setback against Morocco, slowly, steadily, the Germans step up a gear and roll on, exactly according to plan. Against a massed defence, in which Lamrani and Benkhrif barely move out of their own penalty box, the Germans advance, shots rain in, and the goalkeeper Allal performs the greatest prolonged series of goalkeeping heroics of the tournament. But, such is the will of God. In the sixty-fifth minute Seeler scores an acrobatic goal, swinging at the ball in a crowded area while falling backwards.

Allal has done well, but with substitute wingers Grabowski and Lohr now on and flying, it is only a matter of time. In the seventy-eighth minute, Grabowski crosses from the right. It looks overhit, but it's deliberate: the ball sails over the box to Lohr on the left, who then sends a looping reverse header back across the face of the goal. The keeper is at sixes and sevens, the defenders rooted to the spot. 'Tom's' header arcs over, comes off the bar and Müller springs from a standing position to head home. The gallant Moroccans submit at 2–1 but earn themselves a great deal of credit.

The Germans have demonstrated their ability to effect a reversal of fortune with clinical efficiency. For England, though they don't know it yet, the ground of León and the exact manner of those German goals will assume major significance...

Ten miles from the Azteca, in the Maria Barbara Motel, which backs on to a noisy eight-lane motorway, sit the part-timers of El Salvador. Their home is a half-built concrete shell, the staff fawn over the far richer guests from America, and there is yet no restaurant or room service – bus boys working in relays from a restaurant up the street. But, as El Salvador insist, they are happy. After all, they will be the best-supported team (aside from the hosts) in Mexico, with one in five of the visiting fans coming from their homeland – 40,000 in all. They, like their team, will have arrived by bus.

The players have extra reason to be happy. After a resolved dispute with their FA, they have learned they will get £300 a man for playing in the group matches, plus £100 extra for every point earned in Group One. Tellingly, there is no contingency for advancement beyond that. Still, with Salvador Mariona in defence, Ramon Martínez in attack and their best player, Mauricio Rodríguez, another goal addict ('He danced with laughter, shaking a gollywog hairdo,' says Desmond Hackett in the *Daily Express*), they'll give it their best shot. Coach Gregorio Bundio, an Argentinian, has tried to instil in them a Latin close-passing style. What more can they do?

Their first opponents, Belgium, are going to be difficult to overcome. Much better than their 3–1 February defeat by England

164

suggests, they are built in the West German style – hard and fast. Like all the European teams, heat and altitude could be a problem, but having come through their own qualifying Group of Death, knocking out Spain and Yugoslavia, they, along with Romania, are another team for which the label 'dark horses' might carry weight. Under their forceful coach Raymond Goethals, they have got a solid platform based on useful midfielders Odilon Polleunis and Van Moer – the 'Billy Bremner of Belgium'. There are other quality players – Johan Devrindt and Wilfred Puis. Their star is undoubtedly striker Paul van Himst. He is something of a prodigy. In the mighty Anderlecht team by sixteen, he won his first international cap at seventeen – debuting in a 1962 World Cup qualifier against Sweden – and was Belgian Footballer of the Year in his first full season. And though he didn't score in the Fairs Cup Final against Arsenal, he's a striker of true world class, linking well with Devrindt.

Like El Salvador, the Belgians have been having their own football war – bloodless, admittedly. Three rival groups of players in the squad have been vying for the affections (and subsidies) of German boot manufacturers. Two of the groups have been rewarded by rival companies, the other one hasn't and is resentful.

On 3 June in a half-full, subdued Azteca, despite the best efforts of their fans, El Salvador succumb to the Belgians 3–0. Belgium take the ball and keep it for virtually the whole of the match, and goals by Van Moer (two) and Lambert put paid to the Salvadoreans, for whom it still stands as a heroic moment.

As Belgium know, the big test is the next one, Saturday's encounter between themselves and the Soviet Union. As the two quality teams in the group, in theory it is the championship decider. Mexico, on paper, are not in the same class and should finish third. Though Mexico's home advantage is enormous, especially given the stifling atmosphere and climatic conditions. The sheer will to win and that vast Azteca crowd – vociferous, hostile and worth far more than the proverbial extra goal start – is one hell of a boon. If this competition will go down as the first thirteen-man tournament, Mexico must feel like they're taking the field with all of them on it already.

After their uninspired performance against Mexico in the curtain raiser, the strongly fancied Russians now find themselves underwhelming most observers. The *Daily Mail*, ahead of the clash with

Belgium, and given that Belgium are the only team with a win (albeit against El Salvador), try to put a dramatic spin on the whole thing. 'Russia facing fight for survival,' they proclaim, which is hardly fair. But their manager Gavril Katchalin does not underestimate the challenge. Another draw and it could be a three-way split between Russia, Belgium and Mexico. And, if it goes to goal average, it could all come down to how many each side whack past the Salvadoreans.

The Russians should not beat themselves up too much. Though not the sexiest team, a massive 90,000 still swell the Azteca to watch Mexico's rivals do battle. And what they see is a Soviet team firing on all cylinders. Whereas the noon kick-off at the Azteca had been played in blazing sunshine, the late afternoon start brings with it a similar case of four o'clock shadow to that at Guadalajara, cutting the pitch right down the middle, goalmouth to goalmouth. Belgium are in all white, Russia in their usual red tops, but with black shorts, according to a loosely applied FIFA diktat that, in addition to shirts, neither shorts nor socks should clash.

Belgium kick off and the game begins at a frantic European pace. Only a few minutes in, Belgium nearly get off to a great start. A cross comes over from the right and the unmarked number 8, Van Moer, with a free header, plants it straight at goalie Kavazashvili, who deflects it straight back out to him. Almost impossible to miss, Van Moer takes an awkward straight-legged swing at it with his wrong foot and blasts it against the crossbar, the ball bouncing back into play but out of harm's way.

Belgium will not get a better chance to take the lead. On fourteen minutes, up at the other end, Bishovets, in full cry, takes a shot from twenty-five yards and it cannons into the net past the helpless goalie Piot, wearing a big floppy cap more suitable to a street urchin in a Charlie Chaplin film.

In the second half the conditions start to take their toll. The Belgians, who, bizarrely, are wearing long sleeves, roll them up and puff hard. The Russians, in their old-fashioned outfit, just suck it up and switch into machine mode. Fortunately, the shade now completely covers the pitch, but its still tough going. Russia mark their dominance with a goal by Asatiani on fifty-nine minutes. The big number 11, moving in from the inside-left position on the corner of the box, takes the ball, holds, feints and then streaks through, accurately placing a left-foot shot into the far corner of the net, beyond Piot and his mighty cap. Six minutes later, from a similar position on the right, Bishovets takes it, bamboozles three Belgian defenders and unleashes a screamer of a shot into the top left-hand corner: 3–0.

If the Belgians believe it is over, they have another think coming. Contrary to the dreary Russian stereotype, this is a flair team they're up against. The Russian number 21, Khmelnitski, hares down the left, passes over to Evriuzhikhin on the right, who chips it back in for the still thundering Khmelnitski to steer a diving, glancing header along the ground into the net, causing the winger to get quite animated in his celebration.

To their credit, the Belgians don't give up, but with all players dead on their feet there are few challenges going in by now. The crowd are already filing out. Five minutes from time and with the game at walking pace, number 11 Van Moer jinks inside from the right wing, runs to the centre and takes a left-foot shot from thirty yards. It arcs towards the goal, dips under the keeper, hits the post and bounces out. Only a handful of games into the tournament, it is evident that long-range shots are causing all sorts of problems, deceiving goalkeepers left, right and centre. From three yards, Lambert can't miss. Before rows of empty seats behind the Russian goal, he thumps in the rebound, turns and walks away solemnly. Van Himst gives him a pat on the back, but it is an empty gesture.

Poor old Belgium. With Van Moer and Puis in midfield they had looked good in the early stages, but with a 4–2–4 formation they had left themselves undermanned in the middle. Manager Raymond Goethals, rather churlishly, finds good reason for the defeat, blaming it on the long, thick grass. But it was the same for both teams. The Russians had outplayed them. They were solid in defence, marshalled by Shesternev; the midfield had looked busy, with Muntian and, especially, Asatiani. And their success is not lost on the British press – 'From Russia with love,' coos the *Observer*. 'Top form Russians scare the bookies,' says the *Daily Express*.

The next day Goethals is a little more gracious. 'There's not a team in the tournament that could have lived with them on this form,' he says. 'They were fantastic.'

Belgium will thus have it all to do in the final game against

Mexico, assuming, as is very likely, that Mexico make the most of it against El Salvador ...

El Salvador, being the whipping boys, have generated quite a bit of sympathy among the neutrals. After their first defeat, much attention was given to keeper Alfredo Magaña, who had gamely thrown himself at every Belgian shot, including stopping one with his face. Magaña joked about the defeat, claiming that, had he been playing up front, which he has been known to do on occasion, his team would have won.

Only one thing is absolutely certain about El Salvador – they have the longest anthem in the tournament. As it comes to an end, the Mexican players run off to start the kick-in only to realise that it was merely a dramatic pause and that there are several more bars to follow. They politely come to attention again, wherever they stand. Fortunately for all, the 1970 organisers have done away with the tradition, employed up to and including 1966, of playing the anthems at the end of the game as well.

The chief change to the Mexican team has been brought about by press pressure – the recall of striker Enrique Borja, nephew of President Ordaz himself. In spite of Mexico's nepotistic reconstruction, El Salvador do well. In the bright noonday sunshine they look lively. In the ninth minute Rodríguez hits the post, then Calderón, with successive shots, and the underdogs are enjoying their moment. Indeed, too much for the capacity crowd, which begins to grow increasingly restless, the atmosphere charged with tinderbox combustibility.

Two minutes before half-time, their influence becomes as influential as that of their president. Referee Mahmoud Kandil of the United Arab Republic awards El Salvador a free kick midway inside their own half on the right touchline. As the Salvadorean players move upfield, Pérez, the Mexican midfielder, either misunderstanding the referee or just being impudent, comes across and takes it for *Mexico*. To the aghast El Salvador players who have all pushed forward, Pérez knocks it up to Padilla on the left, who centres. There are two Mexican forwards completely alone in the box, not a defender in sight, quite possibly offside. Borja misses the ball completely and falls flat on his back, but Valdivia is more sure, sidefooting it easily past a disbelieving Magaña. Inexplicably – or rather due to a stadium that erupts with delight, shaking the very earth – the referee allows the goal to stand.

On the pitch, all hell breaks loose. Leaving the ball right where it is, sitting in the back of the net, the El Salvador players, Magaña included, besiege the referee, following him all the way back to the halfway line, extremely agitated and, as the *Daily Express* puts it, invoking the spirit of the time, 'gesticulating like angry strike leaders'.

As linesman Keith Dunstan of Jamaica retrieves the ball and takes it upfield to place on the centre spot, there are still seven players round Kandil, blocking him whichever way he turns. They are furious. The number 9 points up to the VIP box like a wronged tennis player calling for the tournament referee to overrule. Another taps the ball off the spot, forcing the ref to collect it and replace it. With seven players around him, he starts issuing cautions, or threatening them, no one is really sure. Where he would begin with his disciplining, too, is another matter. The El Salvador players volunteer themselves, turning their backs and pointing their fingers at their numbers – 10, 8, 11, 6 and the ref gives up on that strategy. The number 3 rolls the ball back off the spot and, with a huge kick, hoofs it into the stand. The crowd love it, lapping it all up, goading their foe and delighting in their country's first goal. The Mexican players, who have retreated well inside their half, mind their own business.

Fortunately for Kandil, an 'out' presents itself. He checks his watch and blows for half-time. And though the row continues on the way off the pitch with scuffles in the tunnel, he's got himself off the hook.

In the second half, a broken and demoralised El Salvador kick off, play the ball rearward and proceed to try possession football – not intent on scoring, but simply in spoiling the game. But it doesn't work. Their tails up, the Mexicans sweep forward – without nephew Borja, too, who, fluffing his chance at immortality, has been replaced by López. Valdivia beats Magaña with a daisy-cutter from just inside the box and, at the other end, goalkeeper Calderón whips the crowd into a fervour. Later, Fragoso half-volleys home a nod-down by López. Towards the end, Basaguren adds a fourth.

Amid scenes of wild celebration, Mexico are now topping the group, and the whole country works itself into a patriotic fervour.

One supporter who questions the merits of winning under such dodgy circumstances is duly shot dead (following a pattern set by the fatal stabbings of two Mexicans in 1968 who doubted Mexico's ability to win the Olympic football tournament), and everyone is very happy.

No one needs to tell El Salvador about the ramifications of football matches. The next day their captain, Salvador Mariona, issues an apology for his team's behaviour.

To their credit, El Salvador, down and already out, still make a game of it against the USSR. Having already beaten Belgium, Russia just need the points, not the goals, and so, resting several key players, amble to a 2–0 win playing in second gear.

The general public seems uninterested. Only 15,000 turn up, no more than a smattering in a 106,000-capacity stadium. And, as rain begins to pour in the second half, it seems an appropriate backdrop for El Salvador's farewell. They fought a war to get here and nearly caused another one against Mexico. You can't say they didn't make an impression . . .

With Russia through, the final game between Mexico and Belgium is effectively a cup tie, the winner joining the Soviets in the quarter-finals. For Mexico there is an added incentive. If they beat Belgium by two goals, thus winning the group, they will stay based at the massively advantageous Azteca. To advance, Belgium must win. And the thought that they will do so is one – for abiders of law and order – too awful to contemplate.

For the game between Mexico and Belgium, the Azteca is packed to the rafters. When the teams come out, drums and trumpets blare like the prelude to a bullfight, so loudly you can barely hear yourself think.

Both teams are in their change strips, Belgium in all white and Mexico in red shirts, black shorts and socks. They are, much to everyone's secret glee, Borja-less. The players on both sides seem relaxed considering the almost tangible atmosphere. Perhaps, on the part of the Mexicans, it's because they know their fate has been preordained.

From their kick-off, they knock the ball about casually in the midfield. But then, in the fifteenth minute, comes an incident that suggests their thinking is not just wishful. The ball is lobbed forward into the Belgian box and ricochets to Valdivia. Jeck beats him to the ball and slides it into touch and, with the ball at least three yards away, Valdivia falls over Jeck's legs. A couple of Mexicans raise their arms in a half-hearted appeal, but it is enough for the ref. Norberto Angel Coerezza of Argentina blows for a penalty.

The crowd go wild. So do the Belgians. And, making the El Salvador protest in the last Mexican game look like polite objection, the Belgian defenders surround Coerezza and bundle him into the goalnet, the ball again booted into the crowd. The linesman runs over to help his comrade but is blocked out and the Belgians, whose every move was vigorously booed and hissed, now start screeching like savages themselves.

Valdivia decides to lend credibility to the decision by staying down, embellishing it by trying to get to his feet and collapsing, like a hamming pro wrestler. Number 11, Padilla, adding to the melodrama, runs to the touchline and gestures for a stretcher while Valdivia, who'd first been rubbing his leg, now clutches his stomach and writhes.

The Belgians don't let up, pushing the ref this way and that, and Señor Coerezza even swings a defensive punch. The Belgian players mock him, laughing at him, rubbing thumb and forefingers together in bribery gestures. And when the teams go off at half-time, goalie Piot will be booked for his gesticulating.

It takes a full two minutes for the game to be restarted. But the ball is placed, Peña takes the spot-kick and the stadium explodes as Piot dives to his left but doesn't quite reach it.

It was illegal, for Fragoso had run right into the area when the kick was taken, but then it was never a penalty anyway. The crowd don't care: newspapers are set on fire, sombreros are set on fire and flung out to fly like crippled spacecraft in some Hollywood B-picture, the people in the lower tiers praying that they are not on the flight path.

All Mexico have to do now is keep eleven men behind the ball for the rest of the game and hope that an angry Belgium fail to find a way through. Ten minutes from the end, Belgium get their best chance. Substitute Devrindt beats Calderón with a lob, but it just misses. The stadium is thick with smoke, even thicker with abuse for the Belgians who have been ground down throughout. And so it remains, 1–0, and Mexico are through to the quarter-finals. The Azteca has never witnessed such euphoria.

At the post-match press conference, Cárdenas, looking cool in shades and chewing gum, salutes the victory and says he hopes that they'll play the Italians. The chainsmoking Goethals, meanwhile, boycotts it, lest he say anything he might regret. He puts out a statement instead: 'The penalty was the worst I have ever seen,' he rants. 'Nor have I ever experienced such a hostile, biased crowd.'

The Mexicans refuse to let anyone rain on their parade.

'After the match we were down in the tunnel area trying to speak to Piot,' remembers David Lacey. 'The Mexican officials in charge of the press conference almost got the armed guards to usher us away.'

It is the biggest moment in Mexican sporting history, the biggest party Mexico has seen since the last revolution. And, just to embellish proceedings, that very day, Mexican Pedro Rodríguez wins the Belgian Grand Prix (in a British-built BRM car).

That night over a million people take to the streets in one amorphous mass of celebration. The Zócalo Square is packed, the huge ornate statues and fountains along the Paseo de la Reforma are scaled and, in the true spirit of sporting triumph, cars are wrecked, windows are smashed and buses set on fire. It takes the Belgian coach four hours to drive out of the ground alone. Motorcycle fans hurtle at break-neck speed into the throng in a celebratory frenzy, mowing down revellers. By morning there will be six dead, 8,200 hurt and hundreds of thousands of dollars' worth of damage. Absolute bedlam.

'Not merely because a very average football team had reached the last eight but because it was for the first time in a long time they'd been able to go out and stamp and shout and jump up and down,' says Lacey, stuck somewhere in the middle of it all. 'Just the joy they had at being able to express themselves on *anything*.'

The victory is all too much for one happy chappy, the warden of a maximum-security prison in Chilpancingo. Running around firing a gun in the air, he releases 142 of Mexico's most dangerous criminals in a patriotic frenzy – this used as a mitigating circumstance at his subsequent trial and acquittal.

'I've never seen an evening like that evening,' adds Barry Davies. 'The place was absolutely jumping. People of every age, size, description who could lay his hands on a Mexican flag and could beat on something – "ME-HI-CO . . .!" '

In Group Two Italy and Uruguay look the favourites. Neither play with the passion of Israel or Sweden, who, for all their efforts, lack the ability to control a game totally and smother it to their satisfaction, as do both Italy and Uruguay.

Of the two heavyweights, Uruguay look the better, if only because Italy had seemed a little shaky against Sweden. The test now is the game between them which, given their attributes, looks to be a stifling, slow war of attrition. Uruguay are now without Rocha, who looks certain to miss the rest of the tournament. Italy are minus centre half Commuardo Niccolai, who was carried off against Sweden, but have a strong replacement in Roberto 'Baby-face' Rosato of AC Milan.

There is a common approach towards the game from both sides. With each having notched up one win already and both confident of victory in their final games – they'll quite happily settle for a draw. The winners will stay in Toluca, tucked away where you can carry on doing your business quietly, perhaps progressing through the tournament by stealth, benefiting from higher altitude when coming down to the Azteca for the semi-final. Go to the Azteca now, however, and at least you'll feel like you're in a World Cup. The only team either would be reluctant to play in the Azteca would be Mexico, with the ferocious crowd and inevitably susceptible referee. However, Uruguay and Italy are both used to being the bad boys.

At any rate, neither seems to care. Both teams know exactly which side their bread is buttered. A draw it shall be, and a 0–0 one at that. Stocky little Luis Cubilla, who had tormented Israel, barely breaks into a dribble – certainly tries none of his flashy bending free kicks that had drawn gasps in the first game. Indeed, the Uruguayan forwards generally, who had peppered the Israel goal and had poor old Vissoker flapping at everything, seem under strict orders to keep the lid on it. For Italy Riva, too, seems on a tight rein in a Rivera-less 7–2–1 formation.

The 35,000 crowd in Puebla, there to see two of the favourites go hammer and tongs at each other, respond with boos, catcalls and howls. The teams don't give a damn. It's a job well done.

You can't blame the Israelis and the Swedes for getting a little miffed about all this. Sweden had at least tried to make a game of it against the Italians, the lone Azzurri goal a goalkeeping mistake more than anything conjured out of great attacking play. The amateurs of Israel, too, certainly gave mighty Uruguay a run for their money. The only solution for each team in the vain hope of qualifying now is to go at it blood and thunder in the hope of a victory and the off-chance one of the favourites slips up in the last game.

The enthusiasm is perhaps a little excessive, both sides making it a trying afternoon for Ethiopian ref Seyouri Tarekegn, who at times loses control of the game. There is a litany of fouls and off-the-ball incidents, each side as bad as the other. By half-time, the tiny 5,000 Toluca crowd have barely seen anything resembling a football match. Throw in the preceding day's lack of spectacle at Puebla and they might be forgiven for asking when, if ever, the World Cup is coming to town.

In the fifty-fourth minute they get a rare glimpse of it. The Swedish right back Selander runs up the right wing, squares across the box and Turesson turns it in. With the Swedes sneering in their celebrations, the blood pounds hard in Israeli temples and they throw everything forward. Soon Spiegler is through on goal, challenging for a difficult ball. The keeper, S. G. Larsson (who replaced Hellström after his poor display in the opener), dives to get there first, but doesn't gather it cleanly. And, as Spiegler lunges at the loose ball, he kicks Larsson in the head. There is no intent to foul, and, though it undoubtedly hurts, it looks worse than it is. Larsson thinks about it for a second, realises how it probably appears, and flings himself melodramatically to the turf. With the clock ticking, Spiegler has no time for such nonsense. He picks up the ball, places it for a free kick and urges the Swedes to get on with it. The Swedes, meanwhile, descend on him and, with Spiegler's hand half extended for a make-up handshake, one defender takes his thumb and bends it back against his wrist. As another ruck breaks out the ref calls the captains together.

Spiegler soon gets his revenge. From about twenty-five yards out he blasts an equaliser past Larsson in a manner similar to the goal that beat Hellström in the first game: yet another long-range deceiver.

The 1–1 draw is fair but not beneficial to either party, though it is greeted with joy in the Israeli camp, whose expectations so far have been more than exceeded.

Written off now as out, both Sweden and Israel nevertheless still have slim chances of advancing. Italy need just a point against Israel to win the group. The Swedes can join them if they beat Uruguay by two clear goals – Uruguay so far having conceded none. No one's banking on it, but stranger things have happened . . .

Chapter 11

The Boys from Brazil

Sunday, 7 June 1970

England, or rather Sir Alf Ramsey, claim to be not particularly impressed with Brazil's performance against Czechoslovakia. Possibly kidology, but then Ramsey has never really given himself over to anything so sophisticated as gamesmanship. Indeed, in a TV interview before departing for Mexico he stated that he would *never* cheat, not even at tiddlywinks.

Ramsey is not alone in his assessment of Brazil. The *Daily Mail*, not for the first time somewhat out of step with the other newspapers, proclaims, 'England smile at shoddy spectacular,' and 'Brazil score four in farce.'

Privately, of course, England are taking Brazil extremely seriously. Beating them will not only prove that they are better than the pretenders, but give an enormous psychological advantage should they meet in the final. Plus, the winners of the group will get to stay in Guadalajara through the quarters and semis.

Though right now England have a more immediate concern – getting Keith Newton and Terry Cooper ready for the big showdown. The loss of a first-choice player – *two* first-choice players – would be a vexing question for any manager. But whereas most sides would be breathing a gentle sigh that it was only a full back who was out – not the most crucial position on the pitch – under Ramsey the full back has become linchpin. Maybe it's because Ramsey was one himself and knows what a thankless task it is. In Alf's new England, the number 2 and 3 shirts are king, and have been ever since he devised a system of play that did away with the traditional outside right and left – hence the 'wingless wonders'.

Not that Alf is anti-winger. Indeed, he's tried several over the years. John Connelly, Terry Paine and Ian Callaghan all played in the group stages in 1966. Peter Thompson and Ian Storey-Moore have featured in the run-up to 1970. Alf has remarked in the past that, had he found wide players good enough, he'd have used them without hesitation. But the days of Finney and Matthews are no more (and, with club sides now aping Ramsey's strategy, good wingers are at a premium). But if England could win the World Cup without wingers last time, there's no reason to think they can't do so again.

Alf's methodology stems from his old days as Ipswich manager. It was hit upon largely by default. The wide players he inherited there – basically Third Division journeymen – were either too old or too slow to take on top-class defenders as Ipswich rose up through the Football League. Rather than subject his wingers to constant failure in their attempts to beat their man, get to the by-line and cross the ball, he avoided the problem altogether by getting his wide players to stay deep and hit high diagonal balls into the box instead – and it had worked a treat.

It had carried over into the England set-up, and with this method he developed his attacking strategy around the type of forward player who could cope with such service – tall, good in the air, and could play with his back to the goal, absorbing kicks from his marker while positioning himself to take delivery, either heading it at goal himself or knocking it down for a nippier colleague. Geoff Hurst was such a player, fitting this pattern far better than a smaller goalpoacher like Jimmy Greaves and retaining the position ever since – even though, on balance, Greaves was far the superior marksman.

The emergence of the 4–3–3 system had confused critics at first as it prevented them from applying traditional positional labels to players like Peters and Ball, who could attack and defend, play wide if need be, and baffled those who saw Bobby Charlton wearing number 9, a 'centre forward', yet playing as the fulcrum of midfield.

In 1970 England tend to play 4–4–2 rather than 4–3–3, and the positional duties are now so familiar, so clearly defined, that new players can slot into the team without any difficulty. Everyone knows his job and Ramsey has picked reserve players who play virtually the same way as the ones they are called upon to replace; footballing doppelgängers to a degree – Bobby Charlton/Colin Bell, Brian Labone/Jack Charlton, Alan Mullery/Nobby Stiles, Bobby

Moore/Norman Hunter, Geoff Hurst/Jeff Astle – and it's a system that suits everyone. Football is a simple game.

At the back there are two central defenders – one to mark (Labone), one to sweep up (Moore). The midfield consists of a deep-lying screener of the defence (Mullery), Ball and Peters on the right and left, Charlton in the centre, pushing up when on attack. And then there are the forwards – Hurst as the afore-mentioned target man and Lee as his bustling side-kick.

But crucially, in the absence of the conventional winger, the part of pumping in the cross ball has now fallen to the full backs: Newton (right) and Cooper (left). When England break and while Moore, Labone and Mullery hold, it is Newton or Cooper who will be found galloping down the wing, collecting a weighted lay-off and running at his opposite number, waiting for the chance to bang the ball into the box – the 'overlapping' full back, as this new role is denoted.

Cooper, in particular, has become a great practitioner of the art, perhaps not surprisingly because he was a left winger when he started out – discarded by Wolves, not faring too well at Leeds either, till Don Revie had a hunch that he might work better in defence. Having become the permanent replacement for Ray Wilson in the England team, he's quietly becoming a bit of a star, too, and is often mentioned by the foreign press as a world-class player alongside Moore, Banks and Charlton (and leaving hapless Wolves to splash out £80,000 on Derek Parkin).

'I remember my first cap against France in '69. I said, "How do you want me to play?" ' says Cooper, making light of it. 'Alf said, "Just go and play like you do for Leeds." And it was easy with the lad that played alongside me, of course, Bobby Moore. Bob used to break the attack up and he'd give me the ball and say, "Go on, Tel, you get at 'em." It was great.'

Cooper, so it seems, will be fit for Brazil. And while the likely loss of Newton is a blow, Wright came on and did well against Romania and there's every reason to believe he can do the same job again.

After their raucous night out on Tuesday, the England squad trains hard at the Atlas club with a good deal of laddish banter to enliven the proceedings. For those with hangovers – which was most of them – the dull and overcast weather was a blessed relief.

And so the training has continued, with all thought now geared to stepping out at noon on Sunday.

'We won't give them any room,' Bobby Moore tells the press. With England currently rock solid at the back, the best defence in the world – although the Italians would disagree – it is highly unlikely Brazil will be afforded the luxury they enjoyed against the wide-open Czechs.

Plus, England have reason to be heartened. The Czechs opened the scoring in the game and could, quite easily, have added about another three had they been more accurate. Of course, England know that Pelé is great, but he comes in and out of a game. The real danger, the *generalissimo*, is Gérson. Shut him up and the flow of chances will be restricted. Good news, then: word is emerging that Gérson, who came off against Czechoslovakia, might not be fit for Sunday.

But there are chastening statistics for England to bear in mind. In the England–Romania game there were only seventeen shots on target by both sides all game. In the Brazil–Czechoslovakia game there were sixty-seven, most of them by Brazil. England's defence will have to be on alert. And it is reckoned in some circles that when you want to place an immovable object in the way of an irresistible force you need only call for one man. Once again, the *Daily Mail* leads the crusade – 'Nobby needed for this job,' it screams, insisting that Terrible Stiles be employed to 'do a Eusebio' (Stiles had marked the Portuguese star out of the '66 semi-final) and work his shin-dappling against Mr do Nascimento.

Alf is unlikely to concur but, Nobby or not, England have a new bounce about them. And just to put that extra spring in their step, on Thursday the Colombian government announces that the Bobby Moore theft case is officially dropped, the conditional nature of Moore's release no longer applicable. 'It was an accusation that needed proof,' says Dr Arturo Caparoso, a Colombian embassy official in Mexico City. 'It was never proved. Moore has no obligation with the embassy. There never was much case.'

Of course, unbeknown at this point, there will be attempts to reopen the case further down the line. But this is an official pardon. The Colombian government itself declares him innocent; nothing that the England camp, FIFA, all the participating parties, and the whole nation back home didn't know already.

For all its confidence in Nobby, the *Daily Mail* is less sure about England's chances overall. 'Sorry, but England won't win the cup!' it claims, having consulted top astrologer Roger Elliot, who's been busy processing all the relevant planetary information. In 1966 everything came good when England exploded into Jupiter smiles on the day they won the trophy. Now, unfortunately, they are mired in the gloom of Saturn. The best they can hope for is third place. It's Brazil and Russia for whom the stars are in alignment.

What the heavens have in store for Messrs Heath and Wilson is anyone's guess, though, frankly, the election's meriting barely a look-in, and the opinion polls are all over the place. Add them all up though and they amount to one thing – Labour are 4.5 per cent in front. 'Tories need a miracle now,' says the *Observer* rather hopefully. Though the proverbial week is a long time in politics.

Wilson has egg on his face again over the confrontation with the nation's doctors and their demand for a 15 per cent pay rise. Heath, meanwhile, is still smarting from the cricket tour being called off and trying to keep the lid on Enoch Powell ('I wouldn't be opposed to a bit more coloured immigration, as long as his name was Pelé,' says a cartoon bovver-boy in the *Daily Mirror*).

The most serious piece of aggro (which could seriously influence the election) is the looming strike in Fleet Street, with the unresolved dispute there threatening to shut down all national newspapers from Tuesday, 9 June – the union SOGAT's 25 per cent pay claim not yet having been met. With talks breaking down, it seems extremely unlikely anything will be settled by the time of the deadline.

Not all are sold on the country's pussyfooting centrist course. Jack Straw, president of the National Union of Students, says he'll vote Labour but doesn't care much for either party scrabbling 'for the same illusory middle ground'. 'For me,' he says, 'it is only through socialism that the world's most pressing economic and social problems can ever be resolved' ...

In the great fuss over the England–Brazil game, people have tended to forget about the other game in the group, which could still have bearing.

On paper, Romania against Czechoslovakia is not exactly a sexy proposition: a dour Eastern European grind. Not so to the locals, however. And on Saturday night a healthy 53,000 turn out to watch the encounter – more than saw the opening England and Brazil games. Maybe it's a sense that the phoney war's now over, or perhaps they've turned out in force to offer encouragement to two sides who, one way or another, could still have a hand in England's demise, especially if one of them emerges with two points.

Both England and Brazil, of course, will be hoping that they cancel each other out with a draw. All the better if it's 0–0. Their hopes will not be without foundation. With the exception of Russia, the Eastern Bloc countries in the tournament so far have not done well: the Czechs, Romanians and Bulgarians all lost their opening games.

The dreariness is not apparent in the surroundings. The Jalisco Stadium, Guadalajara, at noon on Saturday, is as much a blaze of heat and colour as was the opening ceremony at the Azteca. Plus, there's real passion in the way the two teams square up to each other, both in the knowledge that, while the victor still has a chance of advancing to the quarter-finals, for the losers it's bye-bye.

Romania have dropped midfielder Tataru, still exhausted from the England game, and have brought in nippy right winger Neagu. The Czechs are without injured midfielder Hagara and have replaced the banana-shooting forward Adamec, who starts on the bench for disciplinary reasons. Giant, black-clad goalie Viktor is replaced by Vencel.

The Czechs still have nippy Petras. And, as a statement of intent, he does exactly what he did against Brazil. After only three minutes he bamboozles the flat-footed Romanian defence and heads home a Vesely cross. This is only Petras's third full international and already his second goal of the World Cup. Given that he was sent off on his debut in the play-off against Hungary his nascent international career has been pretty eventful. With a three-match ban imposed after the Hungary game, Czechoslovakia even arranged a series of innocuous friendlies just so he would be eligible by the World Cup.

He's quite eye-catching is Petras. In contrast to his conservative teammates, there is something of the peacenik about the twenty-three-year-old locksmith (his day job) – shirt untucked, socks round ankles, sandy hair flapping. On scoring he immediately goes 'into his religious routine', as the *Daily Express* puts it. 'There could have been another prayer meeting after nine minutes,' it continues, pointing to a subsequent Petras miss. Perhaps he was asking for divine help with his digestion. While England have borne the brunt of the criticism for bringing their own food, it has been revealed that the Czechs have imported their own chef to ensure that their players are all fed two steaks a day.

For Romania, the inclusion of the winger Neagu seems to be paying dividends, and as they mount a comeback he makes life difficult for the Czech left back Zlocha, setting up several chances.

As the second half gets under way, the Romanians have a renewed sense of purpose about them. The Czech strategy seems to be to consolidate their goal lead by getting men back behind the ball and looking for Petras on the break. Under normal conditions, it might have worked, but the Czech players, as they showed against Brazil, are not physically cut out for this tournament and become sluggish midway through the half, opening up the game. They bring on Adamec in attack but – stomachs laden with sirloin – they are flagging.

At the end of the first half, for Romania, Dumitrache had hit the bar, warning that a goal might come, and eventually it does. With Nunweiller and Dembrowski scurrying around in the middle, eventually they craft a move from which Neagu turns his marker and fires one in. Then, twelve minutes from the end, Neagu does his stuff once more, dances into the box and is clumsily brought down by Zlocha. The Mexican official, Mr de Leo, the 'four-off' ref, awards a penalty and it is converted by Dumitrache: 2–1 to Romania.

At the end, the ailing Czechs collapse. Barring a miracle, they are out. Romania are still in with a shout ...

For England the result is ambiguous. There are no thoughts of losing to Brazil, naturally, but given such an eventuality, or even if the points are split, then England will be putting themselves under a lot of pressure to win their final game.

Whatever the case, England now know they're in a competition, with Guadalajara in the full throes of World Cup frenzy, their own fans – indulged by the tourist board with free trips to the local tequila factory – mixing merrily with the Brazilians, gathering at the evening watering holes to sing songs together. Any fears that there might be even the remotest bit of trouble have proved unfounded. Local chief of police Colonel Luis Ruvalcaba Hernández, who plays trumpet in a mariachi band, seems unconcerned with such notions. The embassy in Mexico City has sent a British consul 'troubleshooter', Second Secretary Charles Tarrant, to look after the British subjects should they get arrested or become sick, but his only job so far has been to settle a domestic dispute: one football fan husband threatened to leave his wife but was persuaded to stay for the games, (*she* being the one intent on remaining). Irritatingly, for all the hospitality, the British tabloids can't resist pointing out that it was the British who gave the natives the Beautiful Game in the first place, introduced by a Cornish tin miner called Pengelley a hundred years ago (there are still a Frederick, Albert and William Pengelley who work at the Real del Monte mines at Pachuca).

Interest in the forthcoming big match between champions and challengers extends into every facet of Guadalajaran life. The local weekly cockfight and bullfight, which are big news, are expecting dips in attendance due to clashing with Sunday's game. Even the elderly widow of Pancho Villa, who lives near Guadalajara, is known to be showing interest in it. A New Orleans businessman is negotiating to take the two finalists – which he assumes will be England and Brazil – on a tour of the USA.

While there is little or no antagonism between the fans, the passion is becoming a problem. England are having a spot of bother with their own supporters: in the early hours of Friday morning, armed police had to remove some fifty-odd rowdy sombrero-wearing Englanders who had taken over the pool at the Hilton for a midnight swim – this after a 10.30 p.m. curfew placed on the players, all desperately trying to get some shut-eye. And observers remark on how easy it is for the packs of Mexican press, fans and anyone who cares to wander in and out of the hotel, making as much noise as they like round the clock. England could soon regret coming to a city-centre hotel – which, presented with a choice, the players had opted for – rather than locking themselves away in a self-contained camp as many other teams have done.

The Brazilian approach could not be more different. The Suites Caribe, their forty-room motel, a mock-hacienda affair, has been entirely commandeered for their use and is guarded like a fortress. The players can be seen at a distance lounging about on the balcony, but that's as close as anyone can get. They have a fifteen-strong security force watching over them run by Chief Security Officer Major Guarani, part of the military regime. Guarani was the one responsible for turfing João Saldanha off the plane at Rio.

Even a military man, though, can let his short back and sides down when national pride is to be celebrated. Thus, on the day after Brazil's victory over Czechoslovakia, the security cordon is lifted to allow accredited press into the motel for a few hours, provided they have the two official passes required – the FIFA one and the one that the Brazilian FA has issued, the only camp to insist on double jeopardy. Not even the Brazilian press has got through thus far, and so, for the handful allowed in, it is a rare treat. In PR terms, of course, it is a great move, and while the visiting journalists get to fawn over Pelé and have him sign autographs for them, they can also fill their papers with glowing copy about the Brazilian team, right on the eve of the big game.

Paradoxically, for all the machinations of the military dictatorship that surround the Brazilian camp, it is England who score the political own goal. On Friday, when a bunch of Brazilian journalists seek an audience with Ramsey, they are chased away from the Hilton at gunpoint by armed Mexican police.

England can only wish that the same guards exercise such caution on Saturday. For that night good-natured enthusiasm turns into organised chaos. It is common practice in Latin America and deemed perfectly within the realms of gamesmanship to deny your opponents a decent night's kip before a big game. And England, with a busy, open hotel, right in the centre of Guadalajara, pay the penalty. All night long hundreds of Mexican fans lay siege to the Hilton chanting 'Mexico' and 'Brazil' relentlessly and noisily. They blast car horns, beat on dustbin lids and hammer anything else that can send up an almighty din right through till dawn. Mysteriously, the Mexican police, who had been so diligent in shooing away the Brazilian press, now offer no resistance whatsoever as a crowd of Mexican fans runs riot all over the Hilton, at one point even working their way up to the twelfth floor, England's level, banging on some of the doors. With the whole storey appropriated for England's use, some of the England players at the front, the street side, are switched in the middle of the night to rooms at the back. Though the shape of the hotel, accessible three quarters of the way round, still does not afford them much respite from the mob below.

'All night there were about two or three hundred fans outside – horns, klaxons going off,' says Brian Labone. 'And the police didn't do a thing about it. Not making that our excuse, but we didn't get a wink of sleep. We resorted to throwing milk cartons down at the buggers.'

'If you'd have hit someone on the head, it could have been dangerous,' chuckles Jack Charlton. 'And we got bollocked over that. But it *was* frustrating.'

At about 4 a.m. a decoy is attempted by getting some England fans to dress in tracksuits and drive out of the vehicle access gate in the team bus. The crowd follows and the ruse works for a while, though soon the chants go up again.

The long and short of it is that the players are deprived of some essential shut eye. Some, the nervous, light sleepers like Bobby Charlton, manage a couple of hours at best. Banks gets barely a wink. In the morning a furious Ramsey, having already lodged a protest this time yesterday, does so again to FIFA and the Mexican government, but it will not save England now and neither body says they can do much about it.

Up till then, England's preparation had gone well. Off the training pitch they had spent Friday and Saturday nights at the TV studios watching films of their game against Romania and the Brazil–Czechoslovakia encounter. They reserved a chuckle for their old chum Mocanu and his innocent fairy-godmother act against the Czechs – so different from the chap they had encountered four days before. Thrown in for recreational purposes was the elephantine motor-racing film *Grand Prix* which, at three hours, was spread over the two nights. The lads were not particularly impressed – it was keeping them from their cards.

Some have been indulging in their own private pursuits. For Thompson and Sadler, who have carried on diligently with the training, indulging Alf's request that they not flaunt their freedom to break curfews, the only stand they have made is against the order to stay out of the sun. Indeed, the two men are, by now, several shades darker than their colleagues, who are still corralled into the shade by Harold Shepherdson after training. 'Alf told me off. He said, "You should set an example to the rest of the lads,"' says Peter Thompson. 'What I used to do was go up to the roof of the Hilton and lay there. I went up there one day and I fell over somebody. It was Bobby Moore. *He* was up there.'

By now, all the players are in good spirits, except for one: Peter Osgood. On Saturday before the training session, Ramsey announces that the team that finished against Romania will be the one to start against Brazil. Ramsey is never questioned, his word gospel. So, with Newton still crocked, Wright will be starting, as will Osgood, who came on for Francis Lee in the second half. Osgood is beside himself with joy and, in the practice, plays like a demon. Two hours later, at the team meeting, Alf confirms the line-up. Wright is in, sure, but not Osgood. Worse, he is not even among the five subs: Bonetti, Hughes, Astle, Bell and, pleasing the *Daily Mail*, Nobby Stiles. Moore sees that Osgood is upset and has a quiet word with Ramsey, whose original utterance about the prospective line-up had been an innocent slip. Osgood lets his displeasure be known.

Aside from that, England are ready, and, on Sunday morning, they leave the Hilton in their blue boiler suits (like 'trustees out on parole', according to the *Sunday Times*'s Brian Glanville). The atmosphere at the stadium is electric, carnival-like, as fans parade before the game, the England supporters waving their flags, all in good fun. In the stadium Ken Bailey, he of the Union Jack waistcoat, hunting jacket and top hat, messes around with the locals and poses for photographs. There are 72,000 here for this one; the noise is one of vibrant expectancy.

In the bowels of the stadium it's business as usual. The players go through their little routines – Moore calm, quietly urging on the team; Ball getting worked up; Stiles, suiting up for the first time, praying; Bobby Charlton and brother Jack puffing away on pre-match cigarettes; the squad players on hand to gee the lads up, fetch tie-ups, dispense more ciggies, help Doc Phillips lug his twenty flasks of Gatorade, before taking their places in the stand.

The players have been through the drill enough times not to need too much of a team talk. One piece of news perks them up: forty-five minutes before kick-off, as the team sheets are handed in, Ramsey confirms what they had hoped – Gérson is out, the twenty-nine-year-old's strained right thigh not deemed worthy of the risk. He had been having round-the-clock treatment, electronic massages, everything, and had willingly volunteered to sacrifice himself against England, even if it meant missing the rest of the tournament. The fast and leggy Paulo Cézar is in Gérson's place, but, as England will discover, it has necessitated a reshuffle: Rivelino will move in from the left to fill Gérson's architect slot in the centre; Cézar, pretty much a left winger, will be going wide. Ramsey has a word with Tommy Wright. Though Rivelino normally plays on the left, he is not a dribbler; Cézar will run at you, taking you on the outside, Ramsey warns. The Brazilians, they are all told, must be kept out of the England box at all costs.

Then Alf gives them his cryptic pep-talk. 'Do you like gold, boys?' he asks them. A few quizzical faces are pulled, some grin at each other, some nod. 'Well the ball's a lump of gold today,' says Alf. 'Don't give it away.'

'I can remember at quarter to twelve the buzzer going to come out into the passageway to go out together, and looking to my right to see who I was walking out against, and it was Pelé,' says Terry Cooper. 'I remember thinking, Bloody hell, he's like a pocket battleship. Look at his thighs. Jesus, if you run into him . . . And then I turned round and looked at the others! That stood out, how physically strong they were, as well as technically superb.'

And so England and Brazil emerge into a cacophony of 72,000 voices (including 5,000 England fans) and the teams line up for the anthems. 'I looked across at the Brazil side and thought, You'll not get a much better side than this ever, ever, ever,' says Alan Ball. 'Just awesome. I just remember thinking, We've got to be on our knock here today.' You can barely hear 'God Save the Queen' but it doesn't matter. Sleep deprivation aside, England have never been so prepared for a game in their lives. This is their first serious test since lifting the trophy in 1966, the most anticipated international in four years. All Mexico is gripped, all Brazil is gripped. England, of course, too . . .

Back home they've even got Mexican weather. At Chester Zoo the elephants have to be hosed down hourly; the polar bears and penguins are completely confused. But even as the temperature hits the eighties there's no one outdoors. The country has come to a standstill: no cars, no buses, no taxis, no people; cinemas are empty, parks are deserted as the nation gathers round its TVs waiting for the big showdown.

This is no ordinary game: as Bobby Moore and Carlos Alberto shake hands in the middle, do the toss and conduct the ritual exchange of pennants – or, in England's case, a wooden shield bearing the three-lions crest – they are surrounded by photographers who swamp the centre circle. The two captains indulge them with a Kodak moment, arms around each other's shoulders, but then it's back to their respective corners for the heavyweight encounter.

The players check out their opposite numbers. Terry Cooper glances at Jairzinho. 'We sort of acknowledged one another. He was probably two or three inches taller than me and I thought, Jesus Christ, you know, I've got me hands full today. If I whack him he's going to come back at me.'

On the pitch at the Jalisco Stadium it is 98 degrees and not yet noon. By the end of the game it will be well over 100. 'England will have to watch themselves in this heat,' declares Hugh Johns as England kick off.

It begins with slow possession stuff – Charlton to Ball to Lee to Mullery to Wright. Charlton runs around in the middle, the ball comes to Pelé and then, just as a statement of intent, Mullery thunders in and clatters him to the ground. Pelé ignores the outstretched hand of faux apology, and a smirking Mullery pats him on the head as the Brazilian sits on the deck.

As an England attack peters out, Félix, the ropy keeper, plays it out – Carlos Alberto to Tostão to Rivelino to Pelé. A rare miskick from the maestro is picked up by Peters in his own half and he lays it off to Ball, who strokes it square to Charlton, who taps it wide to Wright. 'England showing no signs of tension. A lot of control,' says Coleman on the Beeb, and all is going well.

England's first attack – Wright plays it to the inside-right position to Lee; a back-heel flick to Charlton, evading Paulo Cézar and Clodoaldo; Charlton pings it with his left-foot over to the right wing to Hurst, who has drawn centre back Piazza with him; a nod down to Lee; Lee to Ball; first-time lay-off to Wright, who plays it back to Lee on the right. Hurst has now run back into the middle, creating space, and Lee – seeming to have learned from the evidence of the games so far – fires a cracking long-range shot, but it goes straight to Félix, who just stands there and catches it at chest height.

Félix rolls it out to Carlos Alberto, who plays it to Jairzinho on the wing. Suddenly England are experiencing the Brazilians in full flight. The powerful Brazilian number 7 (who, according to Hugh McIlvanney, 'would not look out of place among the better welterweights at Angelo Dundee's gym'), runs at Cooper, beats him and gets round the back. 'Oh, and he left Cooper standing,' panics Coleman as Jairzinho carries himself to the by-line and crosses, tumbling out of play as he does so. The cross is one of perfection. Running in at the far post about eight yards out, Pelé, in full cry, makes an extraordinary leap, comprehensively outjumps Wright, makes optimum contact with the ball and, with textbook precision, drives his powerful header downwards, just inside the foot of Banks's right-hand post. Pelé is already shouting, 'Goal', and the people in the stands behind have now risen to their feet in exaltation. But the man from Stoke City is having none of it. Flatfooted by the cross, Banks somehow defies the laws of physics and, from a standing position, facing slightly the wrong way, flings himself to his right, such that his whole body is now at 45 degrees to the ground, head downward. Somehow, *somehow* he makes contact with the ball with his right palm and, incredibly, flips it up over the bar. 'Pelé ... what a save ... *Gordon Banks*,' screams Coleman, nearly bursting his microphone. 'And a fantastic save by Gordon Banks ... *what a fantastic save by Gordon Banks*,' yells Hugh Johns, in simultaneous rapture.

Pelé just stands there, barely able to believe it. It is beyond anything he, or anyone, has ever seen. Banks gets up, as if he had just been taking part in some routine training exercise. Moore slaps him on the backside. Mullery pats him on the head. 'Why didn't you catch it?' quips the England number 4, and Banks gives him a choice mouthful.

The corner amounts to nothing – too short, the ball is intercepted by Moore, who casually strokes it out to Ball to begin all over again. But the stadium is still abuzz.

The game is not yet eleven minutes old. What's more, England are taming the Brazilians. It's as though, with that nervous opening encounter against Romania out of their system, and with this game not being do or die, they can play with an unleashed freedom. 'We knew we could match them at keep-ball, passing the ball, holding the ball up, which is what you've got to do in that heat,' says Alan Ball, 'and play a different style to how we would play in England. We *knew* we could match them at their game, in their climate.'

Moore is looking imperial at the back, running through his world-class repertoire, and the Brazilians know it. Jairzinho plays it to Carlos Alberto who elegantly crosses from deep. Moore casually strides across to head it down to Ball. A cross from Wright is headed away by Brito, Labone plays it back in, Peters fluffs it and the ball arcs back to the centre circle. As Moore goes for the header, Jairzinho challenges with a raised knee right into the England captain's back. Moore, absolutely furious, and in considerable pain, does not let himself stoop to the undignified level of taking the bait. He simply draws a deep breath, bends over, exhales, calms himself and walks away. Such intimidation will only make him play better.

And so it does. A chip from Carlos Alberto to Jairzinho? Moore nods it down and strokes it out to Peters. Paulo Cézar haring down the left and skinning Wright? Moore gets it away. Tostão running through? Moore's there again to block him and play it off to Cooper. 'And again Moore with the decisive tackle,' says Johns, and Pelé ruffles his hair as he gets up. 'Both sides showing each other a lot of respect.'

England step up a gear. On twenty-three minutes a cross from Wright is hooked on by Lee but Peters chooses to head harmlessly over rather than chest and shoot. On thirty-two minutes Mullery puts his foot on the ball in the middle, finds Wright on an overlap almost at the corner flag – giving weight to Ramsey's criticism about the shortening of the pitch. Falling backwards as Everaldo rushes in, Wright crosses first time to the near post. Hurst goes up for the header but doesn't make it. Little Piazza is nowhere near him but takes out insurance, making a spectacular flailing lunge just in case a goal is scored and he can look at least as if he was trying to do something.

Lee, flying in, takes a diving header, Félix muffs it and Lee goes for a second attempt. The pounce is legitimate but he clobbers Félix in the face with his knee. The stadium erupts. All are on their feet. The surrounding players – beardy Brito and Carlos Alberto – rush in. Lee kneels over Félix and shows concern. 'Lee had to go for it. It was a fifty–fifty ball,' says Coleman, which seems only fair, or at least to the 5,000 England fans, mainly in the upper tier, all in their souvenir straw boaters with Mexico '70 hat bands. Not content to leave it to the rule of law, Carlos Alberto flicks Lee in the face. Rivelino, the gunman, backs him up. Hurst tries to mediate and the referee runs over. Abraham Klein of Israel was not an obvious choice to officiate such a high-profile encounter, but he gets in there quickly. Félix is still down cradling the ball. A yellow card is shown to Lee – dangerous play. Charlton and Peters arrive on the scene and Charlton tries to keep the Brazilians at bay. Carlos Alberto flings him away. Charlton put his hands up as if to say, 'OK, OK.' Pelé comes over. The trainer runs on with a bucket and sponge. He is a massive black man with a shaven head. In a former life, perhaps, he could have been one of Cleopatra's eunuch guards. Félix seems to be faking it.

The game restarts. Within thirty seconds Lee gathers the ball centrally and midway inside the Brazil half. Rivelino swings but can't get him, though Carlos Alberto does, body-checking the Manchester City man and, for good measure, studiously scraping studs down Lee's left shin as he tumbles. The situation is reversed. This time Charlton picks up the ball and storms over, absolutely incensed, to confront Carlos Alberto – most un-Charlton-like. But there are four gold shirts screening him – 2, 3, 11, 5: Brito, Piazza, Rivelino, Clodoaldo. Referee Klein intervenes. Tries to show who's boss. The Brazilian captain is warned but not booked. And Harold Shepherdson is on, nursing the stricken Lee. Pelé steps in to lend the ref authority. The Game must stay Beautiful.

The niggles continue: Mullery is lucky not to concede a penalty when he brings down Pelé in the box. But, in spite of such physical stuff, it is a veritable masterclass in football, and the Brazilians are coming back into it. Clodoaldo pings a shot that Banks spills round his left-hand post. And Pelé is starting to look lively. 'El Rey Pelé,' exclaims Hugh Johns, entering into the full spirit of the occasion.

As the whistle goes for half-time, there is no doubt about the spectacle. 'A most entertaining first half full of football,' says David Coleman as the teams troop off. 'The match is in a most delicate situation. One goal could swing it.' Coleman reckons England have problems when Brazil's wingers get the ball. Don Revie, flying co-pilot, agrees. They're not giving Cooper and Wright the chance to go on the overlap.

But let's not forget Banksie. Says Coleman, 'Banks surely deserves a knighthood for stopping that shot from Pelé.'

Brazil, though, have a trick up their sleeve. An old, old tactic. When England come out for the second half, they find they have no opponents. For a full five minutes, with the fierce sun burning directly above (there being no shade at all for the noon kick-offs), the players stand there waiting for Brazil. Hurst, Ball, Charlton and Lee face each other, hands on hips, wondering what the hell is going on. Mullery and Moore chat. Cooper and Wright sit on the ground. Banks leans against the post in a six-inch strip of shade cast by the crossbar – the only bit in the whole stadium.

Is this Brazilian gamesmanship? The absence of officials, too, suggests that it might be England who are out prematurely. Or maybe it's some local Mexican chicanery.

While England fry, there is ample time for some more thoughts on the game. Mercer says Labone is the key man on Tostão; that Charlton must deliver the ball a bit quicker. Revie wants them to get forward faster, too. Coleman requires more long balls because the keeper is suspect in the air. And still England sit there.

Eventually Brazil come up the steps, ambling casually, crossing themselves to wild applause, praying, going through their little rituals, ensuring that their 'lucky foot' hits the pitch first – like a colony of obsessive-compulsives.

Tostão kicks off to Pelé, crossing himself again as he does so. England go at them: Lee plays it up to Ball for a one–two and some bagatelle in the Brazilian box, but England don't seem to have quite the same zip about them now. Sun? Altitude? More probably the lack of a decent night's kip.

Pelé threatens in one move, then Banks stops a swinger from Jairzinho. At the other end a Charlton shot dips over the bar. Tostão, with his little legs turning frantically, charges through. Moore relieves him of possession and nonchalantly brings it out. 'And again Bobby Moore there to stop him,' says Hugh Johns. 'What a superb bloke to have in your side.'

England, however, are feeling the pressure. They must be, because Moore even has a little tug on Jairzinho's shirt as he charges through, grinning like a Cheshire cat when the ref fails to spot it. Coleman has observed a chink in the England armour: 'Ten minutes gone and England at the moment going through an uncomfortable period,' he says. Brazil have noticed it, too. They turn the screw, and Jairzinho runs clean through the England defence and is alone on goal. True to his reputation, Banks speeds out to beat him to the ball on the edge of the area and hoof it into the stands, then turns furiously, screaming in protest at the referee. Jairzinho, craftily, had kept his right foot up, studs showing, raking them down Banks's thigh.

Another attack: Rivelino shoots, Banks saves, and Brazil are playing with a swagger now. Coleman, in his remarkably prescient manner, provides some hasty rediagnosis: 'And England at the moment are struggling for survival.' The England defence are on the back foot, trying to get to grips with all the interchanging going on among the Brazilian forwards. 'There'd always been a problem of European sides marking South Americans,' says Brian Labone. 'They didn't really have any fixed positions. They would play where they were, so you'd have a succession of players coming at you. But they weren't like the recognised European number nines, you know.'

Down the left, Paulo Cézar plays it to Rivelino in the centre, who finds Carlos Alberto striding down the right. Peters comes over to jockey, rather cosmetically, and Carlos Alberto plays a square ball in to Tostão, now shuffling along on the edge of the D. Sensing the danger, Labone comes out to block and, as Tostão shoots, keeps big and doesn't flinch, the ball blasting back off his shoulder. Charlton and Ball are both upfield, ahead of the ball, while Mullery has tracked Pelé back into England's box. For a brief second, the middle is empty. Tostão goes and retrieves the ball at his leisure and springs a new offensive while England zone around the penalty area. Tostão plays it wide on the left to Paulo Cézar, who is being shadowed by Wright. He returns it to Tostão. With the England midfield haring back, Ball charges in and the Little Coin repays him with a well-judged right elbow to the face. The England number 8 stops dead in his tracks, literally gobsmacked. With the forward now on the edge of the England box, Moore comes out to put out the fire and shapes to hustle him. Whether by accident or design, little Tostão succeeds in nutmegging the England captain. Wright rushes in, skids and lands on his backside, and as Moore comes back again to cover, Tostão nonchalantly puts his foot on the ball, spins 360 degrees and chips it across the box. It is hopeful more than anything, but like a heat-seeking missile it finds its way to the target – the feet of Pelé. With Moore having come over to block Tostão and now out of position, and Mullery coming across to cover the ground in the centre, everyone has been pulled rightwards. Labone is still in Pelé's way but, with no cover, doesn't know whether to hold or lunge. Peters next to him is equally indecisive and Pelé, seizing the moment, simply side-foots it square, rolling it to Jairzinho. Cooper tries to intercept, but he slips over. Jairzinho waits, takes a step to the right and, while Banks charges out to fling himself at the striker's feet, thumps a hard shot over him into the opposite top corner. Goal.

Coleman offers a dumbfounded fifteen seconds of silence. On Mexican Telesistema, commentator Angel Fernandez, who is Brazilian, extends his breathless 'Goooooooooooooal!' to a full thirty-five seconds. The vast majority of the 72,000 fans in the stadium are delirious.

The ball rolls back out of the net to Mullery, who flicks it up and drop-kicks it into the air in disgust. Colin Bell, who had been warming up on the touchline, can only stand in dismay as Jairzinho dances past him trailing a conga of excited teammates – Paulo Cézar, Rivelino, Pelé – who, just for good measure, jig round the back of the England bench, all sitting there with stern faces.

Banks, dripping with sweat and looking dejected, picks himself up. His face says it all. Brazil's goal was well rehearsed but luck was with them – the lucky ricochet, the two slips, the fortuitous nutmeg, the elbow. 'There was a blatant foul by Tostão on myself,' says Ball. 'I was very disappointed that the ref didn't spot it, or the linesman. I've gone to challenge him and he's elbowed me in the face very, very blatantly.'

But England *had* left themselves undermanned in midfield for a crucial moment and, in defence, Moore had too much problem-solving to do because of others' dithering.

In his goalmouth Félix hops up and down like a rabbit. Maybe he has sunstroke. In 100-degree heat, the eccentric keeper is dressed in his customary thick black tracksuit top with another shirt underneath.

There are still thirty minutes to go. England go for broke and make a double substitution: Bell for Charlton, Astle for Lee. Charlton is now only one cap short of Billy Wright's record, and together with Moore has equalled the England record of playing in three world series, along with Tom Finney and Billy Wright. They are part of an elite group. Until this tournament began, only a handful had even played in two – Jimmy Dickinson, Stanley Matthews, Bryan Douglas, Jimmy Greaves, Johnny Haynes, Jimmy Mullen, Ray Wilson. Such thoughts are far from anyone's mind at present.

English crosses rain in, shots rain in. With Astle on now beside Hurst, England revert to the less sophisticated tactic of playing in high centres; with the Brazilian defence looking this shaky, it is worth a crack. A cross comes over to Astle, the big number 22, on the right-hand side of the box, who, with his first touch, heads it back to Ball on the edge of the area. Running in fast and trying to volley it with his left foot, Ball swings but finds only air. It was a good chance.

It is end-to-end stuff now as England try to claw their way back into the match. But it's tough: Moore blocks Tostão, Pelé has a pop, Banks palms down another one from Jairzinho. Pelé, however, starts to fade and so, crucially, does Jairzinho, leaving Cooper to push forward. Félix fluffs another shot and then, when Ball hits one over, proceeds to time-waste – 'Very dodgy keeper, this Félix,' says Hugh Johns.

In the middle, Bell is caught between two stools and the ball bounces back to Moore, who brings it forward. Pelé runs right across him, knocking him off his stride and giving away a free kick.

With twenty-five minutes to go, Jairzinho is set free on the right, midway inside the England half. It is a classic counter-attack, England having pushed up. Jairzinho is one-on-one with Moore, and Tostão is to his left as an option should he choose not to go it alone, which he surely will.

With Jairzinho in full cry, Moore simply tracks the winger back, waits for his chance and then, seizing the moment, makes the tackle with a stiff right leg, taking the ball cleanly with the outside of his boot and sending Jairzinho tumbling into the box – candy from a baby. 'Good tackle by Moore,' blurts Coleman. 'The perfect timing.' Years later it will still be replayed as one of the greatest interceptions ever made – all conducted in the head, supremely effortless in its execution.

Unfortunately, what follows is at odds with such brilliance.

Moore looks up, trots forward and strokes the ball to Cooper, who plays a one–two with Bell. The ball from Cooper is hit in high, Piazza and Everaldo collide, Everaldo swings at it and misses, and the ball is knocked straight down to Astle, less than ten yards out and with the net at his mercy, Félix stranded. Astle pulls the trigger, shoots with his left and misses the goal altogether, the ball trickling harmlessly wide of the far post. Coleman is furious: 'You can't win matches if you miss open goals.'

That one sequence says it all. England are rock solid, brilliant at the back and impotent up front. 'To be fair to Jeff Astle, he'd only just come on,' says Cooper. But to miss an open goal from a few feet out is something that will haunt Astle – and his teammates – for years to come.

'I remember in '68 he'd whacked one in from about twenty yards against Everton in the Cup Final, scored the winning goal,' says Labone, 'so I would have liked that to have been reversed.'

There is an end-of-term feeling about the stadium now. Results are coming in on the Tannoy from other games. Great buzzes surge round the stadium as the Mexican goals against El Salvador are reported. A Mexican *and* a Brazilian victory. An England defeat. This is all too much.

Brazil make a substitution. Number 13, Roberto, is on for Tostão, and pretty soon forces a save from Banks, diving to his right again.

Another chance for England: in the seventy-seventh minute Mullery lobs a high ball into the box, Astle nods it down and Ball shoots with his right this time. It's on target with Félix beaten, but Brito, running out, is able to get a faint deflection on to it. Painfully, it grazes the top of the bar.

In a last-ditch attempt to salvage something, England throw everyone forward. Even Bobby Moore goes up, taking the corner. Bell then has a parting but limp shot from long range. To outdo him, right at the end, Pelé tries to chip Banks rather impudently ('This man's clairvoyant,' says Coleman). And, just to show what a frustrating lunchtime it's been, Peters takes a spiteful kick at Pelé right on the final whistle which under normal circumstances might have got him in trouble with the ref, as well as with Carlos and the Gunman.

It's over. Brazil have won. And, after shaking hands with Labone, Pelé runs over to Bobby Moore and grabs his face with both hands for an affectionate squeeze. They hug, exchange shirts. It is rather poignant that it has been Pelé going up to acclaim Moore rather than the vanquished saluting the conqueror. Rather more can be read into the hug between Rivelino and Tostão, boots in hand. They know that they've just beaten both the World Champions and the only team in the competition that can come close to them.

'A single brilliant move by Brazil,' as the Radio 1 commentary has it, 'a momentary lapse in the English defence, and England have lost.'

The difference between the two has been the finishing. 'England have played enormously well and created a number of chances they should have tucked away,' says Revie. Indeed, Brazil had four chances, scored one. England had six, scored none. Good enough for the crowd, who go bananas. Surrounded by photographers, someone or other tries to present Pelé with some kind of award in the centre circle, but no one's really interested, the photographers relishing the affection between the world's greatest forward and the international game's best defender, who've fought a magnificent duel.

Legend will have it that the words exchanged between them were to the effect that they wish each other well and that the two sides will renew acquaintance in two weeks' time in the Azteca, though one England player claims that Pelé – whose English at this point is not great, though better, naturally, than Moore's Portuguese – simply says, 'You no thief, Bobby.' Either way, the sentiment is the same.

Joe Mercer sums it up best: 'Brazil won and England lost – but football won. What a great game.'

'It was a fantastic game of football by two teams that had total respect for each other,' says Alan Ball. 'Indeed, a little bit of fear comes with that respect.'

As Moore trudges off wearing Pelé's sodden shirt, the mask slips a little. Grim realisation that, though they are still nominally World Champions, Brazil are in the driving seat.

'Probably the best team I've ever played against. Probably the best team I've ever seen all around,' says Cooper.

Back in the dressing room, Moore does his best to lift the team. The mood is downcast, naturally – always is when the lads lose –

but they can draw satisfaction from it. If that was the best the world has to offer, they should hold their heads high.

'Even though we lost the game we came out of it with a better reputation than we went into it with,' says Emlyn Hughes.

'There was no way Brazil were a better team than England that day,' adds Jack Charlton.

But the players, inevitably, are exhausted. Not fair to play in such heat and at noon – and with no sleep. Dr Phillips points out that an American Army manual forbids training when the temperature is over 85 degrees. And there are bruises, too. By consensus, the Brazilians were far more physical than the Romanians and a great deal more skilful at it. 'Brazil weren't any good boys, no they bloody weren't, don't kid yourself,' says Hughes. 'They could bloody crunch and tackle and go over the top.'

The England players have each lost around ten pounds in body fluid – tough for Alan Mullery and Martin Peters, who have been selected by the doping monitors to provide the random urine samples. They will be quite a while.

In the minutes after the game and with brief satellite time to England, Hugh Johns gets a few precious seconds with Ramsey. Alf agrees with and repeats Johns's assessment: 'Bad result, excellent performance,' he says. 'But all is not lost. We have another match on Thursday and we hope to recover what we lost today.' The necessary compliments follow about the Brazil forward line but, he says, his boys were flagging a little, and Brazil scored while the subs were warming up.

Ramsey, as he always insists, doesn't like singling out players in a team game, but can't hold back about his number 1: 'The greatest goalkeeper in the world, no doubt about it.'

So, the lads are tired, but he has three full days before the Czech game, and they are very confident still. All the players will be fit but he might make tactical changes, he says, to freshen it up.

He's not the only one who's pleased. Hugh Johns grabs a passing Sir Matt Busby. 'As a lover of football I enjoyed every minute of it,' he says, handing special praise to the ref. Unusually for a Scotsman, he generously refers to England as 'we' but says he thinks that it is Brazil who will win the World Cup: 'Brazil ... or England ... or Russia or Uruguay.'

In the full post-match press conference, both managers give

more elaborate prognoses. 'The best team did not win today,' says Ramsey, rather unsportingly. 'Brazil were very good in an even match. They took their one chance, which is where we failed. There was really nothing between the teams in ability, technique and planning.' And he gets in a dig about the ill-will that had brought them a restless night: 'We expected peace and quiet but we found bedlam.' If you thought the players were knackered at half-time, well they certainly are now.

Zagalo, in the fortunate position of victor, can afford to be magnanimous. 'The match was in doubt right up to the final whistle,' he says. 'At no moment did I think our victory was certain. Anything could have happened at any moment . . . It was a difficult match. We had to play hard, precise and more scientific soccer. It was not like the ballet performance against Czechoslovakia.'

Would he like to see a repeat of the match on 21 June?

'Yes,' he replies. 'On videotape.'

Despite fatigue, Ramsey gives the players another night off as a reward for their exertions and allows them to attend a cocktail reception at the Hilton, to which the World Cup wives are invited, as are Emlyn Hughes's parents and Gordon Banks's relatives, who have also come over. They're all proud of Gordon, of course, and with special reason. Next Saturday, in the Queen's Birthday Honours List, he'll be getting an OBE. It had been hinted at for a while, but Ramsey had received the official call and taken him aside one morning after training, though Banksie had had to keep it quiet till after the match lest it break concentration. (He will be in interesting company. When the list is published on 13 June, Jock Stein becomes a CBE, Sir Laurence Olivier – who'll have a singing part in *Guys and Dolls* at the Old Vic in December – becomes a life peer, Sybil Thorndike is a dame, Richard Burton receives a CBE and David Frost and Nyree Dawn Porter will be OBEs.)

Even the Mexicans are full of praise for England's keeper. Despite their antipathy towards England, they have already started giving him a new name – 'El Magnifico' – on the strength of that fantastic save from Pelé. And Pelé's been raving about Banks, too.

In England, of course, they've known about Banks's abilities for quite a while: 'safe as the Banks of England' as the old joke goes.

He's a strange chap, is Banks: odd looking with broad Eurasian features, his goalkeeping skills are born of countless hours of painstaking practice. Brilliant reflexes definitely, but the thing that characterises his work is his general unfussiness. Nothing fancy, just safe, his goalkeeping is based on anticipation and the narrowing of angles. As the old cliché goes, he makes it look easy – far more thoughtful in his goalkeeping than some of the Flash Harrys who go for the spectacular save or punch just for showmanship. And it says something that even Peter Bonetti and Alex Stepney have no qualms about acknowledging his superiority. It must be a frustrating business, for that pair would walk right into any other national side. Indeed, it would be fair to say that, of the top six keepers in the tournament, three of them are in the England squad.

For all his talents, and there is little doubt that he is the world's best keeper – with only Uruguay's Mazurkiewicz coming close on occasion – Banks has never played for a big club; never even won any major domestic silverware. The Football League is currently blessed with some outstanding keepers: Pat Jennings at Spurs, Joe Corrigan at Manchester City, newcomer Ray Clemence at Liverpool and Banks's own protégé at Leicester, young Peter Shilton. But while they (with the exception of Shilton) are all winning or challenging for honours, Banks has chosen to ply his trade at two unfashionable Midlands clubs – Cities Leicester and Stoke.

He very nearly wasn't a goalkeeper at all. As a kid in Sheffield he was a centre half and only switched to going 'in nets' when his local parks team was short. Getting a liking for it and modelling himself on his two heroes, Bert Trautmann of Manchester City and Bert Williams of Wolves, he was spotted by a Chesterfield scout at sixteen, though he carried on bricklaying to hedge his bets. When he broke his arm playing for Chesterfield's third team he thought it might be over (he still has a screw in a bone, but on recovery it soon became obvious he was a talent and a half). Though with all players of his age – Banks is now 32 – football was put on hold while he did two years' National Service, in the Royal Signals Corps, and when posted near Hannover he met his German wife Ursula. His stint in the army has always gone down well with the punters, most of whom over the age of thirty have done their bit for Queen and country. And now Banks is on top of the world.

El Magnifico humbly accepts the plaudits and says he'd rather be celebrating on the back of a win, but still ...

*

Domestic football, indeed domestic sport, seems a million miles away at the moment. Lester Piggott and Nijinsky win the Derby; in the run-up to Wimbledon, unknown Czech player Jan Kodes wins the French Open; the Rest of the World team to take on England's cricketers numbers four Springboks, including Graeme Pollock and Eddie Barlow; Birmingham City face a League inquiry when new boss Freddie Goodwin tries to take coach Willie Bell from Brighton, even though Bell is still registered as a Brighton player.

Also, and rather unfortunately given the hoo-ha over the cricket tour, it is revealed that, as soon as the World Cup's over, and after only a short stopover, Bobby Moore and Geoff Hurst will be off to do a week's coaching in South Africa, taking up an offer from the South African FA in Johannesburg. They protest that they'll be coaching black kids as well as white, but FIFA, beyond whose jurisdiction the SAFA operates, will not be very happy. Nor will a lot of the general public...

Chapter 12

'Going Bent'

Monday, 8 June 1970

Having slept on it, the England players mull over yesterday's match. Ball mutters about Astle's miss (though not his own). Peters ventures that England might have had some kind of hoodoo placed on them, especially in the light of the game on tour last year when they were leading against Brazil and also lost.

On the streets of Brazil there is less conjecture – the favourites have now shown themselves superior to the reigning champions. In Rio there are wild celebrations. A giant banner reading 'THE LION IS NO MATCH FOR THE ANTS' is paraded through the heaving throng. In the palaces of Brasilia, the generals breathe a collective sigh of relief.

As for the question of a hex, though, the failure of rain to materialise, as it has tended to do in the late stages of games in Guadalajara, may have had supernatural overtones. Says Frank Clough of the *Sun*, 'A Brazilian journalist told me that the primitives back home would have been beating the Macumba drum all night.'

One should not underestimate the role of mysticism in Brazilian football. One São Paulo newspaper goes into great and diagrammatic detail about how the foot of Jesus himself kept the ball out of the Brazilian goal. No wonder Astle missed. Many Brazilians, particularly in the north-east, *do* practise Umbanda and Candomblé, ancient African voodoo rites that, in the dark days of slavery, had been dressed up in the Catholic codes to appease colonial masters. According to such superstitions, fated moments (and buses) are apt to come in threes. For all the euphoria, enthusiasm is tempered in some circles. Just as Zagalo is believed by some to be cursed, so has arisen the notion that, having beaten England twice now in the last twelve months, the portents are not necessarily good should the two teams renew acquaintance in the final.

'Zagalo was a bit of a voodoo man himself,' says Ken Jones. 'They were very lucky to beat England in Rio in '69, and it could have gone either way in Guadalajara. So if they'd met in the final it would have been the third game.'

In Britain there is less equivocation about the match. 'OH BALL, OH ASTLE, OH ENGLAND,' mourns the *Daily Express*, bemoaning the English misses that could have swung the result the other way. Though it generously hails the 'peacock players of Brazil' and, pursuing the bestial theme, the goal taken 'cobra style' by Jairzinho. 'The difference between the two teams was that when England attacked it was always with poise and elegance,' says Desmond Hackett. 'When the Brazilians played forward it was like a rifle squad at full fire.' And, let us not forget Banks's save: 'The greatest goalkeeper in the world had outwitted Pelé, the greatest striker on earth.'

The *Sun*, in rather camp fashion, devotes its whole front page to the header, 'WEEP FOR ENGLAND'S GLORY BOYS', with a picture of Bobby Moore traipsing off the pitch in Pelé's shirt, and bleating that after this gladiatorial romp, their jerseys 'darkened with sweat', it was enough to make grown men break down sobbing.

Still, all is not lost. According to the back page statisticians of Fleet Street, if Romania beat Brazil 2–0 and England turn over the Czechs by a three-goal advantage, England will still win the group. As the *Sun* points out, that may be a tad optimistic. 'Lucky dip could put us out!' they wail again, with Peter Batt pessimistically casting ahead to the fact that, if both games end in draws, depending on the scores, England and Romania could be tossing a coin to see who gets second place.

But there is enough cheer generally to suggest that, even though England have only once beaten Brazil – in a friendly at Wembley in 1956 – it's even money to suggest that they'll meet again in the final. 'Everybody after that game thought it would be an England–Brazil final,' says Jack Charlton. 'Everybody thought it. And *we* thought it, to tell you the truth.'

It will be a cataclysmic showdown. As Brian James in the *Daily Mail* puts it, 'The apostles of adventure against the disciples of discipline.'

But uh-oh, trouble. Just when Abraham Klein had given a shining example of how to referee a match, renewing faith in the officiating for the impending, and inevitably heated, knock-out stages of the tournament, a scandal has broken out. It begins in petty, though perhaps understandable, fashion, when the Italians discover that the ref for their game against Israel – Henry Landauer of the USA (formerly of Stuttgart, West Germany) – has a Jewish father. Fearing favouritism to their opponents, they ask FIFA to switch Landauer with another official. Though dismissing Italian objections as spurious, FIFA are obliged to comply. They reluctantly swap Landauer with Brazilian referee Airton de Moraes, who would have been doing the Uruguay–Sweden game.

Nothing too problematic there. But as the hours progress towards the respective kick-offs, the plot thickens. The question of Landauer's ethnicity, it seems, though genuinely raised by Italy, is not the prime motive for the switch. Just as everyone has always expected in Britain, that word which is deemed synonymous with officiating in Latin America has cropped up – bribery. A rumour had already been flying round the press watering-holes of Toluca and Puebla that de Moraes was caught up in something – whispers that he might be the recipient of a large cash sum to ensure the safe passage of fellow South Americans Uruguay into the quarter-finals. And though there is no evidence to suggest impropriety by de Moraes, FIFA acts swiftly. Thus, the game at Puebla on 10 June between Uruguay and Sweden goes ahead with Landauer in charge.

In a hastily convened press conference in Mexico City the following morning, Sir Stanley Rous issues a statement explaining his actions.

'The rumour was so widespread that I decided to interview Mr de Moraes personally but could not contact him until nine o'clock yesterday morning,' he states, having duly interrogated the referee, together with Ken Aston, at the Hotel Maria Isabel. Both men were absolutely convinced that de Moraes – a forty-one-year-old finance secretary from Rio – was entirely innocent, but didn't want to lay FIFA open to accusations. 'When the referee appointments were made, the president of the Referees' Committee and I were told of a plot to discredit Mr de Moraes by suggesting that if a sum of money was paid to him by the officials of one of the teams, he would favour that team. We did not believe the allegations, having implicit faith in the honesty of the referees selected for the tournament.'

The issue, it seems, was the result of malicious gossip planted by a jealous Brazilian colleague of de Moraes – a journalist, it turns out – this matter communicated to FIFA by a Swedish businessman, Bjore Lantz.

Under the circumstances, Rous's speedy resolution of the problem seems logical, but the Uruguayans do not like it, not one bit. There is the re-emergence of the old suspicion that the refs had been switched to benefit the Europeans. Plus, didn't action over the matter imply that the Uruguayans *were* crooked?

On the day of the Sweden game, when Uruguay arrive at the stadium in Puebla and learn of the last-minute change, they stage an angry press conference, their fury vented by Alfredo Fernández, head of the Uruguayan delegation. The team only takes the field under protest.

'I do not intend to answer the accusations against me by Mr Fernández,' replies Rous, 'nor his reasons for disapproval of my action. I am surprised at his attitude about something which was done for the benefit of his team.'

As it happens, the Swedes might wish they'd been given de Moraes after all. Before a Puebla crowd of 15,000, a good many noisy and colourful supporters from Uruguay among that number, an under-strength and injury-depleted Sweden give Uruguay all they've got.

The game begins well for the Scandinavians. After only thirty seconds, Leif Eriksson hits the post. The pattern continues – close shaves, side-netting, one-handed saves from Mazurkiewicz. But then things begin to go against them. When Ancheta hacks down Kindvall in the box, referee Landauer only awards an indirect free kick. Then, soon after, Kindvall puts the ball in the net, only to have it disallowed for no explicable reason.

Uruguay do not look good, but as the second half progresses they exert their customary and brutal stranglehold on the game. Sweden do not give up. In the second minute of injury-time, a cross comes in from the right and Swedish substitute Grahn heads in. The Swedes go wild. Mazurkiewicz sits down, disconsolate; defenders shake their heads and rub the backs of their necks.

Sweden have won 1–0, but the referee has denied them the necessary two-goal advantage they needed to advance. Given the favourable refereeing – Uruguay treated with kid gloves – some would argue that the Uruguayan protest beforehand was a useful strategic investment. Sweden's vain hope of progress now lies with the unlikely prospect of Israel thrashing Italy.

Italy, though, have no intention of letting the spectre of North Korea loom again. The Toluca crowd may have clasped Israel to their bosoms, but the love is not apparent on the terraces, where there is even some scuffling. On the pitch, too, it gets physical. When Israel's David Primo jumps with both knees into Boninsegna's back, Italian fans hurl cushions, bottle tops and paper cups. But the Mexicans, shouting for the Israelis, are in the majority and there are cheers when Boninsegna is later booked in a retaliatory fracas. There is wild enthusiasm too when Ethiopian linesman Tarekegn, the ref who had lost control of the Sweden–Israel game, flags to disallow two Italian goals, including one by Riva. There is certainly no cordial welcome extended to Rivera for his one and only appearance in the group games.

While Italy step up a gear in the second half, the end result is an almost compulsory 0–0 draw. It does the trick: Uruguay's slip-up means Italy have won the group.

Israel can hold their heads high. They have contained both Italy and Sweden and run Uruguay close. Italy, meanwhile, advance to the quarter-finals on the strength of two 0–0 draws and having scored just one goal in the other game – a fluffed one at that . . .

In cynical old England it doesn't lake long for the pleasant satisfaction of the Brazil feast to be followed by the indigestion of suspected foul play. It has started to dawn on everyone, especially the more excitable elements of the popular press, that Brazil, already through with maximum points, might employ another dirty Latin trick and throw their last game against Romania – thus allowing the Romanians to qualify at England's expense. This is no mere tittle-tattle. The *Daily Mail* even traces this concern to a high-up within the England camp itself, though by refusing to name him does not exclude the possibility that it simply made him up. 'I am worried about this,' the anonymous blazer is said to have uttered after Sunday's match. 'After the game we gave them, Brazil won't want us still in the tournament if they can help it.'

Naturally, it is scoffed at by the Brazilians, who are angered by the suggestion that they might 'go bent'. First, they don't do that sort of thing. Second, and most importantly, it would be sheer folly. If Romania beat *them* by two goals and England beat Czechoslovakia, they themselves will be out. Given that their game against Romania is on Wednesday 10th, the day before England play Czechoslovakia, taking a dive will advantageously gift the champions a specific target to achieve. Footballing suicide. Far better to win the group, stay in Guadalajara and let the runners-up decamp to León for the quarter-final against the winners of Group Four.

The Brazilians have injuries – Gérson is still doubtful, as now is Rivelino – but their intention is to play for a win. Ordinarily, they might have been expected to rest their star, Pelé, and spare him the boot of Mocanu, but with Gérson and Rivelino missing, Pelé will have to play. There is even talk that second keeper Ado might come in for the hapless Félix, though reports from observers suggest he may be an even worse prospect.

For Ramsey and his players, talk of Brazilian fixing has never been seriously entertained. England's fate lies in their own hands. The Czechs are already out, having nothing to play for, and are now, apparently, racked by internal disputes – a faction of players declaring no confidence in their manager, Marko, claiming that their preparation, steaks and all, was insufficient for the job in hand. (They did not arrive in Mexico till the 17th, already whittled down to a straight twenty-two, and no acclimatisation – 'Acclimatisation? We went to Font Remeu in France in February. That was sufficient,' says Milan Michalik, president of the Czech FA. 'They are all strong and healthy.')

But a wounded animal, as Ramsey knows, is often the most dangerous. And pride can be a great motivator. The Czechs, still lingering under the shadow of the Soviet suppression of the Prague spring, are a patriotic bunch. Ramsey's main problem is a tactical one. An obvious one at that. His defence is sound, but even against a suspect Brazilian back line his attack was found shooting blanks. 'We didn't finish as well as we should. We were like a cat on hot bricks inside the eight-yard box,' he tells the Birmingham *Evening Mail*. He would never for one minute concede that he had boobed by axing Thompson and Coates, but, having already committed himself to shaking up his team, the odds are that new faces will be introduced up front, with Astle, Clarke and Osgood all hopeful of a start.

With a couple of days to ruminate on the new formation, there is much speculation about other possibilities. Newton's fit again, so should come back (though Wright did pretty well against Brazil). But will Ramsey rest Bobby Charlton, the player he seems to have reserved the cotton-wool treatment for? To do so would deny him the chance of equalling Billy Wright's international appearance record . . .

Such hypothesising is now done blindly. For back home, true to their word, at 1.30 a.m. on the morning of Wednesday 10th – the deadline for print industry peace talks – the union SOGAT calls its 23,000 members out on strike. In defiance of mediation by Barbara Castle and Vic Feather, there will be no newspapers printed in London and Manchester – effectively no national press for the first time in fifteen years, and with little prospect of a resolution before the weekend.

For a country hooked on the World Cup, this is not good news. For those in the North-west, where there is no ITV either, it is particularly grim. Worse, a strike at the Tetley-Walker brewery in Warrington has left hundreds of pubs and clubs in the region without beer – Morecambe and Blackpool are almost dry.

Though industrial action is a way of life in Britain.

The British Medical Guild go ahead with their pay protest, doctors refusing to sign sick notes. At Ford's Halewood plant, 20 workers walk out when the temperature reaches 80 degrees, resulting in 650 workers sent home and one hour's production lost. British Leyland lay off over 2,000 at Longbridge because of an unofficial strike by four inspectors over the positioning of a table. At Heathrow, 200 BEA ground staff and ground hostesses walk out because of abuse from passengers – 24 flights are cancelled. In London a conductor abandons his number 88 bus and its fifteen passengers when he refuses to pay fares for his two children, citing an 'unwritten rule' that allows transport workers' families not to pay, along with 'blind people and cripples'. The end of a long-running strike at the Pilkington glass works in St Helens still leaves the plant, and the town, under a pall of acrimony.

But there is some cheer.

On Saturday 13th the Tetley-Walkers workers get back on the job. Not that the pubs are doing a particularly roaring trade at present. Landlords report a marked dip in clientele as people prefer to do their drinking at home in front of the telly. Churches report no marked difference in attendance, but perhaps a few prayers are diverted to Mexico.

In the run-up to the election, politicians are finding themselves even less able to draw a crowd than usual. When Foreign Secretary Michael Stewart speaks in Peterborough at 7 p.m. on 7 June – kick-off time against Brazil – fewer than fifty people turn up. When Chancellor Roy Jenkins and Minister for Sport Denis Howell share a platform in Birmingham on the same day, they bring their meeting forward so that their audience (and they) can catch the game. Even so, there are still only a hundred punters there.

All other news is relegated to insignificance. The Liberal Election Broadcast? No thank you. E. M. Forster dead at ninety-one (slipping away around the time that Moore was swapping shirts with Pelé)? Poor bugger, had a good innings. Catch BBC1's *Mission: Impossible* (the 'new thriller series starring Peter Graves')? Maybe next week.

British climber Don Williams claims he saw an abominable snowman on the slopes of Annapurna One and watched it for a full thirty minutes. He could have taken pictures, drunk tea with it and brought it home to meet his mother for all anyone cares at this current moment in time.

For some, the lure of Mexico has become such an obsession that they've dropped everything to go there. Mark Hemming, a twenty-five-year-old fitter from Lutterworth, Leicestershire, takes girl-friend Linda (twenty-four, from Coventry) to Guadalajara to get married, aided in their celebrations there by Charlie Cooke and Roger Hunt.

But for the majority, their window on Mexico is the telly. And a sterling job the broadcasters are making of it, too, so everyone reckons. The *Sun* heaps praise on the Beeb's mastery at com-mentated tension – from fevered frenzy on the one hand to dra-matic silence on the other. The first half against Brazil was 'So silent', says TV critic Peter Barnard, 'that you could hear Coleman drop a generalisation.'

By common consensus, however, it is ITV which has come of

age. While ITV could always compete admirably with the BBC when it came to commentary – the distinguished Hugh Johns being every bit the equal of the Beeb's venerable Kenneth Wolstenholme, the BBC had always been streets ahead in the ratings. (Who now remembers Johns's words as Hurst scored England's fourth in 1966?) There is still a sort of snobbery at play, ITV regarded as the grubby commercial upstart, trying to ape the BBC but not doing it quite as well. In 1966 the only frills were the new-fangled device called 'action replay', or perhaps a polite interview with a player or manager after the game, and ITV had little scope to craft the essential gimmickry with which to trump its mighty rival. By 1970, though, things have begun to change in terms of presentation. The concept of analysis has come in, with the advent of the professional pundit.

On ITV, the popularity of opinionated ex-Fulham player and former Coventry manager Jimmy Hill – forever replaying controversial action and talking of 'truth by television' – had given the station some big pointers as to how to compete. And so, for Mexico '70, ITV has unleashed its secret weapon – 'The Panel'. Like the BBC, before and after games, and during half-times, ITV's live broadcast has cut back to the studios for discussion. But this time there is no pale imitation of the Beeb, with its boring bunch of polite studio stiffs (Brian Clough excepted) – almost literally in the case of Ray Wilson who, just given a free transfer by Fourth Division Oldham, has announced he will be going into the family undertaking business in Huddersfield. No one could accuse Brian Moore of hosting some civilised tea party with the old boys. Instead, from the studio at London Weekend Television (known to all as 'the fishbowl'), he has been introducing the verbal equivalent of all-in wrestling with the hugely egotistical likes of Malcolm Allison, Pat Crerand and Derek Dougan. And, in a late addition to proceedings, Bob McNab, who was initially only invited on for one show, but was retained as he became the designated whipping-boy.

'We beat the BBC hands down. That was a masterstroke,' says Hugh Johns. 'I don't think it really mattered what the games were like at all. The punters were tuning in to see what they were going to do to little Bob McNab ... The big thing was that anything Bob said they took to pieces. Poor little Bob was being bullied by those chaps. LWT was deluged with letters, mostly from mums and grandmas, saying, "You've got to lay off this fella, he's too nice." So they kept him on.'

Not that the BBC haven't scored over their rivals elsewhere. Given that a lot of people can't stay up too late, and in a pre-video recorder age at that, Frank Bough's highlights package, *Good Morning Mexico*, is going down a treat. Bough has sealed his own fate – breakfast TV.

With the live matches, viewers everywhere are bemused by the halo of glare that appears around each player's head and shoulders. Leonard Matthews, manager of ATV, in the Birmingham *Evening Mail*, reckons one shouldn't get too pernickety. 'There are problems enough in getting the pictures from the grounds to the transmitters and on to the satellites,' he says. 'It must be remembered, too, that British reception involves converting the South American 525 picture standards to our own 625 lines – and converting upwards is more difficult than the other way round.'

Hell, World Cup TV has even saved lives.

'WORLD CUP FEVER SAVES SOUTHSEA WOMAN,' screams the Portsmouth *Evening News*, detailing the experience of Mrs Constance Hodgekins, 'who follows the World Cup closely'. There's a picture of the pensioner beaming, next to a twisted lump of melted metal. When her TV was on the blink, threatening her enjoyment of the coming game, it was her trip to the call box to summon the engineer that removed her from the ensuing domestic explosion.

Britain – where 25 million people, half the population, watched the Brazil game – is not the only land glued to the gogglebox. Indeed, most European nations are taking live satellite broadcasts. In Italy it's sixty hours, with eleven matches late at night. French state TV has eighteen matches, eleven live. Most countries in Western Europe are screening thirty to forty hours in total. The Soviet Union takes thirty hours either live or the next day to avoid too much disruption to production lines. In most of Eastern Europe they also have thirty hours live. In Poland every news bulletin is accompanied by ten minutes of footage.

Mexico, naturally, has all-out service. There is substantial coverage in the rest of Latin America, too. In Chile there are seventy hours broadcast over three channels. In Brazil, President Médici has ordered official radio programmes to be put back so as not to interfere with reports. Though in Argentina, where, on 9 June, there is a coup, things have been a tad disrupted.

Even in soccer-eschewing North America, though not live, twelve cities have closed-circuit TV in fee-paying auditoriums. The England–Brazil game is a sell-out in New York City, where 25,000 watch it at Madison Square Garden (5,000 poor souls are locked out).

In Asia the matches are on live during the following working morning, but the high cost of coverage means that many countries are reliant on videotape flown from Mexico. In Hong Kong they're all broadcast three days late.

Not all are happy about it. In Norway travel agents complain that people are postponing holidays in their mountain and seaside huts, where there is no TV reception, till after the tournament. In Sweden a second channel is being opened up to provide alternative TV and sociologists there predict many husband and wife battles. Austria ends its coverage at 1.30 a.m. to avoid wrecking the ensuing working day. And in Switzerland announcers constantly apologise for the upset to regular programming. In Colombia there was concern that the games would interrupt Sunday children's programmes, but the kids, it turns out, would rather watch soccer.

The build-up to England–Czechoslovakia continues. In the absence of the national papers the provincial rags scramble for any bit of news they can get coming out of the England camp. The Birmingham *Evening Mail* has fun with Alan Ball, in a white coat, who's suddenly assumed the role of team hairdresser – 'The barber of Guadalajara' – with Ballie merrily cutting Geoff Hurst's hair ('When it comes to the parting of the ways,' says the caption, 'Czechoslovakia, it is hoped, will be trimmed to size'). At the Camino Real Hotel – home of many of the visiting FA officials, Football League players and managers – the Liverpool *Echo* interviews Fred Hughes, Emlyn's father, the former Rugby League player, in Mexico to see his 'soccer son' (as opposed to his 'rugby son', David, who plays for Barrow). Fred is strictly an oval ball man, a former Great Britain Rugby League international who toured Australia as a front forward in 1946. He confesses he was rather disappointed when Emlyn opted for the Association code, though it was obvious after a few schoolboy Rugby League matches 'he would not be one of us'. Fred's not particularly taken with the pansy game of footer – doesn't like all the play-acting and disputed decisions. 'If there was a rugby match here tomorrow and Brazil were also playing in another stadium, I know which one I'd choose,' he says. But he and Mrs Hughes are extremely proud of Emlyn and have flown all the way out here even though there's only a slim chance (if Cooper gets crocked) of their boy getting a run-out.

'I was desperate to play,' says Emlyn. 'It's the only regret I've got in the game, that I didn't play in a World Cup Finals. I was substitute for two of the games.'

Hugh Johns of ITV manages to grab some of the England players for a few words outside the Hilton. And in what must be one of televised sport's most amusing bloopers burps loudly into the mic in front of Alan Mullery, exclaiming, 'Oh Christ, bloody peanuts.' Mullery, in his boiler suit, which the players never seem to be out of, and in front of some lush palm trees, says he thinks Romania can make it difficult for Brazil,

Will they 'sell' it to eliminate England?

No way, says Mullery, 'They want to win all their games.' But Romania will make it tough, he warns, 'They played eight back in defence and kicked a bit,' he says. That Mocanu 'put some stick about . . . and with the temperamental Latin American people, they [Brazil] won't like this too much, I don't think.' He adds that if Romania had played against England like they did against Czecho-slovakia then it would have been a more entertaining game.

Brian Labone echoes the sentiments, says that England have a good chance, will beat Czechoslovakia, and that Brazil will over-come Romania.

What was it like in 96 degrees against Brazil?

'I thought it was a hundred and ninety-six!' he quips, but adds that England were comfortable. 'The game only bore out what we already knew,' he says – that Brazil have world-class forwards but their defence is still suspect. 'If we played Brazil tomorrow, the game would still be open.' Better to beat them in the final.

Casting ahead, he says he thought Czechoslovakia would be the dark horses, but they haven't lasted the pace – not been out here long enough. Petras is good, but they all seem to flag. 'We reckon we could lose Czechoslovakia and still qualify,' he says, 'but that wouldn't be the right way to do it.'

'The best of British luck,' concludes Johns.

With time on their hands, the Mexican press goes to work on England and, indeed, all of the visiting teams – except for Brazil, of course. All are reported boozing and brawling round the clock. England pay no attention. They will go into the game with confidence sky high. Ramsey adds that all are fit, with the exception of Osgood, who was affected by the heat while watching Sunday's game from the stands and landed himself a blinding headache – officially 'sunstroke'. It is only some years later that Osgood lets the truth be known. So disgruntled at missing out on the Brazil game was he that he went out that night, on his own, and, by his own admission, got roaring drunk. It is a costly demonstration. Going into a new decade when he might have been expected to be one of England's leading lights, he will not start an international for Ramsey again until November 1973, his best days behind him.

Alf will reserve judgement on his team until after the Brazil–Romania game, which the squad will watch at the Jalisco. He expresses no concern about the other group games, or whom England will play, toeing the party line that you have to beat the best if you want to win the damned thing. Secretly he knows what the outcome will be. Brazil will win, leaving England with just a point needed to see them through. By the end of the evening he'll also know the result of the West Germany–Peru game in Group Four, played simultaneously, thus revealing England's quarter-final opponents before they take the field against the Czechs the next day.

Ramsey has already dispatched FA people to check out accommodation in León, which, for all the preparation that went into the tournament seems a rather last-minute arrangement. Still, despite it all, Ramsey is philosophical: 'I was in León in 1967,' he says. 'There will not be so many people there, either in the stadium or outside our hotel. We might be able to sleep at nights.'

And at training England are in good spirits once again, zipping around, no England team ever looking leaner or fitter. But they will not be winning the award for fair play. Francis Lee's booking against Brazil has blemished their otherwise spotless record with a minus point. There are still six countries with zero points at this juncture – Belgium, Bulgaria, Italy, Mexico, Peru and West Germany – though this is all ahead of the final round of games.

On Tuesday Bobby Moore and Bobby Charlton go to pay a social call on their old pal Pelé at the Brazilian HQ. Not even the likes of these two are above the security cordon, kept sweating in the car for fifteen minutes by Guarani's pistol-brandishing guards before they're allowed through. Such an object of worship has the Suites Caribe become that the Mexicans now want to rename the hotel Casa de Brasileros...

And so to the business in hand. The question of Brazil taking a dive has also been disrespectful to the Romanians. Their coach Angelo Nicolescu admits that, on the evidence so far, it will be a tall order to beat Brazil, but they will be doing their utmost, acknowledging that the Brazilian defence is not as good as England's.

As it turns out, Romania *do* get goals, two of them, which is more than England ever threatened. But it is not enough.

In a changed strip of light blue shirts, white shorts and red socks, the Romanians do well, though near the start the pattern is laid down. Pelé, strolling through on the edge of the penalty arc, is tackled and takes an unconvincing tumble. Had the incoming Lucescu not made a wild, but unconnecting, swing at him, the referee might not have done anything, but the free kick is given.

Tostão places the ball, Pelé walks backwards ten paces, like a long-jumper reversing from his mark. Tostão walks over the ball, but no one is remotely fooled that it is anyone other than Pelé who is going to take it – except for the Romanian defence, who stand there like lemons as Pelé charges forward and sends in a waist-high screamer that swerves round the wall. The bemused defenders all turn to see the inevitable: the ball sailing past Adamache.

Not long after, Paulo Cézar – in the side again – jinks down the left, pings the ball across the box and there is Jairzinho to tap it in, to keep his goal-a-game record going. For Brazil, it's business as usual, their under-strength team making light work of a defence England had struggled to crack open.

Romania, however, do not give up. With thirty-four minutes gone, the number 5, Dinu, lobs from deep into the Brazil box, Dumitrache goes for it, and Carlos Alberto, Brito and Piazza are typically ineffective as the Romanian centre forward belts it – Félix diving over it as it slides into the net. Sloppy defending of the worst order. Romania are not out of this tournament yet. If they nick a point, the Czechs still might do them a favour tomorrow.

Their joy is short-lived. As the second half gets under way, with the notorious Jalisco shadow now creeping right across the pitch, Carlos Alberto crosses from the right and little Tostão, darting in at the near post, impudently back-heels it with his right foot over Dinu. Pelé, running into the goalmouth, strokes it home. Romanian defenders argue and gesticulate at each other, but no one's really to blame. There's no legislating for genius like that.

Romania throw everyone forward and Satmareanu, the number 2, charges down the right wing, putting in a cross for an unchallenged Dembrowski to head in. With not a defender in sight – the old culprits Brito and Piazza just in vague proximity – it might have been any one of three Romanians who converted. And, for a rare moment, sensing that Brazil are just coasting, the Mexican crowd give them the bird. Despite a valiant rally by the Romanians, Brazil have done exactly what they needed to do – conceded two and scored three . . .

Peru, still enduring the trauma from back home, have already won everyone's hearts in León. An Australian scientist posits the theory that the terrible earthquake may have been caused by a French A-bomb test in the Pacific upsetting the tectonic plates – in which case it's a good job Les Bleus didn't qualify for Mexico. For all their footballing heroics, all the players care about is the plight of their loved ones. Some have still received no news. It's something of a miracle they can play at all, though in terms of keeping up national morale they have more than discharged their duty.

Walter Winterbottom, Ramsey's England predecessor, here to see the show, has already dubbed Peru the 'New Magyars'. Everyone else is calling them the 'New Brazil'.

In their second game Peru beat Morocco 3–0 – though the team was perhaps not quite as convincing as the scoreline suggests. The Africans, as they had done against Germany, made life tough for the South Americans in the first half and kept it to 0–0. Morocco's coach Vidinic admitted that his players were overawed by the big names in the German team and would be less inhibited against the Peruvians, their feat all the more impressive given that their goalie Allal, who had performed heroics against Müller and co., was patched up to play at the last minute, pumped full of painkillers for an ankle injury. A shrewd throw from the keeper nearly set up an early Moroccan goal. But with Peru starting to dominate play in the second half and the Moroccans wilting, the rest seemed inevitable. On sixty-six minutes Cubillas put Peru ahead. It was only three minutes later when the South Americans executed the killer blow with a mind-blowing multi-man move of one–twos and blind-side running, the ball finishing up with Challe, who beat two defenders and dummied before belting a screaming riser past Allal. Then, ten minutes from time, Cubillas added another to conclude the victory and put himself, briefly, on top of the goalscoring chart. And what a goal: ending another mesmerising piece of interpassing, he hit the ball so hard that it made Rivelino look like a nancy boy.

In the final, meaningless match of the group, watched by just 5,000 people, Morocco and Bulgaria will play to a 1–1 draw. For the amateurs of Morocco – as for Israel – their performances in this World Cup have been exceptional. Morocco can go home with their heads held high. They have heralded the arrival of a new footballing continent. African soccer is here to stay.

The next day it is the Germans' turn to assert supremacy in what has already been by far and away the most entertaining, free-scoring group, a fact sadly not reflected by the crowds. Only 7,000 watched the Peru–Morocco game. Only an extra thousand filed in the next day to see the Germans take on Bulgaria, though the German PR people had done a good job, the locals won over with sackfuls of German flags and merchandise. And, in the same manner as the England fans in Guadalajara, 2,000 or so Germans have been intent on revelling in the World Cup carnival, making their voices heard, blowing cheap little plastic horns and waving their black, red and gold colours, sunning their wobbly beer bellies.

For the Bulgaria game, a contingent in the crowd, on-leave servicemen, sit with a big banner reading, 'Luftwaffe grüsst die Deutsche elf' – the air force salutes the German eleven – the question of the Luftwaffe and saluting probably not the most comforting selection of words for anyone who was on the wrong end of the Blitz. But, then again, their goal machine, Gerd Müller, is nicknamed Der Bomber.

The question of Seeler has been vexing the Germans. In April the murder of a German diplomat had shocked the world. Ambassador Karl von Spreti, envoy to Guatemala, was kidnapped and held to ransom for £300,000 and the release of twenty-five political prisoners by a left-wing guerrilla organisation, Tuparos. Then they killed him anyway. On 30 May, the very eve of the tournament, an anonymous call made to Schoen threatened a similar fate for Seeler. No one is sure if it is the same group or another terrorist organisation, but a trace on the line suggested the call represents a genuine threat. (Very genuine. On 11 June the West German ambassador to Brazil will be kidnapped, sending West German Foreign Minister Walter Scheel into a frenzy to arrange his release.)

The Germans are staying at a desert spa twenty miles outside León at the village of Comanjilla. With its wooded grounds and hot-spring pools, it would normally be an idyllic spot, but the area is now crawling with forty-odd machine-gun- and grenade-toting Mexican special police.

Seeler, however, shows no signs of stress. Indeed, the German camp is in exceedingly good spirits, larking about in the sun, enjoying the pool and all those luxuries denied to England. So relaxed are the Germans that Schoen, on the day of the Bulgaria game, and after consulting Seeler, even throws the camp open to autograph hunters – much to the consternation of the security heavies.

'He is a marvel,' Schoen says of Seeler to the *Observer*. 'He has been in the winter of his career so many times. This must be his fourth spring.'

Spring isn't an appropriate metaphor for the German team, for, in playing terms, the weather has caused West Germany the most damage. They are coming off the worst winter that German football has ever suffered: forty-six Bundesliga games were postponed in 1969–70, every team in the top division facing a Leeds United-like schedule to clear the decks in time for Mexico. It has played havoc with the process of squad get-togethers, and, for all the good intentions of the Deutsche Fussball Bund, the team has managed only four matches since January, including going down 2–0 to Spain in Seville the following month.

Having scraped his players off the floor, Schoen has crucially, and in complete juxtaposition to England, decided to treat the group stage of the tournament as a recuperative mini-holiday, conscious of the mistake of four years ago when they were 'played in', as he puts it, before they reached England, rather than starting out ragged and building to a peak as the tournament progressed. Schoen has simply told his players to keep it simple and workmanlike in the opening three games and avoid the flash stuff, which cost them the early goal against Morocco.

And so, true to form, in the Germans' second game, once again the opposition – Bulgaria – takes the lead. The Germans, though, as they demonstrate, are dab hands at coming from behind. In an open and flowing game they prevail 5–2, with Müller getting a hat-trick.

They are through. As the headline in the *Daily Express* puts it, 'GAY GERMANS MARCH ON.'

After the game, ITV gets to interview Schoen back at the team hotel. Relaxing in a deckchair, while his lads lark about in the water, Schoen says he's pleased that they're into the next round. Not that they're easing up, by any means. What could be better than to beat Peru, win the group, and spend an extra few restful days in León for the quarter-final?

Whom would they prefer, England or Brazil?

'Both teams are hardly welcome,' he says. He saw them play each other on TV and was impressed with England. Thought they were unlucky to lose. Still, they will give it their best shot.

The Peruvians, too, fancy their chances. And quite a few are banking on them. Forget staying in León, what bigger incentive is there for winning the group than avoiding Brazil? In other words, both teams are playing for the right to face England. Some Peruvian ex-pats make the six-hour dusty and bumpy journey up from the capital to see the game. But even with 2,000 supporters of either side in the stadium, the attendance only reaches 16,000, a sad turnout for what promises to be one of the ties of the early rounds.

It was rumoured that Müller had pulled a thigh muscle and would miss the game but the Peruvians have no such luck. In the eighteenth minute, in thoroughly predictable fashion, he pops up to net a Libuda cross and leave keeper Rubiños – the weakest link in the Peru team – suspecting that it's going to be one of those days.

The Germans are playing in their change strip of emerald-green shirts and white shorts, which has an interesting story behind it. Pariahs in international football after the Second World War, the Republic of Ireland were the first team to invite the new West German nation over for a friendly and, when the German shirts went missing, loaned them a set of their own. The Germans have honoured the gesture by maintaining the Irish colours as their second strip ever since. They need no Irish luck today and, though they look different, there's something very familiar about their play.

Seven minutes later Lohr goes down the left, crosses it and there's that man Müller again, running back up the field in celebration, arms aloft, with a big grin plastered all over his swarthy Teutonic chops. In the thirty-seventh minute a cross comes over from Seeler and Müller and his short, fat, hairy legs are there. Another hat-trick.

Peru get one back in the second half when Schnellinger brings down de la Torre on the edge of the area. The kick by Cubillas hits the wall, deflects badly and bobbles past Maier, who had gone the wrong way.

Peru may be good, but there are no doubts about who are the masters here. Germany have scored ten goals in the opening round, Müller has got seven, including his consecutive hat-tricks, equalling the record of Hungarian Sandor Kocsis (though Cubillas, notably, has got four himself).

Provided England don't slip up against the Czechs, then, they're in for a rematch of the 1966 final . . .

Chapter 13

The Divine Baldy

So who's to play? Astle, Osgood, Clarke, maybe Nobby? Who'll be dropped? Lee, who's been huffing and puffing? Peters, who's not quite been the player of his reputation? Will Ramsey throw on an extra forward and go 4–3–3, or stick with the more solid midfield base of a 4–4–2? Will he get people to run themselves out and use his subs tactically?

Alf's not saying. At least not until forty-five minutes before kick-off. Only one person is definitely in the side – Bobby Charlton. For, without going as far as confirming it, Ramsey has given every indication that, against Czechoslovakia, the England number 9 will be taking the field to win his 105th cap.

The magic figure of 105 has been ingrained on the nation's minds for quite some time. And, especially since his hundredth cap against Northern Ireland, the words 'Bobby' and 'Charlton' have barely passed without a commentator or pundit mentioning the impending equalling of the English appearance record. For Hugh Johns and the ITV brigade, the facts have been easily committed to memory – at the Jalisco Stadium there are exactly 105 accursed concrete steps on the steep climb up to the commentary position. Johns's co-commentator – and co-climber – is none other than the great Billy Wright himself, whose magnificent record may very soon be surpassed. Wright, a true gentleman, has been making some very complimentary remarks about Charlton, ranking him alongside Wilf Mannion, Tom Finney and Stanley Matthews as one of England's greatest-ever players, and adding, rather modestly, how, in his case, all he had to do was defend – unlike Bobby, who's there in the middle directing things, a far more demanding exercise.

The pair's careers are inextricably entwined. It was Wright who was England captain when Charlton made his international debut in 1958. The two shared a room on England duty. And, marking the transition from one era to another, it was on Wright's hundredth appearance, against Scotland at Wembley, a year later, that young Charlton scored his first international goal – with his head, at that. Just to round out the occasion, Wright's wife gave birth on the same day.

Charlton, now thirty-two, is still something of an enigma. A completely different character to his cocky and confident brother Jack, the mental scars of the terrible Munich air crash, which he survived, still run deep, making him something of a sensitive, introverted personality. Prematurely balding, with a habitual and nervous habit of smoothing down the flap of blond strands across his pate, even during games, he seems like a man out of a different time (which, to a degree, he is, having arrived on the scene in the fifties and of that generation when smoking thirty a day – which he does – was not considered detrimental to athletic performance). For English football, there's been no finer ambassador over the past decade. Foreigners have always taken Charlton to be the ultimate English gentleman and have never quite reconciled his mild-mannered demeanour and physical delicacy with his playing prowess – especially his long-range shooting ability.

One Mexican newspaper recently published a *World Cup Guide for Women*, introducing them to the tournament and detailing the main characters in the game. Under 'Bobby Charlton' is the following entry: 'A slight, wispy-haired Englishman who, off the field, looks as though a breeze would knock him over, but on the field becomes, in Latin eyes, a combination of Genghis Khan and Ivan the Terrible.' He is known locally as 'El Calvo Divino' – The Divine Baldy.

After the final England training session in advance of the Czech game, and against the strains of a mariachi band blaring from a nearby cantina, Hugh Johns and Billy Wright manage to grab the man of the moment. The Divine Baldy is his usual modest self. 'I think generally I'm just proud that British football at this present time is having such a golden era,' he says, pointing out the haul of European club trophies that British sides have amassed in the last two or three years. He says that his first cap, against Scotland, 'could have been my first and last'.

'I never set my sights on any record till ninety-seven caps,' says Charlton. 'Then everyone seemed to be mentioning it.' There's nothing really remarkable about it. As a forward he's been able to avoid injury, and in the modern era they play more games and it's much easier to travel; in Billy's day they would only play five or six England matches a season. In future years someone will come along who'll win 125, 130, 180 caps, no trouble at all.

Charlton admits he's been very fortunate to play against some of the true greats – Yashin, Beckenbauer, Seeler, Di Stefano. But if he was going to single out any particular England moment – apart from 1966, of course – it would be, rather poignantly, the 4–2 win over Czechoslovakia in May 1963, the start of a change of the playing system and a long winning streak.

Charlton is also England's leading goalscorer. Will he go from forty-nine to fifty goals against Czechoslovakia in 1970? Well, who knows?

For the Czechs there is a more certain fate. After a disastrous World Cup and a thwarted players' revolution, the managerial axe will swing hard. Out will go captain Alexander Horvath, Andres Kvasnak and Karel Jokl, with ninety-one caps between them. Back will come Ivo Viktor (an army officer and economist) between the sticks. But make no mistake: despite all the internal ructions, the Czechs are well up for it.

'Well, you saw us against Brazil and Romania. I don't think we could play any worse with the new boys,' says coach Josef Marko at a pre-match press conference. 'The newcomers will fight to the last whistle in an effort to blast England right out of the stadium. You need strong stomachs to play against men like Cooper, Mullery and Moore [and to digest all that red meat, one supposes]. A victory over England will save us from complete disaster.'

The target is now absolutely plain: the Czechs need to win by four clear goals to snatch second spot; England need only a draw to qualify. If England lose 2–0, however, they will be level with Romania and will have to endure the unthinkable tie-breaker of a coin toss. They can take comfort from the fact that the last time they lost by more than the odd goal was six years and sixty matches ago – against, wouldn't you know it, Brazil (5–1 in Rio).

'I know the prospect of beating England by four goals seems impossible, but I think the younger players I'm bringing in are more likely to achieve a miracle than the older ones,' says Marko.

On Wednesday, after training and a round of golf, the England squad go to the TV studios again to watch West Germany versus Peru. They know exactly what the future holds in store for them now. Get the crucial point against the Czechs and they'll be facing the Germans in León.

'I don't think the Germans are better now than they were in 1966,' Moore declares the next morning. 'Müller looks a bit useful, but he hasn't been up against any great defences. Basically the Brazil result hasn't changed things for us. We play every game to win and it will be the same tonight against Czechoslovakia.'

Jack Charlton, who's talking like he might be a surprise selection, catching everyone unawares, says that at least there's no conjecture any more: 'Now we know exactly what we have to do to get through to the semi-finals.'

Big Jack's selection may raise a few eyebrows, but he's always had his fans. There's something about him, that absolute positivity and confidence that's infectious. Plus, he's as tough as nails. A latecomer to top-level League football, joining Leeds before their amazing rise, thirty years old when he played his first international, he's heard all the criticism before. But he knows he's good at what he does: Footballer of the Year in 1968, a League Championship medal the following season, too many cups to mention. And, in the twilight of his career at almost thirty-five, anyone who's anyone in the game reckons he will be a great manager when he finally hangs up his boots.

This year, the 'Giraffe' has been a fantastic player, too. 'I'd had a great season at Leeds, probably the best season in my life,' he says. And were it not for injury, or the fact that he'd been so otherwise engaged with Leeds, he'd have won many more caps.

Alf likes Jack. Jack tells it like it is. Doesn't mess about. 'I remember saying to Alf one day, "Why did you pick me to play for England?"' Jack remembers. 'He said, "Well, I've watched you play many times and I know you won't trust Bobby Moore." I said, "What are you talking about?" He said, "If the goalkeeper gave you the ball, you would give it back to him and say, 'Kick the bloody thing.' But if Bobby Moore was joining the attack and going through into midfield with the ball, you would always go across and cover him. If he made a mistake, you would go and retrieve it," which was sensible and he was right. I was always the header of the ball, Bobby the reader of the game.'

Although Jack's now lost his place to Brian Labone as the first-choice stopper alongside Moore, he can still be relied upon to dish it out when the going gets tough. Indeed, Jack has said on several occasions that if he can't stop a forward by fair means, then he will do so by foul. There is something very earthy and Leeds United about it all, but that's what Jack does: no airs and graces; if you want artistry, speak to brother Bobby. As Our Kid creates, so Big Jack destroys. And, just for good measure, he even keeps a little black book listing forwards due for some retributive justice.

It is unlikely there are any Czech names on Jack's hit-list, but with Labone in need of a rest from his exertions in the Brazil game, and more than likely required for the big quarter-final push, there might well be soon . . .

In the Jalisco Stadium at 4 p.m., local time, on Thursday, 11 June, England line up against Czechoslovakia. With 35,000 spectators in place, the ground is only half full (or half empty), hardly surprising given this is the least consequential of the Group Three games.

Ramsey has made his changes. Sentiment perhaps has caused him to play Bobby Charlton. Though Alf is never usually given over to such stuff. Maybe Alf has already decided something of which Charlton is not fully aware – that after this series, his England career will be over, every game from now on potentially his last. Charlton would have seemed an obvious choice if key players were going to be rested – give the indefatigable Bell a run-out instead. Bell *is* in, but for Ball, perhaps an indicator of whom Alf acknowledges now as his most important playmaker: the little Everton man on the bench, champing at the bit, his strength to be used sparingly before the quarter-final.

In defence Newton's back for Wright. And, as had been hinted, reliable old Jack gets his chance. He hadn't been expected to make it this far. As the team pensioner, it was assumed he would wilt with the early training, but Jack is from solid Northumberland mining stock and he'll be doing his bit all right. And so now brother Bobby's crowning moment will be a family affair.

Up front, as observers had been guessing from the training exercises, there are changes. Lee and Hurst sit it out while Astle and

Clarke get a turn. For Clarke it is a hell of a game in which to be making his debut, the fifty-fourth capped player of Ramsey's reign. As he explains, under Alf it has always been a question of progression: 'The only England manager that's done his job properly.'

He had been something of a sensation. In 1966–67 he scored four goals on his England under-23 debut in an 8–0 victory over Wales at Molineux, home of Wolves, his local boyhood heroes. 'For three years I'm playing for the under-23s, I'm knocking goals in. I'm selected for the full squads,' he says. 'But I remember saying to my wife, "If I don't get a cap in the next year [1969–70], I'm not going to Mexico." ' Indeed, concerned by this possibility, his transfer from relegated Leicester to Leeds in the summer of 1969 was inspired largely by his wish not to fall out of the England frame.

Alf, though, was simply doing what he always did. As manager of the under-23s, too, he would pick you, watch you perform, step you up to the full squad, with the odd run-out in an FA XI game or Football League representative match, take you on tour. You were an established part of the outfit, primed to slot in when the moment came without any major panic.

'I remember the day before the Czech match, we were on the training ground, Alf coming over to me. He says to me, "I'm gonna play you tomorrow, Allan." And so obviously I'm elated – "Smashin', Alf." He says, "I think you're ready now, son." I thought, Ready? I've been ready for three years!'

Clarke might have been expected to get a late run-out against Brazil, but had been laid low by a stomach bug, confined to bed, and had to watch the match on TV in the hotel room, joined by his best mate Billy Bremner, in town for the tournament as part of a *TV Times*-sponsored junket. Still, this is a big honour; on his wife's birthday, too, their fourth wedding anniversary. A grand day out for 'Sniffer', the man who's had such a dazzling first season with Leeds.

So it's an unfamiliar-looking England – and in more ways than one. Because the Czechs also wear an all-white strip and won the toss for colours, it is England who must change. Now it's light blue for England, a sort of pastel-hued version of their usual outfit, with the same big red numbers on the back. Still England, but not quite the same.

The French ref Roger Machin blows the whistle, and England

kick off – Astle to Clarke, back to Mullery, and immediately apparent is the difficulty with visibility. The notorious Jalisco shadow had caused problems in the game against Romania, though a haze had taken the edge off its sharpness. Today, with a clear blue sky and the sun burning fiercely, it is the worst it has been so far. In the first half Cooper finds himself charging down the wing in a blinding white glare; Newton, by comparison, is playing in the dark. It is also 98 degrees and extremely humid.

From the England bench, which has been shifted across to the shady touchline, in the first few minutes the problems are obvious as several England players hit passes straight to their opponents, including a beautifully executed lay-off from Colin Bell to Capkovic. The pale blue shirts, it seems, in this light, are barely distinguishable from the white of the Czechs. It's the same for both sides, of course, but, short of voluntarily going shirts and skins, not really an option in an international match, the game suffers.

As the match begins at a brisk pace and the ball pings around from man to man, it is all starting to resemble a pub match. Plus, the Czechs, quite patently, are set on winning it. Straight away the lively Petras charges down the right wing, requiring a crucial sliding tackle by Cooper to halt him. And with the number 18, Vesely, buzzing, England are forced to man the pumps at the back, requiring some speedy covering.

'You're never as quick and determined when you're sweating your bollocks off and trying to get your breath,' says Jack Charlton.

And so the problems continue. Moore, running out with the ball, plays an inch-perfect pass to a Czech midfielder. 'England not finding the players at all well,' comments Hugh Johns, fully aware of the problems.

The game is live on ITV, only highlights appearing on the BBC. The third channel are flying solo on this. Good for them, but not for those in the Granada region, with that station off the air. The people of Lancashire will have to make do with the radio, avoid the result till the highlights or – good heavens! – hop in their cars and drive to Yorkshire.

The game wears on, the ball bounces back and forth, and Hurst, hunched over on the bench next to Ramsey, and desperately disappointed he didn't get a start, seems to be watching it through his fingers. No wonder he's angry that he is not playing: he was promised £1,000 by an Essex businessman if he scored a hat-trick in this match.

'A tremendous tense period for these players as they test each other out,' says Johns. And he's absolutely right. To find the ball, Clarke has started coming very deep. On the left-hand side, Peters, Cooper and Charlton try a little short passing exchange which unravels against a solid Czech defence. At the other end Moore does his usual snuffing-out routine, though in the process of chasing down Capkovic he accidentally handles in his own box. To the chagrin of the Czech number 21, referee Machin doesn't spot it.

By the time the first quarter of the game has lapsed, it is obvious that the Czechs are doing all the running. And, yet again, a pass is played straight to the opposition – by Cooper this time.

Bobby Charlton mounts a counter-offensive, lobs one into the box from the right, a cross-cum-shot, in the hope that Astle might reach it: no joy. Cooper floats one in for Astle, who tries a very ungainly, un-Brazilian lunge, vaguely approximating an overhead kick. And, with similar balls being pumped up to Clarke, it seems that England's sole strategy in offence is based on the long ball into the box. Primitive stuff.

Maybe there is a method in all this. Sit back, let the Czechs run at you and then hit them with the occasional aerial bombardment, or, in the second half, hope that the Czechs begin their traditional flagging routine. If this is the plan, then England are flying by the seat of their pants. Number 10, Adamec, steams into the England box, stopped only by a Jack Charlton sliding tackle. Then, number 2 Dobias, another overlapping full back, plays Cooper at his own game. England have simply run out of ideas.

'Mullery, drilling it inside for Colin Bell, and that wasn't so far away,' yells Johns enthusiastically as Bell at least has a crack, firing from twenty-five yards out only to see the ball caught by the giant black-clad Viktor underneath the Czech bar. Bell is pushing up now: he heads a Cooper cross over, the ball skimming the top of his blond thatch. Then he finds Clarke, who fires wide.

The Czechs continue to give as good as they get. Dobias plays a long ball to number 21, Capkovic, their left winger from Slovan Bratislava, who easily beats Jack Charlton and shoots wide, the lanky Leeds man furious with Newton for leaving what should have been his man. Big Jack, fired up, starts joining the attack, and a corner from brother Bobby is picked right off his head by the goalie.

Capkovic again threatens, beats Mullery and squares for Petras to fire high and wide. A corner follows from Adamec which curls straight under Banks's crossbar before being headed away. 'Oh, a naughty one,' says Johns, 'and Newton right off the line.'

Cooper, on the back foot now, seems troubled by a big grass burn on his right thigh – an occupational hazard for a defender on a dry, hard surface – hitching his shorts up and out of harm's way, and the England midfield, all at sixes and sevens, gives the big Czech number 9, Kuna, licence to stroll around the middle.

Another attack: Hagara, the number 4, unleashed on the left, crosses for Adamec to hit over. 'Well, the Czechs are getting in there far too often for Sir Alf Ramsey's peace of mind,' says Johns.

The crowd do not enjoy the spectacle and the catcalls begin. The jeers merely increase when Cooper's boot comes off after a scrap with Vesely. Cooper sits down, delaying a throw-in, to put his boot back on, and the ref chases him off the field of play. England seem disinclined to go forward and take people on. There seems fat chance of Bobby Charlton getting his fiftieth goal today. And just when it couldn't get any uglier, electrical storms over the Atlantic start breaking up the picture for the folks back home.

The Czechs knock it about – Dobias, Adamec, Kuna, Migas. Pollak, the number 17, in his first World Cup game, looks very comfortable on the ball. Then, in the forty-third minute, a sudden burst of excitement. Bell, on the right, sees Clarke breaking free on the left and hits him with an inch-perfect ball. 'Clarke and he's in the clear,' screams Johns. 'Clarke is closing in now, *Clarke...*' Sniffer darts inside the defender, just like he does every Saturday for Leeds, and shapes to pick his spot. Migas thunders in and hoofs it away for a corner.

Almost on half-time, Peters is brought down just outside the box and England get a free kick in a prime position. After seeing several examples of Brazilians and Peruvians doing amazing things, bending shots round walls, with lots of theatrical feinting before-hand, England's imagination stretches as far as Bobby Charlton chipping it over the wall in the hope that Astle can get his nut on it. You can hardly hear the half-time whistle for the 35,000 other ones in the stands.

Unfortunately, the second half doesn't begin with any signs of encouragement. England run into culs-de-sac, the Czechs begin to look frustrated. And then, an amazing piece of good fortune. Four minutes into the second half, Cooper runs down the left and plays it across field, over to his counterpart Newton on the right. Unmarked, Newton comes forward. 'Newton faced by Hagara. One–two with Bell...' It happens quickly but Johns spots it, and so, luckily, does the ref: 'Handball in the box, *penalty!*' As Bell had gathered from Newton just inside the area and challenged the Czech number 4, Hagara, the defender had taken a tumble, landed on the ball, and knocked it with his outstretched arm. Unlucky, sure, but a penalty none the less. That the Czechs do not offer up much protest suggests they are of the same opinion.

Allan Clarke, on his full debut and in the absence of Hurst and Lee, the regular takers, steps up. To the viewers back home it might be a surprise that Clarke is taking it at all, especially given the significance for Bobby Charlton, who's spot-kicked before for England.

'I remember Alf's team talk for the Czech match and he's telling us all what he wants us to do, what he doesn't want us to do and a bit of information about the Czech side,' says Clarke. 'And just as he's finishing, he says, "Now if we have a penalty, who'll take it?" Now although I've been with them for three years, I'm still relatively new. I was waiting for one of the more experienced players to put their hand up – thirty seconds, it seemed like a lifetime. Anyway, there's nothing coming and so I say, "I'll take 'em, Alf." He says, "Good lad." '

Clarke – who's taken penalties for Walsall, Fulham and Leicester (though not Leeds, where Johnny Giles does it) – does not believe that penalties should be missed. He calmly side-foots it hard to Viktor's left, the keeper going the wrong way. 'Clarke, there it is, one–nothing,' says Johns. Astle, Peters and Bell, who are thankful for Sniffer's nerve, leap all over him. Clarke looks well chuffed.

At the Clarke family home in Willenhall in the Black Country, Allan Clarke's mother knew he'd score. She had a premonition, at least according to the Birmingham *Evening Mail*. 'I told people about it and when I learned that he would play against Czecho-slovakia, I felt that was it,' says Mrs Alice Clarke. And so overjoyed was she when her twenty-four-year-old son popped the ball in, she stood up and knocked a glass of water across the room. 'As soon as I saw the ref award a penalty and Allan pick up the ball I gasped,' she says. 'No one feels the same way as a mother at such a time, but my husband Frank said, "Don't worry, he will score."' Also watching are brother Derek, the Wolves player, and siblings Margaret, Kelvin and Wayne – as well as neighbours Mr and Mrs George Worthington, whose TV is broken.

Says Mrs Clarke, 'When the players ran out and I could see my boy lining up in the middle of the pitch with the ball at his feet, I could not help crying. It was a very emotional moment.'

'She was a very proud mum,' says Clarke.

The Jalisco crowd, though, do not like the outcome at all and jeer the ref. The 3,000 or 4,000 England fans suddenly find their voice. All of a sudden it seems we might have a game on our hands.

If only. It soon reverts to type, with just a touch of bile applied by the Czechs now, whose cause is lost unless they can score five in the next forty minutes.

Amazingly, England manage to string a full six passes together from the back before Cooper is hacked down from behind by Vesely. Cooper squares up to him and is dragged off by Peters. The next time Vesely comes near him, the ref's looking the other way and Cooper makes his point.

'Some of the England passing is too bad to be true,' says Johns. 'Perhaps if they've got to get a bad game out of their system, it wouldn't be bad if this was it.'

On sixty minutes Osgood comes on, dutifully handing in his official slip to the linesman, entering the field of play and eagerly ordering off Astle himself, explaining to the referee what's just happened. It will take a while for him to see any action. The ball is in the crowd and they keep it. A new one is found and it is obviously to Petras's liking as he forces Banks to tip it over the bar. At the other end, Osgood and Clarke chase the same openings and get in each other's way. Then, a faint hope when Peters chips it in, Bell rounds the keeper and taps it in the net, only to be given offside, the defence already having stopped.

Things get more encouraging when Ball comes on for Bobby Charlton in the sixty-fifth minute, and instantly reveals what a dynamo he is for the team; Charlton is booed as he shuffles off. In the seventy-fourth minute Clarke picks up a loose ball, plays it to

Ball thirty yards out and he shoots and hits the bar. Bad luck.

For England, the quarter-finals are in sight, but the Czechs don't give up. Kuna takes a far more imaginative free kick than Charlton managed and curls it past the far post, against the stanchion, fooling the crowd for a moment who yell, 'Goal.' Nine minutes from time Dobias nutmegs Osgood and shoots from long range. Banks goes to catch it at head height, it slips through his gloves and clatters against the bar, then to the feet of Jack Charlton, who taps it back to Banks and safety. 'Well, you don't often see Gordon Banks make a mistake like that . . . what a let-off for England,' says Johns, though the world number one had already had his concentration broken before that when he had to go behind the goal and appeal for the Mexican fans to stop pelting him with orange peel, drinks and coins.

The Cooper/Vesely contretemps continues. Adamec has a long-range pop that sails into the England supporters: they do as the locals and keep it. Shortly afterwards, the Mexicans do the same again, perhaps in the hope that this dreadful game will be abandoned. But with yet another ball – the fourth of the match – thrown on from the bench, and with the shadow now right across the pitch, the game ends, Osgood nobbled right on the final whistle.

None of it matters. England, through Clarke's penalty, have notched up their fifty-first win under Ramsey. 'Les Cocker told me in the dressing room afterwards, "Alf was funny, you know," ' chuckles Clarke. 'He says, "You know when you were placing the ball? Alf turned to me. He says, 'Will he score, Les?' " So Les turns to Alf, he says, "Put your mortgage on him." '

After the match, in what is becoming the usual drill, Ramsey comes through and the British commentator, in this case Johns, is waiting for him for the brief satellite interview – a couple of moulded-plastic canteen chairs pulled up for the purpose.

The result was satisfying, but surely the game wasn't very good, was it? 'I don't think so,' agrees Alf. 'We've played a lot better and lost. Our football was not up to the standard of the last two matches.' But, he says, 'in qualifying, now you'll see a little more freedom of expression from the players'.

Well, at least they've got that bad game out of their system now, eh? Well, yes, Ramsey says, but it was the nervous tension and the bad light which affected concentration. 'Certainly in terms of colour,' says Alf. 'I think the choice, and it was my choice, of pale blue as a second colour was a bad one. Where I sat looking from the shade into the sun it was very difficult to distinguish the players.'

Now it's the Germans on Sunday. 'Always a tremendous battle,' explains Alf. 'The opposition is very strong, very good. I have every confidence that we will qualify for the semi-finals.'

Back home, though, none are particularly impressed. 'All's well that ends well, but England must drop the disguise,' says the Liverpool *Echo*. 'On the spot England scrape in,' says the Birmingham *Evening Mail*, at least extracting some fun from the situation by saying that on ITV it was 'quite like old times with Jimmy Hill urging on the sky blues'.

It was bad, everyone knows it, but we're through. Though the Czech manager says afterwards that he wasn't impressed with England, and they'd better watch it. 'I think it is very difficult for history to repeat itself and the German team have been improving much more than England in the tournament.'

The Liverpool *Echo* seems to agree: 'The ten-goal Teutons of West Germany smugly predict that if England cannot do any better than score twice in three qualifying matches, they can expect to have their Anglo-Saxon noses rubbed into the turf of the small but well-manicured stadium at León when the teams clash in Sunday's quarter-final.'

After the match, back at the Hilton, Bobby Charlton is presented with a special gold medal for sportsmanship by the governor of Jalisco State, Francisco Medina Ascensio. On a small, raised platform, against the backdrop of a Union Jack and a Mexican tricolour, Charlton talks about his 'many happy hours in Mexico'; is very touched; says everyone is saying nice things about him; adds he will treasure this award even more than a second World Cup winner's medal, should he win one in ten days' time. Later, even the diplomatic Charlton admits that it was a terrible game and that the Czechs were the better side.

Perhaps the Birmingham *Evening Mail*'s closing remark is a tad premature: 'England still do not know for certain whether they will play their semi-final in Guadalajara or Mexico City.'

With no national papers to report the match and problems with TV transmission, it seems only appropriate that this dreadful game will slip into a media black hole . . .

Chapter 14

Nacho

Friday, 12 June 1970

And so the losers go home: Belgium, El Salvador, Israel, Sweden, Czechoslovakia, Romania, Bulgaria and Morocco. Some can consider themselves unlucky. Sweden might feel irked at the denial of a goal in that last game against Uruguay. Belgium will be particularly incensed by that dodgy penalty awarded to Mexico.

Indeed, Van Himst and Puis announce that, in sheer disgust, they will quit international football (though Van Himst will ultimately return). The penalty is the second robbery this week. At the Hotel Maria Isabel, the FIFA HQ, a ten-foot high fibre-glass promotional football was stolen from the roof.

There are already casualties among the departed. Czech manager Josef Marko has announced that he will be standing down from the national job to take up a post with Slovan Bratislava. He is not very happy with his players. 'They let me down. I treated them with kid gloves because I thought they were men,' he snarls. 'I know now I should have used the iron fist.' (No sign yet of the velvet revolution.)

The Czech footballing authorities, due to the threatened mutiny in Mexico, will disqualify most of the squad from the international scene till the end of 1971.

And so it is the conquerors of Belgium and Sweden – Mexico and Italy – who must square up in one of four quarter-finals which will be played simultaneously at noon, local time, on Sunday, 14 June. As Belgium and El Salvador know only too well, the atmosphere of the Azteca has been extremely good to the Mexican team, as have the referees, who have fallen under the crowd's persuasive spell. With up to 112,000 screaming fans, the pitch's ankle-deep grass and benevolent officials on their side, the Mexicans fear no one.

But there is a problem for Mexico. Though level on points with Russia, and with equal goal difference, it is the Russians who won Group One, due to a superior goal tally. Therefore, by rights, it is they who should be staying put in the capital while Mexico go off to face Italy at Toluca. The Mexican FA, sensing this eventuality, have been lobbying FIFA hard for some time to remain at 'home' and let the Soviets traipse off to the sticks instead. What's the point in Russia and Uruguay playing before a third-full Azteca, they argue, when Mexico and Italy could fill the stadium ten times over? Surely it is logical from a spectator and commercial point of view. Indeed, and quite surprisingly, the Italian FA itself confesses it would rather play at the Azteca, too, instead of crappy old Toluca. 'Toluca does not offer any guarantees for the public and players. The field is bad and the stands are insufficient,' announces Franco Bertoldi, secretary of the Italian FA.

Just to seal the argument, the Mexicans cite the precedent that has already been set by Evil England, who, scheduled to play their 1966 semi-final with Portugal at Goodison Park, successfully petitioned FIFA to let them stay at Wembley on exactly the same basis (Russia and West Germany thus played in Liverpool, annoying all those people who'd bought tickets thinking they'd be seeing England).

The argument is not without reason, though against the spirit of the draw. With Rous eager not to face a repeated accusation of manipulation and mindful that he's already taken a tough line with the Uruguayans over the refereeing scandal, he would prefer not to yield. However, and for all his prior hard-line attitude, he does the diplomatic equivalent of deferring to his linesman. Lots will be drawn to decide who'll stay put.

On the morning of Friday 12th, in the Hotel Maria Isabel, where the original draw was made, the great deed takes place, televised to a nail-biting nation. No one – the country, officials, even the Russians – thinks for one minute that the draw will not be fixed to give Mexico the advantage. The Russians are probably already packing. But lo and behold, it's the Soviet Union whose name comes out of the hat.

Livid, the Mexicans protest and mount an appeal, but with the clock ticking and only hours to sort out travelling arrangements, FIFA abides by the decision. Russia will stay at the Azteca.

The governor of Toluca, Hank González, again raises the question of safety. Now that his small mountain outpost is going to be besieged, he implements emergency security measures. He appeals for Mexican fans not to come to Toluca unless they have tickets, spurred on no doubt by the scenes of rioting in Mexico City, not wishing them to be visited upon his town. What's more, knowing that at least 10,000 more than the stipulated 106,000 have been cramming in for the games at the Azteca, the tiny Bombonera Stadium with its capacity of 30,000 – no moat, flimsy chicken-wire fencing, creaking stands and the maze of narrow streets around it – will pose a serious safety threat.

'We will not allow more people than the stadium can take to watch the match on Sunday,' says Gonzalez. 'All precautionary measures to prevent gate-crashing will be taken.' He orders TVs to be placed in public parks throughout Toluca, enlists the army to adopt a siege posture with a military cordon around the stadium and urges the town to batten down the hatches.

At least that's the official line. It turns out Toluca, a venue not originally considered for the World Cup, was awarded the right to stage games in return for political favours to the government done by González, a rising star of the ruling PRI party. Now it is González's duty to get the game switched back to Mexico City.

None of this washes with FIFA . . .

At the Azteca on Sunday afternoon, the Mexicans have been proven correct in their assessment. Although there are 75,000 people there, in such a vast cauldron this still leaves huge tracts of empty seats. Most of the people inside have got half an ear on what's going on at Toluca, the stadium abuzz more from news on the Tannoy, or the thousands of transistor radios in the crowd all tuned in to events in Toluca – all far more exciting than what's happening on the pitch down below.

The USSR have much the better record in this tournament than Uruguay, though the fact that they got the Azteca and the Mexicans didn't – plus the fact that they're communists – immediately makes them the villains of the piece. And, just to ram it home, the Uruguayans, Latin brethren, enter the field holding a giant Mexican flag. Otherwise, though – as evidenced by results in Group Two –

the Uruguayans care little for spectacle. In fact, seemingly not too bothered by the Swedish defeat, their manager Eduardo Hohberg reaffirms their limited ambition: 'Our objective when we left Montevideo was to get to the quarter-finals,' he tells the *Guardian*. 'We have managed to do so.'

As an Argentinian, Hohberg is one of a number of 'foreign' coaches now in the international game. In this tournament alone we have had Morocco coached by a Yugoslav, El Salvador run by another Argentinian Chilean, Israel managed by a German-born Jew and Peru bossed by a Brazilian. Of course, there is no question of it ever happening in England.

For the sake of football, then, and especially on behalf of the Swedes and the Israelis, the neutrals want a Russian win.

Of course, with Uruguay involved, the game is dull. Russia's bright attacking thrusts, led by Bishovets and Evriuzhikhin, run into brick walls, the Uruguayans marshalling themselves to get ten men back behind the ball whenever they lose possession and prepared to kick out whenever a man is beaten. The crowd, not particularly interested anyway, becomes even less so. At ninety minutes, it is hardly surprising that the score is that old Uruguayan party-piece, 0–0.

But the Uruguayans know exactly what they're doing – letting the Russians, struggling in the heat, gradually burn themselves out. As the teams take breaks before extra-time, it is evident which side has got the legs for the coming thirty minutes. The Russians loll around on the turf, many of them at the point of exhaustion, while the coaching staff plies them with water and fans them with towels. They look completely spent. Plus, crucially, they have already used both their subs and removed their star orchestrater Asatiani back in the seventy-first minute.

The Uruguayans, by comparison, look like a little dark commando outfit, sitting on their haunches while Hohberg spells out the tactics for extra-time – like troops about to burst off the landing craft and take the beach.

The game doesn't improve, just slows. We are within seconds now of the end. With no means of a tie-breaker, it will come down to the toss of a coin, a horrible way to exit.

FIFA have recently recommended to their International Board that for the next World Cup a system of penalty kicks be used to decide a stalemate – best of five, then sudden death. For now, it's still down to heads or tails.

What with winning the draw to stay at the Azteca, the Russians must already be thinking they'd used up their luck when, with Ubiñas looking on, Bishovets cuts inside Ancheta in the box and places a shot past Mazurkiewicz's right. A goal at last. Or not. To a man, Uruguayan right arms shoot up and the ref – Laurens van Ravens of Holland – blows for a questionable offside. Bishovets cannot believe it, stands there dumbfounded, and the Uruguayan number 3, Matosas, walks up to him and claps sarcastically in his face.

Immediately, the number 10 Maneiro taps it to Ubiñas, midway inside the Russian half, and he sends a long far-post cross into the Russian box. In the thin air the ball overshoots, Ancheta and Shesternev jump for it. It bobbles down, Ancheta chases it, there is a scramble between him and defenders Afonin and Logofet and the ball rolls out of play over the goal line.

Or does it? The Russians all stop, two Uruguayans even turn away, but Ancheta pulls it back, runs it along the line, flicks it up at the near post and the unmarked Espárrago, who's only just come on, nods the ball into the net without any real conviction – Dzodzuashvili, Kiselev and Kaplichni absolutely static. Waiting to see whether it has been a goal kick or a corner, the Russians are suddenly horrified to observe the ref running back, pointing to the centre circle. *Goal.*

The Uruguayans, naturally, are wild with joy. They did, after all, do the correct thing and merely play to the whistle. But the Russians lose it completely. To have come so far, to be dead on their feet and to have just had a seemingly good one of their own ruled out at the other end ... They besiege the ref and jostle him. The goalie Kavazashvili charges off to the linesman, Scotland's Bob Davidson, the man who kept his flag down, and tries to drag him into proceedings. Bishovets and Khmelnitski flap their arms most emphatically. The Russian number 12, sub Kiselev, makes irate gestures. But it is all in vain. Uruguay go through. Russia are out. And, according to word in their camp, they now have only a dispute over bonuses to occupy them on the long flight back to Moscow.

In Montevideo, the headline of the daily newspaper *Novedades* reads, 'URUGUAY FOR THE SEMI-FINALS, AFONIN FOR SIBER-IA . . .'

Away from the Azteca it's a whole different box of tricks for Mexico. Not that the supporters aren't vocal enough, absolutely worked into a frenzy and chanting 'ME-HI-CO! ME-HI-CO!' inside the tiny Bombonera. The suspicions of the governor have proven correct. There are way too many people in here. Along one side of the pitch fans are, quite literally, hanging off the rafters and edging along the thin ledges that support the advertising hoardings. It's like the third round of the FA Cup when a Southern League side is entertaining one of the big boys – only without all the green parkas.

Mexico take the field in their red and black change strip (their green and white deemed too similar to Italy's outfit on black-and-white TV, which is what most people have). Within minutes of kicking off, as Bertini runs down the right and is hacked down, the Mexicans seem set on demonstrating that they've got the muscle to take on the Italians, if not the skill.

Italy, though, have got something to prove. Having scored that paltry solitary goal in qualifying and failing even to net against humble Israel, those multi-million-lira price tags are looking a little inflated. And dare anyone mention North Korea? In the twelfth minute, the colour collectively drains from the Italian national face as Fragoso turns and beats Rosato, runs into the box and finds González. A static Italian defence can only watch helplessly as the Mexican forward taps it past Albertosi. Rosato, de Sisti, Burgnich and Facchetti are motionless. They stare at each other in disbelief, shaking shameful heads as González is leapt upon by his team-mates.

The joy is short-lived. The roar has barely subsided when Riva finds Boninsegna on the wing. Chased by Guzmán and the tall Padilla, he manages to keep it from going over the deadball line (possibly with help from his hand). With number 5 Pérez shooing him away, he plays it to Domenghini, who aims a low, harmless, bobbling shot at the Mexican goal. Calderón dives right over it: 1–1. The whole nation is silent.

Calderón, wearing kneepads for this game, lies face down, the-atrically. Some defenders appeal belatedly for handball and Valdivia and Padilla try to drag the ref to the linesman. The captain Peña angrily berates his keeper, who lies there guiltily adjusting his new leg wear. As the protest continues, the ref goes for his cards and the Mexicans back down in the stand-off while the delighted Domenghini is mobbed by Mazzola, de Sisti and Bertini. The Italians now mean business.

In the sixty-fifth minute Riva, at last with space to run, charges at three defenders in the inside-left position – suddenly and recognisably like the man all Italy loves. The shot is rather hopeful, but Calderón is way, way too late getting down: 2–1. Again Peña scolds his keeper. 'It's these damn kneepads,' Calderón seems to be saying.

Then Rivera, on at half-time for Mazzola, gives the crowd a glimpse of what all the fuss is about, as he comes into the left-hand side of the box, jinks inside two defenders and hits the ball low, but not particularly hard, at Calderón's near post. If there's one thing you can say about old Nacho, it's that he's consistent. He should gather it, and does get a hand to it, but he lets it spill under him: 3–1.

Rivera disappears under a pile of Italian bodies, the Mexicans collapse and Peña goes to bawl at Calderón and his kneepads but figures it's not really worth it any more. A banner behind the goal boldly proclaims, 'Adelante México', but there is faint hope of victory now.

Thirteen minutes from time, Rivera, the bit between his teeth, runs half the length of the pitch against retreating defenders, then finds Riva. Calderón comes unnecessarily and half-heartedly out to the edge of the area to challenge, when he'd have been better off leaving it to his old mate Peña, who was poised to make the tackle. Riva rounds them both and casually pings a shot between the legs of the covering Guzmán on the line. The scorer lies there in celebration as paper cups, corks, coins and fruit rain down on him. Boninsegna and Domenghini help him up and saunter off in triumph.

Because the Mexican and Italian flags are virtually identical, the Italian fans had remained rather inconspicuous till now. Time to declare themselves. And, just for once, you can hear a chant of 'Italia, Italia'.

For Mexico, it was fun while it lasted, but away from the Azteca at this Third Division ground, they were made to look, in international terms, like a Third Division side. Now the Mexican fans can all go off and support Brazil.

'They accepted defeat very well,' remembers Barry Davies, who commentated on the game. 'I don't think any sane football supporter would have expected any more than what happened. There was a huge expectation which was way above the ability of the side, but they surprised a few people. There was a resignation that, "OK, we had the dream, and we enjoyed it when it was on and eventually we had to wake up." '

The critics like what they have seen of Italy. This is the stuff that everyone wants, not that boring defensive numbness, and with the star players suddenly equal to their reputations. 'Italy at last showed the form which won them the European Nations Cup two years ago and ruthlessly exposed the mediocrity of the host country by winning 4–1,' writes David Lacey in the *Guardian*. 'Away from the hordes of the Aztec Stadium, Mexico were revealed as a ponderous, plodding side with predictable ideas and a defence which became increasingly at the mercy of Riva and the elegant Italian attack...'

Peru move out of the Guanajuato Hotel near León and head west for Guadalajara. It is like walking into the lions' den: Brazil at home, free-flowing goals and a true force to be reckoned with. Intriguingly, Brazil's games at the group stage all came against European teams who are practitioners of the solid defence, putting them under little attacking pressure. How would Brazil fare against a team fashioned in their own image? An outfit who would throw men forward with scant regard for their own defensive frailties?

Brazil have been nursing injuries – Clodoaldo with a bruised right thigh, Everaldo with a twisted ankle. But they have Gérson and his left foot back (so accurate 'he could stir tea with it', according to Tommy Docherty), which means Paulo Cézar will have to stand down and Rivelino can go back on the left. By match day, Clodoaldo has pulled through, too, though left back Everaldo fails to recover in time, meaning a start for Marco Antonio. Peru, meanwhile, are at full strength and have brought back their powerful winger Baylon – Jimmy Hill's boy – who missed the last two games.

Before the match, the Peruvians, complete with their little boy mascot, sing their national anthem for all it's worth, right hand on heart. But they will need something extra special if they are going to pull it off here today.

Brazil, now playing their fourth game on the Jalisco Stadium pitch, set about the game as if it is a Sunday afternoon stroll – little Tostão kicking off to Pelé, who plays it wide to skipper Carlos Alberto, who knocks it to the ambling Gérson. Such is the understanding between the Brazilians that Gérson is still looking down, tying the drawstring on his shorts, when he casually and without even bothering to look up plays an inch-perfect ball off to the slim, elegant Clodoaldo.

Peru, though, show that they're no mugs by stroking it around the middle and begin to wrong-foot the notorious Brazilian defence, forcing an early corner. But it doesn't take long, seven minutes, for the inevitable to happen. Tostão, given freedom to run around in front of the Peruvian defence, in exactly the same area from which he started the move for the goal against England, sends the ball left to Rivelino, attacking on the edge of the Peruvian box. Perhaps in awe of the pistol that Playboy packs, the defender commits the cardinal sin of not facing down the ball but turning his back. Rivelino's fierce left-foot drive sails into the far corner of the net past an insipid dive by keeper Rubiños.

Minutes later, from a short corner on the left, Tostão plays a one–two with Rivelino and, cutting inside along the goal line, and unchallenged, he sends in a low centre-cum-shot across the face of the goal. If Peru are the new Brazil, then Rubiños is certainly the new Félix, for he lets this soft effort go under his body at the near post: 2–0, an elementary goalkeeping error.

Then, bizarrely, perhaps in honour of his new protégé, Félix lets Peru's Gallardo score an almost identical goal at the other end. It's 2–1, but it is not looking good for the men from the Andes.

In the second half, with the Mexican crowd behind them, Brazil step up a gear. After six minutes, Pelé runs down the right, crosses, and Tostão taps it in. He gets a clout on the side of the head as he falls – always a worry where Tostão is concerned – but not enough to prevent him leaping to his feet and clutching his temple as Pelé hoists him high.

But Peru – 'The Diddymen' as the Liverpool *Echo* have taken to calling them – do not give up. As Fuentes and substitute Sotil charge into the box, both flummoxing our old friends Brito and

Piazza, the ball bounces out to Cubillas. While the first two strikers take a tumble, possibly arousing a claim for at least one penalty, Cubillas fires it home, no argument: 3–2.

All that remains is for the customary goal from Jairzinho. Fifteen minutes from the end he runs in from the left, sees Rubiños go AWOL and scores from a tight angle: 4–2. Rubiños is so embarrassed that he goes and hides behind a post.

Brazil have made a semi-final date with Uruguay . . .

After the Peru game the German players had celebrated by throwing Helmut Schoen into the pool fully clothed, making him ten minutes late (and sopping wet) for his press conference. The question of any England player even contemplating such a move with Sir Alf does not even bear thinking about. But they're happy campers, the Germans, and with the pool to themselves, too.

Not that it's all japes. Given the treat of a day off after their group game with Peru, the players passed up the offer. With light training only proposed, they opt instead for the hard stuff.

The news from the camp, at which the press has been made most welcome, is respectful yet quietly confident. As for Müller's seven goals and the double hat-trick, the noises are predictable. 'I don't care who scores as long as the ball goes in,' says the twenty-four-year-old forward. 'I am not a bit concerned about whether I win the scoring title.'

Schoen is still concerned about the ejection of team masseur Erich Deuser from the Peru game by Mexican referee Abel Aguilar – the report stating it had been for coming on to the pitch without permission. The first caution of Group Four and it goes to a trainer, though it is of only minor note compared with the big game the Germans now face. All thoughts must be concentrated on England. Schoen went to Guadalajara to watch the England–Czechoslovakia game, and though he will not be as disingenuous to say what a wonderful match it was, he concedes that Ramsey's side will be a very tough cookie. 'England will be hard to beat. We know just how good their defence is,' he says. 'But we have the advantages here. We are used to the conditions. We know the ground. England, to me, look a little tired, a little jaded. I think this time we will win.' He adds, rather pointedly, 'I do not believe in defensive football. Any side which concentrates mainly on preventing the opposition from scoring is risking World Cup suicide. We know the game against England will be a physical affair. It always is because our football is so alike. But it will not be dirty. Both teams can give and take knocks.'

That the German camp is so open is down to the fact that they have employed a full-time press officer – Dr Wilfried Gerhardt – to liaise with media, officials and public alike, leaving Schoen to get on with the business of managing the team, a move Ramsey would have done well to emulate, by all accounts. It has worked well. The locals – and this is a phrase not used lightly – *love* the Germans. Every TV shot is of smiling players splashing about in the pool, laughing themselves silly. The locals are happy to wave the thousands of paper German flags that have been distributed, and the centre of León, decked out in red, black and gold bunting, looks more like a setting for the Oktoberfest.

Back home, the pundits are already reminding everyone that the Germans have only ever beaten England once – that game in Hannover, the one that didn't really count. However, as they say in this business, you're only as good as your last game. But in footballing terms – as well as other affairs – England and Germany go back a long way. The two sides took part in what was probably, though unofficially, the greatest, certainly most symbolic, football match ever played – that between British and German troops on the Somme on Christmas Eve in the Great War.

There have been other important encounters. At the first international in 1901, England won 12–0 at White Hart Lane. Later, infamously, on 14 May 1938, at the height of appeasement, England played in the Nazi shrine of the Berlin Olympic Stadium. In front of Goering and Goebbels, the players were cajoled by the British ambassador – much to their anger – into giving the Nazi salute. England won 6–3.

On 26 May 1956, on their first return to the same stadium, against *West* Germany now, the new World Cup holders, England again triumphed, this time 3–1 (with goals by Edwards, Granger and Haynes). Then, of course, came 1966, with Alf, who had done his bit for King and country in the great dust-up of 1939–45, telling his lads before extra-time to stay on their feet, so as not to let 'these Germans' know they were tired.

Curiously, in 1970, only twenty-five years after World War Two's end, and with many people involved in the World Cup either having taken part in the conflict or certainly growing up through it (Harold Shepherdson was in the Green Howards; commentators Kenneth Wolstenholme and Hugh Johns were, respectively, RAF and Fleet Air Arm pilots; Sepp Herberger, Schoen's protégé, was a Hitler darling; Israeli manager Emanuel Shefer, as mentioned earlier, survived a Nazi death camp), the war is barely mentioned at all in dispatches from this or any other game involving the Germans.

Perhaps – with half of Europe still under Soviet occupation – the war is still too close for comfort. Maybe, now that there are two Germanys, the western half has been deemed the 'good' side. Or, perchance, it's just that people have yet to transpose crude nationalism on to an inoffensive ball game. 'The Germans came over in 1954 and we beat them at Wembley,' remembers David Lacey. 'Nobody booed them or reminded them who won the war or anything. It would have been considered the height of bad manners.'

Even for old duffers like Alf, there seems to be a sort of modernistic approach, a willingness to embrace the Technicolor future, rather than dwell on a recent painful past.

Admittedly, not all are quite so caught up in the spirit of enlightenment. 'England's World Cup convoy advances to the field of León today with the field marshal of football, Sir Alf Ramsey, wondering if the time has come to change his strategy and call up the artillery,' says the Liverpool *Echo*, full of tales of intended German annihilation. 'While West Germany, encamped sixteen miles from here in a desert dug-out that might have been a relic from Rommel, await the World Champions, England have some thinking to do. [The Germans] are confident, almost arrogantly so ... Walking around the one-horse, leather-manufacturing town of León – the speciality is, aptly, gun holsters – one would think that the Germans had already won this World Cup, as well as the last one and the war' ...

Oh well, can't have everything ...

On the bus on the way back from the Czechoslovakia game, the English players ribbed Banks about his error. It turns out that the ball had been swerving all over the place, the likes of which he'd never seen before. He retorted that with such a dull game and millions dozing off at home, it was the sort of thing needed to wake them up. The joy at getting through to the quarter-finals is tempered by the obvious chagrin of Alf Ramsey, who, despite his public words of a professional job well done, is angered at the standard of the performance.

That evening, the players who didn't feature are kept on the Atlas training pitch until well after sundown. When Geoff Hurst makes a comment about not minding playing in the dark, Ramsey snaps that, judging from the game, it looked like they were used to it. In his heart of hearts Ramsey knows there were serious shortcomings against Czechoslovakia and that the German game is going to be very tough indeed. After a meal, the players are sent to their rooms at 8.30 p.m. It is not the usual Ramsey approach. His successes have always been based on relaxed teams oozing confidence. But tough love can work, too.

Unfortunately, the Mexican authorities are not making the transition to León easy on England. Prospective accommodation, which had been ear-marked in advance, is now suddenly 'full'. 'Well, that was a whole fiasco really because the Mexicans had put every obstruction in our way,' says Dr Phillips. 'We wanted to fly up. They wouldn't let us. They said the airport at León wasn't big enough, which was a load of nonsense because the Germans had flown direct from Germany. It's easy to say afterwards, but I think that was a time when we needed some really strong administrators.'

What's more, there is now no room at any León inn till Saturday night. England's pre-match preparation for the game will therefore be a five-hour bus journey across the desert.

With every single roadblock – both literal and metaphorical – thrown up, Ramsey needs to keep his players fresh and do the worrying himself. On Friday, after light training, he takes the players to the TV centre to watch more videotape of the West Germans in action. Then, finally, he lets the players go to Guadalajara Country Club.

A swank place with its £1,500 a year membership, the players had been angling to go there for a while. It seems it has become quite a British hang-out, with a few familiar football faces – Joe Mercer, Don Revie, Bobby Hope of West Brom, John Greig and Colin Stein of Rangers, Terry Hennessey of Derby, Gary Sprake of Leeds, Peter Rodrigues of Leicester, Chris Lawler of Liverpool, Jimmy Greenhoff of Stoke, Johnny Giles and Billy Bremner of Leeds, Hugh Curran of Wolves and the 'World Cup wives' – Frances Bonetti, Judith Hurst, Tina Moore and Cathy Peters – all there at one time or another. They are also joined by a late arrival, Scotland manager Bobby Brown, whom the Scottish FA have reluctantly and parsimoniously allowed to come out only from the quarter-finals onwards.

When Bremner and Giles get in the pool and casually head the ball back and forth to each other about 200 times to enthralled Mexican onlookers, Mercer jokes that they are merely England supporters – wait till you see what the players can do.

For those England players, the golf course is the main attraction, with Peter Osgood and Jeff Astle having a race in the carts and Alan Ball geeing everyone up for the big game to come. Although it's fun for a short while, the players get the sense that they are very much interlopers at a party that has been going on in their absence in Guadalajara for the past ten days.

The presence of players' wives here is of particular concern. 'Alf would say afterwards that that was the biggest mistake he made,' says Dr Phillips. Ramsey had nullified his argument against it by bringing his own wife with him, but it is becoming a divisive issue – distracting for the four England players concerned, and perhaps resented to a degree by those who've had to leave their womenfolk behind. 'Alf wasn't happy mainly because it appeared that those four players could afford to take their wives and maybe the others couldn't,' says Ken Jones. 'But he couldn't do anything about it because Vicky [Mrs Ramsey] was out there.'

Visits have been severely restricted due to the nature of the training programme and the whole business of squad togetherness. But, of course, among twenty-four young men, where mickey-taking is rife, some of the lads have taken considerable delight in winding up Moore, Peters, Hurst and Bonetti about the presence of their wives.

'That caused a lot of aggro with the other players,' adds Phillips of the presence of the four wives. 'When we got back from training, the husbands would be waiting to phone their wives and the other players were ribbing them.'

In the final days at Guadalajara, Bonetti has become particularly agitated.

Nevertheless, the noises coming out of the England training camp regarding the big game are all the correct ones: 'Now it's sudden death. That's our sort of scene,' declares Bobby Moore, messing around with a tennis racket.

'How's morale?' asks the BBC.

'Very, very high. The lads are very confident,' he says. 'We know we've got a difficult job ahead and we know the people at home are wanting us to do very well. Naturally, we want to do well for them as well as for ourselves. And if we have our way, we'll be bringing the cup back again.'

The pundits, by and large, think that England have come through their sticky patch and, if they can play like they did against Brazil, should have no trouble seeing off the Germans.

'They'll have the look of World Champions again on Sunday,' says Roger Hunt, in his column for the Liverpool *Echo*. 'Maybe I'm wrong but I have a feeling that all will be well and that England will play like the champions they looked against the same opponents, West Germany, four years ago. And I hope to renew acquaintance with my old adversaries and be the first to commiserate with them on Germany's defeat in the quarter-finals.'

England will take everything with them when they leave Guadalajara on Saturday and move lock, stock and barrel to León. They will only be there for one game. If they progress to the semis, as everyone hopes, they will at last get the chance to step out in the magnificent Azteca. But the Guanajuato Stadium in León should be to their liking. Though half the capacity of Guadalajara's Jalisco and with a pitch temperature slightly hotter, it doesn't have the same concrete reflective quality and stagnant, lifeless air. Instead, with its open terraces, it has cooling breezes blowing across the surface and none of the sapping humidity. With its tight pitch and steep stands it (like the stadium at Toluca) mirrors a Football League ground, albeit a decent one.

All very well, but there is still the question of the accommodation. 'León was a cock-up in more ways than one because the FA had cocked-up the hotel arrangements,' says Ken Jones. Indeed, given that the Germans have, in customary fashion, pre-booked their hotels all the way through to the final, it seems remarkably short-sighted that, for all the effort that went into England's pre-tournament planning, such a likely eventuality as finishing runner-up in their group has not been budgeted for. 'Alf was inclined to leave that sort of thing to the admin people,' adds Jones. 'They got there, there was no hotel. They ended up staying in a motel with the German wives and girlfriends . . . I remember Wilf Gerhardt saying, "I don't understand, this could have been done months ago." ' (For their sins, some of the travelling British press end up renting spare cells at the local monastery.)

'We stayed in the motel where the Bulgarians had stayed,' says Phillips. 'And it wasn't very good. We didn't have a choice. We were just told, "That's where you have to go." '

The Motel Estancia does not have the same luxurious quality as the Hilton, with chalet-type rooms round another forbidden pool, but it'll have to do.

The composition of the team, as ever, is up for debate. How the hell do you stop Müller? Though Jack Charlton overcame a shaky start against the Czechs, it is generally assumed that Ramsey will restore Labone alongside Moore in the heart of the defence to do the key marking job. 'Müller is the old-fashioned centre forward, straight up and down the middle,' says Hunt. 'Brian has taken care of better players than that in the First Division.'

Given that the Germans play a similar type of game, England should be happy playing above walking pace, too, maybe with the out-of-sorts Peters jettisoned for the livelier Bell. This still, quite obviously, leaves a lack of punch in attack. Clarke was cool on his debut, and could be retained at the expense of Lee, who's been huffing and puffing.

'Alf had said that anyone who couldn't handle the heat, couldn't handle the altitude, in the games wouldn't play,' says Jack Charlton. 'And yet the guy in my opinion who came through best of all in the heat was Peter Osgood, just because of the way he played the game in his space, but Alf [always] played Frannie Lee. In some of the games, Frannie Lee was on his way back from the attack when we were attacking again. Frannie was the one. He couldn't handle the heat.'

Perhaps Clarke will be played anyway as a third attacker as England employ a more offensive 4–3–3. Ramsey hints at this before departure, but, as ever, nothing will be confirmed till the last possible moment.

The postbag at the Liverpool *Echo* is full of suggestions: wingers should have been retained; drop Lee and play Astle; Emlyn's England's only salvation; stick Nobby in, Big Jack too; English players are too one-footed; over-trained; under-trained; England should have declined the invitation in the first place and refused to go to Mexico because the dice are so obviously loaded against them.

And, of course, the air is already ripe with the whiff of Latin foul play. The scheduled referee is Angel Coerezza, an Argentinian, no less – though inevitable fears that he will be out to avenge his countryman Rattin are somewhat offset by the fact that it was a German ref who sent off the Argentinian captain back in 1966. (Of greater concern, perhaps, should be that it was Coerezza who gave the Mexicans that dodgy penalty against Belgium.)

Not all are wildly enthusiastic about England's chances. 'I fear the odds are against us,' says Reg Dury in the *News of the World*, sticking his head above the parapet. The facts bear out his concern. West Germany are on a roll, have scored ten goals (England can only count a miserable one from open play), have had a trouble-free stay at their Comanjilla spa and are playing at 'home' with the crowd solidly behind them. Hugh McIlvanney in the *Observer* tells it like it is: there 'should be little chance of interrupting West Germany's confident progress to the semi-finals . . . It will be hard for them to accept they are no longer the strongest team in Europe, let alone the world,' he says of England. 'And all the harder for Sir Alf Ramsey because any success the Germans enjoy tomorrow will be inseparable from their use of the conventional wingers he has scorned for so long . . .'

What a crucial week for England. What a crucial week for Britain. The day after Wednesday's semi-finals, the nation will go to the polls. The weekend aggregate poll shows Labour 7.3 per cent in the lead (that's a 100-seat majority) but with the Tories gaining fast, despite (or perhaps because of) Enoch Powell, who keeps blathering on about 'the enemies within', the strange forces aiming 'at the actual destruction of our nation and society', and the fact that the country is facing a greater danger from lefties and immigrants than was ever posed by the Nazis.

Business as usual, in other words. Though on the front page of Sunday's *Observer*, a small late item makes rather alarming reading. It says simply, 'Gordon Banks ill . . .'

Chapter 15

Montezuma's Revenge

Saturday, 13 June 1970

What exactly happened to Gordon Banks remains a mystery. Banks is still not sure himself, but his well-being in the ensuing twenty-four hours will have a direct bearing on England's retention of their world crown. Foul play or simply 'just one of those things', it is a matter that will never be fully resolved.

What is clear is that, on the evening of Friday 12th, the day before travel, Banks feels a little under the weather. Although he's sure he'll be fine, he reports to Dr Phillips, who duly catalogues his complaint as 'loosening of the stools' – 'the runs' to the layman – gives him the necessary anti-diarrhoea medication and packs him off to bed.

It is not an isolated incident. Across the team camps of the World Cup, players have been stricken at one point or another. In probably the worst incident just about the whole Israeli team was crocked for a couple of days.

In the England party, though, due to extreme medical prudence, the players have got off lightly. There has been the odd bit of 'dicky tummy', more often from a player feeling the effects of the sun, exacerbated by the strenuous demands being placed on a sports-man's body in such heat and humidity. But the general pattern has been for such an affliction to pass quickly. Allan Clarke missed the Brazil game with a similar ailment but was right as rain within twenty-four hours. Keith Newton and Bobby Charlton had the same trouble as Banks only yesterday but are now on the road to recovery. On this basis, there is absolutely no reason to believe that, still with two full nights' sleep ahead of him, Banks will not be fit for Sunday's game.

Only one thing does everyone know, it can't possibly be the food that's to blame, for exposure to ingested local bacteria has been virtually eliminated as a possibility. Despite the derision heaped on them for shipping their own victuals, England can at least rest assured that not one morsel of local fare – 'foreign muck', to the less diplomatic – has passed a player's lips. And if it was the Findus that had done it, they'd have all gone down together.

Any health fears are allayed when, at breakfast early Saturday morning, Charlton, Newton and Banks have all recovered sufficiently and are ready for the 150-mile road journey which should get them to León at lunchtime, with a scheduled light training session on the Guanajuato Stadium pitch in the afternoon.

Unfortunately, the morning optimism is soon dispelled. As lively as the coach trip is, with its various card schools and cocky banter, it is all lost on Banks who, sitting at the back, begins to suffer a relapse. After an hour or so, he's groaning with stomach cramps and looking like death warmed up. Dr Phillips is duly summoned and he dishes out the necessary anti-nausea pills. This time Alex Stepney is detailed to look after Banks and dole out more tablets as necessary. Banks simply does his best to reach the destination – as he would later put it – 'without disgracing myself'.

'At the end of this coach trip Banksie wasn't feeling too well,' says Stepney. 'When we arrived at the hotel, Sir Alf, Dr Phillips, Harold Shepherdson and Les Cocker had been in confab about Gordon because there was concern. Alf came to me, he said, "Alex, I'd like you to room with Gordon and keep an eye on him in the night to see how he is."'

Banks is now so weak that Stepney, the assigned nursemaid and Banks's bag carrier, helps Dr Phillips walk Banks to the room and tuck him straight up in bed.

'Gordon is feeling off colour,' comes Ramsey's official statement, once word gets out. 'We have had players like this before and normally they recover after a few hours' rest.'

Meanwhile, the team go off and have their training session on the pitch at the Guanajuato, which is only a few hundred yards away from the motel, across the highway. They are suitably impressed by the lush, smooth playing surface and raring to get out and do their stuff on it tomorrow.

By the evening, and to great relief, Banks seems well enough to give hope to Ramsey that he'll be out there, too. 'I remember being with Gordon the night before – Terry Cooper and myself – and he was sound,' says Norman Hunter. 'He was absolutely fine.'

Stepney duly does his duty, listening for every move through the night, and, apart from getting up a couple of times to go to the loo – just routine stuff – by morning Banks seems all right. 'So I said to him, "Are you OK?" And he said, "Yeah, I think I'll have a bit of breakfast and go for a walk," and that was it,' explains Stepney.

After breakfast, Banks goes through a few stretching exercises and catching routines with Les Cocker. The lads had never doubted that Banksie would pull through after a good night's kip and now England's number 1 seems his normal self.

At 10 a.m. Ramsey gathers the players in his chalet for the final team meeting, ahead of the noon kick-off. Last orders before battle. The players have already been given hints as to the identity of the starting eleven, but anyone back home who'd been hoping for something radical will be disappointed. For a game of this importance, Ramsey has opted for experience. It will be his favoured first eleven that takes the field, the side that started against Romania. And, crucially, England's number 1 will still be in goal – Banks, Newton, Cooper, Mullery, Labone, Moore, Lee, Ball, Charlton, Hurst and Peters

Says Stepney, 'Gordon was in and Peter was sub again, so that was it.'

Not all the players are entirely happy with the selection.

'When he put the board up for the German game he picked Brian Labone,' remembers Jack Charlton. 'That surprised me greatly. I thought, He thinks I can't handle the heat. I could handle it as well as anybody else. And it surprised Brian as well, because he came to me and sort of apologised. He said, "I never expected to be playing, I thought *you* would be playing," and all this. I didn't even get on the bench for the German game.' ('He's got a funny memory, Jack,' says Labone with a laugh. 'No bloody way at all. No way at all. I was in possession, he was number two. They were saving Jack for the final, no doubt!')

Though the line-up doesn't stay that way for long. As the players clamber on to Sid Brown's coach for the short hop over the road, Ramsey sidles up to Bonetti and gives him some simple but rather surprising news – 'You're in.'

Says Stepney, 'I thought I'd go back to the chalet and get my camera. Take a few pictures of the game and the lads. So I do no more than just stroll back to my room and Banksie's gone. He's in the bog and everything's coming out both ends. He just said, "I can't do anything, I'm gone." And he's so weak, so white, so I ran straight out and saw Dr Phillips and, of course, we got Alf.'

Ramsey's remedy is straightforward. 'He got Peter and he said, "Right, Peter, you'll be playing and, Alex, you'll be substitute," and that was it,' says Stepney. 'So Peter had no time to think about it. We were going across straight into the game, the dressing rooms. I don't think there was any doubt in anybody's mind. Peter had always been a good goalkeeper. There were no worries about that.'

And though El Magnifico does his best for one last gallant attempt at selection by hobbling round the hotel pool on the arm of the good doctor, unfortunately he's a lost cause. A blow, sure, but not the end of the world. For, as all the players attest, in Peter Bonetti England have a more than capable deputy, an exceptional keeper. Indeed, one who would walk into any other international team. There should be absolutely no doubting Bonetti's class. Not even Banks can boast an international record like his. In his six games for England thus far, Bonetti has conceded a solitary goal. He's never let England down. 'It didn't shake confidence,' asserts Ball.

Banks's deputy in the 1966 squad, too, Bonetti got his debut on the eve of that tournament in a 2–0 away win in Denmark. Ten months later he was impeccable in a brace of clean-sheet victories over Spain (at Wembley) and Austria (in Vienna). He conceded one goal in the notable 2–1 away win in Madrid in the quarter-finals of the European Nations Cup in May 1968. And during this great cup-winning season at Chelsea, in the run-up to Mexico, Bonetti has played in the away win over Holland and the home victory against Portugal, conceding no goals. Six games for England; a solitary goal let in.

You can't really argue with figures like that, even though a game or two every twelve months seems to be the pattern. And while everyone, Bonetti included, knows that Banks is The Man, there is no one more capable of filling his gloves than 'The Cat' – Bonetti so nicknamed for his amazing agility and lightning reflexes.

Bonetti, however, looks a little startled. Some of the players ask him if he is OK. Of course he is, he tells them. For all the best-laid plans, and for all Bonetti's abilities, England are now playing with a keeper who has not been in a competitive match for six weeks – the last one was the FA Cup Final – and has just been given less than two hours' notice to prepare himself mentally for the biggest game of his life.

'I do remember it being a hell of a shock to Peter,' says David Sadler. 'I think Peter had become used to being the number two. Everybody acknowledged Banksie was the top world goalkeeper. I think Peter had accepted his part as the bridesmaid well before we got to Mexico. Gordon was never injured, always there. It really did shake him up when he realised Gordon was ill and he would have to play. Everything was attuned to *not* playing. It was pretty hard for him to take.'

The mental aspect should not be underestimated. You can be as fit as you like, but, as any keeper will tell you, it demands intense concentration and complete psychological ease to perform between the sticks at this level. In the only position where ninety minutes' outstanding work can be undone by a split second lapse, you've got to think fit as well as *be* fit.

'I don't think mentally Peter was in tune for it,' says Norman Hunter. 'You know what I mean?'

You can only blame the management here. A contingency plan, announced the night before, would have eased any stand-in considerably. And Ramsey, with the clock ticking to this huge match, must be secretly rueing the experience wasted on Gordon West on the 1969 tour – it being tough to dole out opportunities with such a specialist position. (According to one member of the England party, it was at this point that England lost the World Cup, having squandered the opportunity to give Bonetti a feel of World Cup conditions instead.) This, though, is just the way Ramsey is. As Emlyn Hughes says, you're professionals, you're there to do a job. There was no time for the molly-coddling of reserve players. 'He wasn't one that said, "Get yourself warmed up there," ' says Hughes. 'He just said, "You're on." '

And so, with Stepney abandoning his nursing duties rather hurriedly to grab his boots and step up to the bench (joining Wright, Hunter, Bell and Clarke), England set off for their date with destiny...

*

At noon on 14 June 1970 England and West Germany line up against each other on the field of the Guanajuato Stadium, León. It is six weeks shy of four years since that immortal day at Wembley. England's reputation as World Champions, and everything they've achieved in the interim, is owed to their performance against their opponents on that occasion. It seems only fitting, then, that for their most important game since, it should be the same opposition standing against them today.

There are even five veterans of the '66 final on either side – Moore, Charlton, Ball, Hurst, Peters for England; Hottges, Schnellinger, Beckenbauer, Overath, Seeler for West Germany. There should have been one more for England with Banks.

Both sides are relieved by the pleasant breeze, which takes the edge off the heat. England are also no doubt heartened by the fact that there are only 30,000 hostile voices ranged against them instead of the usual 72,000, and, although the support is largely with the Germans, along one side of the pitch, in the section opposite the main stand, there is a healthy chunk of 2,000 Englanders. With Ken Bailey in their midst, they are more vocal and conspicuous than had been evident in the bowl of the Jalisco. Decked out in red, white and blue, and with Union Jacks wafting in the summer air, they are a celebratory presence, more akin to the promenaders at Last Night of the Proms than fierce partisans.

Yesterday, because of the colour clash between the two white-shirted teams, the managers tossed to see who would change strips; again it is England who must don their alternative kit. FIFA regulations dictate that all teams travel with three strips to mix and match for every eventuality. This time England, in preference to their light blue attire of four days ago, plump for their third alternative – the rather more familiar red shirts, white shorts, red socks combination. It is the very outfit they sported on that glorious Wembley afternoon (albeit now in the new aertex fabric).

With there being little problem of glare and shadows, the kind that caused such confusion at Guadalajara, and especially after all the propaganda about dark colours and heat retention, the argument for abandoning the light blue is a little disingenuous. But, what the hell, we're talking history here. For England, if there is a talismanic association with the scarlet shirts when it comes to playing the Germans, then maybe – just maybe – the sight of the

Thin Red Line will also strike fear into the hearts of the foe. Long after this tournament, future generations of England teams and their fans will come to associate mythic properties to the famous red shirt, clinging to it like a lucky family heirloom, though it will yield them little success in return – England developing a pathological fear of playing Germany in the process. In his heart of hearts Ramsey, a pragmatist, knows that England will beat their opponents – Germany or otherwise – because they are better foot-ballers and for no other reason than that. But perhaps even he feels that, what with the Bobby Moore incident, the hostility of the Mexicans, and now the sidelining of Banks, they need all the luck they can get.

England win the toss and opt to play with the wind – right to left from the commentary position – and Germany kick off.

Back home, a record British TV audience of 30 million people sits down, beers in hand, hoping, praying, that England are going to get well and truly stuck in this time and at last show the rest of the World Cup what they're made of.

They are not to be disappointed. Within seconds the ball comes out to Martin Peters on the left-hand side of the halfway line. Perhaps chastened by the criticism of his play in the tournament thus far (though probably not), but more likely fired up, knowing that it's do or die, Peters goes in for a challenge on Libuda so hard that it bursts the ball. The play continues through the midfield, back across the pitch to the right-hand side – Peters to Cooper to Charlton to Ball to Lee, who is hacked down by Hottges – by which time the ball is about as spherical as a peanut, wobbling erratically across the lush turf. As the play stops for the free kick, Bobby Moore calls referee Coerezza over, throws the orange ball up against the sky so that he can observe its asymmetry, though the ref does his traditional bit of dithering before making the obvious decision – replacing the damn thing. A new ball is lobbed on, which, as the game progresses, seems only in slightly better shape than its predecessor, though the players never complain.

So, after a false start, England are off again. And with the match beginning at a far healthier and more familiar pace than in previous games – wouldn't you know it? – England are starting to look very good indeed. This is cup-tie stuff, with a clear objective in mind, none of that lily-livered poncing around for points of the group games. Mullery and Ball look busy and robust in the midfield, Charlton is strolling about in the middle, hair flapping in the wind, fronds of comb-over flowing off his left temple, and within minutes Keith Newton pelts down the right on a textbook overlap, sending over a cross. Maier and his enormo-mitts are flapping at a ball that any self-respecting keeper would have gathered up with minimal fuss. 'Oh, the goalkeeper. We've got a feeling this man couldn't deal with crosses,' says David Coleman rather hopefully, and, with Gerd Müller running round like a little lost toddler in a department store, wayward beneath the towering Labone, Moore and Newton, those 30 million Englishmen back home can settle back on their sofas.

It gets better. Charlton receives it, steadies himself, crosses for Hurst, who plays it back for Lee. Maier makes another terrible mess as Lee runs in to snap up the half chance. In a near reconstruction of the Félix incident, Lee's spontaneous interception results in a clash, clipping Maier unintentionally and harmlessly with his hand. Though Maier has clearly been studying The Master and tears a leaf out of his book. He milks it for all it's worth, rolling around in cod torment, while his teammates rush in to lambaste little Frannie. The reaction works. Angel Coerezza, a man easily influenced, is straight over and brandishing a yellow card – Lee's second in consecutive starts. Nothing to be unduly alarmed about, FIFA has no policy on suspensions nor a points system to go with it and will only punish a player if he is deemed to have displayed too much ill-discipline for the tournament's good. Nevertheless, Lee had better keep his nose clean from now on.

Coerezza, however, is perhaps underrated and it doesn't take long for the legislative standard to be laid down. Ball and Mullery interchange, Ball is chopped down, and Müller, Lee's corporeal counterpart, follows chunky Frannie into the notebook. The game will be a clean one from now on and, with a healthy ebb and flow, makes for an entertaining exhibition of all that's good about the Northern European game – as long as you're a neutral.

Charlton, of course, is playing in his 106th international, and has now become the most capped Englishman of all time. Curiously, this has been little mentioned. It's the first international in about his last ten for which he has not been the subject of some kind of presentation, the weight of history seemingly lifted after the Czech game. The new-found freedom has found him suddenly in his stride – alert, darting, looking like the Manchester United star of legend, especially in that red shirt, and gagging for the elusive fiftieth goal. He takes a long-range peg with his left, though just a grass cutter, which Maier still feels the need to overelaborate upon.

Müller shows a glimpse of tit-for-tat genius with a snapshot at the other end, but with Bonetti showing some good, safe handling and unfussy distribution, playing it out through Moore to build from the back, the Germans look a pale imitation of the conquerors that we have seen so far. Beckenbauer has his hands full chasing Charlton; the gangly Fichtel looks worried every time Hurst jumps and beats him to a high ball; Seeler barks at his men but to little avail; Libuda, Lohr – Stan and Tom – are quiet.

For England, everything is coming good. Mercifully, Peters, who has borne a good deal of criticism for his ineffectuality, is industrious, linking play down the left, setting off Cooper to run and beat Vogts. In the thirty-second minute, just as everyone is agreeing with Ramsey and saying, 'Well, who the hell needs wingers anyway?' Keith Newton bursts out of defence, takes an Alan Mullery pass, and sets off on a rangy right-flank run. Cleverly declining the obvious high ball to the near post and Hurst's head, he spots Mullery continuing his charge, chips a low, inch-perfect pass ahead of his unbreaking stride, and the Spurs midfielder, taking it on the half-volley with his right foot, hammers it hard past Maier.

'Mullery! *Alan Mullery!*' screams Hugh Johns on ITV in a state of near commentator orgasm, and Mullery walks back, with hands aloft and a cheeky grin, yelling, 'Fucking yeah,' while Hurst runs in to embrace him. It's Mullery's first goal for England. And you couldn't score a more satisfying or more important one. The German defenders protest to the ref, though about what no one really knows. The Union Jacks wave in the ecstatic England section. Banks may be ill, but it's just what the doctor ordered.

The Germans, though, are accustomed to coming from behind: with the exception of the Peru game, it seems they don't really get going until someone has rubbed their noses in it. Troops are duly marshalled, Beckenbauer and Overath get more active in the middle, and 'The Kaiser' has a weak pop which Bonetti, safe as houses, gathers up. There is a brief scare when Charlton and Hottges clash with a sickening thud, laying both men out, with each clutching a shin, but they both thankfully get over it.

Beckenbauer and the thoughtful Overath then assert themselves, and Mullery has to start dropping back to retrieve the ball from his defenders. There's a mix-up when he and Moore go for the same ball and collide in the box. Hurst, too, is having to work harder, making more and more diversionary runs to lose his marker. At this rate, England will have to pace themselves to keep on top of it all, but there is no doubt who is the better team. And, as Lee is hacked down for what looks an obvious penalty, there would be nothing to suggest another goal isn't in the offing – but the ref doesn't give it.

As the half-time whistle goes, England go in 1–0 up. The Germans look anguished. And all those unpatriotic naysayers are beginning to eat their words.

'Well, what a great feeling it is to sit here and feel that England are in command of this game,' blurts Don Revie, gushing about Moore, the rock man, the player of the tournament.

'Our back four are playing magnificent,' echoes Joe Mercer, no lover of the adverb, as Coleman cuts back to Frank Bough in London. These Germans, they've got nothing.

Within seconds of the restart, the Germans, however, show they mean business. Having already done a Brazil and kept England waiting in the sun for them to come out, they set about things with a renewed sense of purpose. 'The Germans showing more enterprise,' says Coleman as, once again, they try to bring themselves back into it. At the back, Schulz, another '66 veteran, is on to stiffen their resolve and take over defensive duties from Fichtel, who is shifted left in a reshuffle, with Hottges going off. But it appears to be a case of rearranging the deck-chairs on the *Titanic*. England press on, and another attack is thwarted by an Oscarworthy roll by Maier. 'Much of this fine acting technique seems to be instilled in German players,' says Hugh Johns, while knowing nods are exchanged among ITV viewers across the land.

The crowd gets agitated. People at the back start raining rubbish down on those at the front who are standing up and blocking their view. And they get very frustrated with England, who, with Peters and Cooper combining, are thwarting every advance that darling Libuda makes.

Their woe is compounded five minutes into the second half.

Newton again makes a burst down the right, crosses low, and the newly invigorated Peters ghosts in at the far post, his speciality. 'Newton, number two, and it's through ... *Peters*,' cries Coleman as an admittedly mishit shot from the midfielder bounces into the German net. '*Geoff Hurst*,' yells Johns, before swiftly correcting himself. At last the Azteca looms. England will surely be going there to meet the winners of Italy and Mexico on Wednesday.

Germany now, with absolutely nothing to lose, are the proverbial wounded beast. They go for the jugular. Cooper has been containing the formerly fizzing Libuda, but is beginning to tire. Indeed, for all the marvellous execution of the overlapping fullback system, it is an incredibly taxing role. Cooper and Newton must fulfil a dual function: full back and winger. It requires constant fifty-, seventy-five-yard sprints up and down the pitch – back and forth, back and forth, up with the attack, back to defend. It is tough enough under normal circumstances, but in these conditions it's absolutely draining. For all England's formidable armour, it is their Achilles heel. And, what's more, the Germans know it. On fifty-seven minutes Schoen makes a shrewd tactical switch and pulls off Libuda, replacing him with the fresh legs of Grabowski – that's a brand-new, fresh-legged winger against a tiring defender.

Not that there's anything to be concerned about immediately. Cooper could be on crutches and it'd still take some doing to beat him. And besides, behind him there's a trusty man in a yellow shirt the Germans will have to beat.

Grabowski runs down the right flank and plays a diagonal cross in. 'And good handling by Bonetti,' says Coleman. 'Just think how many caps Bonetti might have had if Gordon Banks hadn't been around.'

But nippy Grabowski knows what he's doing. He darts around on the right, he pops up on the left, and Newton and especially Cooper, unable to get forward so much, devoting more attention to their defensive responsibilities now, are leaving Hurst and Lee in short supply up front. 'Libuda never had a bloody kick,' says Cooper. 'But Grabowski was a different type of player, more of a "jinker". To be fair to him, the last fifteen minutes, I was out on my feet. Probably I should have been substituted.'

Coleman again employs his ominous gift of foresight. 'This is a period for England now that could prove a little bit difficult,' he says, 'with Germany forced to gamble.'

Not that Ramsey is going to be taking any chances. Going into the last quarter and with England surely cruising through, he decides to make a tactical switch. On the bench, the subs, between themselves, reckon it might be Hunter who's about to get his first taste of the action, coming on for the knackered Cooper – though Alf has never been one to take gambles, this would be an untried exchange. Plus, England don't look in any great peril.

Indeed, no sooner is there activity on the bench than England start knocking passes together, twenty-three consecutive ones, playing keep-ball, not letting the Germans get a sniff ('England really giving the Germans the runaround,' says Coleman, revising his synopsis of a couple of minutes ago). But England are also getting a little cocky. 'When our second one went in, I ran round the field shouting to the Germans, "Good night, God bless, see you in Munich," ' says Alan Ball afterwards to Peter Batt of the *Sun*.

Bobby Charlton does not like this 'foreign' possession nonsense, tells the lads to get on with it, stick to the plan, but Ramsey doesn't want Charlton overexerting himself, getting all agitated out there – the next week is going to be one hell of a physical test. Ramsey sends for Colin Bell. And so, having played well on his record-breaking appearance, Charlton will be given his standard breather, Bell coming on in his stead, a switch that they have enacted many times before without cause for complaint.

Charlton spots Bell on the sideline, the message comes back to him that he is to be brought off, and no sooner is Bell jiggling on the spot, waiting for a break in play to replace El Calvo Divino, than Fichtel tries an optimistic blaster of a shot from long range and catches Lee right in the unmentionables. Lee doubles over and hits the turf. Overath retrieves the ball, finds Beckenbauer and The Kaiser gathers the ball on the right-hand side, midway into the England half. For once he manages to side-step the terrier-like Mullery, who's been snapping at him all day, and, pretty much because it's the only option available to him, pings a hopeful shot from distance at the England goal. It bobbles along ineffectively but has caught the defence unawares. Agonisingly, as Bonetti goes down to his right to smother it, it squeezes, Sprake-like, nay Calderón-like, under his body. 'Really it was nothing,' says Hunter.

'Peter would have thrown his cap on it nine times out of ten.'

It's 2–1. There are twenty-one minutes to go.

'I was yelling my head off at Terry Cooper,' says Jack Charlton, watching from the stands, 'because we were winning two–nil and Terry went on one of his runs and he ran the ball right through, nearly to their goalkeeper. The ball bounced back to Beckenbauer. Franz ran and ran and ran and, because Terry couldn't get back, Alan Mullery was left in the left-back position and didn't know whether the ball was going to be played wide down the outside or the guy was going to come inside him. He just sort of over-cooked it a little bit too far to the left. It was a stupid, soft, silly goal.'

Bell is on for the restart. He must be feeling like a bit of a jinx. This is the second big game in which he's watched from the touchline, waiting to come on for Charlton, while England have conceded a crucial goal. Charlton, who is firing on all cylinders, is not happy with the change, but will – as they all do – obey Alf without hesitation. And so, on his 106th appearance, playing the game of his life, he makes his exit. The move has not yet assumed any great significance.

But Bell, number 19, looks to be a good introduction as he adds some dynamism to the midfield, fired up, running at the German defence, taking a pop himself. In a move that looks to have sealed it, he makes a foray down the right, crossing for Hurst, who dives low beyond Schulz to flick a glancing header at the near post. Maier is beaten, defenders' hearts sink, and the encroaching Lee is already jumping, arms aloft in triumph. 'Hurst. It *must* be there,' yells Hugh Johns on ITV. But the ball, agonisingly, grazes the woodwork and bobbles behind for a goal kick.

There is more activity on the England bench: surely now another defender to shore up the back line and see out the remaining minutes. Hunter for Cooper, maybe? Perhaps Wright for Newton. Hunter strips off. No problem. This last patch is going to be tough, with the Germans giving it everything they've got.

Müller, who has been frustratingly shepherded by Moore and Labone ('Moore constantly winning in these battles with Gerdi Müller,' says Johns) and taken to making petulant swings whenever robbed of the ball, suddenly beats Keith Newton and blasts one in. Bonetti makes a fantastic save at point-blank range. 'If Banks got the OBE, Bonetti will be knighted ... What a *great save*,' coos Coleman.

Newton goes down injured, but England still counter. Again Bell had a chance. And, as the Germans muster, Hunter warms up ('Hunter who gives away so little,' says Coleman). But who's going off? Must be Newton, Coleman reckons, he's hobbling. But no, it's Peters. Strange choice – central defender for a left-sided midfielder. Newton is still down when Hunter hands his chit of paper to the ref. Peters yells to the England bench, pointing out Newton. Hadn't they better wait to see if he's OK first? From a distance it looks like Peters is refusing to come off, and while Dr Phillips is on attending to the right back, who's crocked his knee again, the one that kept him out of the Brazil game, England have twelve players on the pitch. But Newton soon gets up and starts walking it off, and Peters retires. (He later confesses that he was carrying a knock, too, and it was therefore a good move to bring him off and, crucially, that Ramsey had told him it was no slight on his performance but, like Charlton, he was saving him for the semis.)

So Hunter, who sometimes plays in midfield for Leeds as a defensive anchor man, is on. Anyway, surely Alf knows what he's doing. It's at least another body back behind the ball for the final ten minutes. But the team looks a little unbalanced. Instead of taking a station midway up on the left, Hunter, relaying instructions to his teammates, adopts a reflexive defensive position and starts marking the same space as Cooper. Though it's all by design.

Hunter remembers the instructions: 'Get out there and do battle and stop them from playing and help "TC" really, because old "TC" was tired,' he says. 'Grabowski was running at him and with me playing with Terry, I'd try to secure it down the left-hand side.'

'Well, I tell you how tired *I* felt,' says Alan Ball. 'And my game was a stamina game. When he put Norman Hunter and Colin Bell on, I thought, That's brilliant, he's brought some legs on to help. Bobby, fantastic footballer. Martin, fantastic footballer. But, two–nil up, I'd have made exactly the same decision. Strong, fresh legs in the middle of the pitch.'

Hunter, a stalwart of all-conquering Leeds United, he of the 'bites yer legs' reputation, was unfortunate that his time on the international scene coincided with that of the great Bobby Moore – like Bonetti, Hunter is a bridesmaid. 'It was part of what I was used to because I went with England for nine years,' he explains. 'I didn't play too many games and rightly so because I was understudy to one of the best players in the world. As long as Bob was fit, he was going to play. Deep in your heart you knew you'd only get on either in midfield or if Bobby got injured. You want to play, but you want to be picked for the side on merit. You don't want anyone to get injured to get in.'

Unfortunately, Hunter's first touch is not his best – 'It came off my studs and went for a throw-in,' he says. And, for it, the Germans pile forward. 'England now under terrible pressure,' anguishes Coleman. From the ensuing German attack, Labone hits an insufficient clearance to Schnellinger on the German left and the blond defender lofts a ball into the box over the England back row. The red-shirted defenders, for one split second and for the first time in the game, are flat-footed. Seeler, who, along with Müller, looks suspiciously offside, is running backwards and falling over. But, somehow, as he tumbles to the ground, he catches the ball with the side of his head and makes just enough contact to flick it up and see it arc over Bonetti, who's motionless in the no man's land between the German forward and his own goal line.

'Seeler, a goal,' yelps Coleman disbelievingly. 'Brilliantly taken by Seeler. And England are letting this go. England are now struggling in a match they never looked like losing.' His words are spot on, and the German delight at this unexpected turn of events is manifest in the joyous mobbing of their captain. He's only three caps away from equalling the German record of seventy-one appearances. And, while Seeler celebrates, his English counterpart, Charlton, sits on the grass against an advertising hoarding with the subs, a frustrated man – boots off, a towel fastened round his head like an Arab sheikh.

'There was no way that was ever intended to be a header towards the goal,' grumbles Labone. 'Defenders make excuses, but I think we were a bit unlucky.'

There are only eight minutes left on the clock now. Beckenbauer goes close. Overath goes close. English hearts are in English mouths. Bell bursts into the box and narrowly misses. Words are muttered everywhere about 'stamina' and 'character', and then, painfully, the whistle blows. A late German equaliser, 2–2 and extra-time, exactly the same as '66.

This time, though, the England players will not be staying on their feet to kid the enemy in some psychological war. These are different conditions entirely. The team sprawls on the touchline, in the shade of the main stand, with Phillips, Charlton and Peters plying the drinks and Ramsey calmly giving the orders. Nothing more to be said other than get out there and give it your all.

Big Jack, a superstitious sort and an uncomfortable spectator, had already been getting worried. It's that hex again, the belief that no player from Leeds United was destined to win anything that season. All too much to bear. 'When it got to two–one I left the stadium, went down the road to a café and had a cup of coffee,' he says. 'There was about ten minutes to go. I waited for the crowd to come out and the crowd didn't come out. And I thought, Oh shit, they must have scored.'

On the restart, Cooper has a long-range crack. Maier saves. But Cooper is going to kill himself if he makes another eighty-yard sprint like that. And with Grabowski still with plenty more juice in the tank, it's looking risky to do so.

German crosses come in from either flank, but still the England centre backs beat back the challenge of Müller and Seeler. With the England midfield now misshapen, Ball running around in the middle on his own, and Beckenbauer freed of his detail to shadow Charlton, England are no longer in control of the match.

'They'd put their best player, Beckenbauer, on Bobby Charlton, so he never had a kick because wherever Bob went, Beckenbauer was trying to stop him,' says Cooper. 'So it suited us, because, though it nullified Bob, Beckenbauer was their most creative player.'

The dreadful prospect of a coin toss looms, but no side would ever settle for anything so ignoble. The Germans have a dig – a long-range dipping shot comes in from Beckenbauer which Bonetti tips over the bar. For England, Bell crosses for Hurst again. Then Norman Hunter, number 18, doing his best in his new-found role as a left-sided midfielder, goes on a dribble down the wing. It is not pretty but mighty effective, simply blasting his way through two defensive tackles that very nearly remove limbs from his adversaries, before finding Ball in a dangerous position. 'Oh, Hunter's making himself felt,' chortles Coleman at the carnage.

More action – Hunter shoots and misses, Grabowski teases, Moore tidies up. And though Hurst continues to threaten from the high ball, the German goalie has suddenly expanded his talent into the full capacity of his huge gloves.

'Maier no longer making mistakes,' says Coleman, as he plucks another off Big Geoff's bonce.

Lee takes another tumble in the box. Penalty? Possibly, but not given. Hunter crosses with his right, his wrong foot. 'Ball's not going to be able to grow enough to reach that,' says Coleman. Hunter takes a corner, a good one, too. Labone nods down to Hurst but a free kick is given for some off-the-ball hanky-panky by Lee.

End of the first period. The teams change around quickly.

Grabowski on the right threatens again. Cooper is back-pedalling. West Germany are driving forward in one final break-out. Grabowski leaves Cooper trailing but now himself seems to be flagging. He puts in a cross but, fortunately for England, the ball sails way over the goalmouth. He's completely overhit it. Or has he? This little ploy has been used successfully in every game, catching defenders flat-footed each time. The über-cross is merely part one of a double-whammy, in effect a long cross-field pass setting up the *real* cross to come back in from the left. And, sure enough, that's exactly what happens. On the left-hand side of the box, left winger Lohr, 'Tom', is waiting. He outleaps a confused Newton, and Grabowski's lofty ball is refashioned into a headed centre straight across the face of the England goal. Bonetti is on his line and helpless. Müller, who has done nothing all game, suddenly sneaks in between Moore and Labone. Without waiting for it to fall for him, as many strikers might, he instinctively leaps, spins in the air, and volleys the ball in from shoulder height. Unbelievably, West Germany are in the lead.

Coleman is absolutely silent for a full fifteen seconds. Labone falls to his haunches glaring at Bonetti, who looks absolutely forlorn ('Müller didn't miss many from six yards, did he?' says Labone). And Moore, rarely given to displays of emotion, just jerks himself around and walks away.

'Perfect cross after Grabowski had beaten Terry Cooper,' says Coleman, voice cracking, struggling to maintain that essential stiffness of upper lip. 'And those balls are always trouble.'

Can England get back into it now? They have eleven and a half minutes in which to do so. And for England fans watching all around the world, it is sheer torture.

But wait! Lee takes on a defender on the by-line, pulls it back to Hurst and it's in the net! It is disallowed for Lee carrying the ball out of play.

Then Bell goes down, blatantly clattered over by Beckenbauer when through on goal. '*Penalty!*' screams Coleman. This time it looks a dead cert, the clearest one of the whole World Cup so far. But for Beckenbauer it was a worthwhile gamble. '*And he didn't give it!*'

All the Germans have to do now is play for time. The ball goes into the stand and the Mexicans delay throwing it back for a precious few seconds while Ball has a temper tantrum on the touchline. Then Maier, in a minor collision with Labone, stays down writhing. 'And he's milking it for all it's worth,' spits Coleman, as Bobby Charlton runs up to hoof the ball back on to the pitch, urging them to get on with it.

A minute later Maier's doing it again. Hunter crosses, Hurst nods down for Ball on his left, and he shoots wide. Then, Newton has a dig and one of Maier's gloves seems to act of its own free will to tip it over the bar. 'Surely this must be England's last chance,' wails Coleman and Mullery blasts the ball over the German goal from the corner. The German fans at that end adopt the Mexican habit of keeping and hiding the ball. But it doesn't matter. The whistle goes.

Coleman can barely form the words. 'Germany have beaten England and gained revenge for 1966.'

And, just to rub in the humiliation, the pitch is invaded by lots of fat men blowing plastic bugles and wearing Alpine hats, one of whom is trailing a banner saying just that – 'This is revenge for the Wembley robbery of 1966.'

The players can hardly believe it. Hands are shaken. Ramsey and Schoen embrace, then Alf leads Charlton off in tears. Ball, for once, is absolutely speechless. And, as a stadium full of Germans and partisan Mexicans erupts in a carnival of *schadenfreude*, England, King's of World Football, abdicate. Their greatest football era is over.

Over in Toluca, the British media covering the Italy–Mexico game, but with one eye on the rickety manual scoreboard relaying results from the other games, can only assume that the man responsible for updating it has made a mistake. Either that or he's doing it to whip up the crowd.

The England dressing room is like a morgue – the worst atmosphere that any player there will ever experience. 'It was disbelief,' says Ball. 'A bizarre, bizarre game. All my time – I played seventy-two times for England – I never, ever witnessed again going through the emotions and how it was towards the end of that game. It was like a dream. This can't possibly have happened. Their goals were freak goals. Seeler off the back of his head. Things happened in that game that don't normally happen.'

Some players are in tears. Others are so exhausted they can barely keep their eyes open. The rest just sit there in stunned silence. No one blames anyone for the errors.

'I've never been in a dressing room like it in my life,' says Alex Stepney. 'No one spoke. We didn't know what to say. And Alf, the man he was, made a fantastic speech. He said, "You've done me proud, you've done yourselves proud, you didn't deserve that," and he went round and shook every player by the hand and said, "Thank you very much for everything you've done." '

It sounds strangely like an epitaph. For himself? Some of the older players maybe, for whom this may well be their last game? With the debris of battle all around, Alf goes off to meet his public.

In the press-conference room there is a hell of a hubbub brewing. A buzz goes round – 'Ramsey, Ramsey' – among the gathered international TV crews. With the game running into extra-time, it has completely thrown out the satellite window. And because there is now only a two-minute slot for transmission to the UK, BBC and ITV must work fast and double up, Coleman going first. But he is rather agitated. In the chaotic TV room there are hundreds of people milling around, no one really intent on getting on with the business in hand, just gleeful in the main that England have been knocked out. With Alf on his way for his quick few words, there are no cameraman and no soundman. Coleman, no doubt in a state of mental anguish over England's sudden demise, raves at the Mexican technicians so hard that a recording of his ultra-blue rantings is bootlegged and will be circulated among BBC TV personnel for years to come.

In the nick of time, though, it's all set up. Ramsey plonks himself down, a mic is clipped to his tracksuit. He doesn't even need to be asked a question for him to begin. 'They took advantage of our mistakes,' he says, with a distant look on his face, his state one of torpor. 'When it was two–nil it was all over, they were dead. They were brought back into the game by a very unfortunate goal. Ten minutes later we gave away another simple goal and their tails were up.'

It would be cruel to pile on too many 'what-ifs?' – Hurst's post-scraper, the penalty, the substitutions, everything else. The end result is that it doesn't really matter.

'Good luck to the Germans,' says Ramsey. 'Good luck to them in the next round.'

Despite all that has just happened, he still believes England are one of the best teams in the tournament. 'It was a game we shouldn't have lost,' he says. 'I don't think I've ever seen England give three goals away.' What's more, *our* goals were 'beautiful goals'.

But there are no regrets: 'In exactly the same match with exactly the same players I would do exactly the same thing.'

And now, he says, he has things to do, plans to make, letters to write. They will be flying home on Tuesday and there is no question of Ramsey staying behind. His place is with his players.

And his future as England manager? Will he carry on?

That one sure enough snaps Alf out of it. The eyes acquire their customary steely glare. 'Is there any reason why I shouldn't?' he growls.

Schoen gives Hugh Johns the polite but Germanic version of the same story. It 'was very hard work', but even at 2–0 down they never thought they'd lost it. 'I always believed in my team ... We have played under circumstances we didn't have in England,' he digs. He thanks the Mexicans for their support and now looks forward to the Italy game.

Later, at the Guadalajara Hilton, Gerald Sinstadt sits on the sun loungers with Bobby Robson and Bertie Mee. They didn't see the England game live. Football connoisseurs, they couldn't resist the chance of staying in Guadalajara and catching Brazil and Peru, two Latin sides, going at each other. Neither will knock Alf, his tactics or his team selection. It's something deeper down in our footballing culture that has failed us, they muse. And Mee trots out a phrase that will be much heard over the following thirty years: 'It's got to be an evolutionary process that starts at school.'

There is still one England player who remains blissfully unaware of it all. Because the quarter-final games were played simultaneously and Mexican TV chose to air the Mexico–Italy and Brazil–Peru games live, the others follow immediately on tape delay. Gordon Banks, propped up in bed in his motel room, is only an hour into the England–West Germany broadcast when Alex Stepney walks in with the longest face he's ever seen. With England 2–0 up on TV and cruising, Banks asks what's up? When Stepney reveals the awful truth and Banks demands a second opinion, Dr Phillips adopts his most sympathetic bedside manner and confirms it...

Back at the motel, the evening is strange, funereal, awkward even, given that there is a huge German contingent there, with their players' wives doing their best to start a party. But it's nothing a few drinks won't sort out.

Gradually the players wander out of their chalets, beers in hand, trunks on, and jump in the pool – partaking of what had been simple forbidden pleasures.

Alf is nowhere to be seen.

'After the game I went looking for Alf and I couldn't find him,' says Ken Jones. 'I said, "Has anyone seen him?" The players are flopped out by the pool. Eventually I find him in his chalet with Cyril Broderick, who was the Cook's travel guy. And Cyril used to wear an England tracksuit; he was in danger of becoming the first travel agent to take a throw-in in a World Cup match. Broderick was pissed and was under the shower in his tracksuit. And I walked in and there were these champagne bottles. I said to Alf, "I don't know what to say." He said, "Do you want a drink?" and I said, "Please." And he said, "Pour it your fuckin' self." He looked at me and he said, "It had to be *him*. Of all the players to lose, it had to be *him*." '

As if to rub it in, Banks, feeling a lot better, ventures out for a cagey walk. By tomorrow he will be absolutely fine.

Alf's not a big drinker so he quickly loosens up. Soon he's telling tales of the old days, wandering around the pool or going room to room to check on the players. Most, now, with still a few hours of sun at their disposal, are intent on making the remaining time a holiday. In a weird way, they are happy to be going home. 'It'd been a long season,' says Hunter. 'We didn't want to go home, but the minute that final whistle blew all everybody was thinking about was going home, because we were tired, very tired.'

'Peter Bonetti was absolutely devastated. He'd thought he'd let the lads down,' says Allan Clarke. 'But Peter was a great keeper. So going up to him, I said, "Well done, Peter, you've got us home early." It made him feel even worse.'

Harold Wilson calls the León motel to tell Ramsey hard luck. It was a 'magnificent performance', he assures, though hardly, from the PM's view, conducive to the national feelgood factor (except, perhaps, in Scotland).

As the evening wears on, the wake, inevitably, becomes a party – players joking, singing raucous songs and dealing with it all in a rather heartening old-fashioned English way. 'After about five or six drinks everybody had played fabulous and they were the luckiest team in the world,' says Peter Thompson. 'Alf just disappeared and let us get on with it.'

No one is singled out for blame – they'll all fight and die together. And when Müller and Brazil show up, well, it's grab a drink, boys, and good on yer for Wednesday.

Not all the England players are present, however. Immediately after the match, having gathered their things, Bobby Moore, Martin Peters, Geoff Hurst and Peter Bonetti had obtained permission to go on holiday with their wives, for a premature version of a pre-planned victory jaunt to Acapulco on the Pacific coast. There is confusion when Moore's phone call to wife Tina is cut off. Thus, when the four players arrive back at Guadalajara en route to reclaim their womenfolk, they discover that they have already departed, assuming the rendezvous to be in Acapulco itself. England have lost their wives as well as the World Cup.

Wanting to be on his own, or at least away from the players while he grieves over the match, Hurst cadges a ride with journalist Brian Glanville of the *Sunday Times*. The forward is too exhausted to speak. They stop in the desert at a dusty village to buy a Coke, circumstances that couldn't be more different from what he experienced a few hours before.

That night, the party wears on and others from the Guadalajaran contingent of British players join the knees up (Charlie Cooke, reportedly, was distraught after the game – a hell of a thing for one from north of the border, eulogised by Hugh McIlvanney in his famous piece, 'Even the Scots had tears in their eyes'). At one point, a plastic Union Jack bowler hat blows into the pool. It is upturned, filling with water and sinking fast. Bobby Charlton dives in to rescue it: a more poignant gesture you could not have asked for.

After a month of eating and living together, billeted away to achieve the absolute peak of physical fitness, with one goal in mind, it's suddenly all over. They'll be flying out on Tuesday. By Wednesday morning they'll be home ...

Back home, England is in mourning. On BBC1, as Nana Maskouri does her best to soothe the nation's spirits, her plaintive Greek warbling is lost on the country's stunned households. That night, on a hastily rearranged edition of ITV's *World Cup '70*, as the jolly Latin music begins to herald the usual highlights package, the programme does not reveal the usual slap-happy panel ready to feast on another night of exotic football. Instead comes a sombre Brian Moore, intoning to the camera as if he was announcing a royal death. 'England and Sir Alf Ramsey are out of the World Cup,' he states, with doe-eyed misery, showing a reel of those happy goals from 1966, now further consigned to history.

The programme will pick over the bones of what happened and pose questions as to the fate of Alf Ramsey, being spoken about now as if he had already passed away. And for good measure the show features a clip of Alf reading what is tantamount to his own obituary – his farewell speech on 28 May, the eve of tournament: 'Myself and the players will be judged and assessed on what they do on the playing field,' he says. Cut to Hugh Johns yelling, 'Pelé ... Jairzinho ... there it is,' and a clip from the end of the Germany game – 'The Argentinian referee calls an end to it and England, the World Champions, are out of the 1970 World Cup.'

ITV have been busy. They've already conducted a vox pop outside a London pub straight after the game. 'When he pulled off Charlton and Peters, he left the midfield and Beckenbauer all to his self,' says one young geezer; 'He thinks too much about defence'; 'Needs wingers'; 'Great manager ... about time he said, "Ta-ta," ' add others.

Back in the studio, on a board are listed Ramsey's England achievements – P71 W44 D18 L8. Under '1970', in a box optimistically reserved for insertion of the words 'World Champions', there now sits a big question-mark.

'Will he go on to face more battles in Munich in 1974?' asks Brian Moore.

'He's taken it very well,' says Jimmy Hill – said all the right things, no blame on the players. 'A first-class PR job.'

But they worry for him, for Alf's a bit of a loner.

Malcolm Allison, in a flashy pink shirt, silk tie, blue jacket, adds, 'A loner is a man who'll take all the credit and all the flak ... He's an independent man, he asks no favours of anybody ... A great man.'

They know Alf would never reveal what he's feeling inside. 'He never shows it,' says Bob McNab.

And Pat Crerand, suitably bedecked in black tie and kerchief, says he knew that, in private, after the '66 final, Alf 'broke down with happiness'.

Derek Dougan insists that the PR stuff should never have been Alf's responsibility. And Allison, puffing on a big cigar, blows smoke in the Irishman's face, calling him, much to his annoyance, 'Doog'. 'Malcolm would have been on the box every bloody second,' snaps Dougan angrily, and Allison keeps it going by winding Doog up about his shirt.

'The FA aren't bright enough to realise that they need someone to handle the press,' says Allison. And Hill says it's a consequence of the fact that Ramsey was the 'first man to do it his way, with complete control'.

Crerand says British football has gone backwards since '66.

So why, then, it is asked, are our clubs doing so well in Europe?

'Because we play against peasants,' says Allison, and Hill threatens him with a yellow card, saying they'll get lots of angry letters with comments like that.

Bob McNab is awfully quiet. Come on, Bob, tell us, they say – *you're* part of the England set-up, is Alf a good manager or what?

'Don't give me the nice stuff,' growls Crerand. 'Does he know the game?'

'I think he does,' says McNab.

Think or know?

And they break off to trail the Brazil–Uruguay semi-final. There's still a World Cup going on, you know.

Other things have been happening, though you'd never know it: Trooping the Colour; the ongoing Granada strike; in Brazil, forty political prisoners are flown to Algiers in exchange for the kidnapped West German ambassador Ehrenfried Von Holleben; in a big athletics bash at Edinburgh, Lilian Board and the British ladies win the 4 × 800 relay and set a new world record; Boycott is not picked for the England Test side; in Argentina, Brigadier-General Roberto Marcelo Levingston is named the new president following a coup; and, perhaps most importantly, Harold Wilson intervenes to settle the newspaper strike, with SOGAT accepting a £5 million settlement from 1 July. Sixty-five million copies of national and London evening papers were lost in the dispute. All Monday's first editions tell the same sad story: 'ENGLAND OUT OF WORLD CUP' (*Guardian* and *The Times*); 'DE-THRONED' (*Daily Mail*); 'WE JUST GAVE IT AWAY' (*Sun*). Most carry the famous snap from behind the goal of Bonetti in his number 12 jersey, flailing vainly as Müller contorts in mid-air to put the ball past him.

'The tragedy of it all was that England sacrificed a lead of two goals when it appeared right and just they would play Italy in the semi-finals,' says Albert Barham of the *Guardian*. 'It was a battle of wits, will-power and stamina. And it was stamina perhaps which lost this game.'

The Times is magnanimous – 'West Germany emerge worthy winners,' they claim. Even the *Daily Mail* is generous to England's foe – 'If it had to be then better to lose to such fighters.'

The *Sun*, however, lambastes England as 'Millionaires who threw away their fortune' and closes with something of an open invitation: 'Now', it says, 'for the big inquest.'

Perhaps the more ominous announcement comes from Len Shipman, president of the Football League and chairman of the FA's International Committee: 'One must give them praise for the good things they have done – some magnificently – but after being two goals ahead they definitely should have been capable of staying in front,' he says. 'He [Ramsey] achieved much for England in bringing us the World Cup in 1966. We will always thank him for that.'

In other words, they can't wait to get shot of him . . .

So what *did* happen to Gordon Banks? Speculation has ranged over the years from the mundane to the outlandish – with poisoning a favoured explanation. Mexican spite, perhaps. Even a CIA-backed conspiracy has been vaunted – England's keeper drugged to ensure Brazil's triumph (and Latin American stability) – or as part of a guarantee to Mexico to secure a lucrative US media deal.

'I wouldn't have a clue whether he was Mickey-Finned or not,' says Brian Labone. 'Gordon liked a little bit of sunshine. Whether he'd sneaked out and got a little bit of sun on the back of the neck, I don't know.'

The more likely scenario, as Banks and others later suggest, is that when he was hosting his mum and an aunt after the Czechoslovakia game, he may have inadvertently taken ice in a Coke.

'I still believe they got at Banksie,' says Hugh Johns. 'It just seemed too bloody coincidental. For this one exceptionally important game in León, when we'd already seen the effect that the Germans had had on the local people there, there seemed every reason to believe there was some skulduggery. There were so many things that you said to yourself, "I wonder." '

'It does make you wonder whether some of the stories about him being nobbled or got at are true,' says David Sadler.

Dr Phillips dismisses the wilder suppositions, given that the course of the illness ran similarly for Bobby Charlton and Keith Newton. 'I treated them and they were better to play in the match against Germany. Gordon started a day later and wasn't able to play against Germany, but the following day was better.'

It is no surprise to find that, at the Guadalajara Hilton, the three ailing players – Banks, Bobby Charlton and Keith Newton – were roommates.

Years later, Dr Phillips has a conversation with David Coleman, who, with Don Revie and Joe Mercer – the BBC commentary team – was also staying at the Hilton. Another theory arises, which, for Phillips, is certainly food for thought.

'I should think about 1976, David said to me that he was convinced, though he didn't have any evidence for it, that room service was taking place in some of the bedrooms,' says Phillips. 'Now all the players were barred from having room service. But David was convinced that some of the players had had room service and that it was probably the food that had upset them.'

And so England went out of the World Cup ...

Chapter 16

Back Home

Tuesday, 16 June 1970

As the hours wear on after that momentous contest, reaction comes in from around the world. From Mexico, it is as expected – 'THE CHAMPIONS ARE DEAD. GO HOME ENGLAND,' squeals *Esto*, rather spitefully. Elsewhere, comment is far more complimentary: 'Fantastic! Incredible! Unbelievable! Marvellous! Extraordinary!' says France's *L'Equipe*. Germany's *Bild Zeitung* is understandably ecstatic – 'BOYS, YOU ARE THE GREATEST!' it declares, ending its report with 'When England, after a mighty last effort, slunk off the ground, it was a sad goodbye to a wonderful team who showed, quite clearly, that they deserved to wear the champion's crown of four years.'

Others papers, in Brazil in particular, reveal a genuine tinge of sadness at England's departure, even if it doesn't quite square with popular opinion. 'I think the Brazilians were bloody dancing in the streets when we went out,' says Emlyn Hughes. 'Because they were frightened of England. They knew we were the only side that could have beaten them.' But the sentiment is appreciated, with Brazilian journalists according England the ultimate accolade of nominating three players in their World XI – Banks, Moore and Cooper. After all he's been through, and then to come out and play like he has, special affection is reserved for the England captain. 'The most perfect and most correct defender I have ever seen,' declares Mário Zagalo publicly. 'Give me Banks and Bobby Moore and no team on earth could beat us.' Which is very nice, but doesn't say a lot for his faith in Messrs Félix, Brito and Piazza.

Within the England squad, the post-match analysis has been ongoing ever since the final whistle, but still it is more lament than criticism. No one will hear a single bad word about Bonetti – 'You *never* blame the goalkeeper,' says Jack Charlton. No one questions the substitutions – 'It made so much *sense*, bearing in mind the conditions,' says David Sadler. 'You've got to remember that it's a hundred degrees,' adds Brian Labone. 'We were having a game two days later, so we had to look ahead. And we were coasting.'

Indeed, each player will only blame himself. 'I had a pretty good game,' says Labone again. 'Müller only got *one* kick. I know all centre halves says this, but it happened to be the winner.'

Generally, though, there is just that air of despondency. 'You don't lose games like that,' says Alan Ball. 'That's what I can't understand.' The Everton midfielder seems to have taken defeat particularly hard. After the match the players were, quite cruelly and unnecessarily, presented with a set of medals for reaching the last eight. On the bus back to Mexico City, Ball takes his and goes to throw it out of the window, stopping only on the insistence of Dr Phillips, who says if Ball wants to get rid of it, he might as well hand it to him so that he can give it to his kids.

When the team rolls up at Mexico City airport on the morning of Tuesday, 16 June, after a six-hour coach ride, there is still a long overnight flight awaiting them to London, where they are scheduled to land at 7.10 the following morning. This time, though, they will be boarding a plane with no big send-off.

Still, with drinks permitted now, the long retreat will be a little more bearable. The beers have been flowing freely ever since they left the stadium and will continue to do so all the way to Heathrow ('Some were in a hell of a state,' says Peter Thompson). And, once they are safely up in the air, the lads seem happy to be going home.

For some it will mark a move to a new phase in their footballing lives. Somewhere over the Atlantic, at a convenient point in the proceedings, Ramsey walks up the aisle and takes a seat next to Bobby Charlton. He simply thanks him for everything he's ever done for England. The message is only implied but completely acknowledged. Charlton has played his last game for his country. There will be no ceremonial retirement, no announcement of his departure: simply, the next time the official squad invitations go out from the FA, there will not be one landing on the doormat of R. Charlton OBE. Charlton understands perfectly. This is the Ramsey way.

As it happens, brother Jack has been thinking along similar lines.

'We had a few beers on the bus. And now we had a drink or two on the plane,' he remembers. 'Alf was sat on his own at the back of the plane. So I went back down to him, and I said, "Can I have a word, Alf?" And he said, "Yes." I said to him, "Listen, Alf, I've been with you for six years and I've enjoyed every bit of it, it's really been great. But I'm thirty-four. I think it's time I called it a day with the England team." And he just looked at me and said, "I totally agree." And that was Alf. So it was my last game for England and it was Our Kid's.' Jack will be leaving international football with quite a record, though, as he proudly states: 'I never lost a game in a World Cup.'

Ramsey will now be facing a new battle of his own, for, as he knows only too well, he is flying straight into the belly of the beast. 'This is one plane I did not want to be catching,' he tells Norman Giller of the *Daily Express*, one of the several journalists flying back with the party. 'I was convinced we would be making our final preparations for the semi-final today. I am bitterly disappointed because I know the players I have with me now are good enough to have won the championship. They are still the champions in my eyes. I appreciate that the people at home are sick over elimination. Believe me, nobody – and I mean nobody – feels it as badly as I do.'

The *Daily Express* gamely chooses to seek an optimistic escape route out of the misery: 'MUNICH HERE WE COME!' it declares the next day, as if this Mexican affair was but a minor blip in English football dominance. But while Ramsey even makes some positive noises about England's chances for 1974 himself – how they've got some great young players coming through – it all rings rather hollow. As people are now beginning to realise, England's failure means that the VIP pass has been withdrawn: Munich will involve England having to go through a qualifying tournament, something they have not experienced since the 1961–62 season, and something, as the Scots will tell you, that is by no means easy.

Ramsey's immediate concern does not extend to such stuff. It must be to protect his players from the impending media storm, with special regard, it seems, for the well-being of Bobby Moore. The Bogotá incident has been almost forgotten in the light of everything else, but inevitably, and especially without any great footballing triumph to write about now, it will run and run ('It still hangs over Bob to this day,' says Jack Charlton). Moore will find himself taking time off from West Ham at the start of the 1970–71 season simply to get away from it all.

But still, there are a great many people behind Alf and the boys. The papers are full of letters of support. And Ramsey must find it heartening that the public welcome at Heathrow Terminal 3 on Wednesday, 17 June is as raucous and goodwilled as it would have been had England come back with the trophy. Several hundred fans have slept overnight, others had begun rolling up with the first train at 5.30 a.m., and there are banners aplenty welcoming home the lads, telling them 'well done', and, optimistically again, wishing them all the best for the next one.

However, any expectations of a smooth ride from the press are dashed when one reporter asks Ramsey straight away, with a sardonic grin, 'Glad to be back home, Alf?'

'If you ask a stupid question you'll get a stupid answer,' snaps Ramsey as the inevitable media scrum ensues. And with that he is bundled by police into a waiting car and sped straight to a press conference at a West London hotel.

In a light brown suit, white shirt, black tie, he tries to cut a dignified figure, but the experience of the last couple of days, the lack of sleep and the aggression of the Fourth Estate do not foster a cordial atmosphere.

'*I* am rude?' he replies, disbelieving, when it is put to him that he is not being entirely cooperative. 'They stick their faces in front of me, they stick these things in front of me and so forth and so forth [waving an angry hand at the microphones and cameras all about him], and *I'm* being rude? There isn't a word invented that would describe the mannerisms of some of the people I've been confronted with. And yet *I'm* rude.'

'It was definitely not the sort of reaction to win friends and influence people,' quips the *Daily Mirror* the next day.

Not all eyes are on Alf. Gordon Banks is stopped and made a presentation, which he accepts, on behalf of the team – a silver disc to mark the 250,000 sales of the 'Back Home' single – before dashing for an airport coach chased by a pack of screaming girls. Big Jack Charlton, in his blazer and trilby, runs a gauntlet of backslaps, quipping with the immigration staff about how he's going to go fishing and sink a few pints. Brother Bobby, despite all that's just happened to him on the ground and in the air, valiantly defends his England boss, saying that the lads are all 100 per cent behind him and that his own substitution was perfectly in order. Ball, still in a state of shock, protests to the BBC how England should have won: 'We had them dead, they were dead men,' he says – but that no way will Ramsey resign: 'No chance of that. Who can take his place?'

But the knives are sharpening, and while some like the great Hugh McIlvanney still see poetry in the heart-rending drama of the quarter-final exit, others are beating the war drums. Malcolm Allison has been particularly scathing, ridiculing Ramsey's tactics: 'Ramsey has kept the same pattern since his days at Ipswich, as far back as 1957,' he tells the *Sun*. Hans Keller on Radio Four's *PM* blasts the England team as the product of a 'Second Division mind'.

Irrespective of the inevitable brickbats – naive use of substitutes, lack of attacking inspiration, ill-advised abandonment of wingers – Alf's real struggle would now seem to be with the powers that be at the FA. Without having a leg to stand on in the last four years (Alf vindicating his dictatorship with silverware), the men at Lancaster Gate are now anxious to reclaim their lost power. 'RAMSEY – THE MAN ALONE,' says the *News of the World*, sensing the political wind.

'When England failed in Mexico, the little dogs began yapping,' says Frank Butler. 'Having slapped Sir Alf Ramsey on the back when England won the World Cup, they now want his head on a block.'

The press conference lasts seventy minutes. Alf, bristling, says all that you'd ever expect him to say and defends his players to the hilt. 'They could not have given me more had they tried,' he says, and if you don't believe they gave their all, he adds, then watch them over the coming season. He genuinely fears that some of them gave so much they might suffer. (Interestingly, Arsenal, who will do the Double, had no players in the England party.)

'I would select exactly the same players if the World Cup were to be played again tomorrow,' he asserts. 'They did not let England down in any way and I am immensely proud of them. The only thing we lacked in Mexico was luck.'

Alf might need a bit of it himself. For, after having restated that he will not resign, he seems intent on being hoist by his own petard.

Can England learn anything from Brazil?

'I don't think we can,' says Alf. 'I have read all the glowing things that have been said about them and they indeed have some brilliant players, but you will find it difficult to improve on what we have here in England at League and international level...'

After wanting out of football altogether – for about five minutes – Martin Peters decides to cut short his trip to Acapulco and head back to Mexico City for the Wednesday semi-final between Italy and West Germany – if only to see the Germans get a tonking. He, like most of the erstwhile competitors, is rather jealous of the conditions, for – and against predictions – Mexico City is comparatively cool and has suddenly found itself sitting under a slate-grey, thundery sky, with great foreboding booms rumbling overhead. The weather will remain like this for the rest of the World Cup, at odds with all that has gone before. Some locals suspect a mystical reason for it all, harking back to something lurking deep within Mexico's soul. When the Conquistadores came to the New World, they founded their capital on the seat of the old Aztec Empire – once a magnificent city of gold situated on an island in the middle of a great lake. Ever since, it is claimed, the periodic earthquakes and epidemics that blight Mexico City have been the result of the Aztec gods trying to eject the Spaniards' descendants. Now their wrath has been incurred again – angry that their sacred spot should be used for such frivolous mortal sport, and in an arena that takes their name in vain. The gods will try to turn the city back into the lake it once was. Given that they have already put paid to Gordon Banks, they are a power to be reckoned with.

No such stuff in Guadalajara. There it's as sunny as it ever was. And while Peters is in the capital, pulling on a sweater, Bobby Moore has gone back to the Jalisco, joining the ITV team to co-commentate at the other semi-final between Brazil and Uruguay, followed by the third-place play-off and then the final itself.

In the spirit of the tournament, ITV and BBC tossed a coin for the semi-final, with each side showing the highlights of the other game later. The plum choice, for which ITV opt, is the Guadalajara game. And so the Beeb are left with seconds: Italy versus West Germany. Some consolation prize: it must be one they're still rubbing their hands over.

On the day of the semis, a pre-planned and rather hopeful Radio Rentals ad in most of the British newspapers asks, 'Are you nervous about tonight's game?' The answer, of course, is absolutely not, although when it comes to events in the Azteca, where England would have been playing, there is a certain interest in how well the Germans will do, the nation torn between hopes for a retributive thrashing by the Italians and wishes that they'll now go all the way, thus making England's exit appear less of a disaster.

In West Germany itself, after beating the champions, naturally there are high hopes: 'With this team, we need not fear anybody,' says Cologne's *Kölnische Rundschau*.

Not all Germany is in rapture. It is all too much for one thirty-three-year-old Englishman, a resident of Dusseldorf, who is seriously injured when throwing himself in despair from his second-floor window. On a less tragic note, the fictitious Terry Collier, he of *The Likely Lads*, will soon be citing England's defeat as the reason for divorcing his German wife.

Despite their sterling performance against England, the Germans know they've got a hell of a job on their hands to beat Italy. A period of extra-time is a crippling handicap to carry into your next encounter. Team doctor Hans Schoeberth and masseur Erich Deuser, the one who was yellow-carded earlier, have been working round the clock to soothe weary limbs. Already it seems that Hottges won't make it, his knee, damaged in the England game, failing to have made a sufficient recovery. Others have problems, too, though will most likely play on regardless: Seeler and Maier have thigh injuries, Beckenbauer has bruised feet, Müller is just crocked generally.

Tactically it will be the usual stuff – wingers to the fore. It seems likely, from training-ground observations, that they will deploy Vogts to man-mark Riva. Across the land, the bier-kellers are abuzz – and awash – with expectation.

In Italy they are brimming with confidence, too. Turin's *Stampa Sera* borrows a line from the national anthem – 'AT LAST ITALY HAS AWAKENED' – and announces that a record TV audience of 18 million watched the quarter-final with Mexico, one in three of the population. And, though it wasn't scheduled, state TV programmers reran the game on Monday just for the hell of it.

The tourists in Italy's beautiful cities had the streets to themselves on Sunday afternoon. By evening every square and fountain heaved with celebrating fans, flags waved from the pillions of Vespas, and tiny Fiat cars, crammed full with as many people as was possible, drove around parping horns till dawn.

'We won because the team found its form and Luigi Riva was again the great Luigi Riva,' Valcareggi declared in his post-match press conference, and the whole of Italy (with the exception of Mazzola, who keeps getting substituted for Rivera at half-time, even though he's playing well) is now hoping that golden boys Riva and Rivera can do the business once again.

The press swarms all over the Parc des Princes Hotel, where the Italians have been throughout. Rivera poses in a ridiculously small pair of trunks; Riva is in a sharp T-shirt and razor-creased trousers.

Pedigree must favour the Italians, the European Champions, though the sheer exuberance and will to win of the Germans and their massive goal haul, despite their weariness, might just get them through. In either case, it should be a hell of a match.

At the start of the game the rumbles of thunder deepen (like an opening day in August in England). Ninety-five thousand have filed in to see the game, and Italy are at full strength. Germany have brought back Hamburg defender Schulz to replace Hottges. They've also chosen to deploy Grabowski from the outset rather than bring him on later, reserving Libuda this time for that purpose. Fichtel has been replaced at the back by Patzke, who played half a game against Peru. As is becoming an apparent feature of modern football, there are rival players on the pitch who play for the same club – Schnellinger, Roberto Rosato and Gianni Rivera all suit up in the red and black stripes of AC Milan in their day jobs.

Italy kick off and, uncharacteristically, go on the attack – Mazzola to de Sisti, to Bertini, to Burgnich. After the dour defensive misery of the group games, the victory over Mexico and now this exuberant start have suggested that, for Italy, it has all been part of a plan, saving themselves for the do or die of the knock-outs. On eight minutes, they prove their worth.

Boninsegna, of Inter Milan, once with Riva at Cagliari, intercepts a header by Vogts and shoots from twenty yards out with his left foot. The ball flies in past Maier's right hand. Italy are in front. The forward, who's only in Mexico because of the withdrawal of Anastasi, assumes a Corcovado-Christ-like stance, standing there with his arms out wide, as Mazzola and Riva congregate to absorb a bit of his spirit.

Italy's ability to shut up shop completely, which they might now well be advised to do, is beyond question, but it is early days yet, a long time to hold out in a defensive pattern. The tall number 3, Facchetti, their captain, herds his celebrating players back for the kick-off.

Uwe Seeler employs that old, familiar palms-down gesture. 'Keep calm,' he's saying, 'keep calm.' West Germany – or 'Western Germany', as David Coleman calls them – have been behind in four of their five games so far. They've given the opposition their customary goal start, now let the game begin.

Thus commences a period of German attacking that continues through the rest of the first half and well into the second. Seeler leaps all over the place, winning balls in the air he's no right to; Libuda comes on for Lohr (with Grabowski switching to the left), running at Facchetti, who's trying his best to thwart him; little Cera is throwing himself into every challenge; hatchet-man de Sisti is doing all he can within the bounds of criminal law to beat them back.

'There's no side that's ever fought harder in any World Cup match than these Germans,' yelps Coleman.

A hell of an offensive is mounted; it's just unfortunate it's against the strongest defensive team in the competition. With the Italians again making their luxurious political substitution at half-time of Rivera for Mazzola, they proceed to keep the Germans at bay.

Into the last quarter, having run at the defence on a few occasions from the right side of midfield, Beckenbauer – who would give Bobby Moore a run for his money in immaculate presentation – tries it again. He collects the ball, sees space before him and charges. He evades a tackle by Facchetti and, suddenly, he's through into the area, with Müller and Seeler waiting for the square ball, when he is hacked down from behind by Cera – half kick, half body-check, totally effective. A goal-scoring opportunity has clearly been denied by a blatant offence in the box. Surely a penalty. Probably a sending off.

Thus follows a cowardly piece of refereeing. Arturo Yamasaki of Mexico (of Japanese extraction, via Peru), fearing the weight of such a crucial decision, gives that tired old referee's cop-out of the free kick on the edge of the area. Cera is not even cautioned.

The Italians look mighty relieved. The Germans are incensed.

With the clock ticking, they have been denied a sure equaliser in either event. Müller is so angry that he physically manhandles the ref, shoving him in the chest with his stubby little hands, lucky not to get marching orders himself. Schulz and Overath muscle in, too. And for all the German protestations, the Italians stand there shrugging like a bunch of choirboys.

Beckenbauer hasn't been to the Maier school of pitch theatrics. Rather than rolling around, writhing in mock agony, lending weight to his teammates' arguments, he just lies there, face down and motionless. With him it can only mean one thing – he is genuinely hurt. And when he is eventually helped to a sitting position, the German trainer discovers he has dislocated his right shoulder.

Once again Seeler tries to calm his team, who are now behaving more Italian than the Italians. Müller clutches his temples as if in the throes of demonic possession; Overath waves two fingers – a very Anglo-Saxon gesture – in the referee's face. Meanwhile, de Sisti stands there, pouting innocently, explaining with overly mannered gestures how silly Beckenbauer fell down the stairs/walked into a door, and, obviously, the incident occurred on the wrong side of the white line. Any fool could see that. Beckenbauer is helped to his feet with his right arm dangling limply by his side. With West Germany having already made their second substitution, Beckenbauer insists he can play on. It's the only thing to do. He can't get into anything physical but he can still kick the ball. No point in pulling him off.

Overath places the ball. Held, the winger, another veteran of '66, who came on for defender Patzke in the sixty-fifth minute (making it three flankers on the German team now), is open. Schnellinger (or 'Shellinger' as Joe Mercer calls him) is free, too. One of them will receive the tap sideways from Overath to blast at the Italian goal. It's Held who gets the crack, and with his right foot he takes a swing at it. But the Italian wall, which was never remotely ten yards back, charges out fast and narrows the angle. With only a slim edge of goal to aim at, Held places it rather than thumps it. The shot rolls weakly wide of Albertosi's right-hand post.

The game wears on. It's fever-pitch stuff now. Riva nearly puts it beyond doubt on a swift break with a diving header. But the Germans continue to press. Joe Mercer and Don Revie, Coleman's co-pilots, are gibbering wrecks. Mercer has started referring to the Germans as 'we'.

They throw everything forward. Little Grabowski, now with licence to roam anywhere, is through on goal and rugby-tackled to the ground by de Sisti. The ref does nothing. 'And de Sisti almost had his trousers off with that tackle,' exclaims Hugh Johns.

The kitchen sink duly follows, but, for Germany, the war is over. With time running out, Burgnich goes down in his own box after an innocuous challenge. 'Again the dying-swan act by Burgnich,' says Johns. More time is frittered away. It's the end.

Or is it? In the second minute of injury time, with just about every player bar Maier now up in the Italian box, Grabowski on the left bangs a cross over with his wrong foot, which proves to be every bit as lethal as his right one. The ball is sent on a collision course with Schnellinger, the blond left back rushing in like a madman and launching himself feet-first at the far post. Isaac Newton himself could not have devised a more perfect study of time and motion. Schnellinger, flying horizontally, like a missile, connects and rockets the ball in. For the second game running the Germans have snatched a goal at the death. For the second game running it is 1966 all over again.

'*Unbelievable*,' screams Coleman. 'As long as people play football they're going to talk about this match.'

'This game is really alive, absolutely *alive*,' yells Johns.

Schnellinger, like Seeler playing in his fourth World Cup, just lies there on the ground, his arms above him, while Müller rolls on top of him like a hairy Sunday morning lover. The Italians, dumbfounded, look at each other with arms open wide, as if to ask, 'How?' The pile of white-shirted bodies in front of Albertosi builds to a pyramid and Maier runs the full length of the pitch to form its peak. Beckenbauer lumbers over, duff arm flapping. Grabowski, who can barely walk by this stage, gets a sudden spurt of euphoric adrenaline and sets off on a dash around the perimeter of the pitch worthy of a 400-metre sprinter. The Italian bench look like they've seen ghosts. Boninsegna collapses to the turf, curls into a foetal position and weeps.

At full time the BBC cut back to Gordon Banks in a Manchester studio. The satellite link is bad. Banksie says something about it being 'very exciting'. 'The understatement of 1970,' splutters

Coleman. 'It's electric,' blubbers Revie. 'The atmosphere now is really boiling.'

The ninety minutes over, both sides retreat to their benches and collapse while drinks are administered and the poor Germans, now into their second come-from-behind extra-time encounter in four days, lie with their socks round ankles, getting their legs stretched by teammates and massages for cramped calves. For Beckenbauer there's nothing to do but patch him up and send him out for the duration. The German bench grab reels of bandages and improvise a makeshift Boy Scout sling, with the German midfielder's injured arm bound tight across his chest, right hand to left clavicle. It's the only way. Beckenbauer won't hear of standing down. 'It looks like he's done his shoulder a fair bit of mischief,' says Johns.

No one wants to get to the final (or especially go out) on a coin toss, and so Italy, the most defence-minded team in the tournament, must now attack. They kick off again and soon the Germans are staging their first advance. Held goes down the left wing but the attack breaks down. From the ensuing corner, taken by Libuda, the ball is nodded down harmlessly. It falls to substitute defender Poletti, who has come on fresh for extra-time. He chests it back casually to his goalkeeper. But he hasn't seen Müller. Like a cheetah who explodes from behind a tree to pick off a straggling antelope, Müller nips in between the two and gets his foot to the ball, sending it trickling agonisingly past Albertosi, barely making it over the goal line: 2–1 to West Germany, and little Müller is jumping for joy.

'The Italians complaining,' says Coleman. 'They may become victims of their own temperament.' De Sisti – not before time – gets booked for not retreating at a free kick soon after.

Italy's turn to attack. Rivera takes a free kick. Craftily he flicks it into the air. Held, in his own box, carelessly kicks at it, it lands at the feet of defender Burgnich, who has been thrown forward in desperation. On the edge of the six-yard box he cannot miss. He may be offside but no one's whistling, and he tucks it away before leaping higher than would seem humanly possible: 2–2. Schulz screams at Held for his costly error.

The pendulum has swung Italy's way, and the Azzurri attack down the left. Domenghini finds Vogts backing off rather than committing himself and he sends a hopeful centre over to Riva, in the 'D' of the German box. Faced by an exhausted Schnellinger, Riva takes a step to the left, swings his billion-lira boot and brings the ball cunningly across the goal to Maier's left, just as the keeper was moving right. 'He took it so well. His left foot is like a rifle,' says Uncle David: 3–2 to Italy. Boninsegna, having bawled his eyes out not a few minutes before, is now so overcome with joy he runs in and nearly blasts the ball clean through the German net in celebration.

Players on either side can hardly walk now, let alone run. Challenges go in late or are missed altogether. Vogts clumsily brings down Riva more through exhaustion than design. Both men can hardly get to their feet. Rivera hacks down Vogts more through design than exhaustion. Forwards find themselves with tons of space but no reserves of energy to exploit it.

Dark now, because of the thunder clouds, the floodlights are on – for the only time in the tournament.

In the final period the Germans, with nothing to lose, dig deep and throw wounded bodies forward. 'Can the Germans do it yet again?' asks Coleman. Overath takes a free kick which loops on to Seeler's head. The German captain nods down, but the header is so powerful that it bounces up and over the bar, helped on its way by Albertosi. From the resultant corner by Libuda, a cross is sent to the far post, hoping, just hoping, that Seeler can meet it again. Amazingly, he outjumps Poletti and dispatches the ball towards goal, sailing to Albertosi's top left-hand corner. The keeper looks to have it covered, but out of nowhere Müller leaps, arms by his side, like a performing seal, to deflect the ball beyond Albertosi's reach: 3–3.

Müller explodes with delight. Beckenbauer winces in pain as he congratulates him. Although it's hardly at the forefront of anyone's mind, that's ten World Cup goals. Müller's only three shy of Juste Fontaine's record thirteen, and at this rate anything's possible.

'What can you say about this?' burbles Coleman.

The crowd – having never witnessed such a thrilling game of football in their lives – are wild with joy. Müller bounces back down the pitch. The Germans, too tired to run to him, simply embrace the nearest teammate so that the field now looks like an alfresco tea dance.

Though it is short-lived. True to the old cliché about being vulnerable in the aftermath of a goal, the Germans provide a text-book example.

Within seconds of the restart, Riva gets the ball on the left. With everything he's got, he runs to the by-line and pulls it back. The defence is static and Rivera is there to tap it casually home. The easiest goal he'll ever score. So simple that he can't seem to comprehend the enormity of what he's just done.

Nine minutes to go: 4–3 to Italy.

Maier beats his fists on the floor like a spoilt child wronged by Santa. Coleman, for the second time in four days, is lost for words.

All the Italians have to do now is waste time. Having failed to do so in normal time, they are not going to make the same mistake again. From the kick-off the Germans give it their last, aching all. Bertini goes down, clutching his throat like he's just been stran-gled – more time gone. The giant stadium digital clock signals one minute left. Nothing yet is impossible in this game, but even the Germans know that they can't work any more miracles. The crowd are counting down – '*Diez . . . nueve . . . once.*' Held makes one last kamikaze run at the Italian defence, but it is too late. Italy are in the final.

The Germans are beyond tears and stagger around in zombie-like disbelief. The Italians break down. Boninsegna lies flat out, soddening the sod once more with his blubbering, though this time with tears of joy. The speed with which middle-aged manager Valcareggi runs across the pitch to hug his boys makes you realise just how spent and sluggish the players all were.

'This is one of the most exciting semi-finals that the World Cup can ever have witnessed,' says Johns. Ninety-five thousand people are on their feet in celebration of the 120 minutes of amazing football they have just experienced. 'Italy go into the final,' says Coleman, 'in a match, really, that will live for ever.'

The critics, of course, have a field day. Brian Glanville calls it 'basketball' football and cites the Italian press's reaction to Sch-oen's premature substitutions – 'DANKE SCHOEN!' Bobby Robson, in the *Daily Mail*, says that though it was a fantastic spectacle, it was a nightmare from a coach's point of view as never have so many technical errors been made in one game. One German critic, seeing humour in it all, suggests that in future, in the interests of entertainment, no crowds should be let into a game until two teams have played a full ninety minutes of football first.

'The odd thing is, had Schnellinger not got that late equaliser, it would have been written off as a rather dull, uneventful match won by the side with the Method,' says David Lacey.

All anyone who saw it knows is that, played to its entirety, they have just witnessed the most thrilling World Cup match that has ever been played.

'In a dream I watched the semi-final, Italy–Germany – an absolute *dream*,' says Alan Ball. 'I couldn't believe I was sat back home in England. It was one of the real tough weeks of my football life, that . . .'

With all the obsession with the Germans in the last few days, everyone seems to have forgotten about Brazil. The darlings, though, are not going to let anyone upstage them.

'We're just too good for the rest of them,' boasts Brazil's *Jornal dos Brasil*, as the team squares up to its old enemy Uruguay.

While Uruguay are not going to be anyone's monkey, they're not making it easy on themselves. Upset with FIFA already over the question of the switched referee, they have now kicked and screamed about the fact that, having upped from Puebla/Toluca to go to Mexico City to play Russia, with extra-time to boot, they now have to travel again to Guadalajara – their fourth venue of the tournament, León being the only ground they haven't visited. Brazil, meanwhile, get the cushy number of staying put, playing their fifth consecutive game at the Jalisco.

Uruguay wants this semi-final to be played at the Azteca, arguing that this is where the tournament is headed anyway – whoever wins the semi-final would have to travel for the final, might as well do it now. And though they may have a point, they create an almighty stink. It is rumoured at one point that the Uruguayan FA has threatened to withdraw from the competition altogether, with FIFA putting the Russians on stand-by. Though any notion of a boycott does not last long. But, once again, Uruguay have been diverting their energies away from the business in hand.

To make a point, they snub an official reception laid on in their honour and, as usual, the governor of Jalisco, who's done nothing but give out medals and make people welcome, is being told to get stuffed by a bunch of ungrateful foreigners. Any floating supporters among the locals who have not yet cast their affections for Brazil have now had their minds made up for them.

Brazil do not help matters by insinuating that the referee, José Ortiz de Mendibil of Spain, has been out boozing with the Uruguayans. But they are still a hard, professional outfit, able to close down a game at will. Not that they ever win any friends in the process.

Brazil knows it's got a leaking defence. England had the chances to beat them but somehow didn't. Zagalo just hopes that Uruguay play some open football like Peru did, enabling Brazil to get at them – though this is not a particularly Uruguayan trait.

Being superstitious types, the Brazilian team is worried about Uruguay for a more important reason: they are their bogey team. The 1950 World Cup still casts a shadow across Brazilian football. With that year's tournament staged in Brazil, and with the Maracanã Stadium built as the great temple of football in which the home team would be anointed World Champions, it was Uruguay who gave Brazil its greatest footballing humiliation. Going into the final game (the final stages being on a league basis that year), Brazil hosted Uruguay in what was prematurely and arrogantly assumed to be Brazil's greatest hour. Uruguay clearly hadn't read the script. The men from Montevideo won 2–1 and 200,000 spectators could hardly believe what was happening.

Going into a period of genuine mourning, the Brazilian players, broken and humiliated men, became pariahs, chased out of public life altogether. Some died in poverty and solitude. Brazil even permanently abandoned their traditional all-white strip, adopting for the next World Cup a combination of canary yellow, green and light blue, the colours of the national flag, the ones they sport today – thus expunging that previous Brazilian team from record.

Uruguay had won the World Cup in the first ever tournament, too: 1930 . . . 1950 . . . 1970? The Brazilians are getting paranoid.

Only one thing is certain: between Italy, Uruguay and Brazil, whoever wins the Jules Rimet Trophy will, as third-time winners, keep it for ever.

At Guadalajara, in blazing sunshine, the holy trinity of Pelé, Gérson and Tostão lines up to kick off. They start stroking the ball around in their customary lazy fashion. With Everaldo, the number

16, returning at left back, this is Brazil's full-strength side, the one that took the field against Czechoslovakia fourteen days ago and has been unavailable ever since.

Uruguay field the same side that started against Russia, keeping their goalscorer Espárrago on the bench. With the vibrant crowd banging their drums, the scene seems set for some more 'samba football'.

Though not from Brazil. In the first few minutes, they seem strangely out of sorts. Pelé, with a direct free kick on the edge of the area, blasts the ball high by at least ten feet. 'Pelé, oooh my goodness, what a shocker,' says Kenneth Wolstenholme.

In the nineteenth minute, Ubiñas and Cubilla combine on the Uruguayan right, switch play to find Morales on the left, and he sends a cross into the box as Cubilla runs in. In just about the same position from which Jairzinho has scored all his goals, running in from the inside-right position, unchallenged and with Piazza, Brito and co. mere bystanders, the strong Uruguayan forward sends a shot to Félix's right. The goalkeeper's dive is not even worthy of the name: it amounts to falling to his knees and adopting a position akin to praying to Mecca, after the ball has already passed him. Goal to Uruguay.

Cubilla is ecstatic, having waltzed past Piazza as if he wasn't even there, he runs over to the touchline, chased by overjoyed teammates. The crowd is dead silent – apart from a small cluster of Uruguayan fans waving their light blue and white flags, who are now rather conspicuous. Pelé goes into the net to retrieve the ball and brings it to the centre spot, encouraging his teammates as he runs back through the ranks.

But it seems Germany are not the only ones in need of a goal deficit to make themselves play. The magic slowly returns. Rivelino, who seems to be taking command in a way that he hasn't done before, finds Everaldo, who passes to Clodoaldo, who plays it to Tostão on the left wing, the Uruguayan defence back-pedalling. Tostão plays a return to Clodoaldo, who runs past Ancheta to fire a sweet right-foot shot past Mazurkiewicz: 1–1.

Clodoaldo, the unsung hero of the Brazilian side, is mobbed by Pelé and Jairzinho. They've all been willing him a goal but Clodoaldo is too unselfish to snatch at unnecessary chances. This time, though, the goal was for the taking. The Brazilians ooze happiness;

the Uruguayans look grim; just like their respective styles of play. With the crowd now in rapture, you get the feeling that Brazil are about to put on a show.

Pelé certainly does. Uruguay's chief defensive ploy had been to put Montero Castillo on him and give Jairzinho a kick whenever he gets the ball, by Mújica in particular, who is booked by referee de Mendibil. Maneiro commits a nasty foul on Rivelino and also gets yellow-carded.

Carlos Alberto, who can be quite petulant, takes the bait, getting booked himself for a foul on Morales, but Pelé is able to elevate himself above such stuff. As if to show that he belongs on a different footballing plane, early in the second half he performs a quite extraordinary trick. After blasting over a free kick, Mazurkiewicz sends the goal kick out. Pelé, about forty yards from goal, shapes to receive it, but rather than chest it down to control and play it off to someone, he simply takes a cracking volley and fires the ball right back to where it came from. Mazurkiewicz saves. 'And Pelé's done it again,' says Wolstenholme. 'Isn't it incredible? He's taking snap shots from midfield.'

It is probably more memorable than the goals. Not that they are unremarkable. There is, after all, still one custom yet to be observed. And, sure enough, it is. With fifteen minutes to go Tostão plays a deep pass to the onrushing Jairzinho in his usual position, running into the area diagonally from the right. Sheer pace and body strength get him past Matosas and he slots it into the far corner: 2–1. A goal a game for Jairzinho.

The party begins.

Uruguay start pushing up and Brazil still look frail at the back. But Uruguay, seeking an equaliser, have now left themselves exposed. As if Pelé's audacious volley were not enough, he tops it with a move that will go down as one of the great moments of individual brilliance in this or any World Cup. As a deep ball is played up to the box from the left-hand side of midfield, with Pelé making a diagonal run from deep right, Mazurkiewicz, the Uruguayan keeper, rushes out to intercept. Pelé simply continues on his run into the area, stepping over the ball completely as it crosses his path. With the player going to the keeper's right and the ball to his left, poor Mazurkiewicz falls for the dummy, following the man not the ball. Pelé rounds the keeper, then darts off to his right to turn and belt the ball into the goal. Though even the Master cannot get everything perfect. With the goalside photographers suddenly on their feet and rushing the touchline in sheer spellbound admiration, and with Ancheta sliding in to block the shot on the line, Pelé tries to place it in the far corner. 'Oh what genius,' cries Wolstenholme. Too well hit from too tight an angle, it misses the post by an inch, but it doesn't really matter.

Uruguay have brought on Espárrago in the hope that he can do to Brazil what he did to Russia, but it is desperate stuff. In the last seconds of the match Pelé, on the edge of the box, lays it off to Rivelino, whose swerving shot flies into the net on Mazurkiewicz's left at ferocious speed. There are forty seconds left and Rivelino runs like a wild man to the Brazilian bench where the subs and coaches charge out to join the celebrations. Referee de Mendibil has to pull the players back on to the pitch and sub Marco Antonio, his partying interrupted, suddenly issues a scowl that could fell the faint-hearted.

De Mendibil restores order, but there is barely time to restart the match. Brazil, getting better each game, and tossing aside top-quality opposition as if practising against the local Girl Guides, have won, as everyone expected they would . . .

Uh-oh. Whatever happened to Labour's seven-point lead? Seems that a nation buoyant and self-confident has suddenly decided to don the hair shirt. Couldn't be anything to do with the football, could it?

Since England went out, the pace has heated up in the general election, not that anyone's paid much attention, even if it *has* started to get a little nasty. Wilson and Heath have been exchanging sharp words about the economy; Enoch Powell's thrown in his ha'peth by slamming the Common Market and stirring up trouble about the arrival of 500 Ugandan Asians; even Mrs Wilson gets injured in the fray when a police horse treads on her foot in Manchester.

With attention diverted to the fields of Mexico, the polls are all over the shop. While *The Times*'s Marplan and the *Telegraph*'s Gallup have Labour in the lead (9.6 and 7 per cent, respectively), elsewhere the government's popularity is falling. Now the *Evening Standard* gives it a new slant by putting the Conservatives 1 per cent ahead. And by Wednesday, the eve of the big day, even the Labour-supporting *Daily Mirror*, which had always gifted Wilson a comfortable start, gives its final verdict in its Harris poll: 'Neck and neck.'

Such a shame that all the last-minute stumping comes on semi-final night. For, as Cliff Michelmore and the folks at *Election '70* keep trying to tell us, the battle is as tight as anything Italy and Germany can offer.

And on Friday morning, just as it was last Sunday, the result that no one thought was possible: defeat has been snatched from the jaws of victory. 'HEATH IN, LABOUR OUT,' as the *Daily Mail* puts it, with pictures of a smiling Ted and a miserable Harold supping a commiseratory pint. Within hours the Pickfords vans are rolling up Downing Street. The Prime Minister, who had made much political capital out of the 1966 World Cup victory, is now experiencing the corollary of Mexico 1970. Poor old Wilson, he must wonder what he's done wrong: the jobless total is down to about 550,000 and, last time he looked, the country was feeling rather good about itself. Apart from all those damn strikes. In the post-match analysis the pundits believe too many people stayed at home, and that's what sunk Labour. The proverbial week has been a long time in politics.

Not that Heath is escaping the football analogies, with much fuss about his 'new team', whom he's going to name in his 'squad'. In un-Ramsey-ish fashion Heath reveals the new way forward and includes a young right winger, a forty-four-year-old ex-research chemist and lawyer named Margaret Hilda Thatcher, as Secretary of State for Education.

Much is made of that fact Uncle Ted will be coming into the office a bachelor ('Hostess needed at number 10,' declares the *Guardian*) and Heath will have his work cut out in other ways. Despite making pledges outside his new address about uniting a divided nation, already the unions are sharpening their knives – GPO workers, dockers, even deck-chair attendants in London's royal parks are threatening strike action. And within days the new cabinet is facing further rioting in Ulster after the ham-fisted arrest of Bernadette Devlin. With curfews and hasty shoot-on-sight orders imposed, the politics of Northern Ireland look set to dominate as never before.

But then the nation gets back to its usual idle fascinations. In the Mediterranean, Aristotle Onassis has been running around with Maria Callas again, behind Jackie's back; in Los Angeles the Manson trial gets under way; at Ascot, women wearing trousers are permitted entry to the enclosure for the first time; British Leyland reveals its new 'luxury car that can plough through thick mud' – the Range Rover, 'half brother of the Land Rover'; and at the pictures, people return to see the latest releases – *Paint Your Wagon*, *The Battle of Britain*, *The Lion in Winter*, *Hello, Dolly*. Though not, perhaps, the critically pummelled *Ned Kelly*, starring Mick Jagger.

Thank heaven for small mercies, too. Twenty-five-year-old Tony Jacklin wins the US Open. And, with the end of the four-week Granada blackout, *Coronation Street* returns to the nation's screens (with a repeat of the last episode so that viewers can refresh their memories).

In the papers, the next time a headline reads 'SHAMEFUL SURRENDER BY ENGLAND' (*Daily Mirror*), it will refer to the collapse of the batting against the Rest of the World at Lords...

Chapter 17

El Rey Pelé

Sunday, 21 June 1970

The third-place play-off is a meaningless affair, an exercise in humiliation for two teams who have given their all and would rather be remembered going down fighting in the heat of battle rather than have their remains exhibited so disrespectfully. Especially as it has become, more often than not, an excuse to run out the reserves – give a taste of the action to the squad players yet to get their studs muddy.

Thankfully, then, West Germany and Uruguay flout convention. Not wishing to have their reputations diminished in any way, both countries field their strongest available teams at the Azteca on the eve of the final. For Uruguay, it is the luxury of the eleven who took to the pitch against Brazil, their first-choice line-up. For the Germans, in all white today, their bravura performances of the extraordinary past six days have meant casualties. In comes keeper Horst Wolter, and Wolfgang Weber, another veteran from '66 who came on for Beckenbauer against Bulgaria, once more deputises for the wounded number 4. Fichtel comes back in for Schulz, and, of the four wingers, Libuda and Held get the nod.

The match, in front of 60,000 fans, is surprisingly competitive, too, though the giving of quarter is not a traditional feature of games involving Uruguay. And it is spiced up by the presence of Wolter, who proves to be another Félix disciple in his erraticism – but who pulls off a couple of blinding saves when the chips are down.

The goal that decides the game, 1–0 in Germany's favour, is tremendously familiar in its execution – the long cross from the right from Libuda, the ball headed back across the box (here by Seeler, who outleaps the taller Ubiñas and Fontes) flat-footing defenders, and there, as ever, is Müller, lurking in the six-yard box. But Müller is looking jaded this time. With two defenders, Matosas and Ancheta, right up his hairy backside, Müller can't turn and shoot, so lays it back to Overath, who blasts it in with his left. Mazurkiewicz just gets a touch. There are only twenty-six minutes gone but there will be no more goals. Uruguay hit the woodwork and have enough chances to pull it back, but the only impressions they make are a few farewell stud marks on German shins.

At the end, with half the team now in swapped, drenched Uruguayan shirts, the Germans, looking gaunt and drained but plastering on happy faces, do a lap of honour with bunches of flowers, the players holding up a big Mexican flag. The gesture is appreciated, and while Uruguay slink off down the tunnel, back to stage their next protest (and having moved cities yet again), West Germany receive a standing ovation. England's conquerors have played a World Cup of honour. The next morning they drive off in the rain. Surely, as hosts, they will be strongly fancied in Munich in four years' time . . .

The performance of Germany may well give heart to Italy. Otherwise the odds are against them: there's the partisan crowd for one, and the fact that every team that has come through a strenuous extra-time battle (West Germany against England, Uruguay against Russia) has crashed out in the next game. The press in the neutral countries do their best to make a heavyweight clash out of the big finale, but of all the pundits and analysts pushed to select the victors, there are very few who don't go for Brazil – with their fifteen goals in five games so far. Indeed, it would be almost inappropriate and contravening the spirit of the competition for Italy to come in and spoil the party.

In England, it still rankles. 'Got to give credit to the Germans, but I think we'd have beaten Italy,' says Terry Cooper. 'We'd have been too strong mentally for them. It'd have been a good, good final. That was maddening, that the Germans went and lost to Italy.'

'We were the only two who were going to the final that year,' adds Alan Ball, still smarting. 'I personally believe it would have been an England–Brazil final and it could have gone either way.'

The last time Brazil and Italy met in a World Cup match was the semi-final in 1938, Italy winning 2–1 in Marseilles on the way to lift the trophy for the second time and Mussolini posing triumphantly with the players on their return. That, of course, was a footballing lifetime ago. Still, Italy have an outstanding international record – twice World Cup winners, the current European Champions, and they have only lost one of their twenty-seven internationals since the North Korean debacle of '66 (going down to Bulgaria in Sofia), their presence in the final exemplifying what all the experts were saying about World Cup 1970: the great showdown between Europe and Latin America; the old versus the new; defence versus attack; cynicism against optimism; conservatism against flamboyance.

You'd never have believed it in the group games, but now, having found their scoring boots, Italy could still do it. 'Four years ago we had good players but this present side is more experienced and has more faith in itself,' Gianni Facchetti tells the *Guardian*. 'Over the last few years we have been getting good results. We used to be a team of pilgrims, but this eleven has got a lot of confidence in its ability to do well.'

Facchetti, Albertosi and Mazzola are the only survivors from the dreaded North Korea game. They will be doing everything in their power finally to lay that nightmare to rest. Facchetti, no doubt, regrets those stupid lapses that gifted the Germans some easy goals and word is that Rosato, who man-marked Müller and is considered to have had a good game (though Müller *did* score two goals), will be given a specialist job again. It could be against Pelé, Tostão or Jairzinho: no one will really know until the game kicks off. Babyface got a bit of a knock in the semi-final but will definitely be OK on the big day.

One thing is certain: Italy will be suffering from their extra-time exertions – especially when they were kept up all night with phone calls and well-wishing telegrams. But Italy will be hoping to do what they did against the Germans – let the Brazilians come at them and then, with swift play by the likes of Boninsegna (who did well against the slow Schulz) and Riva, exploit the acres of space, with de Sisti and Domenghini charging forward in support.

Not that Brazil have got it all easy either: still living in the shadows of the '58 and '62 World Cup-winning teams, their '66 side, too, was barracked on its return. The weight of expectation now bears heavily, certainly if that first half against Uruguay is anything to go by. Also, for the first time, they are the ones doing the travelling, Italy staying at 'home', based in the same hotel they've occupied for the duration. Italy will just have to hope that the famously dodgy Brazilian defence and its eccentric keeper live up to their reputations. But if they're hoping to nick a goal and shut up shop history is against them. No final to date has produced fewer than three goals. None has been drawn, either. (Just in case, a replay has been scheduled for Tuesday, if required.)

Brazil, however, are not as naive as everyone thinks. If their defenders are unable to mark and make tackles in the conventional sense, then their deficiencies are compensated for by the work rate of teammates. Throughout the game against Uruguay, players swapped positions, dropped deep to pull defenders with them and gave opposing markers a confusing time. Jairzinho popped up on the left wing, Rivelino came to the right, Tostão, with his busy little runs, drifted off to the flanks, Pelé spent part of the game almost as a centre back and Gérson traded duties with Clodoaldo, in the holding role, enabling him to launch the run from which Clodoaldo scored. Tostão has already had to change his game radically to suit Pelé; submission to the group cause is paramount. And, of course, there is Pelé, marshalling the troops and, crucially, for the first time in his illustrious career, surviving every game.

The fates seem determined that this will be Pelé's moment. The last time Brazil won it – in 1962 – they beat England on the way. And this time, as in 1958, they seem to be building to a climactic performance.

But oh, how everyone wishes that such gifted players – on both sides – would stop all that dreadful play-acting. Famous Dutch referee Leo Horn, in the *Observer*, blames Herr Tschenscher in the opening game for allowing all this to happen. 'He was heavily briefed but the fault was that they had not understood that if you give a German strict instructions then he will click his heels and carry them out very strictly indeed,' he says. In which case Horn won't be pleased that, while talk was of either Bob Davidson or Laurens van Ravens doing the final, it has been awarded instead to East German Rudi Glockner – in only his seventh international.

Whatever happens, for Mexico it will be a celebration. Not only have they staged a great World Cup, but unofficial statistics, released on the morning of the final by the local press, reveal Mexico to be the fifth-best team in the world. According to a complicated points system they have invented, based on games played, points and goals scored, they are superior even to Uruguay, who reached the semis, and bettered only by Brazil (first), West Germany (second), Italy (third) and the USSR (fourth). Poor old England languish at eighth.

What's more, they've advocated that the new World Cup trophy, which will now definitely be needed, given that Brazil or Italy get to keep the present one, be called the Aztec Cup – conflicting with the plans of the Brazilian FA (and working on the basis that Brazil must merely go through the motions in this final), who want it dubbed the Pelé Cup . . .

Just as meteorological gloom had descended for the Azteca semi-final, so for three nights before El Gran Final itself there have been fierce thunderstorms over Mexico City. On Sunday morning it continues in a similar vein, with slate-grey skies and booms of thunder still rolling in the distance. Not that it's holding anyone back. For hours before the game, the area around the Azteca has been closed off, the drab heavens and every drenched street and thoroughfare offset with jammed hordes of brightly coloured Brazilian supporters and the handful of those sporting the red, white and green of Italy.

Before the match, the spectators, many of whom are now under vividly coloured cagoules and pac-a-macs, are treated to the same tin-pot military parade as in the opening ceremony. On the field are tethered five massive helium balloons – one for each of the semi-finalists and one for hosts Mexico (no doubt also to mark their new standing in world football), each done out in national colours. At about 11.45 a.m. local time (leading up to a 7 p.m. BST kick-off) come the teams, marching out together, side-by-side up the ramp from the underground dressing rooms behind one goal. They stop briefly – and bizarrely – as a Brazilian sailor vaults the barrier and asks the Brazilian players if he can snap them with his box camera. The whole team stops, poses and smiles, then continues on its way.

Out in the arena, the edge of the playing area has been decorously laid with flowers. Big bazooka mics jut out occasionally, set there to pick up the onfield action.

As the teams arrive at the VIP box for the presentations and anthems, they take a photocall and a bank of photographers snaps away, needing flashbulbs in these conditions. All the talk about heat, and the final ends up like this. Then, while the teams kick in, Facchetti and Carlos Alberto shake hands in the centre circle and exchange pennants, again posing for the photographers while the Italian reserves walk round the pitch dishing out roses to the crowd in a vain effort to win friends.

The players all look tense; Valcareggi looks tense. The Italians win the toss and Facchetti points to the ball with his foot – Italy will kick off. While all this is going on, even the great Riva finds time to run over, grab a bouquet and do a bit of distribution himself.

And so, here it is, the 1970 World Cup Final.

Boninsegna, number 20, kicks to Mazzola, 15, and the game is under way. Straight away, those nerves are immediately apparent, with some cautious stuff by both sides tapping it around the middle. The crowd, waiting for that first flash of Brazilian brilliance, buzzes with expectation as Carlos Alberto plays it up to Jairzinho on the right, who goes at Facchetti and then just backs off, as if probing for weaknesses in the Italian line. Fat chance of that. As Italy did in the opening games, the minute they lose possession, they pack the area behind the ball with bodies.

Albertosi gets his first touch and rolls it out to Mazzola to build an attack from the back. Everaldo jostles him, and when the ball is played inside to Riva, the Brazilians employ the same tactic – bodies, bodies, bodies. Riva, thirty yards out, has a dig anyway. With the ball on his left foot and with Pelé and Gérson running in to block – two not normally known for their defensive contributions – he fires an unexpected screamer at the Brazilian goal. As the ball flies towards the top left-hand corner, Félix, for once, does something useful and leaps acrobatically to tip it over the bar. 'By golly what a shot,' yelps Hugh Johns. First blood to Italy.

Mazzola takes the corner from the right, but it goes straight to Félix, who rolls it out to Carlos Alberto to start another slow, cautious move forward. With some interchanging, Carlos Alberto's cross is nodded down by Cera, who plays it to Mazzola to bring forward, and thus the cycle repeats itself. Everaldo breaks down the left and is immediately surrounded by four players – Domenghini, Mazzola, Rosato and Burgnich. Everaldo shoots: it was going wide, but Albertosi, choosing not to tempt fate when the ball can still swing all over the place, catches it and carries it over the goal line as he lands. The ref gives a goal kick despite the appeals, and the stadium stirs with its first talking point.

Brazil get a corner. Rivelino, 'the man with the left foot', as Johns puts it, takes it and so overhits it that it almost flattens the corner flag on the opposite side. No one's settling.

Riva gets a free header. 'The frailty of the Brazilian defence has already been slightly exposed,' says Johns, aware of their jitters.

But Italy can be sloppy, too. Domenghini takes it down the right, midway inside his own half, and then, for reasons known only to himself, is somehow possessed to play a suicide ball square across the field. Meaning to switch play to the other flank, left back Facchetti had already pushed up in anticipation and Jairzinho rushes in to intercept. It is the quintessential inside-right gallop from which Jairzinho has scored most of his goals. Facchetti, the wily old pro, is not going to let anyone rain on his parade this early in the day: he runs up behind Jairzinho and cleverly brings him down without making it look too blatant, like the Mafioso who can kill without leaving a mark. A free kick to Brazil on the edge of the 'D'. Prime territory for Pelé, who stands over the ball, his St Christopher (who's watched over them from Guadalajara to here) hanging outside his shirt.

The Italians marshal a wall. Gérson and Tostão plant themselves in it and get ready to sprint away at the last minute to leave a couple of gaps. Pelé runs up and over the ball; Rivelino gets the shot and the rifle foot sends the ball sailing high over Albertosi's bar. The Mexican and Brazilian majority in the crowd is frustrated; Italy breathes a sigh of relief.

Brazil try to show willing. Everaldo, in an advanced left-back position, gets the ball. He has time to use it well but, like Domenghini before him, plays a silly square ball inside, intercepted by Rosato. It bounces out to Gérson, who isn't quite acrobatic enough to control it. Boninsegna nips in and runs with it. He plays it wide to Domenghini, and Everaldo scampers back to kick it into touch. There is a sense of purpose about Brazil now, though, true to the formula of such games, pressing forward and losing possession give them a lot of work to do at the back. The drum rhythms, which had been evident before kick-off and then lost in the early tension, pick up again.

At the Jalisco Stadium, Brazil strutted around like they owned the place. At the Azteca they are guests, but they are now starting to make themselves welcome. On the right, they start toying around, playing cat and mouse. Gérson orchestrates, playing short one-touch passes, trying to tease de Sisti out of position, bringing him too far forward, so that he can be picked off with a deft ball in behind. Gérson to Carlos Alberto to Tostão to Gérson to Clodoaldo to Gérson. Gérson sees a chink, space on the right. He releases Carlos Alberto, who runs down the touchline and centres hard. Pelé is running in on a collision course, but Albertosi dives to catch at his feet. Pelé, recognising good goalkeeping when he sees it, pats the Italian on the head. And so it goes – Albertosi out to Domenghini and a new move begins.

Brazil have reason to be concerned. Riva goes down the left, Piazza makes a half-hearted attempt to stop the shot, Félix catches it and then muffs it. Mazzola centres, Riva comes to meet it, Félix shuts his eyes and makes a dreadful double-fisted punch. The ball breaks for Brazil but Pelé is cautioned, just outside the Brazilian area, for a feet-up challenge on de Sisti. Not a popular decision. Gérson and Tostão have been too busy arguing with the Italians to get back. Mazzola takes the free kick and lobs it to an unmarked Riva. He meets it and sends a looping header towards the Brazilian goal. Félix makes a spectacular leap, can't get there, but the ball lands in the side-netting. One half of the ground, just for a second, shrieks with horror at what looks like an Italian goal. Heads are clutched in the crowd, followed by nervous giggles of relief.

Domenghini goes down the right, cuts it inside to Boninsegna. He is brought down by Piazza on the edge of the box. Riva is furious, but the foul is not given.

It's all rather tense now. Something's got to give.

The ball breaks to Tostão on the Brazilian left, he jinks in on number 8, Rosato, and sends a low cross to Pelé. Facchetti dives in head-first and clears for a throw on the Brazilian left. Tostão takes it, casually tosses it to Rivelino, who catches his marker by surprise by not controlling it and bringing it down but by simply swivelling and hitting it on the half-volley with his left boot, banging it on a looping trajectory into the area. Pelé, at the far post, outleaps Bertini with a jump of quite extraordinary athleticism ('a Nureyev leap' according to the *Daily Express*) and heads the ball down past Albertosi's left. Goal to Brazil.

For all that preceded it, only nineteen minutes have so far elapsed. Let the party begin.

'What a beautiful goal for Pelé, El Rey Pelé,' cries Johns.

'He's up there like an eagle,' gushes Bobby Moore, Johns's co-pilot. 'Tremendous header.'

The Azteca explodes with joyous relief. Carlos Alberto comes in to lift the national hero high. Though he's probably not counting, Pelé has just scored his 1,028th senior goal. ('Pelé was lifted high by gay colleagues, their teeth shining brightly in grins of joy and pride,' according to the *Express*, again, the next day.)

Italy have got no choice now. It's do or die. From the restart Mazzola sends it square right to Domenghini who just runs with it and meets no opposition whatsoever. Rivelino doesn't try, Everaldo turns to give chase, Félix stops it.

The swagger is back for Brazil. Jairzinho beats Facchetti and finds Pelé, who now seems intent on strutting his stuff, though Burgnich beats him to it and another counter-attack is on. The ball is pumped up, but Brazil gain possession, then Clodoaldo casually back-heels it, allowing Boninsegna to run on to it. He beats Piazza and sails past him. He's through the middle in a dangerous position on the edge of the area. Félix is off his line like a shot. It wasn't a one-on-one, but he's now made it so. Brito, who has shaved off his beard, according to the declaration that he wouldn't do so till Brazil reached the final, tries to put out the fire by sliding in, but glides right between Felix and the Italian causing the keeper to flinch and take his eye off the ball. Riva is there to swoop, but Boninsegna, momentarily disorientated, spins round and finds himself over the ball, too. For a second it looks like the two Italians will collide and miss the chance altogether, but Riva, sensibly, holds back and lets Boninsegna take the shot into an open goal: 1–1.

Boninsegna is mobbed, Félix blames everybody but himself, and the Brazilian celebration suddenly seems premature.

We've got a game on our hands now and Brazil will have to throw caution to the wind. They kick off – Pelé to Tostão to Rivelino on the left. The moustachioed number 11 tears down the wing and is dispossessed by an absolutely perfect sliding tackle by Bertini that takes ball not man. Not that Rivelino's settling for that, rolling over and over and over. The ref gives a free kick. Rivelino, miraculously OK again, takes it, sending the ball into the box. Tostão, who can't head but forgets for a second, goes, then stops. Albertosi makes a huge punch out that flies half the length of the pitch. What the fist would have done to Tostão's retina does not bear thinking about.

Rivelino, blood up, is booked for a hack on Bertini. For a second it looks like the ref's pulled out the red card.

The ball comes back in to Pelé in the box who turns and shoots. It rolls into the goal but the Italians have stopped. The ref has already blown for half-time. Pelé claims he never heard the whistle. It's a goal, goddammit. No one steals a goal from The King. But the ref is already halfway to the tunnel, marching away purposefully, like his mum's just called him in for tea, taking his ball with him. Italian players surround Pelé to explain the awful truth.

'Well there'd be a bit of booing and shouting if that happened at Elland Road, Don, wouldn't there?' chortles Kenneth Wolstenholme to Don Revie on the BBC.

For the second half, unusually, Brazil come out first. This can mean only one thing – they were given a vicious rollicking by Zagalo. They look anxious but steeled for action, and when the whistle goes they set about Italy with a renewed purpose. They stroke it around now – Gérson to Carlos Alberto to Clodoaldo. Alberto hares down the right, whips in a cross and Pelé is sliding in at the far post, just an inch away from making contact, the striker careening into the side-netting. The crowd are on their feet. For a second it looks like Pelé's hurt. He caught his hand in the net as he slid through, winces, and shakes it. But he's OK. If it wasn't, he certainly wouldn't be shaking it.

Carlos Alberto is starting to spring attacks now down his flank. He runs again and squares it to Gérson, shuffling around with his shirt hanging out. Gérson runs at the Italian centre backs (as much as Gérson runs at all) but he is well marshalled by Cera. The ball spins out and Pelé is accidentally kicked in the head by Burgnich, attempting a high clearance. Penalty!

Hearts are in mouths. The ref this time can't fudge it by giving a kick on the edge of the area as it was well inside. He still, however, has a soft option available – an indirect free kick. Bobby Moore says it *has* to be a penalty. 'Ridiculous decision,' he mutters. There is further concern about Pelé, but again he's fine.

Six Italians form a wall, clutching their testicles, and Albertosi spits on his hands like a cowboy ready for a saloon-bar punch-up. Gérson flicks it, and it hits a defender in the face. Take that! But the wall did well to hold strong. The ball comes out, Facchetti goes off on a run down the left and finds Boninsegna centrally. It is played out to Domenghini, who shoots into the side-netting. Mercifully for Brazil, as Riva and Boninsegna were running in. Domenghini would have done better to square it. Boninsegna, in particular, is not happy. For Brazilian fans the weakness at the back is painful. A cross comes in, Burgnich gets his head to it, but it loops over the bar.

'What an interesting game,' says Don Revie, who's taken to calling Pelé 'Pelly'. 'There's no fireworks really from either team yet.'

And then the sun comes out. As if it were the very essence of their football being, Brazil suddenly switch on. They run at Italy, keeping them on the back foot, and Italy, likewise, revert to type. Rivelino runs through and is hacked down (rolling over and over again). Jairzinho runs through and is hacked down. And, as ever, when Brazil are being manhandled, Carlos Alberto protects his boys like a big brother, clumping down Bertini and then having the temerity to come over and say sorry.

Cera takes a kick to de Sisti, who surges forward. The move ends with another Italian corner. This time it's Mazzola with the looping header and Félix punches it lamely when no one is near him and he could just as easily have caught it. 'Oh, what a feeble punch by Félix. What an incredible man to have behind you,' remarks Hugh Johns.

Unusually, Mazzola is still on the pitch, now probing forward. Has the entry of Rivera been delayed so that Mazzola can burn himself out? We'd expected to see Rivera, not Mazzola, come out for the second half.

It's tense now, and tempers are frayed. Brazil attack and Pelé is held when running through. ' "Did you see what he did to me, boss"?' is Johns's estimate of what the protesting Pelé might be saying to Herr Glockner, who awards a *tiro indirecto*.

Everaldo goes down the left, taps it inside to Jairzinho, who's over on the left himself now. He is tackled by Facchetti, but the ball comes to Gérson who takes it, side-steps Cera and shoots with his left from just outside the area. It is not hard but perfectly placed into the far corner. Albertosi dives full length but can't get there: 2–1. The Parrot is overjoyed and hops off to the touchline, leapt on by squawking teammates.

Italy kick off. Brazil are going to dig in now. Hard, Italian-style tackles come from Brazilian players. Even Pelé is in on it. He chases Domenghini in the centre circle and tackles him from behind. A foul. The Italian number 13 pushes him away. Pelé makes it seem like a punch and goes down. Then, for good measure, clutches his shin. Mazzola then Boninsegna lean over the world's greatest player and scream obscenities at him. The gigantic Brazilian trainer comes on with his magic sponge. Glockner, only half his size, pushes him off. Pelé stands again to a hero's welcome.

The kick is taken by Everaldo to Gérson – 'A lion was left on the loose,' as the *Observer* puts it – who walks with it, then sees Pelé deep at the far post. He sends over an inch-perfect thirty-yarder to Pelé's head. Just like the Germans had been doing for most of their goals, Pelé heads it back across the face of the goal. Facchetti lunges but can't beat Jairzinho to it. Albertosi had opted to stay on his line. He dives out but it is too late. The ball rolls into the net. Jairzinho has scored: 3–1. Not only that: he has become the first player in the history of the World Cup to net in every round of the tournament. He's got seven now, second only to Müller's ten overall.

The Italians protest that it's offside. No one's listening. Jairzinho runs off to the corner where he drops to his knees, crosses himself and gives his thanks to the Good Lord above. Pelé runs after him, leaping and punching the air. Rivelino and Tostão lean over Jairzinho and administer blessings.

'You have never seen a happier fella than Jairzinho,' says Johns. And when they pile on to him even old Gérson manages to get on top. The Italians pursue the ref – how about a foul, then? Obstruction? Hand ball? But nothing will wash. Twenty minutes to go.

Italy are still protesting as they kick off. Socks are round ankles now.

A chant goes up – '*Bra*-sil, *Bra*-sil.'

For the final push Italy bring on another forward, Juliano, of

Napoli, who replaces the now limping midfielder Bertini. They are feeling the effects of that extra half-hour in the semi-final on this thick, sapping grass. West Germany have demonstrated that nothing's impossible, but the eleven men in blue are the only ones who believe that anyone other than Brazil is going to win this thing now. There's only one person working miracles at the moment, and he's got a big green number 10 on his back.

Under the unspoken rules of football, Brazil should sit back now, ride out the last quarter, let the Italians run into culs-de-sac, but they've already had a little go at that and it's not to their liking. It's hot and bright now, like a summer's day on the Copacabana. The time is ripe for showing off. Rivelino, deemed to be utterly one-footed, takes a direct free kick with his right, which seems every bit as powerful as his left. They are showboating and duly irk the Italians by pushing forward in search of more.

Everaldo runs in at speed, Albertosi throws himself at his feet and is hurt. Genuinely, a clonk on the head. He must be so because he's staying down, wasting valuable seconds. Pelé realises this and, the true gentleman, tells the ref to stop the clock to give Italy a fighting chance. He comes over to the goalkeeper, as the trainer rushes on, and puts his palm on Albertosi's forehead, like a laying on of hands. While water is being poured on his face, Albertosi blinks back into dazed reality. Rivera runs on as sub and hands his chit to the ref. Eighty-three minutes have elapsed. There's not a lot he'll be able to do now. And, surprisingly, he's not on for Mazzola but Boninsegna, scorer of the first goal and Italy's most lively forward. Riva has been quiet. They would seem to have sheathed the only weapon they had. Albertosi staggers around; the game goes on.

Still, the Italians give it their all. Three minutes are left when an Azzurri attack breaks down. Brito strokes it out to Clodoaldo to Pelé to Gérson to Clodoaldo again. In his own half and in an area where any English centre half would have been yelling, 'Get rid of it!' Clodoaldo takes on four Italians – Rivera, Domenghini, de Sisti and Rosato – and skips over every one of their tackles. He plays it wide to Rivelino, who hits it down the left touchline to Jairzinho, who's switched flanks again. Jairzinho spins, cuts inside and squares it to Pelé. Facchetti has been following Jairzinho everywhere, which is opening up space for Carlos Alberto when Jairzinho comes out of position. The diversion of Jairzinho to the left has pulled the defence over. Pelé puts his foot on the ball, looks up, and, in a similar fashion to the way he set up the goal against England, simply smiles and rolls the ball to his right. Steaming in like an express train comes Carlos Alberto, and the right back unleashes the hardest-hit shot of the tournament, beating Albertosi and nearly bursting the net. 'Oh, this is great stuff . . . sheer delightful football,' says Wolstenholme. 'And what a great goal that was . . . puts the game surely well beyond the reach of almost any side now,' agrees Johns.

Its 4–1. That's it. And the Italians, who were practically dead anyway, have no way out. Albertosi and Burgnich saunter back to collect the ball and the Brazilian players, to a man, have joined their captain's victory parade, running behind the goal before a delirious crowd, sub Paulo Cézar leaping on top of them as if he's playing king of the castle, all surrounded by the goalside photographers, who have now turned their backs on the game altogether.

The Italian defenders scream abuse – at least let them finish with their dignity intact. But Albertosi looks at his colleagues as if to say, 'Let them have their moment,' while Rudi Glockner, the tough little ref, wades into the bodies to pull the players back on to his pitch.

'It's useless to try to stop Brazilians celebrating,' says Wolstenholme.

Gérson, meanwhile, has run off towards the bench now and has dropped to his knees, sobbing like a baby. Domenghini can't resist patting him on the head – 'There, there, mate.'

Order seemingly restored, Glockner walks back to the centre circle, though as soon as his back is turned, photographers sneak on in his wake, snapping him as he goes.

For all the military hardware on display inside the stadium – and armed military police are absolutely everywhere – there is little attempt at security. Glockner must do it himself, and the best he can manage, with people somehow pouring across the nine-foot moat that separates the stands from the pitch, is keep them back to the touchline. With the pitch completely surrounded now by standing onlookers, it resembles a keenly contested parks match.

With two minutes to go Rivera takes a long shot. Fairly harmless, but Félix spills it. Then Jairzinho dances down the right, but Facchetti is too experienced to throw himself into a tackle, waiting for the Brazilian to surge before robbing him. 'And the devil takes the hindmost at the back,' says Johns.

Brazil regain possession. They start to play keep-ball in their own box. One last throw of the dice and Italy launch an attack: Riva plays the ball to Domenghini to shoot, but it goes way over into the crowd. Whether it's someone eager for a valuable souvenir or just another attempt to help the Brazilians towards the big prize, the ball doesn't come back. Seconds lapse as a replacement is sought.

Seeing Glockner with arms aloft, whistle in mouth, the crowd think it's all over and swarm on to the playing area. Once more Glockner orders them off. 'This game is going to end in chaos,' says Wolstenholme. And he's not wrong.

From the goal kick Félix taps it to the left-hand corner to Brito, who plays it back for Félix to pick up. Rivera comes charging in and, for once, Félix's reflexes are put to constructive use, leaping in the air to avoid the scything legs beneath him. He rolls it to Piazza, who finds Rivelino. That's it. This time the ref signals it's really over.

'There are players on the park, there are spectators on the park. There are now policemen on the park,' says Hugh Johns, doing a Wolstenholme. 'The game is over. Brazil have won it.'

The Italian congratulations don't amount to more than running up and touching the ref before sprinting towards the tunnel as the pitch is swarmed by thousands of fans. It looks scary. The ref orders the players off – quick, quick, quick – but before he can do anything a mob has surrounded Tostão, held him down and stripped him of everything but his underpants – shirt, shorts, socks, boots, the lot. A man in a cape seems to be entertaining the idea of raping him.

Pelé, rather agitated, has his shirt ripped off, is hoisted on to shoulders, has a giant black sombrero placed on his head and is carried off to one end of the ground.

Zagalo, still clutching his clipboard, the blueprint for global football domination, gets carried in the opposite direction, like a sacrificial offering in days of yore.

Tostão, escaping his assaulters and overcome, hugs Félix, the goalkeeper blubbing for all he's worth, till someone tries to pull off one of his gloves and his joy turns to rage. And, out there on the pitch, in the middle of it all, lies Rivelino, who's passed out –

through exhaustion, emotion, who knows? – with the Brazilian trainer splashing water on his face, the known cure for all ills.

Amid the throng, rather incongruously, can be seen Ken Bailey, in his top hat and tails, waving the Union Jack. Paulo Cézar fights an Italian player for the match ball.

Eventually, the police make a half-hearted effort to clear the pitch, or at least cut a corridor through for the Brazil players. And, with fresh shirts found, and in Tostão's case a full set of clothes arriving, the players begin the climb up to the VIP box.

It is not easy. A scuffle breaks out between some of the Brazilian reserves and a couple of military policemen, who seem rather more keen on joining the triumphant parade themselves than letting these bit-parters have their moment.

With Rous, Cañedo and the dignitaries stand President Ordaz, a tray of red medal boxes and, the most important thing of all, the Jules Rimet Trophy. Brazil's now to keep.

Carlos Alberto steps up, accepts it, looks back at his teammates with a knowing wink, plants a smacker on it and then hoists it aloft, turning it around so that the angel can get a good view of the marvellous scene before her. He then brings it over to Pelé and his teammates to kiss. Confetti cascades from the roof. On the way back down the steps, one of the military policemen gets his way and joins in the victory march.

Back home, England players are muttering. 'We were the only team that could have given Brazil a game in the final,' says Brian Labone; 'The only country Brazil were apprehensive about was us,' says Allan Clarke, 'once we were out, they knew they were gonna cruise it'; 'To be honest I think Brazil would have won it, but I think we would have made a better show of it than the old Italians,' adds Terry Cooper.

During the lap of honour, the top part of the Jules Rimet Trophy falls to the ground. A small Mexican boy nips in to scoop it up and disappears into the crowd. Reserve player Dario's sole contribution to the campaign, a valuable one, is to dart into the stand to grab him and wrest it back (while simultaneously in Brasilia – according to the *Observer* – his patron, President Médici, drapes himself in a flag and dashes out to play football in the main square).

With further chaos ensuing in the Azteca, the scoreboard says all that you need to know – 'Brasil: Campeon Del Mundo'.

In the living rooms of England, menfolk get up, go to the kitchen, pour themselves another can of Double Diamond and contemplate mowing the lawn tomorrow.

The wife moves into the TV chair. Wimbledon's started, hasn't it?

Bibliography

Banks, Gordon, with Giller, Norman, *Banks of England* (Arthur Baker, 1980)

Bowler, Dave, *Winning Isn't Everything ... A Biography of Sir Alf Ramsey* (Victor Gollancz, 1998)

Coleman, David, *World Cup '70 Preview* (Purnell, 1970)

Finn, Ralph, *World Cup 1970* (Robert Hale, 1970)

Glanville, Brian, *The Sunday Times History of the World Cup* (Times Newspapers Ltd., 1973)

Jenkins, Garry, *The Beautiful Team: In Search of Pelé & the 1970 Brazilians* (Pocket Books, 1998)

Kapuscinski, Ryszard, *The Soccer War* (Vintage International, 1992)

McIlvanney, Hugh & Hopcraft, Arthur, *World Cup '70* (Eyre & Spottiswoode, 1970)

Peters, Martin, *Mexico '70* (Cassell, 1970)

Powell, Jeff, *Bobby Moore: The Life and Times of a Sporting Hero* (Robson, 1993)

Index

After the competition proper begins games are indexed but individual players are named only if they figure prominently.